CAHOKIA

CAHOKIA
Domination and Ideology in the Mississippian World

EDITED BY

TIMOTHY R. PAUKETAT

THOMAS E. EMERSON

University of Nebraska Press

Lincoln and London

© 1997 by the University of Nebraska Press
All rights reserved
Manufactured in the United States of America
♾ The paper in this book
meets the minimum requirements of American
National Standard for
Information Sciences — Permanence of Paper
for Printed Library Materials,
ANSI Z39.48-1984
Library of Congress Cataloging-in-Publication
Data. Cahokia : domination
and ideology in the Mississippian world / edited
by Timothy R. Pauketat
and Thomas E. Emerson. p. cm. Includes
bibliographical references
and index. ISBN 0-8032-3708-1 (alk. paper)
  1. Cahokia Site (East Saint
Louis, Ill.) 2. Mississippian culture—Illinois—
American Bottom.
3. Indians of North America—Illinois—American
Bottom—Politics and
government. 4. Chiefdoms—Illinois—American
Bottom. 5. Indians
of North America—Illinois—American Bottom—
Antiquities. 6. American
Bottom (Ill.)—Antiquities. I. Pauketat, Timothy R.
II. Emerson, Thomas E., 1945–.
E99.M6815C35 1997 977.3'89–dc20
96-28639 CIP

1001640207

Contents

Contents

List of Illustrations & Tables

CAHOKIA

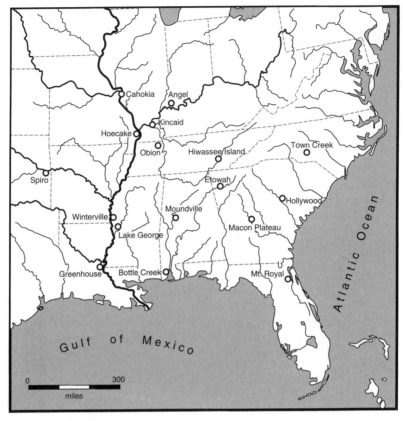

Figure 1.1. Selected Sites in Southeastern North America

Timothy R. Pauketat and Thomas E. Emerson

1

Introduction: Domination and Ideology in the Mississippian World

There was a place in native North America that, far removed in space and time from the Mexican empires and European governments, embodied political order and social inequality of a sort seldom associated with precontact peoples. In this place, and spanning more than a century, a dominant few transcended the community and ruled. The produce of a fertile floodplain was carried to this place, and from this place, the media of a political ideology were dispersed. The place was Cahokia.

Cahokia, more than any of its contemporary "Mississippian" neighbors, was a vortex of native social, political, economic, and religious activity.[1] For a time it was the preeminent cultural center in the Mississippi valley. Its direct and indirect influences on midcontinental and southeastern native communities were varied and widespread, from Minnesota to Oklahoma, Louisiana, and Tennessee. Cahokia as a native center of political and religious activity was, in many respects, not unique. It was one of many such centers in the central Mississippi River valley, and one of hundreds throughout southeastern North America dating between A.D. 1000 and 1600 (figure 1.1). But Cahokia, by almost any measure of polity, economy, or society, was the largest of them all. It was situated at the very northwestern margins of the American Southeast (Emerson 1991a, 233), in a regional setting that has been likened to a "gateway" to the north (J. Kelly 1991a). Its geographic location, moreover, may have been just one of several unique factors involved in its rise to preeminence (Pauketat 1994a).

This book is an explanation of Cahokia and its immediate domain as a phenomenon that contributed to the development of the Mississippian world. The thirteen chapters of this volume constitute a new synthesis of this most important of archaeological places. They seek to establish for the interested layperson and the trained archaeologist the developmental sequence and boundaries of an expansive polity where this sequence and those boundaries involved the complex processes of domination and ideology. Cahokia, we maintain, enables a greater appreciation of the social, political, economic, and cultural factors involved in the origins of complex society. Moreover, a historical and processual analysis, as put forth by authors in this volume, reveals that Cahokia's panregional effects were foundational to the history of midcontinental and southeastern North America before the Europeans set foot in North America.

Cahokia in Historical Context

Archaeology in the American Bottom region, as it is known historically, has proceeded, up to now, with little theoretical direction. The earliest professional archaeology in the region established Cahokia's great size but did little to delineate the timespan covered by Cahokia-Mississippian or the internal complexity of Cahokia and its relationship to archaeological complexes elsewhere in the Mississippi valley or Southeast (cf. Moorehead 1929). James B. Griffin can be credited with formalizing a ceramic chronology and advancing a recognition of Cahokia's relationships with archaeological complexes outside the American Bottom (Griffin 1941, 1949, 1952, 1960).[2] Other excavations in the 1940s and 1950s had little immediate impact upon Cahokian archaeology (Fowler 1989; see Pauketat 1993c; Perino 1971; H. Smith 1977); however, archaeology in the 1960s resulted in a revamped regional chronology and an identification of significant Cahokian community features (see Fowler and Hall 1975; O'Brien 1972a; Porter 1974; Vogel 1975).

Robert Hall (1966, 1975) and Joseph Vogel (1975) identified phases of pre-Mississippian and Mississippian residential occupation at Cahokia, explaining this as evidence of a slow acculturation over centuries of non-Mississippians to a Mississippian lifestyle. Mississippian community features, monumental architecture, and an elite mortuary were documented at Cahokia by excavations of the palisade wall, monumental rotundas, bastioned compounds, Post-Circle Monuments ("woodhenges"), Mound 72, Monks Mound, and other remains (J. Anderson 1977; Bareis 1967, 1975a,

1975b; Benchley 1974, 1975; Chmurny 1973; Fowler 1991; Fowler and Hall 1975; Reed et al. 1968; Salzer 1975; K. Williams 1975; Wittry 1977). During this period, Porter (1974) and Gregg (1975b) conducted excavations at lesser Mississippian centers nearby that, combined with other site-location information (Harn 1971), were part of the basis of Melvin Fowler's (1978) four-tiered settlement hierarchy model (see also Fowler and Hall 1978). Cahokia was seen as a North American case of Precolumbian urbanization (Fowler 1974, 1975, 1989). Taken to an extreme by others, Cahokia was characterized as a little Teotihuacan-on-the-Mississippi, a mercantile city crowded with bureaucrats, priests, engineers, craft specialists, peasants, and marketplaces (Gregg 1975a, 1975b; O'Brien 1972b, 1989, 1991; Yerkes 1991). This extreme view, despite its popular appeal, is not tenable today.

The FAI-270 Highway Mitigation Project in the late 1970s and 1980s modified views of Cahokia-Mississippian through a refinement of the regional chronology and through large-scale excavations at small pre-Mississippian and Mississippian sites in the American Bottom outside of Cahokia proper (Emerson and Jackson 1984, 1987; Emerson et al. 1983; Esarey and Pauketat 1992; Finney 1985; Fortier 1985; Jackson and Hanenberger 1990; Jackson et al. 1992; J. Kelly, Fortier et al. 1987; J. Kelly, Ozuk et al. 1990; McElrath et al. 1987; Milner 1983a, 1983b, 1984a, 1984b; Milner et al. 1984; Stahl 1985; Wittry et al. 1994). James Porter (1974, 1977), while in favor of a Mexican-state model of Cahokia, believed the population density of the region to be far lower than Gregg (1975a; Porter 1974, 184). This view was verified for a segment of rural landscape along the FAI-270 corridor south of Cahokia (Milner 1986). Emerson and Milner (1981, 1982) argued for a modified regional settlement model, one that recognized the diversity of rural habitation sites and a less rigid three-tiered settlement hierarchy (see also Emerson 1991b; Esarey and Pauketat 1992; Milner 1990; Pauketat 1989).

Chiefdoms, Domination and Ideologies

From a comparative or evolutionary perspective, Cahokia is an example of an elaborate nonstate political organization often called a "complex chiefdom" (Earle 1987, 1991a; H. Wright 1984). Complex chiefdoms were centralized polities lacking formal bureaucracies in which social groups or subgroups were hierarchically ranked. Power, inequality, kinship, and cultural identity were negotiated among populations within and between complex chiefdoms (see Earle 1991a). Although domination was not simply political or economic in form, the regional populations associated with complex chiefdoms were, to variable extent, "dominated" by superordinate political elites. Domination was not necessarily recognized as such by subordinates, nor was it static or unchanging. The non-elite subordinates were the source of communal labor and the primary producers of agricultural goods and handcrafted objects. They were the clients more or less attached to powerful chiefly patrons who consumed the labor and products of their non-elite clients (see Brumfiel and Earle 1987).

Such sociopolitical arrangements undoubtedly were viewed by many elite and non-elite people as legitimate, traditional, or entirely natural forms of organization. These elite and non-elite views, along with related beliefs, values, and ideas as they legitimated the social order for particular groups of people, are "ideologies" (see Emerson, chapter 10; McGuire 1992, 138–42; Pauketat 1994a; Pauketat and Emerson 1991). Ideologies are and were not homogeneous and unchanging, nor were they shared by all members of some social formation. We cannot speak of a Cahokian or Mississippian ideology unless by this we mean a process rather than a thing. Chiefly patrons, for instance, probably had to expend considerable effort promulgating their views concerning how the clientele should behave. These elite views may or may not have been accepted by the common masses of local people who, acting according to subordinate and disparate ideologies, might have conceded to or resisted local domination depending on historically shaped attitudes and circumstances. Such historical contingencies make chiefdoms a disparate lot (see Drennan and Uribe, eds., 1987; Earle 1991a), leading some to reject the utility of the chiefdom concept (Yoffee 1993). Even Mississippian chiefdoms were not necessarily identical in form or scale. Their differences were in large measure due to sociohistorical factors, including the particular, localized configurations of ideologies and dominant-subordinate relations (see Barker and Pauketat 1992).

Ideology and domination are integral strands of a cultural fabric (Paynter and McGuire 1991). They are not simply constraints or variables to be weighted equally with economy or environment, nor are they superstructures or epiphenomena or mere tactics selected knowingly by elite agents from their quiver of political weapons. Instead, they are basic structural elements of a cultural tradition expressed in the created spaces, monuments, and artifacts, and reflected in the remains of daily life within a region. As ideology and domination were incorporated within tradition and the everyday world, we may identify a "cultural hegemony" (see Comaroff and Comaroff 1991; Pauketat 1994a). Thus, to begin to speak about how and why Cahokia emerged as the preeminent Mississippian place, the Cahokian hegemony (or the Cahokia-Mississippian cultural tradition) as it was created and re-created in regional and interregional contexts and as it involved ideology and domination is a requisite starting point.

Cahokia-Mississippian Cultural Tradition

A pervasive feature of the period A.D. 1000–1600 in southeastern North America was a distinctive settlement pattern and subsistence base (Smith 1978, 1986, 1990a; Steponaitis 1986). In the so-called American Bottom region around Cahokia, the Mississippi Period is characterized in part by a three-tiered settlement hierarchy and maize-field agriculture (figure 1.2). These characteristics existed during roughly a two-century span (figure 1.3).[3] Archaeologists have broken the span into three principal Mississippian phases, with a fourth Mississippian phase (Sand Prairie), an overlapping Bold Counselor Oneota complex, and later Oneota complexes marking the final two-plus Precolumbian centuries in the region (see Jackson et al. 1992). Other variants or ill-defined cognates of the Mississippian phases have previously been proposed for areas outside the northern American Bottom or for adjacent regions in Illinois and Missouri. These may correspond to social groups or political entities outside the immediate control of Cahokia.

The two-century Mississippian span encapsulates the rise, aggrandizement, and eclipse of the regional Mississippian capital of Cahokia. In the few decades prior to A.D. 1050, the site of Cahokia was already large and expanding, home to a thousand or more people. In overall layout and in its key features, however, Cahokia before A.D. 1050 was not yet Mississippian. This changed dramatically over a brief span of time around A.D. 1050 (Pauketat 1994a). In the next half century, referred to as the Lohmann phase (A.D. 1050–1100), the Cahokian population increased five to ten times what it had been (Pauketat and Lopinot, chapter 6).

The Lohmann phase constitutes the collective appearance or adoption of a suite of southeastern Mississippian attributes, including a town-and-dispersed-homestead settlement pattern, wall-trench architecture, circular

5

Figure 1.2. Mississippian Centers in the Northern American Bottom

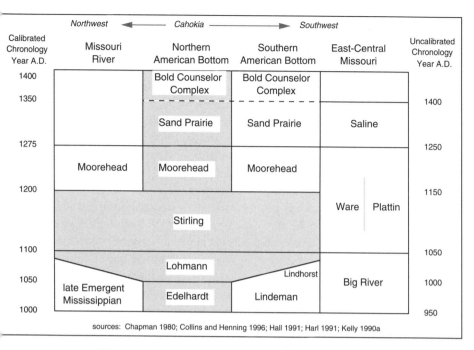

| Calibrated Chronology Year A.D. | Northwest ← — Cahokia — → Southwest | | | | Uncalibrated Chronology Year A.D. |
	Missouri River	Northern American Bottom	Southern American Bottom	East-Central Missouri	
1400		Bold Counselor Complex	Bold Counselor Complex		
1350					1400
		Sand Prairie	Sand Prairie	Saline	
1275					1250
	Moorehead	Moorehead	Moorehead		
1200					1150
		Stirling		Ware | Plattin	
1100					1050
		Lohmann			
1050	late Emergent Mississippian		Lindhorst	Big River	1000
		Edelhardt	Lindeman		
1000					950

sources: Chapman 1980; Collins and Henning 1996; Hall 1991; Harl 1991; Kelly 1990a

Figure 1.3. American Bottom Region Chronology

buildings, and stylistic elements without precedent. At Cahokia, residential areas were reorganized, or new ones established, in areas not previously inhabited (Collins, chapter 7; Pauketat, chapter 2). Large central plazas were constructed, probably at the beginning of this phase (Dalan, chapter 5; Kelly, chapter 8). Lohmann phase refuse includes a diverse array of minerals, rocks, and metal ores, some possibly from Wisconsin, the Ozarks, and down the Mississippi. Distinctively shaped, slipped or plain-surfaced pots made from bottomland clays tempered with crushed mussel shell became common at this time.

A large portion of the regional population—the primary producers—were year-round residents of the rural floodplain, cultivating crops and collecting the aquatic, terrestrial, and avian bounty of nature (Emerson 1992, chapter 9). In the vicinity of Cahokia, of course, this rural settlement pattern *did not precede* either Cahokia, as a Lohmann-phase political capital, or other Mississippian towns or centers. So we must look to the towns for an explanation of regional dynamics (Pauketat and Emerson, chapter 13).

7

These larger Mississippian "towns," centers of local political and administrative activities that sported one or more earthen platform mounds, were situated among rural homesteads, farmsteads, and field houses in the American Bottom proper (Emerson 1991a, 1992; Esarey and Pauketat 1992; Finney 1993; Milner 1990; Pauketat 1994a). Near the center of the northern expanse of bottomland lies the sprawling Central Political-Administrative Complex, including the Cahokia, East St. Louis, and St. Louis sites (figure 1.4; Pauketat 1994a, chapter 4). Within this complex lie some 200 earthen mounds and adjacent rectangular plazas, residential areas, and other elite or communal monuments and mortuaries.

It is not certain whether people living along the margins of the consolidated Lohmann-phase domain, even those only 30 to 100 kilometers away from Cahokia itself, retained political autonomy or identities distinct from the new Cahokian order. By the Stirling phase, however, the entire American Bottom region may have been integrated by the central order, if the homogeneity of material culture is any clue (Emerson 1991a, 234). The Stirling phase is easily recognized because of the decorative motifs, color schemes, monuments, and centrally made wares and objects that characterize it (Emerson 1995, chapter 10; Emerson and Jackson 1984; Holley 1989; Pauketat 1992, 1993c; Pauketat and Emerson 1991). As explained by Emerson (chapter 9), the Stirling-phase settlement pattern may be described as a town-and-dispersed-homestead pattern like the preceding Lohmann phase with certain notable differences.

Residential usage of Cahokia proper continued through the late Stirling phase, but according to Collins (chapter 7) there were shifts in the location of domestic stores and in the configuration of domestic buildings relative to the community as a whole. Central aggrandizement would seem to account for the many mounds, large buildings, compounds, and Post-Circle Monuments or woodhenges of the Stirling phase (Pauketat 1993b, 1994a, 1996). The presence of moderately large communities just outside the capital's limits may signal that some Cahokians were displaced by the many central monuments and public or elite spaces built in the capital's core (e.g., Hanenberger 1990b; Jackson et al. 1992; Pauketat and Koldehoff 1988).

The Moorehead phase is characterized by the lack of a demonstrable three-tiered settlement hierarchy and the depopulation of the American Bottom proper (Pauketat and Lopinot, chapter 6). Cahokia mound-and-plaza groups still were maintained, although fewer in number, and certain special

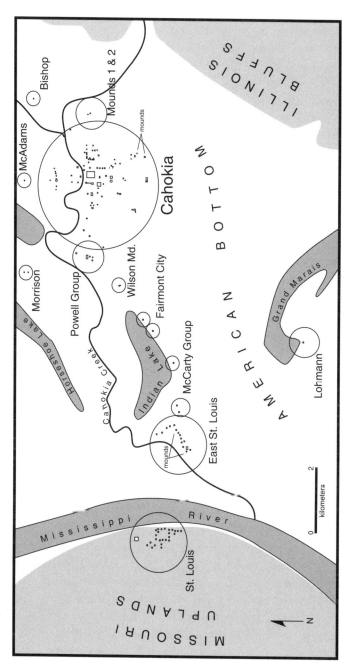

Figure 1.4. Mound Clusters of the Central Political-Administrative Complex

wares and objects, like Ramey Incised jars, Wells plates, sandstone tablets, and shell artifacts, were manufactured past A.D. 1200 (Pauketat 1994a). New decorated bowl and cordmarked jar styles became common at this time, comparable to other forms in Illinois, Missouri, Kentucky, and Tennessee. Exotic materials in Moorehead-phase artifact assemblages by and large include a low-diversity assortment from the eastern Ozarks and southern Illinois (Brad Koldehoff, personal communication, 1995; Pauketat 1992, 39). The last Mississippian phase, Sand Prairie, and the subsequent (and partially coeval) Bold Counselor Oneota occupation are poorly known from scattered residential areas at Cahokia, Sponemann, and a handful of outlying sites (Fowler and Hall 1975; Jackson et al. 1992; Koldehoff 1989). The scattered domestic remains illustrate the small-scale, unstratified social relations that had replaced the centralized hierarchies of earlier years.

The Central Political-Administrative Complex

Brackenridge (1814 [1962]) was the first to describe in some detail the Cahokia, East St. Louis, and St. Louis sites. The St. Louis site, leveled long ago, had included a central cluster of twenty-four mounds and, about 500 meters north, a "single mound, with a broad stage on the river side; it is thirty feet in height, and one hundred and fifty in length; the top is a mere ridge of five or six feet wide" (Brackenridge 1962, 189). As illustrated by Peale (1862), the central cluster consisted of rectangular and circular flat-topped mounds around a plaza, with several circular and one multi-terraced rectangular mound nearby (see Chapman 1980, figure 5.22; Pauketat 1994a, figure 4.1; Williams and Goggin 1956).

Brackenridge (1962, 187) describes his initial encounter with the East St. Louis mounds as follows (see J. Kelly, chapter 8).

> I crossed the Mississippi at St. Louis, and after passing through the wood which borders the river, about half a mile in width, entered an extensive open plain. In 15 minutes, I found myself in the midst of a group of mounds, mostly of a circular shape, and at a distance, resembling enormous haystacks scattered through a meadow. One of the largest which I ascended, was about two hundred paces in circumference at the bottom, the form nearly square, though it had evidently undergone considerable alteration from the washing of the rains. The top was level, with an area sufficient to contain several hundred

Plate 1.1. Monks Mound as viewed from the eastern plaza, 1922. Courtesy of the Museum of Natural History, University of Illinois, Urbana. Photo #26687

men. . . . Around me, I counted forty-five mounds, or pyramids, besides a great number of small artificial elevations; these mounds form something more than a semicircle, about a mile in extent, the open space on the river.

That same day, Brackenridge proceeded to the Cahokia site proper. Upon arrival at Monks Mound, Brackenridge (1962, 187) was awestruck. "When I reached the foot of the principal mound, I was struck with a degree of astonishment, not unlike that which is experienced in contemplating the Egyptian pyramids. What a stupendous pile of earth!''

Brackenridge saw a mound that measures 291 meters by 236 meters at its base and is composed of about 615,000 cubic meters of earth (Muller 1987, 12; Skele 1988). Monks Mound rises to an elevation of 30 meters (100 feet) in three principal terraces and a fourth eroded terrace (plate 1.1). A small circular mound was situated at the summit of the third terrace and a "secondary" rectangular mound was located on the western edge of the first principal terrace (Benchley 1974, 1975). An earthen ramp extends from the east-central portion of the first terrace down to the foot of the mound (plate 1.2). Stretch-

Plate 1.2. Monks Mound in 1892, view from the south. Courtesy of the Missouri Historical Society, St. Louis

ing out from the southern face of Monks Mound, and covering about 19 hectares, is a "Grand" Plaza (plate 1.3; Dalan, chapter 5).

There are many other mounds and several plazas, large and small, adjacent to Monks Mound (figure 1.5). Brackenridge (1962, 188) stated, "I every where observed a great number of small elevations of earth, to the height of a few feet, at regular distances from each other, and which appeared to observe some order; near them I also observed pieces of flint, and fragments of earthen vessels." John Kelly (1991b, chapter 8) recognizes a quadripartitioned central plan at Cahokia and, besides the Grand Plaza, has identified an "East Plaza" and a "West Plaza," each covering approximately 9 hectares (see also Fowler 1989). There is another large plaza, covering around 6 hectares, north of Monks Mound within the "Creek Bottom" group of five mounds (Fowler 1989, 203; see J. Kelly, chapter 8). The northernmost plaza may be associated with the Kunnemann-tract mounds (Holley 1995; Pauketat 1993c). Easternmost and westernmost plazas are probably associated with Mounds 1 and 2 and the Powell group, respectively. The southernmost mounds, perhaps without plazas, include the large Harding tumulus and

Plate 1.3. The Grand Plaza as viewed from the first terrace of Monks Mound looking south, 1922. Courtesy of the Ohio Historical Society

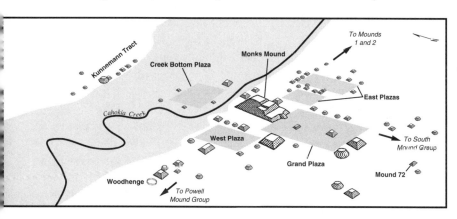

Figure 1.5. Central Cahokia's Mounds and Plazas (used with permission of the Illinois Transportation Archaeological Research Program)

other circular and rectangular platforms in an area with little occupational debris (Fowler 1989, 202; Pauketat and Barker, n.d.).

Fowler (1989) tallies 104 mounds, large and small, circular and rectangular, in the Cahokia (and Powell) group. Circular mounds are often paired with rectangular ones and have been speculated to be "conical" burial mounds (Fowler 1989, 194). It is more likely that the circular and rectangular mounds were surmounted by circular and rectangular buildings, respectively, symbolizing basic cosmological themes of the Mississippian world (Pauketat 1993c, 145). Some mounds were capped with "ridge-top" mantles, apparently marking high-status mortuaries (Fowler 1989, 194; J. Kelly, chapter 8).

Flanking the large plazas and mounds were residential areas, smaller plazas, and other monumental architecture. The identification of such features usually requires archaeological excavation, and thus we have information on their location, shape, and size only from large excavation samples (Collins 1990, chapter 7; J. Kelly, chapter 8; O'Brien 1972; Pauketat 1996, chapter 2; Pauketat and Lopinot, chapter 6). The monumental architecture includes large elite or special-purpose buildings, compounds, and posts. During the Stirling phase, a series of large circles of posts—Post-Circle Monuments or woodhenges—were built one after another to the west of Monks Mound (figures 1.5–1.6; Pauketat 1994a, 1996). There are four commonly recognized Post Circles besides hints of others on Tract 15A and the Dunham Tract (Pauketat 1994a, 1996). The most completely excavated of these, Post Circle 2, was comprised of forty-eight individual posts in a circle that had a diameter of 126 meters (figure 1.6).

Other large town sites, each with one or more mounds and plazas, are scattered outside Cahokia and the central complex in the northern floodplain and adjacent Illinois uplands (figure 1.7). In between and around each town complex were located small rural sites (Emerson, chapter 9). The small rural site includes possible seasonal field house locations, single-family homesteads occupied for several years, and nodal homesteads that evidence longer spans of occupation, larger households, and extradomestic architecture (see figure 1.8; Emerson 1995; Finney 1993; Pauketat 1989).

The architectural and artifactual remains of the central complex, outlying centers, and rural settlements in the American Bottom proper further distinguish a Cahokia-Mississippian pattern from other Mississippian phenomena (cf. Griffin 1985). Rectangular and circular structures were built using wall-

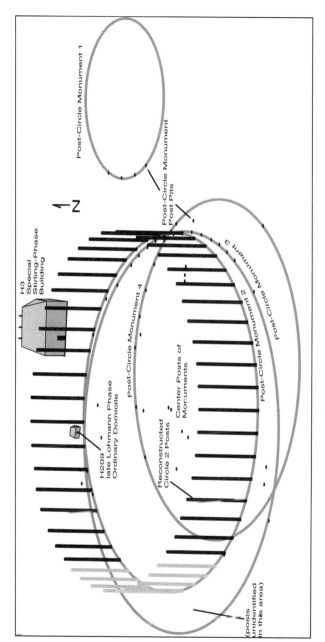

Figure 1.6. Post-Circle Monuments and Associated Buildings (adapted from Pauketat 1994a, figure 4.8)

15

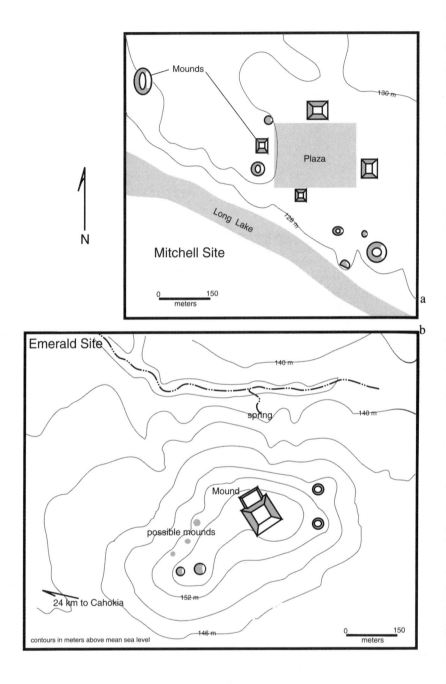

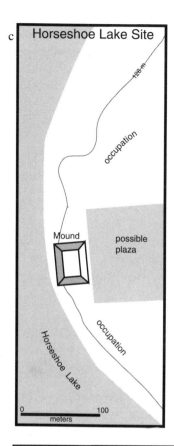

c Horseshoe Lake Site

128 m

occupation

Mound

possible plaza

occupation

Horseshoe Lake

0   100
meters

Figure 1.7. a, b, c. Selected Outlying Political-Administrative Centers in the American Bottom Region

Figure **1.8.** Oblique View of a Mississippian Homestead at the Robert Schneider Site

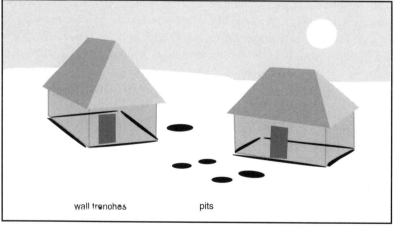

wall trenches   pits

trench techniques. Distinctive shell-tempered and grog-tempered pots were manufactured with diagnostic shapes, finishes, and decorations (Griffin 1949; Holley 1989; Milner et al. 1984; Pauketat 1996; Pauketat and Emerson 1991; Vogel 1975). The local stone-tool industries were based on expedient, small-biface, and microlith technologies and overwhelmingly made use of a high-grade Burlington chert from the Missouri Ozarks (Koldehoff 1987). Hoe, adze, knife, and axe blades manufactured adjacent to chert quarries in Missouri and southern Illinois were imported to the American Bottom as were foreign pots, limited numbers of finished goods, and a plethora of exotic lithic, mineral, and mollusc-shell raw materials (J. Kelly 1991a, 1991b; Pauketat 1994a; Pauketat and Emerson, chapter 13). The latter exotic raw materials were transformed into Cahokian symbols—weapons, tools, figurines, and ornaments—by primary producers and artisans attached to elite American-Bottom patrons (Emerson, chapter 10; Pauketat, chapter 2).

Regional and Interregional Cultural Contexts

Cahokia-manufactured objects and Cahokian styles are occasionally found at locations outside the American Bottom region (see Griffin 1993; papers in Emerson and Lewis, eds., 1991 and Stoltman, ed., 1991). These finds suggest Cahokian contact with and Cahokia-inspired changes among other Mississippian and non-Mississippian peoples to the north, south, east, and west. There is intriguing evidence of limited emigrations out of Cahokia, significant population shifts, and direct exchanges between Cahokians and native groups up to 800 kilometers to the north (Conrad 1991; Emerson 1991a, 1991b; Finney and Stoltman 1991; Green and Rodell 1994; Harn 1991). Farther north and west of the American Bottom are the Aztalan, Mill Creek, Cambria, Silvernale, and Steed-Kisker complexes that, along with other peripheral complexes, provide sometimes equivocal evidence of direct and indirect Cahokian contacts (Gibbon 1974; Gibbon and Dobbs 1991; Goldstein 1991; R. Hall 1967; Henning 1967; J. Kelly 1991a; Rodell 1991; Tiffany 1991a, 1991b). Southern and eastern evidence of possible Cahokian contacts or significant indirect influence seems less apparent but is found in Arkansas, southern Illinois, Tennessee, and Mississippi (Brain 1991; Chapman 1980; Cole et al. 1951; Garland 1992; Griffin 1993; Hargrave et al. 1983, 346–50; Johnson 1987; Lewis 1991; Moffat 1991; Morse and Morse 1983; Williams and Brain 1983).

Interpretations of the evidence for long-distance interaction between Cahokians and other native groups are influenced by our conceptualizations of the scale of Cahokia's political economy and developmental trajectory. Those who are unfamiliar with Cahokian archaeological data or who employ outmoded archaeological scenarios continue to characterize the preeminent Mississippian polity as a mercantile center directly controlling commerce along major waterways (e.g., Dincauze and Hasenstab 1989; Little 1987; O'Brien 1989, 1991; Peregrine 1991; Tiffany 1991a).[4] However, these top-heavy mercantilist perspectives ignore the burgeoning wealth of Cahokian data, as presented in this volume.[5]

This is not to say that an opposite extreme, called "minimalist" by James Stoltman (1991), adequately captures either the internal dynamism of Cahokia-Mississippian or the history of Mississippian–non-Mississippian interactions. While correctly rejecting Cahokia as a mercantile state, an extreme minimalist position also denies the role of ideology and domination in Cahokian development. A minimalist stance, which goes little further than recognizing Cahokia as a Mississippian site like most other Mississippian sites in the American Southeast, begs questions about Cahokia's unique social history and its place within a panregional social formation.

The configuration and extent of Cahokia-Mississippian interaction with outlying regions undoubtedly was a function not only of Cahokian development but of the social histories of outlying groups as well. Given Cahokia's preeminence, however, we may expect that a kind of interregional hegemony had existed. Positing this hegemony as direct and coercive, as in the outmoded mercantilist scenarios above, is not consonant with present-day archaeological data (Milner 1990, 26). But recognizing this hegemony as cultural (and, in local arenas, political) both fits well the archaeological data and, importantly, extends theoretical knowledge about ideology and domination.

Cahokia may be seen as having emerged relative to local social-historical constraints and at the same time as embedded in an interregional political-economic or, better, political-ideological milieu. As outlined by Pauketat in chapter 2, Cahokia's appearance as a regional polity was abrupt, at about A.D. 1050, and involved political domination of a region at the same time as claims to distant cosmological and geographical linkages were emphasized and transformed by a political elite (Pauketat 1994a, 183). There is evidence of massive undertakings at Cahokia itself—the construction of large plazas, the reconstruction of houses according to new plans, the reorganization of community—and of a large-scale demographic transformation (see chapters 2, 5, and 6). A kind of "kinship coalition" or rule by collaboration with political underlings and non-elite possibly enabled this abrupt consolidation of political power (in the sense of Wolf 1966). In short, there were probably benefits for a substantial portion of the regional population in order for this population to concede to such a new centralized political order (Pauketat 1994a, 176). The benefits afforded certain members of the population via this new Cahokian order or hegemony probably would have included an enhancement of their own social power within their social networks vis-à-vis those of their rivals. In such circumstances, the material trappings of Cahokia-Mississippianism would have diffused out of the American Bottom simply because they were symbols of the prestige and power of that place (Pauketat 1994a, 184).

Such a political and ideological logic may be extended beyond the rather artificial boundaries of the American Bottom region to encompass inter-regional interaction (see Pauketat and Emerson, chapter 13). As extralocal linkages would have enhanced the power of Cahokian rulers and would-be authorities in the eyes of the American-Bottom populace, so connections with Cahokia would have enhanced the power of distant political leaders and religious specialists in the eyes of their own followers, far removed from Cahokia (Hall 1991, 21–22). Such long-distance relationships might have included ties between elite trading partners, affines, siblings, or other kin (fictive or actual). Distant leaders might even have been Cahokians by birth, leaving the American Bottom by choice or of necessity, depending on political contingencies (Emerson 1991a, 1991b). Visitors might have arrived at Cahokia for certain life-cycle events, ceremonial homages, quests, or pilgrimages (in the sense of Helms 1992a, 161–62). Cahokians might have sent messengers, emissaries, task groups, or war parties to acquire some resource or achieve some prestigious political end. Cahokian rulers themselves might have traveled to distant realms in search of knowledge, power, and prestige. Success in such searches could have been translated into an increased ability to dominate the American Bottom populace.

Along a myriad of lines of communication, some regular and others intermittent, or through direct encounters with nonlocal peoples, cultural information would have been transmitted. A panalopy of such information might have been accessible to Cahokian lords, affirming their place in the center of the known world and earning them the respect and tribute of primary producers (Helms 1979, 1992b). Distant visitors or trading partners could have left the American Bottom equally enriched by Cahokian information, materialized in various Cahokian media, providing status legitimation for the visitors back home.

This cultural view of interregional interaction is congruent with "prestige-goods" constructs and certain tenets of "world-systems" and "peer-polity" approaches, albeit in less economic terms (cf. Kohl 1987; Renfrew 1987; Rowlands 1987). Regional populations are, from these perspectives, parts of larger social formations with fuzzy, if not undefinable, boundaries not adequately captured by the western notion of "society" (Wolf 1982). The histories of regional populations are articulated with each other such that change in one affects change in others (cf. Spencer 1982, 40–58). This is not to say that all significant change is located within an interregional economy, as criticized earlier. Rather, it is to recognize prestige goods as symbols or markers of political-cultural exchanges that at once supersede yet are subordinate to local political arenas and social and historical factors (Pauketat, chapter 2).

Migrations and Ethnogenesis

Our view of Cahokia's external relations and internal development, with the recognition of interarticulated social histories, places the Cahokian phenomenon central to the genesis of native cultures and ethnicities. By A.D. 1200, emigration may have been occurring from Cahokia and the American Bottom in general (Emerson 1991a, 235; see also Koldehoff 1989; Koldehoff et al. 1993; Milner 1986; Woods and Holley 1991). Such demographic shifts might have been a continuation of an earlier pattern of emigration apparent as Cahokian "intrusions" into distant lands (see papers in Emerson and Lewis, eds., 1991; Stoltman, ed., 1991). Whatever the mechanism for leaving, it is clear that people did leave. By A.D. 1400, if not before, it is likely that nearly all of the Mississippian lineages, clans, or families that had in generations past called the American Bottom home were gone. Only immigrant Oneota hunter-farmers resided in the region (Jackson, Fortier, and Williams 1992). We are left, as were the Illiniwek natives of the eighteenth-century American Bottom, pondering what became of the Mississippians.

The identity of Cahokian descendants is significant not because of modern-day attempts to delimit rights and access the past, but because it furthers our knowledge of how cultural identities are related to (Cahokian) political centralization, interregional interaction, and cultural hegemonies. In this vein, we should first recognize that some native ethnic groups are themselves artifacts of the encounters between Native Americans and Europeans (Fried 1975, 114; Friedman 1992). Second, it is necessary to resist viewing ethnicity or tribal affiliation as immutable cultural qualities, the same in every respect now as in the past. Instead, and especially in light of archaeological evidence from Cahokia and outlying regions, we need to envision contexts in which, over a period of more than five hundred years, a series of relationships were forged that linked diverse people, in some cases homogenizing identities and in others heterogenizing formerly like groups.[6]

At A.D. 1150, the landscape of the Mississippi valley may be broken up into a series of archaeological phases or complexes that, based as they are on the stylistic qualities of material remains, are the current approximations of cultural identities, social organizations, and regional interactions (figure 1.9).[7] Some of these complexes probably represent the culmination of centuries of *in situ* development, with little movement of entire populations from one region to another. However, such migrations are evidenced in the precontact period and include Late Woodland displacements in northern Illinois, southern Wisconsin, and perhaps eastern Iowa immediately preceding, or as a consequence of, contacts with Cahokia-Mississippians (Emerson 1991b; Finney and Stoltman 1991; Goldstein 1991; Griffin 1960). Anderson (chapter 12) postulates political and demographic changes south of Cahokia as a consequence of Cahokian political consolidation. Stephen Williams (1990, 173) has postulated that a general abandonment of the central Mississippi and lower Ohio River valleys occurred during the late fifteenth and early sixteenth centuries (see Emerson and Brown 1992; B. Smith 1986). Such a "vacant quarter" and "site-unit intrusions" are indicative of whole-group migrations well before the Hernando de Soto expedition in A.D. 1539–43.

Migrations of the scale indicated in the upper Midwest or mid-South were, in all likelihood, outcomes of an interregional dynamic involving tensions between native groups with established or emergent ethnic identities (cf. Griffin 1960, 854–56). If, as Friedman (1992) posits, ethnogenesis is dialectically related to hegemony, then the demise of Cahokia might have heralded tensions between diverging social groups, the splintering of groups formerly attached to Mississippian patrons, and the formation of new social

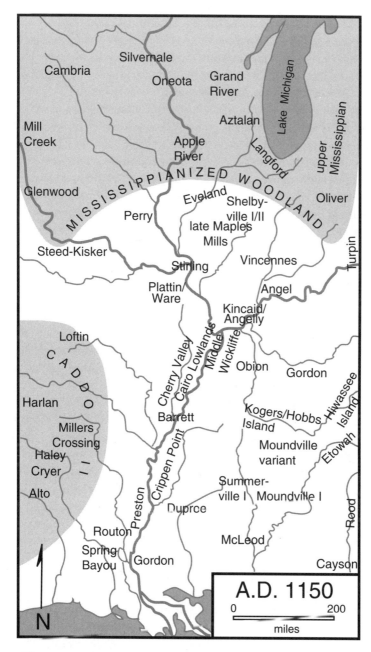

Figure 1.9. Cultural Complexes in the Midcontinent at A.D. 1150

or ethnic borders where none were visible before. Perhaps a vacant quarter was an expression of the substantive social transformations taking place as Mississippian hegemonies, including Cahokia, waxed and waned (in the sense of Anderson 1994a; see S. Williams 1990, 175–78).

By about A.D. 1500, the social landscape of the Mississippi valley was most likely a mosaic of ethnic groups speaking a variety of Siouan, Algonkian, Muskogean, and Caddoan languages (figure 1.10; Haas 1979; Nicklas 1994; Swanton 1979, 10–14). Given Cahokia's location and the evidence for extensive northern interaction, it is plausible that Cahokians were ancestors of multiple Siouan-speaking ethnic groups, Cahokia's interactions being so broad and multidirectional as to make any single ethnic offspring extremely unlikely. Cahokia's population probably splintered in many directions, some moving west and perhaps south, and some moving into the nearby Illinois uplands around A.D. 1200 only to move out again one to two centuries later (Koldehoff 1989; Koldehoff et al. 1993). Population decrease also might have occurred through dropping birth rates.

It has been argued for many years that Oneota groups, subsuming a number of Siouan-speaking populations, emerged out of a tribal milieu affected by Cahokia and related Mississippian developments (Griffin 1960; Hall 1991; Rodell 1991). Certain Oneota peoples may have established consanguinial links with groups or subgroups of Cahokians as early as A.D. 1000 but, given the "intrusion" from the north of a Bold Counselor Oneota occupation in the American Bottom beginning A.D. 1300 (Jackson et al. 1992), it seems unlikely that many migrating Cahokia-Mississippians went north (cf. R. Hall 1991, 19).

Certain Dhegiha-Siouan-speaking people like the Omaha, Osage, Ponca, Winnebago, and Quapaw have origin myths attaching them to lands east of the Mississippi River (Hoffman 1990, 1994). While Mochon (1972) noted the lack of Mississippian qualities among Siouan languages as opposed to Muskogean ones, archaeologists have material-culture and historical reasons to think that Precolumbian ancestors of Dhegihans may have lived in the central Mississippi and lower Ohio river drainages (Duncan 1993; Vehik 1993; see also Drechsel 1994, 37).

The social organization and material culture of Dhegihans include important elements that are Mississippian in character. The Osage possessed an elaborate political and ritual leadership hierarchy (Mathews 1961; Rollings 1992). The Omaha were governed by hereditary chiefs (O'Shea and Lud-

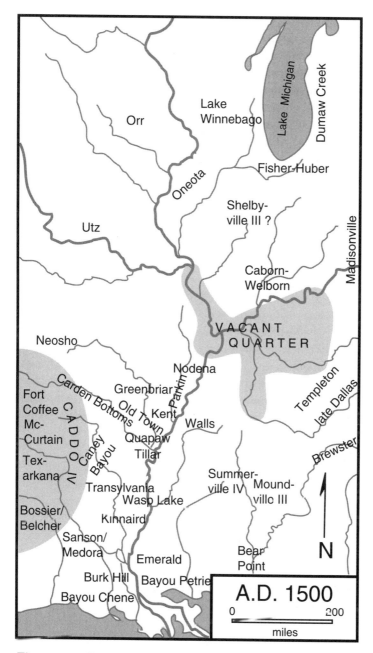

Figure 1.10. Cultural Complexes in the Midcontinent at A.D. 1500

25

wickson 1992). The Hidatsa and Osage played chunky using objects like Cahokian discoidals (Culin 1907; DeBoer 1993; Swanton 1979, 683–86).[8] The long-nosed god maskettes found in the Cahokia region and dispersed throughout the Mississippi valley have possible counterparts in the "Red Horn" or "He-who-wears-human-heads-as-earrings" myths of the Winnebago and Iowa, perhaps also sharing mythical features with the Osage and Pawnee (R. Hall 1989, 240–42). A pictograph in central Missouri depicts this mythical Siouan character, and, along with other petroglyphs in Missouri, might link a Mississippian past with the historic period (Duncan 1993).

To what extent Dhegihan societies were shaped by direct contact or actual Cahokian-Mississippian population movements is unknown at present. In any case, it is plausible that games, myths, sacred objects, and the sociopolitical organization of Dhegihans or other Plains, midwestern, and southeastern native groups were derived in part from interaction with Cahokians or other Mississippians. Cahokians' cultural impacts on native cultural identities, practices, and social histories may have been great, but, along with those of other Mississippian polities, have not been systematically examined. Such an examination, bridging archaeology and ethnohistory, and avoiding the economism of previous Cahokia-periphery models, awaits future researchers. These researchers will undoubtedly bring to bear sophisticated historical perspectives that will depend in part on a well-founded Cahokian social history. Just such a social-historical foundation is established for Cahokia in the following chapters.

Approaching Cahokian Social History

Explaining Cahokia is crucial to North American archaeology, given its place in the larger political and ethnic developments of precontact America and given its world-historical significance. Explanations of Cahokia-Mississippian since the FAI-270 project are rooted in two different perspectives. The first, deterministic in logic, views external causal factors like population growth and environmental change or degradation as having led inexorably to Cahokia's emergence and demise. From this perspective, common to the neoevolutionary thought of the 1970s, population growth was closely linked with environmental stresses, which, in the American Bottom, ranged from the introduction of new strains of maize or the depletion of natural resources to rising water tables (e.g., J. Kelly 1990a; R. Hall 1991; Lopinot and Woods

1993; Milner 1990; Rindos and Johannessen 1991). Synthetic statements from the 1970s to the 1990s, while differing in how regional organization and scale were characterized, share an overemphasis on external environmental, technological, or demographic causes (e.g., Fowler 1974, 1975; Milner 1990, 1991).

The second view, historical in thrust, views the dynamic social and political environment as the mediating force behind Cahokian developments. From this second perspective, inspired largely by Henry Wright (1984) and diffused into the Southeast via his students and advocates, the coalescence of Cahokia, its developmental trajectory, and later fissioning of its populace are explained in part through its political structure (Emerson 1991b; Pauketat 1994a).[9] A Wrightist perspective continues to inform present thinking on Cahokia-Mississippian as analyses of older, previously unpublished Cahokia excavations are completed and additional excavations are conducted at Cahokia, East St. Louis, and related sites (Collins 1990, chapter 7; J. Kelly, chapter 8; Pauketat 1987a, 1987b, 1993c, 1996). The Cahokia-Mississippian phenomenon in all of its cultural, organizational, demographic, economic, environmental, and interregional aspects may be seen, from this vantage point, as a gestalt pinned to political structure, with a historical momentum that was internally generated.[10]

New theoretical ideas and empirical details of the scale and composition of a Cahokian polity and economy are presented in the following chapters. None of the contributors to this volume, and few other Mississippianists, adhere to the notion that Cahokia was a mercantile city or that Cahokian rulers could or did exert significant economic control more than a hundred kilometers in any direction. The scale of a Cahokian political economy was probably little larger than the American Bottom region itself (Pauketat, chapter 2). The Mississippian politics of production, appropriation, and redistribution gave form and rhythm to Cahokian hegemony, as elaborated by Pauketat (chapter 2). Its agricultural economy, as delineated by Lopinot (chapter 3), was geared to the production of local starchy and oily seed crops, maize, and cucurbits. Periodic shortfalls or surfeits of foodstuffs probably were of paramount concern to the political administrators. Choice portions of white-tailed deer underlined the status of the elite in this political economy, according to Kelly (chapter 4).

The emigration of thousands of individuals to early Cahokia entailed community-wide reorganization and monumental undertakings, highlighted by Dalan (chapter 5). The diachronic relationship between central and rural Mississippians is revealed in the demographic shifts suggested by Pauketat and Lopinot (chapter 6). The Lohmann-phase Cahokian landscape featured densely packed houses and outdoor storage facilities, described by Collins (chapter 7). These gradually gave way to Stirling-phase changes in building orientation and the location of domestic stores.

Stirling-phase architectural and monumental features included fairly elaborate domestic zones, ceremonial sanctums, and ritual facilities, evident to Kelly (chapter 8) at the Cahokia and East St. Louis sites. These features were arranged or constructed according to kin-group contingencies, labor constraints, and basic cosmological principles. These same contingencies, constraints, and principles ruled the lives of rural commoners. Their apparent self-sufficiency of production masks an apparent top-down management of rural labor and produce (Emerson, chapter 9). Emerson (chapter 10) sees the Mississippian cosmos incorporated into many media in both rural and central contexts. Pots, pipes, and statues bespeak falcons, serpents, gourds, fire, gender, fertility, nobility, and, in general, the broad cultural themes that defined the Southeast.

There are, in fact, significant correspondences between Cahokia's historical trajectory and that of other southeastern Mississippian polities. Knight (chapter 11) outlines startling parallels between Cahokia and Moundville, in Alabama. The developmental trajectories of both were marked by a rapid political centralization followed by a lengthy period of stability or decline where political capitals were transformed into ritual and mortuary centers for a decentralized population. According to Anderson (chapter 12), in fact, the Cahokian trajectory in certain respects is comparable to many other southeastern chiefdoms. In other respects, however, Anderson and ourselves (chapter 13) recognize Cahokia as a preeminent cultural development that diverged from and disproportionately contributed to the Mississippian world. Its preeminence is attested by its size, its massive mounds, its productive residues, and its icons emulated and scattered to the four winds. It was the most expansive political-cultural phenomenon of the Mississippian world. It had profound impacts on other native groups of southeastern and midcontinental North America.

As presented in the foregoing discussion and as elaborated in subsequent chapters, Cahokian development was based in the configuration of historical factors and the intersection of these factors with the social histories of other

Mississippian and non-Mississippian groups to the north, south, east, and west. Cultural shock waves emanated out from Cahokia, shock waves that, metaphorically speaking, varied in periodicity and amplitude according to the mode and form of Cahokian domination. This domination was comprised of the attempts to administer or to resist the administration of the regional population. The scale and configuration of a Cahokian political economy—the population size, artifact styles, centralized production, rural lifestyle, and monumental constructions—were direct outcomes of the actions of people rooted in their interests or ideologies vis-à-vis domination. Even the dissolution of Cahokia must be seen as part of this same process (Pauketat 1992).

We cannot ultimately say where the thousands of Cahokians went, probably because they did not go any one place or become any one historically known ethnic group. It is likely that Cahokia's ultimate demise and population dispersal were simply a continuation of the established pattern of Cahokian relations with peripheral groups. That is, emigrations probably were as multidirectional and far-flung as Cahokian political and economic relations had been. Cahokia, for a time the premier center of Native America, ultimately—and perhaps appropriately—was itself scattered to the four winds.

Timothy R. Pauketat

2

Cahokian Political
Economy

A Cahokian political economy, as iterated here, encompasses the local and
supralocal configurations of human interactions and ideologies as these
formed the historical landscape of the American Bottom and beyond. This
contrasts with the usual isolation of a "subsistence economy"—domestic
production, exchange, and consumption—from a "political economy"—
the centralized appropriation, production, consumption, and distribution of
goods and services (e.g., Brumfiel and Earle 1987). In Mississippian archaeology, the subsistence economy often has been discussed as if it were an
"adaptation" to southeastern floodplain environments, the economic base
upon which rested the political and religious superstructure of the Mississippian world (e.g., Muller 1986a; B. Smith 1978). The panregional circulation
of finished "nonutilitarian" prestige goods has become the defacto focus of
political and economic analysis, affirming the rift between it and the subsistence economy (e.g., J. Brown, Kerber, and Winters 1990; Cobb 1989, 80–
81; Muller 1987, 18–19; Peregrine 1992).

While such a dichotomy has served a purpose in scholarly discourse, it is
nonetheless artificial and unfortunate because it deemphasizes the mobilization and appropriation of domestic energies within a region as an integral aspect of historical development. It places the intersection of local politics and
the daily lives and labor of rural or low-ranking people outside the realm of
the political economy. When casting an eye on this intersection, it becomes
clear that Cahokian development was more than a mere variant of a Mississippian adaptive pattern and that the political economy involved more than
panregional exchanges of prestige goods. A Cahokian political economy entailed the extension of and resistance to political domination through the negotiation of cultural meanings and the appropriation of labor. The processes

at the core of Cahokian political economy were ideological; that is, change was mediated by ideologies or the sets of values, beliefs, and attitudes shared differentially by groups or subgroups, dominant or subordinate, within a social formation.[1] These core processes at both local and supralocal levels hold the key to a conceptual door to Precolumbian developments in the eastern United States. Unlocking this door requires returning to the beginning of the Mississippian universe in the American Bottom. Through an examination of this beginning and its social and political consequences, I will argue that regional domination was effected through an appropriation of labor and a transformation of cultural meanings and values.

Big Bang in the Bottom

The decades leading up to A.D. 1050 witnessed increased population density, intensified intercommunity activities, and local aggrandizement of small town centers within the northern expanse of the American Bottom (T. R. Pauketat 1994a, 53–63; Pauketat, Rees, and S. L. Pauketat 1996). A plethora of exotic artifacts are found at Cahokia, probably already a chiefly center of a local Emergent Mississippian polity (Emerson 1991a, 234; J. Kelly 1991b). These artifacts are telling of long-distance communications between Cahokia and points as far removed as the Yazoo or Tensas basins in Mississippi and Louisiana. Long-distance ties of this sort were probably a means by which local officials or high-ranking kin groups legitimized their superordinate positions and extended their affinal alliance networks (H. Wright 1984). Affines or other immigrants might have moved into the American Bottom as a consequence of the long-distance ties, an inference warranted in part by pottery evidence. This evidence consists of ubiquitous sherds of exotic-style pots in Cahokian Edelhardt–phase refuse that were probably manufactured locally (Pauketat 1994a, 63, 1994c, 1995). The enlarged kin groups or entourages of prominent Cahokians, perhaps including these exotic potters, may have been fed with provisions supplied to centers, as inferred through comparisons of Cahokian and non-Cahokian faunal assemblages dating to the Emergent Mississippi Period (see L. Kelly 1979, 1990b, chapter 4).

Then, about A.D. 1050, the American Bottom experienced the political and economic equivalent of the Big Bang (Pauketat 1993a). I have identified this Big Bang in the bottom as a consequence of the rapid consolidation of political power or regional control presumably by some subset of the high-ranking Emergent Mississippian population (Pauketat 1994a). The event brought about the abrupt and large-scale transformation of community order, the physical landscape of Cahokia, and the entire northern expanse of American Bottom floodplain. Large plazas were leveled (Dalan, chapter 7), buildings were reconstructed entirely using new (wall-trench) techniques, domestic and community space was reordered, populations became nucleated, and, judging by refuse assemblages, domestic activities were altered (figure 2.1).

Cahokia became the capital of a dynamic three-tiered settlement hierarchy, as defined using site sizes and the differential distributions of exotic or craft goods, architecture, monuments, and mortuary remains (Milner 1990, 21–23; Pauketat 1994a, chapter 4). Outside of Cahokia, large village-level communities, each comprised of a series of flanking courtyard groups, dissipated around A.D. 1050, to be replaced by Mississippian towns with mounds and scattered homesteads (Emerson and Milner 1982; Milner et al. 1984). Early Cahokia Project excavations of domestic refuse and one of two small mounds at the Morrison site suggest that this small Edelhardt-phase town was abandoned at the end of the Edelhardt phase (T. R. Pauketat, Rees, and S. L. Pauketat 1996). This corresponds to an overall decrease in numbers of sites following the Edelhardt phase in the vicinity of the Cahokia site (Lopinot 1993; T. R. Pauketat, Rees, and S. L. Pauketat 1996).

Resistance

Emergent Mississippian courtyard groups, of the sort that disappeared at outlying villages, also were dissolved at Cahokia as part of Lohmann-phase changes (Pauketat 1994a). Presumably, the surging numbers of people immigrating to Cahokia from the surrounding countryside would have facilitated this dissolution (Pauketat and Lopinot, chapter 6). Whether or not it was entirely intentional, the elimination of an element of the social fabric, perhaps the basal social organizational units of pre-Mississippian society, would have been quite a political feat, casting off as it would have the means by which social resistance might have been mobilized against political consolidation. With the demise of the Emergent Mississippian courtyard group and the resettlement of many local people to Cahokia around A.D. 1050, we might reasonably suspect that new decision-making bodies articulated the activities of households and small kin subgroups. High-ranking Cahokians,

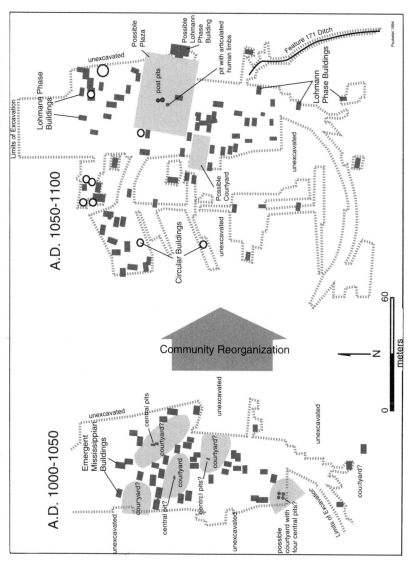

Figure 2.1. Cahokian Community Transformation, Viewed from Tract 15A

33

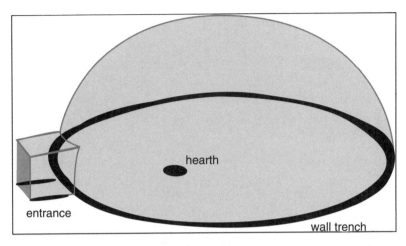

Figure 2.2. Oblique View of Circular Building, Tract 15A, Cahokia

their own identities transformed, may have encouraged the dissolution of the old pre-Mississippian organizations and the redefinition of domestic group relationships by rewarding those who did not resist the new order. Such encouragement would have engendered patron-client relations in the local domain unfettered by pre-Mississippian social structures (Pauketat 1994a, 21–25).

The kinds or degree of resistance to the consolidated Lohmann-phase regime is uncertain from archaeological evidence. Possible reintegrative measures were introduced, like the addition of circular "sweat houses" (figure 2.2), centralized agricultural rites, or even community-wide chunky games, as these probably had been "appropriated" by the central personages of Cahokia beginning with the Lohmann phase (DeBoer 1993, 89–90). Such measures probably helped minimize resistance to the new Lohmann-phase order at Cahokia and throughout the bottom (Emerson, chapter 9; Pauketat 1994a, 122, 174). In the very least, dissentors may not have been treated with rewards or subsidies as given to collaborators.

Resistance might well have been met with more than simple lack of reward. In one pit in Mound 72 were thrown the bodies of thirty-nine individuals, most of whom were male, three of whom had been decapitated and two of whom had arrowheads embedded in their thorax or vertebra (Rose and Cohen 1974). Litter burials of honored dead were placed atop this pit of dishonored dead. Nearby four other beheaded and behanded males were found

(Fowler 1991). These Lohmann-phase victims demonstrate that reckoning with Cahokian patrons sometimes had deadly consequences.

Other Lohmann-phase human remains might have derived from similar reckonings. One early Lohmann-phase pit in the middle of a newly expanded plaza on Tract 15A might contain further evidence of the treatment given those who resisted the new order (figure 2.3). There were thrown the articulated legs and arms of three to four individuals (Miracle 1996b). Another shallow pit (feature 460) on the ICT-II contained a damaged cranium in its approximate center (Milner and Paine 1991, table 2; Pauketat, personal field notes; see Collins 1990). A cranial fragment of a robust male was associated with a special Lohmann-phase building at the Lohmann site, and an adult female missing the right leg below the knee was interred on the floor of another nearby Lohmann phase house, an extremely unusual treatment (Milner 1992b, 153).

Other incidental human bones in Cahokian refuse are not as readily interpreted (e.g., Milner and Paine 1991; Miracle 1996b; Pauketat 1993c, 138). Scattered bits of human bones are occasionally associated with Emergent Mississippian and Mississippian refuse in the American Bottom (L. Kelly 1979; Milner 1984b, 1987). These do not include the qualitatively distinct Lohmann-phase treatments mentioned above, although sampling biases inhibit a clear delineation of phase-specific patterning. Suffice it to say that no articulated limbs, isolated crania, decapitations, or violent deaths are apparent prior to the Lohmann phase.

Central Individuals

It is likely that the threat of coercive force during the Lohmann phase was symbolized by the individuals in central mortuaries. Central individuals include a male on the bead blanket in Mound 72, buried adjacent to other individuals (possibly related to this male) with chunky stones, beads, a pile of mica, a rolled tube of copper sheet, and bundles of several hundred arrows tipped with finely chipped stone points (Fowler 1991). The central Mound 72 male and other isolated-incident burials, as they were unique in some respects and deserving of special treatment, suggests a social order cross-cut by superordinate organizations and political offices other than strict kin-based ones (figure 2.3). Other elite mortuaries at Cahokia, East St. Louis, St. Louis, and Mitchell included communal tombs filled with articulated and

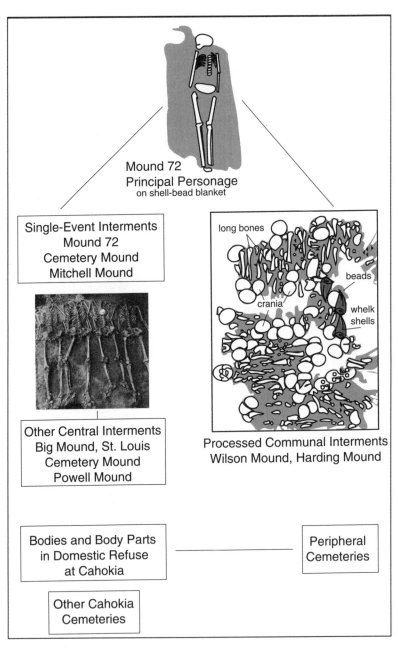

Mound 72
Principal Personage
on shell-bead blanket

Single-Event Interments
Mound 72
Cemetery Mound
Mitchell Mound

long bones

beads

crania

whelk
shells

Other Central Interments
Big Mound, St. Louis
Cemetery Mound
Powell Mound

Processed Communal Interments
Wilson Mound, Harding Mound

Bodies and Body Parts
in Domestic Refuse
at Cahokia

Peripheral
Cemeteries

Other Cahokia
Cemeteries

Figure 2.3. Mortuary Remains of the American Bottom

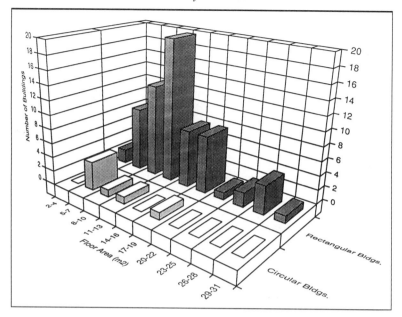

Figure 2.4. Lohmann-Phase Building Sizes from Tract 15A, Cahokia

disarticulated skeletons and associated accoutrements, perhaps processed and collected in charnel houses (Milner 1984c, 479–80). Cahokia itself, and other parts of the sprawling Central Political-Administrative Complex, would have been home to those high-ranking patrons and political officials who exercised regional authority over lesser officeholders and the non-elite masses (Pauketat 1994a, 73–87).

These central individuals probably would have included the managers of communal surpluses or the appropriators of primary produce. They would have received staple goods and labor for their consumption, redistribution, or allocation to fund short-term labor projects or to invest in longer-term transformations of social, economic, and physical landscapes. High-ranking Cahokian patrons and their kin presumably resided in houses that reflected their social prominence. These may have included the 10 percent of sixty-eight Lohmann-phase rectangular buildings in the Cahokia 15A-DT sample that had larger-than-average floor areas, falling within a 20 to 30 square meter range (figure 2.4). Later Stirling-phase buildings in the same sample, presumably the homes of high-ranking households, ranged up to 228 square meters, as large or larger than mound-top buildings (Pauketat 1993c, 1996).

37

There are no other buildings comparable outside of Cahokia at the scattered rural homesteads or the smaller towns where district administrations were centered (Esarey and Pauketat 1992; Milner et al. 1984). Rural domiciles of the Lohmann and Stirling phases were small, like most domestic architecture at Cahokia (Collins 1990; O'Brien 1972a; Pauketat 1996). Rural Lohmann-phase and Stirling-phase floor areas covered no more than 16 square meters and 20 square meters, respectively (e.g., Emerson and Jackson 1984; Jackson and Hanenberger 1990; Jackson, Fortier, and Williams 1992; Milner 1983a). Burials of most people outside of mounds and in rural areas are not elaborate nor do they include wealth accumulations, outside an occasional craft object (Milner 1984c; Pauketat 1994a, 85). Some individuals or isolated body parts even are associated with residential debris within towns, especially Cahokia (Milner 1984c, 1992a; Milner and Paine 1991; Miracle 1996a; Pauketat 1993c, 138). These are perhaps the remains of lower-ranking individuals, the clientele or victims of superordinate patrons.

Subsidized Producers

The size of the region or population dominated or successfully integrated under a Cahokian paramountcy after the Big Bang or at any point in time would have greatly affected the labor that could have been mobilized for mound building, plaza leveling, and craft production. There undoubtedly were political and administrative constraints to the size of the region or population that could be so administered, and the technology did not exist to mobilize labor (and tribute) from far outside the northern American Bottom region on a regular basis (*contra* O'Brien 1991, 1992; Peregrine 1991). It is possible that goods from outside the immediate American Bottom region occasionally were moved into Cahokia (J. Kelly 1991a), but this movement probably would not have affected available labor. Nonetheless, the two hundred earthen mounds of the Cahokia, East St. Louis, and St. Louis sites attest to sizable local labor pools. In number and volume, the earthen monuments far exceed any other flat-topped earthen tumuli concentration in North America.

After the Big Bang, the Lohmann-phase community order featured an increased number of tightly clustered buildings oriented to the cardinal directions around plazas, and a segregation of these buildings by size and shape (Collins, chapter 7; Pauketat 1994a, 1996). The artifactual evidence from the Lohmann phase suggests that domestic activities were altered at Cahokia and across the northern expanse of the American Bottom. In central locations, the data support an increased focus on a few craft-production tasks. Some households within Cahokian subcommunities engaged in the manufacture of axeheads, while others produced shell bead necklaces. At the Lohmann site and rural settlements, shell-bead manufacturing refuse is found only among some domestic refuse, likely a result of temporal or social restrictions in shell-bead manufacture (Pauketat 1987c, 81; 1989, table 6).

Likewise, outside of Cahokia, axehead-making debitage, consisting of St. Francois Mountain basalt and diabase flakes and shatter, is known only in minor amounts from a handful of Lohmann-phase sites around Horseshoe Lake or northwest of Horseshoe Lake (T. R. Pauketat, Rees, and S. L. Pauketat 1996; Charles Rohrbaugh, personal communication, 1993). At the Cahokia, Lohmann, and East St. Louis administrative centers, caches of up to 100 unfinished "hypertrophic" axeheads, made from the St. Francois Mountain rock, were found, which would seem to boast of the ability of a central personage to subsidize such unwieldy and conspicuous objects. These were too massive to be circulated far afield and, except for one known occurrence (Brouk 1978), they are found only in caches at these centers (see Milner 1992b, 157–58; Pauketat 1994a, 98).

Artifact styles new to the region, like notched triangular arrowheads, probably were among those craft goods made by subsidized Lohmann-phase producers. Red-slipped pottery wares and decorated finewares, each group characterized by a distinctive paste recipe, also suggest production by some subsets of the population (Pauketat 1994c). Other Lohmann-phase evidence of the central subsidization of households at Cahokia and other centers is found in the increased quantities of all refuse, including exotic raw materials and craft-production debris in garbage: exotic cherts, copper, mineral crystals, pigments, and pieces of imported adze and knife blades. This density measure probably indicates the production of more refuse and exotic waste per capita, although it may also reflect in part the higher population density of the Lohmann phase (Pauketat and Lopinot, chapter 6). Lohmann-phase lithic refuse, in fact, is more than three times as dense (grams/cubic meter) as the preceding Edelhardt phase (and four times as dense as the subsequent Stirling- and Moorehead-phase deposits) in the Cahokia 15A-DT sample (Pauketat 1996, figure 8.1). Lohmann-phase households at Cahokia appear to have had access to considerably more resources than in the years before A.D. 1050, among these resources being the exotic raw materials that were crafted into finished goods on site.

Household-cluster occupation spans and refuse density further support the inference that households were subsidized by central patrons.[2] Lohmann- and Stirling-phase domiciles at the Cahokia and Lohmann sites typically were reconstructed repeatedly in the same location and are associated with considerably more refuse than most rural domestic zones (see Collins 1990; Milner 1992b, 159; Pauketat 1989, 1996). Whereas rural homesteads, outside of Emerson's "nodal" category (chapter 9), seldom occupied one spot for more than a decade, central household clusters include some that were perhaps occupied for several decades (figure 2.5; cf. Pauketat 1989, table 5). The more abundant refuse of these central domestic clusters might also indicate the increased level of activity at centers. The greater numbers of broken pots associated with central household clusters might signal food preparation for suprahousehold aggregations of people (from outside the center), also a form of central patronage of domestic groups.

Perhaps the diet of centrally located Lohmann-phase households was superior to rural producers. Centripetal mobilizations of animal meat already had occurred during the Emergent Mississippi Period, and, while few Lohmann-phase samples are yet available for quantifying tributary patterns, Stirling-phase samples evince an elite reliance on processed deer meat (L. Kelly, chapter 4). Likewise, data, though equivocal, suggest the Mississippi Period mobilization of maize and some fruits and the consumption of more nutritious foods by the Cahokian elite (Bender et al. 1981; Johannessen and Cross 1993; Lopinot, chapter 3; Pauketat 1994a, 75). Indirect clues in the standardized pastes and distribution of Monks Mound Red seed jars and Ramey Incised jars suggest that goods or medicines were redistributed from centers using pottery containers (Emerson 1989; Pauketat 1994a, 58–60; Pauketat and Emerson 1991). Many of these decorated pots and other finely made wares, probably produced under the aegis of high-ranking patrons, might have been items of value rewarded to the recipients in the same way that "prestige goods" were distributed to followers (see Brumfiel and Earle 1987).

The subsidization of domestic groups at towns, the hints of a division of labor, and the evidence of centripetal and centrifugal mobilizations of goods and comestibles reveal the relationship of some producers to central administrations and of the kinds of returns that producers, attached or not, perhaps expected from these administrations.[3] In fact, given that a political consolidation seems to be at the heart of the changed American Bottom landscape

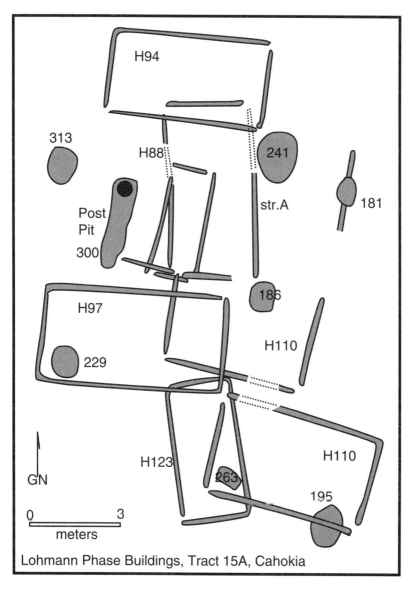

Figure 2.5. Superposed Lohmann-Phase Buildings, Plan View

after A.D. 1050, we might reasonably view the Lohmann-phase dispersion of rural homesteads as a direct consequence of political consolidation and not an adaptation that necessarily preceded the political superstructure (Emerson, chapter 9). In other words, recognizing the homesteads as self-sufficient, in terms of subsistence, does not mean that they were also self-sufficient in social reproduction. In fact, in all probability the Lohmann-phase dispersed homestead pattern was very much linked to the overall political order in a manner reminiscent of, if not more highly integrated than, Bruce Smith's (1978, 490) description of a typical Mississippian settlement-subsistence system.

From our Lohmann-phase vantage point, the presence of occasional craft manufacturing debris at rural homesteads need not signal a decentralized political landscape or a lack of central control over rural production (Muller 1987). Rather, craft-production debris in the Lohmann-phase countryside may indicate a unified political economy in which rural activities were coordinated with the central administrations. This is not to say that the rural craft production was conducted by full-time specialists (*contra* Yerkes 1991). Instead, rural craft activities might have been limited to particular times of the year or to irregular political-ritual events, the shell beads, axeheads, or other items comprising the produce required by Mississippian overlords from rural households.

Local Symbols and the Appropriation of Labor

Intermittent central gatherings probably were an inseparable part of rural Mississippian life. Public agricultural rites, annual festivals, and a variety of other community or life-cycle events likely were conducted within the sacred communal (and elite administered) spaces of the Central Political-Administrative Complex and smaller towns (see Emerson 1989; Jackson, Fortier, and Williams 1992). At the same time, periodic aggregations in towns could account for the regular and incremental construction of mounds. Such aggregations at centers might have gone a long way toward reducing social tensions, mitigating imbalances, resolving disputes, and, generally, restoring balance to the cosmos.

One way of looking at the tremendous central undertakings of the Lohmann phase, then, would be as a negotiation of social tensions that resulted from the rapid and large-scale transformation of the political landscape.

Elsewhere I have argued that the dramatic and pervasive character of the changes that mark the beginning of the Lohmann phase imply that common resistance to them might have been alleviated where patrons collaborated with low-ranking producers such that the interests of both groups were served (Pauketat 1994a, chapter 7). The process whereby this would have been accomplished and perpetuated was necessarily a symbolic one, as it involved a shift in common values, ethical standards, and cultural meanings.

Monuments and Craft Items

Looking across the transformed political landscape of the eleventh century, political symbols were manifest in a variety of media. Mounds, plazas, giant posts, and Post-Circle Monuments or woodhenges were highly visible political symbols, constructed with mobilized community labor (Pauketat 1994b). Monument construction was probably a means to integrate an increasingly stratified Cahokian community while legitimating the sanctity of both the monument and its elite caretakers (Knight 1989a; Pauketat 1993c).

Most of the flat-topped mounds, including the largest tumulus in North America, Monks Mound, were built up by many incremental and often minor-stage enlargements and blanket mantles (figure 2.6; Pauketat 1993c, 142–44).[4] Moreover, each stage or mantle addition saw the reconstruction of the surmounting buildings. In the same way, large posts and the Post-Circle Monument on Tract 15A were emplaced, replaced, or reconstructed frequently (see figure 1.6; Pauketat 1994b). One such cypress post, over a meter in diameter, was found snapped and lying in the bottom of a post pit at the Mitchell site (Porter 1977, figure 60). Cutting, hauling, erection, and removal of these posts, numerous examples (of the size found at Mitchell) also being associated with the Cahokia and East St. Louis sites (figure 2.7), represent a considerable amount of labor. Obviously, building and rebuilding a monument, be it a post, post circle, plaza, mound, or mound-top structure, regularly employed much labor. Thus, the act of monument construction as a regular event was probably as important, if not more so, than the actual monument itself (see Knight 1989a).

During construction events or other centralized rites, Lohmann-phase patrons could have projected the cosmic importance of their roles to the congregated masses. Distributions of goods, valuable objects, and comestibles may have taken place. The valuable objects, perhaps distributed as part of

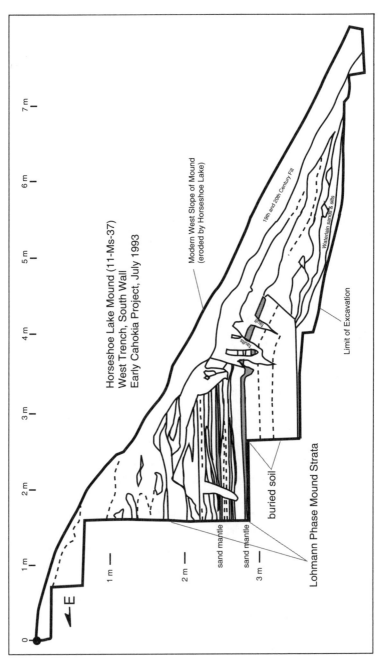

Horseshoe Lake Mound (11-Ms-37)
West Trench, South Wall
Early Cahokia Project, July 1993

Modern West Slope of Mound
(eroded by Horseshoe Lake)

18th and 20th Century Fill

Waterlain sands & silts

fault

faults

Limit of Excavation

buried soil

sand mantle

sand mantle

Lohmann Phase Mound Strata

E

Figure 2.6. Profile of the Horseshoe Lake Site Mound

44

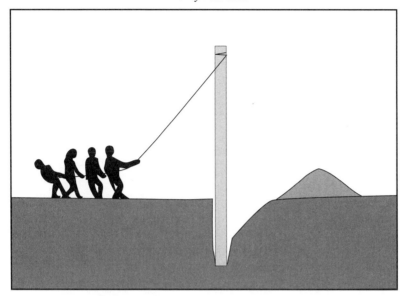

Figure 2.7. Large Post Emplacement Procedure

such centralized events, were symbols of relationships between people. Importantly, as these incorporated religious or supernatural meanings, the material goods also would have been (like monuments) symbols of the inherently powerful supernatural forces beyond the known social world (Helms 1979, 1988, 1992a). Greater access to, or control over, these tangible items, then, would have been a means of legitimating superordinate claims to authority within or over the community.[5]

However, simply to understand the circulation of legitimating symbols as related to political centralization is to miss the dynamism of the Cahokian political economy. As evidenced in the Cahokian data presently available, control over legitimating symbols was not restricted to control over the circulation of finished items from distant sources. Such "prestige goods" as discussed by Brown et al. (1990), Muller (1987), and Peregrine (1992) are apparent in certain archaeological contexts in the American Bottom (J. Kelly 1991a, 1991b). However, based on quantitative measures, such finished items from distant sources plainly constitute a minority of the prestige goods found in the American Bottom (Pauketat 1994a, 92–105, 1997).

The craft items that are found in central mortuaries and at secondary centers and rural homesteads in the American Bottom are most often objects made *inside*, not *outside*, the American Bottom. Local craft items—arrowheads, axeheads, shell beads, carved-stone figurines, and copper ornaments—typically were manufactured from exotic raw materials, thereby incorporating the powerful supralocal meanings affiliated with distant realms into an otherwise local product. For instance, many of the chipped-stone arrowheads found in Mound 72 and in Cahokian refuse were made from exotic cherts or from local cherts in exotic styles. Exotic marine shell, it seems, was commonly used to produce shell beads and necklaces for local (as well as nonlocal) consumption. The ordinary and hypertrophic axeheads cached or made at Cahokia and a few other sites were manufactured from exotic rock, only available 100 kilometers away, while entirely suitable glacial-rock erratics, plentiful in the hills east of the floodplain, were not used. These axeheads do not seem to have been made for exchange outside of the Cahokia region but rather were displayed or distributed within the region (Pauketat 1994a, 98). That the tools were for use within the region contrasts importantly with extant models of prestige-goods economies that emphasize the acquisition of foreign finished objects for local distribution and the elite accumulation of local craft items for exchange with outsiders (e.g., Brown et al. 1990; Peregrine 1992).

Perhaps even better examples of the local production and exchange of objects are the locally made decorated pottery wares and "magicoritual" materials (Emerson 1989). The red-slipped and decorated Monks Mound Red and Ramey Incised wares mentioned earlier, along with a suite of incised fineware pots, incorporated supralocal or supernatural meanings within their forms or decorations. These were *local* products, many subsidized by central patrons, yet also targeted primarily for *local* consumption (see Pauketat and Emerson 1991). As centrally manufactured and centrifugally distributed objects, these pots (along with the other craft items) were *local symbols* of a Cahokian order crafted by central patrons or centrally subsidized households.

The supralocal meanings and centralized production of these local symbols created the value of each object. Other materials, not necessarily manufactured into craft objects, attained value in a manner like the decorated local pots and other centrally made craft items. These included minerals or raw lithic materials having a variety of uses—hematite, galena, Burlington chert from the Crescent Quarry in Missouri, quartz crystal, high-grade sandstone—and plants having ritual uses such as red cedar, tobacco, and jimson-

46

weed (Emerson 1989, 78–84). Given the higher densities or associations of these "magicoritual" materials at and around Cahokia, the distribution or use of an unknown quantity of these was probably regulated by Cahokian patrons. If so, then part of their value most likely was acquired from their association with Cahokia. That is, magicoritual items, too, might have been local symbols of a Cahokian order. These locally available items and raw materials, along with the decorated pots, would have incorporated the supralocal or exotic meanings associated with Cahokia or its rulers (Helms 1993).

The Cahokian Valuation Process

The Cahokian valuation process of reshaping or transforming the exotic idea or raw material (symbol) into the local craft or magicoritual item was, in essence, a negotiation of meaning or a reconciliation of the ideologies of patrons and clients (Pauketat 1997). To the extent that the central ideas or themes of high-ranking patrons were served, this transformation of symbolic value also would have been a homogenization of cultural meanings, values, and beliefs. The resulting local symbol (i.e., craft or magicoritual object) would have conveyed meanings about the American Bottom world that perhaps, as these were associated with the local elite and their supernatural powers, would have affirmed the elite mediation between the distant unknown (exotic) and the locally known (Pauketat and Emerson 1991, 920). As such, local symbols did not merely legitimize the central order but actively created it.

Cahokians and other central administrators, by controlling the production of meaningful symbols that were circulated within their own domains, were in effect attempting to control the array of symbols that would inform the ideologies of the masses. Of course, the same may be said of mounds and other monuments or symbolic media constructed under the aegis of central administrations. The construction of both craft goods and monuments entailed a regular appropriation of communal labor that, as it served to create and legitimize a Cahokia-dominated order, enabled the appropriation of the ideologies of those same laborers.

Monuments and craft items, then, actually express a kind of fetishized labor, since the products of laborers would have been dissociated from their labor. Laborers, to some extent, would have become "alienated" from their own labor and from traditional (Emergent Mississippian) modes of reproducing their labor through a process of symbolic domination by central administrations. The increased construction of mounds during the Stirling phase and other signs of a "divine chiefship" (in which a chiefly social class was expressed in multiple media and diverse contexts) reflects the degree of producer alienation (see Pauketat 1992, 1994a). Furthermore, the enlargement of buildings through the Moorehead phase, such that domestic activities and food stores—both of which had been located outdoors—were kept away from the eyes of the larger community and inside the domicile, signals the same (DeBoer 1988; see Mehrer 1988; Mehrer and Collins 1995; Pauketat 1994a, 182).

Symbolic Transformations through Time and Space

The dispersion of Cahokian values, meanings, and ideas, *qua* local symbols, across time and space shaped the historical landscape of Cahokia and related supralocal developments as it is projected to have done in the local sphere. While Cahokian craft goods were produced primarily for local consumption, they also were used in supralocal exchanges. Cahokian goods are found hundreds of kilometers away from the American Bottom (Pauketat and Emerson, chapter 1), and finished goods from elsewhere are found at Cahokia (J. Kelly 1991a, 1991b). Outside of Cahokia, the value of a Cahokian object would have been transformed such that original Cahokian meanings probably were not fully retained. We may think of this final transformation as occurring with distance from Cahokia, distance both in spatial and temporal terms. The value and meanings of local symbols changed through time as they entered larger networks of exchange or as they were retained as heirlooms (see Brown 1976a, 124–25; Farnsworth and Emerson 1989, 23).

Across the Southeast, early centralized economies or those more at the center of a panregional development might be composed of a higher incidence of local raw-material transformations and internal redistributions of the sort argued to characterize the Lohmann-phase political economy. Later economies, or those peripheral to a panregional formation, might have focused more on the circulation of finished goods from foreign places as so many more of these recirculated goods might have been accessible (cf. Knight, chapter 11). For instance, craft goods made at A.D. 1100 but still circulating a century later in the same region would have been subject to revaluation. Extending this logic, extant monuments at Cahokia would have

48

acquired new meanings over the years as time separated the acts of construction from a revalued earthen icon (Pauketat 1993c, 146–47).

In general, with distance from original value comes revaluation. Barring the complete elimination of the revalued symbols, we may infer that, with more craft goods in circulation, post-Lohmann-phase central administrations at Cahokia shifted some portion of the work force from the creation of local symbols to the control of circulation of revalued symbols. If so, then the subsidization of domestic producers at centers like Cahokia might even have tapered off with time. Moreover, reduced subsidization of craft goods could have engendered ambiguity over meanings, permitting usurpers to gain control over the process of revaluation and hence over labor pools. Such a process might have been closely related to the "falling rate of political expansion" or the "crisis of hierarchization" that I have hypothesized accompanied the divine chiefship of the Stirling phase (Pauketat 1992, 1994a, 186).

Given the revalued, overhierarchized political-economic context of the Stirling phase, however, resistance might have easily surfaced. Of course, resistance to the twelfth-century political landscape, as it would have been based in alienated subordinate ideologies, would not have been the same as it might have been during the Lohmann phase. Perhaps such resistance would have been mobilized against certain officeholders rather than the Cahokian hierarchical structure in general. The bastioned palisade line of the late Stirling and early Moorehead phases at Cahokia may be testimony of severe and violent opposition of the sort that surfaced as a consequence of the process of revaluation.

Certainly, Moorehead phase evidence indicates continued social hierarchy, but without the unequivocal signs of regional control evident up to A.D. 1150. Presumably, the labor pools of the Moorehead phase administrations were considerably reduced from those of the Lohmann and Stirling phases. Perhaps the conflicts that divided the Cahokians of the twelfth and thirteenth centuries were so severe as to drive people out of the region altogether (Emerson 1991a, 227–30). Or perhaps episodic defilement of the sacred center by those who penetrated the palisade resulted in the outmigration of the people who had identified with the center (Anderson 1994a, 80). The continued prominence of Cahokia, however, throughout the Moorehead phase (A.D. 1200–1275) and perhaps into the Sand Prairie phase, also testifies to the inertia of Cahokia as a sacred place. Cahokian sacrality in the thirteenth century A.D., I submit, was in itself a revaluation of a political capital.

49

Cahokia's gradual change from an eleventh-century political capital to a sacred center perhaps is similar to what Knight (chapter 11) has noted for the Moundville site. In fact, much like Moundville, the heart of the Cahokia site (especially the Mound 17–20 area adjacent to Monks Mound) was used as a cemetery area late in its history, during the thirteenth and fourteenth centuries A.D. Unfortunately, only sporadic reports exist from the various individuals' diggings in this portion of the site (Fowler 1989, 75–80; Milner 1984a, 478; see also McAdams 1882, 62; Moorehead 1929, figure 1; Peet 1903; Perino 1980).

The Production of Cahokia

Cahokian domination was a matter of production, a production of local symbols—mounds, posts, craft goods, magicoritual objects, even comestibles—and a homogenized political-ideological landscape legitimating the Mississippian patron-client relationships, and, ultimately, the divine chiefship of the Stirling phase. In fact, Cahokia, and the whole of the Central Political-Administrative Complex, can be usefully viewed not simply as an archaeological site but as a set of symbols or products that were created and re-created over centuries by the populace under the sway of central administrations.

Cahokia was comprised of many media. These media incorporated the supralocal as part and parcel of the local production of Cahokian symbols. Labor was mobilized, and local symbols produced only as high-ranking patrons were able to convert supralocal value, the control of which they would have sought, into local value. Cahokia as product *was* the intersection of local politics and the daily lives of all American-Bottom people. The labor employed to construct and reconstruct mounds and to craft other local symbols exemplify the core processes of Cahokian political economy. The mode of monument construction, the numbers of mounds on which work was prosecuted and the plethora of craft production debris point to the political-economic significance of the intersection of local politics and the masses of rural and central producers.

The labor mobilized for Cahokia's production probably was not matched elsewhere in the Mississippian world. The large labor pools intimated suggest that much of the American Bottom region was dominated or successfully integrated under a Cahokian umbrella as a consequence of the region's Big Bang. There undoubtedly were political and administrative constraints to the size of the region or population that could be so administered. The political organization and the technology to mobilize labor (and tribute) from far outside the northern American Bottom region on a regular basis did not exist, although provisions and finished valuables from a much broader portion of the Mississippi River drainage occasionally might have arrived at Cahokia.

Thus, explanations of Cahokian development cannot rest solely on long-distance exchange or adaptation to environment. These beg the question of how labor was appropriated and, in so doing, fail to comprehend the core mechanisms of a Cahokian political economy. These mechanisms, as they were part of the cultural valuation and revaluation process, perpetuated a consolidated regime and underlay other political tactics, even the use of coercive force. The use of coercive force or the resistance to such force or to the production of Cahokia—witnessed by dismemberments, violent deaths, single-event interments, a bastioned palisade, and arrows or arrowheads in central mortuaries and domestic refuse—was based in a continually redefined cultural logic. Let us not fail to recognize Mississippian political economies for what they were, the products of a cultural process in which local populations were dominated and in which labor was mobilized to create a Mississippian world.

Neal H. Lopinot

3

Cahokian Food Production Reconsidered

A theoretical shift has occurred in which greater primacy is allocated to political and ideological factors in modeling cultural change, particularly for groups other than egalitarian hunter-gatherers. The cloaked ecological "determinism" of neoevolutionists and New Archaeologists has faded as an important theoretical cornerstone since its peak during the late 1960s and early 1970s. Nonetheless, virtually everyone still recognizes the importance of an ecological, or contextual, approach that examines interaction among various temporal and spatial aspects of the physical, biological, and social environments.

All populations obviously must be fed. Consequently activities of non-food-producing sectors of a stratified society (e.g., elites, traders, craftsman, priests) are dependent to a large degree on the organization and input-output of agricultural activities. It follows then that changes in the organization of food production, and therefore any and all elements of the political economy, can be affected by, or must respond to, unexpected interannular or long-term environmental fluctuations (e.g., climatic change) that affect food production.

We must, therefore, evaluate the temporal and spatial webs of social, political, and ideological conditions, as well as impinging "natural" environmental conditions, if we are to gain a better understanding of the rise, short climax, and demise of the complex Cahokian chiefdom. The importance of analyzing subsistence remains and evaluating the relationship of techno-environmental factors and changing human behavior has been among the primary research domains in American Bottom archaeology during the last twenty-five years (e.g., Chmurny 1973; Gregg 1975a; Johannessen 1984,

1988, 1993; Lopinot 1991, 1994; Lopinot and Woods 1993). The body of data that has emerged on numerous facets of late prehistoric lifeways in this region allows a relatively detailed examination of spatial and temporal variability in food acquisition in relation to social, political, and ideological systems. The focus of this chapter is on the role of agriculture in the evolution of the Cahokian chiefdom.

Late Prehistoric Crop Production Models

Archaeologists and archaeobotanists alike have had a tendency to use models of subsistence and concepts of crop production rather loosely, although some recent exceptions can be noted (e.g., Fritz 1990; M. Scarry 1993a). Concepts utilized for cultivational practices in the New World mainly include gardening versus farming and horticulture versus agriculture. The two pairs of concepts are typically correlated with one another. Horticulture is considered to have entailed gardening or relatively small-scale crop production, mostly involving shifting cultivation techniques such as slash-and-burn/swidden or "bush fallow" methods accompanied by frequent group movement (e.g., every two to five years) to new residential locations.

Conversely, agriculture is considered to have involved intensive farming or large-scale crop production, often of alluvial fields that were repeatedly cultivated, with a marked emphasis on surplus production. Irrigation systems, terraces, and raised fields represent various forms of intensive agriculture (Michael Smith 1993); as Fritz (1990, 390) has noted, one might add ridged field systems to this list of labor-intensive farming systems. Ridged fields have been documented for late prehistoric times in southeastern and midwestern North America, including the Cahokia region (Fowler 1969a; Gallagher 1989, 1992; Gallagher et al. 1985; Gallagher and Sasso 1987; A. Kelly 1938, 1964; Riley 1987; Riley and Freimuth 1979: Riley, Moffat, and Freimuth 1981; Sasso et al. 1985).

Woodland populations have generally been viewed as horticulturalists or gardeners, whereas Mississippian populations are viewed as agriculturalists or farmers. Despite the "reluctance for some archaeologists to give up explanatory schemes that are traditional and comfortable" (Scarry 1993a, 4), the ever increasing body of archaeobotanical data for certain contexts necessitates either discard or significant revisions of these interpretations (see

Fritz 1993, 40–43). Johannessen (1993) has aptly argued that many Late Woodland populations, particularly those centered in the central Mississippi Valley, consisted of farmers, not gardeners or hunter-gatherers who supplemented their diets with small-scale food-producing activities. The terms farmers and farmstead have even been used recently to characterize some Middle Woodland peoples and sites in the region (B. Smith 1992a); such a term would have been viewed with much disdain less than a decade ago.

In reality, horticulture or gardening, as opposed to agriculture or farming, represents multifariously conceptualized stages in a continuum of growing human-plant interdependencies that are difficult to classify ethnographically and, even more so, archaeologically. For example, prior to late Emergent Mississippian times when Mill Creek–chert hoe blades were being imported to the American Bottom on a large scale, much of the tillage may have been performed using hoes of shell, limestone, or some other material that often decomposes beyond recognition in open-air deposits (Fortier, Finney, and Lacampagne 1983; L. Kelly 1987, 1990c; Kuttruff 1974; Lopinot, Hufto, and Brown 1982). The influx of hoe blades manufactured from exotic Mill Creek chert may have had little to do with agricultural intensification but instead reflects the establishment of a prestige-goods economy that was essential for validating and perpetuating elite positions.

Zeacentrism

Extant models of crop production, particularly those presented by most archaeologists in general overviews on late prehistoric societies of the Midwest and Midsouth, typically suffer from what I will refer to as "zeacentric bias." Although the recognition of such bias is not new (B. Smith 1992a), the bias must be emphasized for those seeking to understand the development of Cahokian crop-production systems. My criticism is not meant to demean the importance of maize in many late prehistoric contexts, for it became the central element of food production activities throughout much of eastern North America. Yet, many archaeologists have had a tendency to correlate crop plants other than maize with horticulture, while placing maize on an unrivaled agricultural and ceremonial pedestal.

Older models of subsistence emphasized the importance of maize, beans, and squash in the Mississippianization process (Griffin 1967, 189; Willey

1966, 292). Cultivation of this Mesoamerican triad was believed to be a primary thread running through a myriad of cultural diversity in the greater Southeast. Documents derived from early historic encounters with Native American groups throughout much of Eastern North America seem to provide a good basis for projecting similar adaptive strategies back into late prehistoric times when Mississippian populations were almost ubiquitous.

The importance of maize, beans, and squash in late prehistoric subsistence has slowly eroded as the analysis of flotation-recovered plant remains and the reanalysis of pre-flotation collections have demonstrated considerable spatial and temporal variability in late prehistoric adaptive strategies (see Scarry 1993). The common bean now appears to have been grown little if at all prior to the twelfth or thirteenth centuries in the central and lower Mississippi River valley segments (Johannessen 1984; Lopinot 1992a; Morse and Morse 1983; Parker 1994).

Squash, too, has declined in its inferred importance, largely because of its relatively infrequent occurrence in the flotation sample record. Yet, the infrequency of squash remains at most Mississippian sites may belie a much greater importance that is masked by past food preparation, consumption, and discard behaviors (for a caveat, see N. Asch and D. Asch 1975, 117–18). The relatively abundant occurrence of squash rind fragments at some Middle Woodland and Late Woodland sites, and its relatively infrequent occurrence at Mississippian sites, could reflect a shift away from container squashes to food squashes. This is a trend that might be expected in light of the late prehistoric diversification in ceramic vessel forms that included water bottles and various types of jars.

Only one of these three plants continues to be the central element of most late prehistoric subsistence scenarios—maize. It was certainly the dominant grain crop throughout much of the Southeast by the time of the De Soto entrada, as well as in the Northeast. However, the emergence of at least some chiefdom-level polities in the Southeast appears to have occurred largely or entirely in the absence of a maize-centered economy (e.g., Fritz and Kidder 1993; Kidder 1990; Nassaney 1992). In the American Bottom, it does appear to have been one of several crops that underwent intensified production during the emergence of the Cahokian polity, but its achievement of paramount economic status comparable to that described during historic times may, in fact, coincide with the time of Cahokian decentralization or the aftermath or both. (A discussion of this follows later.)

Zeacentric perspectives also appear to be reflected in the recent trend to emphasize some, as yet unknown, religious or ceremonial role for the initial infusion and long period of limited maize cultivation during Middle Woodland and early Late Woodland times. Recent dates have pushed the entrance of maize into the American Bottom region well into the Middle Woodland period (Riley and Walz 1992; Riley et al. 1994). Traditionally, maize required a lengthy period of adjustment due to new environmental conditions imposed by its translocation to temperate eastern North America; this would account for its dietary insignificance until some eight hundred to one thousand years later.

Fritz (1992, 29) has ably argued "that environmental conditions in the Midwest at the time [of maize introduction] would have been, if anything, more favorable to maize agricultural techniques than those of the Southwest," where maize had already made necessary latitudinal adjustments and was presumably the area from which it diffused to eastern North America. Some empirical data have been marshalled to support the "ceremonial" argument (Johannessen 1993; Scarry 1993b), but the inducement of this perspective also appears to reflect a biased view of the expected but long-unfulfilled importance of maize. In other words, the failure of maize to readily dominate subsistence systems after its introduction must reflect some unique religious significance. Alternatively, we must consider the possibility that maize was another cultivated plant that, for a variety of economic, social, and even traditional religious reasons, was little more than a minor garden crop for some 500 to 1,000 years. Given a long-established and elaborating symbiotic relationship with starchy seeds, it may be that people were simply reluctant to cultivate in a large way some new crop that required greater attention, thereby significantly altering deep-rooted scheduling strategies.

The initiation of intensified maize production in the American Bottom area corresponds to what has been referred to as "Formative Emergent Mississippian" (Fortier, Maher, and Williams 1991). However, this, too, may be partly the result of our own chronological manipulations and potentially distorted views about the impacts of maize production on early sociocultural developments in this region. Intensified maize production in the American Bottom itself did not make Emergent Mississippian any more than shell-tempered pottery makes Mississippian. In other words, the intensification of maize production was not an essential economic precondition for Mississippian emergence; it could just as easily have been some other, more nutritious and equally productive crop. In the Cahokia area, maize simply became an important element of a multicropping system that was expanding long before it entered the scene in a major way (Fritz 1993).

Implicit or explicit in most arguments of subsistence has been that the change from horticulture to agriculture was achieved only after maize became an important component of the economy. I attribute this to (1) the residual effects of past perspectives on Mississippian development that emphasized direct or indirect links to prehistoric Mesoamerica where maize was the dietary mainstay; (2) an overdependency on historic records for developing static models about the subsistence behaviors of groups that lived some five hundred to eight hundred years earlier; (3) the fallacious assumption that maize was simply capable of sustaining higher yields than other crops, particularly the starchy seeds; and (4) the long-established emphasis on maize analysis in pre-flotation archaeobotany.

Growing evidence indicates that maize may have been equally or less productive than some of the native crops (Lopinot 1992a; Scarry 1993b; Smith 1987, 1992a), and maize is clearly less nutritious than several of the starchy and oily seeds (e.g., D. Asch and N. Asch 1978, 1985; Crites and Terry 1984). In this regard, the dominance of maize in late prehistoric and protohistoric economies appears to go hand-in-hand with increases in dental and infectious diseases, as well as increases in mortality, especially among weaned children (e.g., Ambrose 1987; Cook 1984; A. Goodman et al. 1984).

Eastern North America was a separate center for the domestication of a suite of crops (Fritz 1990; Smith 1992a), and these crops became the critical components of agricultural intensification in many parts of eastern North America where chiefdoms eventually emerged. The forebearers of Mississippian culture were the Late Woodland or Emergent Mississippian populations or both that were scattered about in the major river valleys of the Midwest and Midsouth. In many places, these groups grew little or no maize whatsoever; in other places, such as the American Bottom, maize became important relatively early and abruptly, but it did not readily displace the existing crop complex.

I have argued elsewhere that the increase in maize cob parts relative to maize kernel parts reflects an increase in the production of mature shellable maize relative to the consumption of green or immature maize (Lopinot 1992a). Thus, proportional increases should reflect greater emphases on

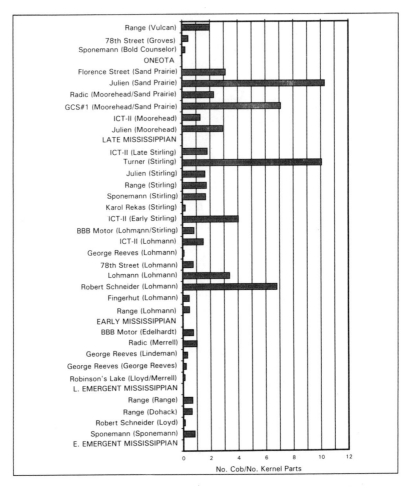

Figure 3.1. Cob-Kernel Part Ratios for American Bottom Sites

maize production and storage. If this argument is correct and maize was the central element of the food-production system, then the proportion of maize cob parts should peak during the climax of the Cahokian polity. Figure 3.1 illustrates an apparent increase in the proportion of maize cob parts throughout the Mississippi Period, with the highest attained during late Mississippian times when the polity was disintegrating. Alone, this could be considered an indication that maize was indeed a subsistence liability and not the golden-grained fuel for the apogee of Mississippian polities. Still, many

58

other changing political, social, and economic factors must have induced the downfall of the Cahokian system.

Cahokian Food Production

In a polity where the vast majority of the people were farmers, ample attention should be given to understanding the types, scale, and organization of food production and land tenure. Unfortunately, most of our data are limited to indirect and sometimes very questionable expressions of activities associated with food production. These relate as much to the types and proportional mix of plants that were cultivated as to the broader systemic interplay among demographic, biological, economic, political, social, and ideological factors.

The linkage of demographic growth to agricultural intensification and technological innovation has been at the forefront of much debate since Boserup's (1965) classic study (e.g., Bronson 1972; Cohen 1977). The development of the Cahokian polity also appears to be related to increases in population density within the American Bottom region, due to some combination of local growth, immigration into the area, and nucleation (Pauketat and Lopinot, chapter 6). Such increases should not be viewed as the cause of agricultural intensification, but more people should correlate with more crop production. In turn, more people and more agriculture should translate into fewer naturally available terrestrial products (e.g., nuts, fleshy tree fruits, fuelwood, and game), particularly in an area marked by a relatively circumscribed bottomland of friable, rich alluvium.

Mississippian food-production activities in the American Bottom are believed to have involved an infield-outfield system with private family gardens near the structures and large communal fields around the settlements (Swanton 1931, 46, 1946, 309; S. Williams 1930, 435–37). Although the Cahokia site was the location for a relatively large and dense population, structures were sufficiently scattered within most of the community limits and immediate periphery to allow for substantial gardening. Some areas of the site considered to represent locations of plazas and plazuelas may have instead comprised structured garden areas, both for the elite residents of the community and groups of non-elites occupying the individual subcommunities scattered throughout the site. For example, the relatively open central portion of the Interpretive Center Tract-II, dating to the Stirling phase, may represent one such garden area (see Collins 1990).

As the population grew during late Emergent Mississippian and early Mississippian times, so too would have the distances of travel to and from outfields. The interconnected network of streams, oxbow lakes, and other canoe-navigable waters would have facilitated travel of people and harvested produce to and from these more distant fields. Surveys of the Horseshoe Lake peninsula indicate that this ridge-and-swale point bar complex was largely abandoned after or during the Lohmann phase (Lopinot 1993; Norris 1975; T. R. Pauketat, Rees, and S. L. Pauketat 1996); it appears to have had a very small resident population during the subsequent Stirling and Moorehead/Sand Prairie phases. This area could have provided a variety of habitats for the production of a diverse assortment of crops by Cahokian residents, particularly occupants of the nearby Powell Tract area.

Despite the diversity in site types and locations, there appears to be considerable similarity among the types of crops represented in the archaeobotanical record. The gross redundancy among archaeobotanical assemblages indicates that similar types of crops were grown and consumed virtually everywhere within the polity, from the small scattered farmsteads in the uplands to the town-and-mound centers in the floodplain. Such a contention, however, may not survive closer study of the proportional representation of various crop residues with respect to landforms and soil types within site catchments, differences in settlement organization, and chronological variability among sites or components thereof.

Similarities in crop production throughout the polity do not lend credence to arguments for specialized production. Nevertheless, we presently lack adequate samples of human skeletal remains representing members of different social ranks and of refuse generated from elite contexts to evaluate adequately this supposition. If elites did manipulate production and consumption to maintain or enhance their societal status, then such social inequalities might be reflected by differences in food acquisition and consumption. In any respect, any redundancy in cropping profiles mainly serves to demonstrate that a large percentage of the population was engaged in intensive multicropping agriculture; it could have little to do with the food tribute demands imposed by elites.

The ability of the elite class to extract tribute from the larger, non-elite farming population, particularly members occupying the scattered farmsteads in the hinterlands considerable distances from the center, is an unresolved question. The answers, if ever found, will vary both temporally and spatially, but they are likely to show that the ebb and flow of tribute in the form of surplus grain was directly or indirectly related to the movement of agricultural implements manufactured from exotic materials, such as Mill Creek–chert hoe blades.

Pauketat (1991, 1994a) has attempted to examine the possibility of maize appropriation by elites. Using kernel-to-cob ratios for a series of sites ranging from rural farmsteads to the administrative centers, he has assumed that elite tribute would occur mainly in the form of shelled mature maize. As such, ratios of kernel-to-cob remains should be higher for elite refuse than for non-elite refuse. He notes the presence of abundant quantities of carbonized maize kernels relative to cob remains at the Lohmann site and perhaps the Horseshoe Lake site, two local town-and-mound centers. In contrast, the greater proportion of cob remains at typical rural sites led Pauketat (1991, 109) to remark that, "while other depositional processes deserve consideration, the paucity of shelled maize at Lohmann- and Stirling-phase homesteads may be a direct reflection of its appropriation by elites at centers."

Diversity in Crop Production

Cultivated plants grown by Cahokians minimally included maize, chenopod, erect knotweed, maygrass, little barley, marsh elder, sunflower, squash, gourd, tobacco, and perhaps amaranth. Seeds of other plants such as black nightshade, "wild bean," and panic grass occur in sufficient abundance, or else in significant proportions of samples at many sites, that they also probably represent encouraged and protected, if not cultivated or produced, food plants. In addition, we must consider the possibility of arboricultural practices as well, especially with respect to persimmon, a favored fruit throughout the Mississippian world, and perhaps to sumac. At the very least, the common representation of such fruits, as well as of other pioneering annual and perennial taxa, in late prehistoric archaeobotanical assemblages is indicative of the "massive disturbance of the landscape by Late Woodland and Mississippian agriculturalists" (Cowan 1985, 219).

Considerable evidence suggests that, besides maize, the four starchy seeds were cultivated in fields, not gardens. Of the starchy seeds, at least chenopod, erect knotweed, and maygrass were cultivated more intensively in the central Mississippi valley than perhaps anywhere else in eastern North America. Relatively intensive cultivation of starchy seeds extends back in

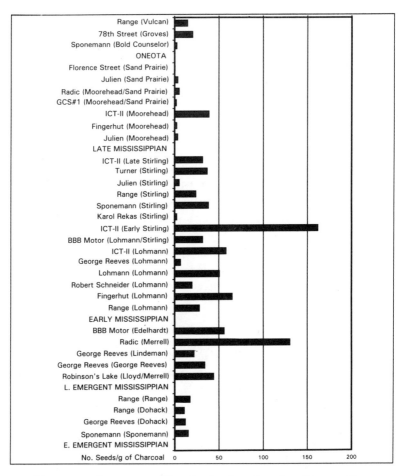

Figure 3.2. Frequency of Starchy Seeds at American Bottom Sites

time to at least the Middle Woodland period in the American Bottom (Parker 1989a).

The proportions of starchy seeds in total seed assemblages are typically 75 to 80 percent or greater for Late Woodland, Emergent Mississippian, and Early Mississippian sites in the American Bottom region (e.g., Johannessen 1988; Parker 1991; see figure 3.2). Similarly high frequencies of starchy seeds are also apparent for contemporaneous sites in the lower Illinois valley (D. Asch and N. Asch 1978; N. Asch and D. Asch 1981), the nearby extreme lower Missouri valley (P. Wright 1986), the lower and central Kaskaskia valley (Dunavan 1993; Ford 1974a), and along the Mississippi River below the southern limits of the American Bottom (Lopinot 1992b). These high percentages reflect considerable emphasis on the production and consumption of starchy seeds relative to other potential seed and fruit foods.

Considerably more well-dated, flotation-recovered assemblages are needed, but there are some indications that late Baytown and early Mississippian groups in the upper part of the lower Mississippi valley also were intensive starchy seed cultivators. Throughout the second half of the first millennium A.D., populations stretching from the Toltec Mound group northward into the Missouri Bootheel and the Ozark Escarpment perhaps emphasized starchy seed cultivation as much as their contemporary American Bottom counterparts (Fritz and Kidder 1993; Lopinot 1995; Wetterstrom 1978). Despite some differences, there are many remarkable similarities; at least around A.D. 900–1050, the similarity of cropping profiles may have been due in part to interaction between the American Bottom and northern portions of the lower Mississippi valley (see J. Kelly 1991a, 1991b).

Another factor to consider is that of a possible history of introgressive hybridization between some indigenous cultivars and their hardier, abundantly occurring native counterparts. The typically small sizes of most sunflower and marshelder achenes from American Bottom Mississippian sites have been noted repeatedly (e.g., Lopinot 1991; Parker 1992a, 1992b, 1994). The archaeological achenes are often distinctly smaller than cultigen achene populations from contemporary sites in other regions, perhaps a reflection of introgressive hybridization with local native, wild plants rather than the discard or loss of aberrant or immature fruits. Today, sunflower and marshelder are very common inhabitants of disturbed habitats in the American Bottom, particularly field borders. Hybridized mixtures, or simply the planting of different cultivars, would provide the genotypic diversity that could buffer against catastrophic destruction from pests and pathogens (Snaydon 1980; Trenbath 1976). Some of the starchy seeds also may have been favorably hybridizing with the native gene pool.

Selection and inbreeding can result in a very highly productive cultivar under favorable conditions, and there is a tendency for one genotype to obtain dominance through natural means. Nevertheless, inbred cultivars also require greater attention and are more susceptible to catastrophic destruction such as drought or flooding. In addition, the cultivation of one or a few such cultivars is not a very good agricultural strategy for a heterogeneous environment like the American Bottom. For the Cahokia site itself, some evidence shows that there was marked emphasis on one or a few varieties of maize during late Stirling times, with a diminished emphasis on starchy seeds (Lopinot 1991).

The relatively diverse crop production system that included both fall-harvested and spring-harvested crops would have served to subdue the effects of most seasonal and interannual environmental perturbations. Greater diversity in cropping also was a more compatible means of utilizing the heterogeneous environment of the American Bottom, particularly that occurring within the catchment of the Cahokia site. This environment included silty clays of low swales and old meander scars; sands, sandy silts, and sandy silt loams of ridges within point bar complexes and on overbank deposits; the alluvial and colluvial silt loams of terraces, mostly occupying a band along the bluffline to the east of Cahokia; and the loessal bluff soils.

Intensification in Crop Production

Archaeobotanical evidence for the intensification of a multicropping system has been presented for the late prehistoric American Bottom, having begun during the Woodland stage and culminating during early Mississippian times (Johannessen 1993; Lopinot 1992a; Scarry 1993b). The evidence includes increased ubiquity indices for known and presumed cultigens, as well as greater densities of crop residues, attended thereafter by declines in both with the diminution of the Cahokian social order. Here, I will examine a few less direct forms of evidence for agricultural intensification.

First, the intensity of cultivation prior to Mississippian times is indicated by the occasional presence of charred masses of starchy seeds in refuse deposits at late prehistoric sites in the American Bottom and the nearby lower Illinois River valley. The earliest-dated masses are from a few early Late Woodland sites (N. Asch and D. Asch 1981; Jackson and Smith 1979), prompting Johannessen (1984, 202) to infer that "these seeds were [becoming] an increasingly important, storable dietary staple." Although greater numbers of earlier sites need to be excavated, such masses seem to be even more common at Emergent Mississippian sites (Johannessen 1985; Lopinot, Fritz, and Kelly 1991; Parker 1989b). These masses perhaps represent cooking accidents, "spoiled" caches that were intentionally burned, or resources that were accidentally charred while being stored in subterranean pits; in any

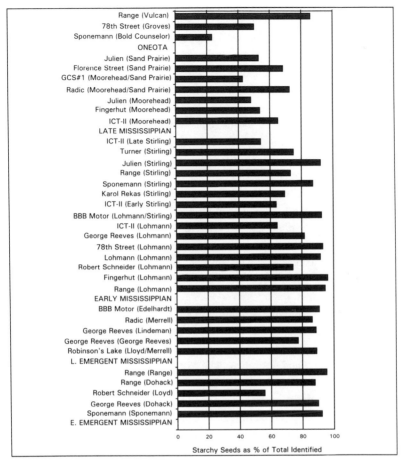

Figure 3.3. Number of Seeds per Gram of Charcoal at American Bottom Sites

respect, their increased appearance in the archaeobotanical record is symptomatic of their increased cultivation and consumption, just as occurrences of cob-filled smudge pits are for maize.

The numbers of seeds per gram of charcoal should indicate the overall importance of starchy seeds, given that the vast majority of all seeds consist of chenopod and erect knotweed achenes, and maygrass and little barley grains. Figure 3.3 shows that the peak production for such seeds was during late Emergent Mississippian and Early Mississippian times, or during the period of political coalescence and the zenith of the Cahokian polity. In turn, the late Mississippian decline would appear to have been attended by a sharp decline in the importance of starchy seeds at the same time maize had gained even greater economic importance. As such, the intensity of agricultural production of the multicropping system correlates well with the emergence and peak of Cahokia.

Other indirect evidence for the relative intensity of agricultural activities relates to storage facilities, both above-ground and subterranean. DeBoer (1988, 9) has commented on "the sheer abundance of storage" represented for American Bottom domestic contexts, compared to that represented in the late prehistoric sequence for Normandy Reservoir, Tennessee. He also discusses considerable variability within and between settlements, as well as throughout the late prehistoric time span, noting that the volumes of storage (cubic meters of subterranean pits/square meters of structure floor space) appear to have waxed and waned on a predictable basis with the emergence, florescence, and subsidence of the Cahokian polity.

As a component of the total food web, nut consumption also can provide some indirect information on agricultural activities. At a general level, it may be assumed that fluctuations in nut exploitation would be inversely related to fluctuations in food production; this is the basic underlying premise for utility of seed and nut ratios. The exploitation of nut masts during late prehistoric times in the American Bottom region appears to have fluctuated greatly, both spatially and temporally (Johannessen 1984; Lopinot 1991; Parker 1992a, 1993, 1994). Overall, however, there does appear to be an inverse correlation between nut exploitation and intensified crop production (figure 3.4). In other words, the emergence of sociopolitical complexity in the American Bottom coincides with a decline in protein-laden hickory nut usage, although there appears to have been a relative peak in consumption of carbohydrate-rich acorns during the Stirling phase (Lopinot 1991; Parker 1992a, 1992b; Whalley 1983, 1984).

Conclusions

The basic stabilizing responses to temporal and spatial variations in resource availability include mobility, storage, exchange, and diversification (Halstead and O'Shea 1989). One or more of these responses could be expected in light of the increased competition and the potential for resource scarcity,

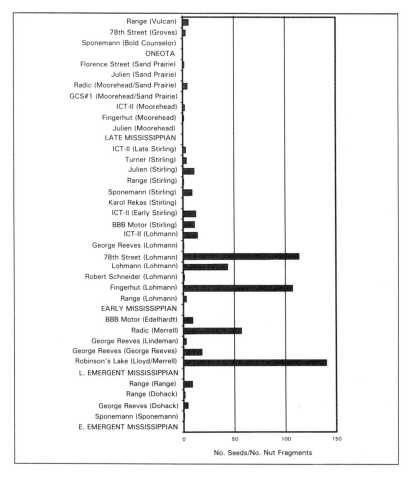

Figure 3.4. Seed-Nut Fragment Ratios for American Bottom Sites

whether those resources were naturally available nuts and fruits, produced foods, agricultural land, or water. Within the Cahokian polity during its zenith, all four responses may have been realized in one way or another. Storage and diversification are the most obvious, whereas mobility may be reflected in attenuated form by the presence of field houses or "growing-season farmsteads." The eventual dispersal of people from the American Bottom during the twelfth to fourteenth centuries A.D. also may represent a response to scarcities in preferred resources. The exchange of foods is difficult to document, but chiefdom-level societies in general and the Cahokian polity in particular provide numerous examples of material-goods exchanges.

The evidence for intensification of agricultural activities in general takes on a variety of forms. Some forms of evidence appear to be more direct and measureable archaeologically, whereas others are indirect and equivocal. In the context of the emerging Cahokian polity, there were probably several other related forms of agricultural intensification besides a heightening emphasis on the existing diversified crop production strategy. These would have included cultivation of marginal areas (e.g., development of ridged fields in low floodplain areas), increased rotation of crops, or even no rotation whatsoever. Such forms of intensification, however, would have meant lower cumulative productivity and higher risks for crop failure.

As stated, the intensification in the American Bottom region included not only maize production, but also that of the starchy seed plants and perhaps several other plants. Maximum production of this complex, but especially of maize, chenopod, and maygrass, seems to correlate well with the emergence and zenith of Cahokia. Therefore, the conclusion is that the diverse mix of field crops supported the unrivaled Cahokian polity during its heyday. The development and greater stability of an economic base for such a relatively large, aggregated population required more than a simple maize-centered agricultural system supplemented by the less predictable products of mother nature.

Lucretia S. Kelly

4

Patterns of Faunal Exploitation at Cahokia

About A.D. 1050 a sudden change in the social structure of the Cahokia site occurred with an abrupt consolidation of the Cahokia region into a political hierarchy (Pauketat 1991, 1994a). Pauketat (1994a, 37) hypothesizes that as a result of this political development there should have been a "qualitative shift in all aspects of social life and in the residues derived from elite-controlled exchange networks." The elite, those individuals at the top of the hierarchy, would not have been self-sufficient. They were non-food-producing specialists who would need to be provisioned with food. This differential access to food resources between the non-food-producing elite and the food-producing general populace should be evident in the faunal assemblages they generated.

By the Emergent Mississippian Edelhardt phase (A.D. 1000–1050), data suggest inhabitants of Cahokia were either being provisioned with deer meat by persons outside the site or they were procuring deer themselves at a distance from the site, returning with only the meatiest portions (Esarey and Pauketat 1992; L. Kelly 1979, 1990b, 1991). It has been demonstrated at other Mississippian chiefdoms in the Southeast (Moundville, Toqua, and Lubbub) that the elite or individuals of higher status were being provisioned with specific, high-quality cuts of deer meat (Bogan 1980; Jackson and Scott 1995; Michals 1990; Scott 1983). Other differences in the faunal assemblage related to status were also observed, particularly at Moundville, where an increase in medium-sized mammals and an increase in the amount of bird, particularly turkey, was found in faunal assemblages from elite contexts (Michals 1990).

Advances in zooarchaeological method and theory have led to the more accurate identification of cultural and taphonomic processes that contribute to the formation of faunal assemblages. Our understanding of urban processes has been enhanced through zooarchaeological studies of complex societies in the Near East and Europe. Similar studies should be applicable at Cahokia, generally considered to represent a complex Mississippian chiefdom with its ranked, if not stratified, political order (Crabtree 1990, 156).

In the past twenty-five years about a dozen faunal studies from different areas and time periods of the Cahokia site have been made. This chapter will review some of the more recently recovered faunal assemblages in terms of the results at the aforementioned Mississippian chiefdoms as well as the application of advanced zooarchaeological methods. The more detailed faunal studies and the refined chronology for the American Bottom now allow for the testing of the hypothesis that changes in faunal exploitation, food distribution, and consumption reflect the social, political, and economic changes that were taking place within the evolving complex chiefdom at Cahokia (Bareis and Porter 1984; Fowler and Hall 1975).

Can it be determined if the observed changes or differences in assemblages are attributable to status differences within the site, to increased site population, or to environmental stress which may have occurred because of the increased consolidation of population into a large site? Because of Cahokia's large size, the relatively small faunal assemblages recovered, particularly from elite contexts, may offer no definitive answers at this time. Although more questions may be raised, this review will refine and develop existing hypotheses about faunal exploitation at the Cahokia site.

Zooarchaeological Studies

To identify differences in status or access to faunal resources, two types of studies are generally employed. The first is the study of body-part distribution for the main vertebrate species, which for Cahokia is deer. If different social classes or segments within the society consumed different cuts of deer meat, this should be reflected in the anatomical parts represented in their refuse (figure 4.1).

The study of body-part distribution necessitates some caution, since many factors, both cultural and noncultural, can play a role in what body parts form an assemblage (Klein 1989; Lyman 1984; Marshall and Pilgram 1991). Noncultural taphonomic factors such as trampling, animal gnawing, and bone density do not appear to be significant for the Cahokia assem-

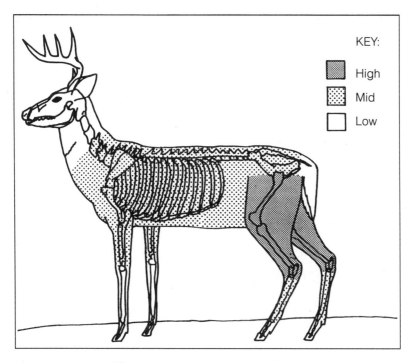

Figure 4.1. Deer Food Utility Indices

blages. Most bones were recovered from feature fill rather than from middens. Features were in most instances filled rapidly with refuse so that trampling and weathering are not considered to be significant taphonomic factors. Little noncultural modification, such as carnivore and rodent gnawing, was observed.

Lyman (1991, 126) states that "*all* taphonomic processes affecting those frequencies [of skeletal parts], not just those involving human behaviors, must be considered." Lyman (1984) has pointed out that many times bone survivorship is directly related to bone density. In other words, bones of higher density tend to survive or be preserved over those with low density. Lyman, Houghton, and Chambers (1992, 559) also "observed that many skeletal parts which have high food utilities . . . also tend to have low structural densities and that many skeletal parts which have low food values tend also to have high structural densities." Because most of the Cahokia deer bone assemblages are comprised of elements of mid-low structural density, a cultural explanation should be investigated rather than a density-mediated explanation, in order to account for the assemblages' compositions.

The cultural explanations for certain body-part representations can be complex and much more difficult to discern. The pattern extant at Cahokia of a high proportion of low density elements and a very low proportion of some very high density bones, such as metapodials, seems meaningful. Although the amount of meat represented by a particular element may have been important in its selection for transport to the Cahokia site, within bone, nutrients may be equally as important. Marshall and Pilgram (1991) have shown a connection between the marrow and fat content of a bone and its representation in a faunal assemblage. The amount of fragmentation of a particular bone has been shown to be relevant to its marrow and fat content as well. However, due to the nature of the data used, the discernment of general patterns is the goal of this paper. General food utility indices of the various parts of the deer are used rather than the more specific indices of marrow and bone grease.

Binford (1978) originally developed a Modified General Utility Index (MGUI) for caribou that gave values to the different bone elements by measuring their associated amount of meat, marrow, and bone grease. This is valid when applied to deer, an artiodactyl similar in structure. Metcalfe and Jones (1988) simplified Binford's MGUI to a Food Utility Index (FUI). Purdue, Styles, amd Masulis (1989), in turn, adjusted the FUI values by dividing them into high, medium, and low categories instead of having them be a continuous variable. They proposed that this grouping calls "attention to the extremes of the FUI spectrum, toward which human behavior may be less variable, leaving a more discernible pattern in the archaeological record" (Purdue et al. 1989, 150). The high, medium, and low categories will be used in this paper. Many zooarchaeologists, when employing these indices, use Binford's %MAUS (Percent Minimal Animal Units). MAUS have been calculated in only one Cahokia study (Miracle 1996a), so NISP (Number of Identified Specimens) and %NISP are being used in this paper. NISP is as good an indicator as MAUS or MNIS (see Marshall and Pilgram 1993). Styles and Purdue (1996) agree with Grayson (1984) that MAU and MNE (Minimum Number of Elements from which MAU is calculated) are subject to similar problems as MNI. The calculations of MNE and MAU are based on whole portions of elements that are rarely found in archaeological assemblages. Because of the fragmentary nature of archaeological bones, it is often difficult to determine

MNE. Therefore, using NISP here will provide relevant data concerning the types of patterns we hope to identify.

The second type of faunal study that can be used to help identify status is the diversity of the taxa represented. Did the different social classes consume different taxa of animals or greater percentages of certain taxa over others? The species composition of the various assemblages will be examined to determine if there are differences in the number of taxa or percentages of taxa represented. Only the species which are felt to be of significant food value are considered; therefore, rodents, reptiles, amphibians, and molluscs were not included in this study, since they represent a very small percentage of the total NISP in all the assemblages used.

The Data

Assemblages from six areas of the Cahokia site are examined. They represent the three Emergent Mississippian phases of Loyd, Merrell, and Edelhardt, and the three subsequent Mississippian phases of Lohmann, Stirling, and Moorehead. Excavations in the East Palisade area resulted in faunal debris from the three Emergent Mississippian components. All these assemblages represent domestic refuse, and all are relatively small. A larger assemblage of Edelhardt phase materials was recovered from the Merrell Tract (L. Kelly 1979) 0.5 kilometers to the west. For purposes of discussion, the East Palisade and Merrell Tract Edelhardt phase materials have been combined in some cases.

The Interpretative Center Tract II (ICT-II) excavations delineated a portion of settlements from the sequentially defined Mississippian components of Lohmann, early and late Stirling, and Moorehead phases. This area of Cahokia is thought to represent a non-elite residential area (Collins 1990). The faunal remains should therefore represent nonspecialized, domestic garbage. Unfortunately, the assemblages, particularly for the early and late Stirling phases, were poorly preserved. Even so, the deer body part representation pattern was not significantly affected by density-mediated attrition. I will explain this later. Because the assemblages from the early and late Stirling ICT-II are relatively small, they have been combined and for the purposes of this paper, the Stirling phase will not be examined by subphase units.

Three small faunal assemblages were recovered from possible elite Stirling phase contexts. The Southern Illinois University at Edwardsville field school in 1992 reexcavated a portion of the trench originally dug by Moorehead (1929) in the Jesse Ramey Mound (Mound 56) located within the Grand Plaza (Dalan, Holley, and Watters 1993). The faunal materials recovered are, in essence, those from Moorehead's backdirt (L. Kelly 1993). Because they are from a mound context and because they are associated with fineware ceramics and other artifacts such as shell beads, the probability is great that they originated from elite individuals. However, these data are from secondary context (mound fill), and it is not possible to determine definitively from where they originated.

The second elite assemblage, from Tract 15A, was recovered from a structure and a midden area believed to be associated with this structure. These have been interpreted as *possible* elite contexts. The individuals residing in this area may have been taking care of a nearby Post-Circle Monument (Pauketat 1991, 1994a). The third is from a structure on the Kunnemann Tract that has been interpreted as an elite context (Pauketat 1993c). The structures from Tract 15A and the Kunnemann Tract are from the early Stirling phase. All the elite areas were excavated prior to the implementation of flotation or water screening recovery techniques. It is, therefore, possible the assemblages are biased toward the recovery of the larger bones and may explain the paucity of fish remains. A flotation sample was taken during the SIU-E field school excavation of the J. Ramey Mound. This yielded some fish bone. The smaller, more fragile bones, however, were possibly destroyed or lost during the original excavations by Moorehead, important when comparing species variety or habitat preferences for these areas.

A single Moorehead phase pit from the East Stockade excavations yielded a small assemblage. For discussion purposes it has been combined with the Moorehead phase materials recovered from the ICT-II.

Data from the FAI-270 Project indicate an increase in the density of settlements within the American Bottom during the Emergent Mississippi Period (J. Kelly 1992b). From the Range site, located 20 kilometers south of Cahokia, the large faunal assemblages recovered from the Late Woodland Patrick and Emergent Mississippian phases indicate that a localization of faunal exploitation occurred in the Emergent Mississippian (L. Kelly 1987, 1990c). Deer remains decrease and the recovery of smaller animals increases. The argument was that this change came about because of increased competition for local resources and because more time was being devoted to the newly acquired maize agriculture. It appears that the inhabitants did not employ as wide a range of faunal exploitation (i.e., they utilized a smaller catchment area) than they had in Late Woodland times (L. Kelly 1990c, 511). This localized pattern would be expected for the Emergent Mississippian at Cahokia as well, although differences may be evident due to the location of the two sites and the size of the occupations.

This evidence supports Speth and Scott's (1989, 74, 77) suggestion that maize agriculture, besides requiring more time "at home" for the inhabitants, may increase the abundance of small mammals available because of habitat alterations. Increased sedentism could lead to rapid depletion of large mammals near the site, and the increased horticultural activities may have prevented or inhibited long-distance hunting. Therefore, this would cause an increase in the procurement of small mammals, fish, and aquatic resources. They state that the availability of fish "can significantly reduce or eliminate the pressure on horticulturalists to travel long distances in search of large game" (Speth and Scott 1989, 77).

The major classes that comprise the Cahokia- and Range-site Emergent Mississippian assemblages are represented by similar percentages. Fish and waterfowl (e.g., aquatic species) procurement was very important (figures 4.2 and 4.3). Fish remains representing similar taxa make up the vast majority of NISP for both sites. The main differences in the two sites are in the mammalian assemblages where more taxa of medium-sized mammals were recovered from the Range site. Although deer remains represent the largest mammalian NISP at both sites, there is a marked contrast in the body part representation, particularly in the low- and mid-FUI percentages. The Range percentages are more consistent with what would be expected if the complete deer were being returned to the site (figure 4.4 and table 4.1). The Cahokia percentages are more consistent with what would be expected if deer were being killed at a distance from the site and the higher utility cuts brought back most often. This is not unexpected, considering the location of the two sites. The Range site is adjacent to the uplands, and the Cahokia site is at a distance of 4 kilometers.

From her analysis of the faunal assemblage from the nearby upland Emergent Mississippian AG Church site, Holt (1993) believes that this site *may* have had ties to Cahokia. For the Merrell phase occupation, the deer remains predominantly represent the extremities. She contrasts these data with the deer remains from the Merrell Tract at Cahokia, which are from the more

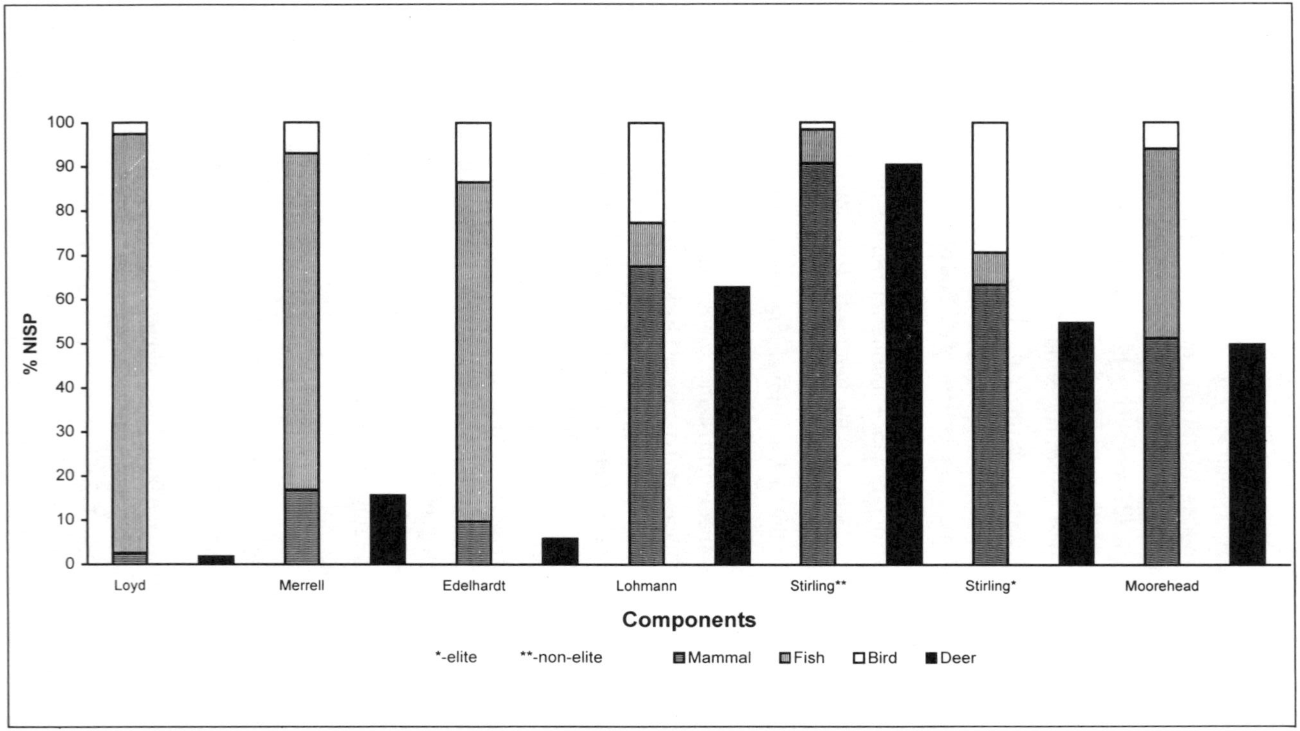

Figure 4.2. Change in %NISP of Major Faunal Classes (Through Time at Cahokia)

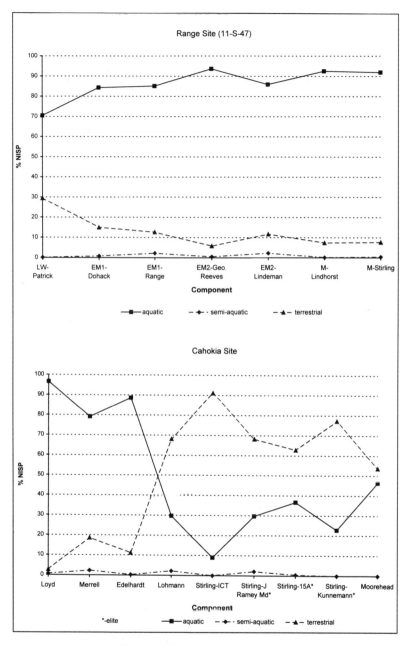

Figure 4.3. %NISP of Vertebrates from Different Habitats

77

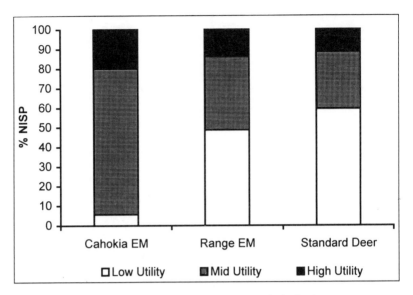

Figure 4.4. Comparison of Emergent Mississippian FUIS
(Range and Cahokia Sites)

"choice" cuts. However, she cautions that due to the small sample sizes of both deer assemblages, more data from other upland sites in the vicinity are needed. Holt notes that bone fragments identified as large mammal from the AG Church site are more than likely the remains of deer. It is possible these could represent the missing torso portions of the deer.

Once the American Bottom population coalesced into the major population centers with their attendant elites by the Lohmann phase, an increase in the deer represented might be expected. Deer, being the most abundant large mammal, could feed more people more efficiently. But, for more deer to be procured, the elite would have had to control wide-ranging hunting territories or a tribute system would have to have been in place whereby deer meat could be obtained. Speth and Scott (1989, 78) indicate one response to reduced community mobility, increased horticultural activity, and changes in the political and demographic environment is to engage in exchange for meat with other people who have greater access to large game.

The floodplain in the vicinity of the Cahokia site consisted of large aquatic, semiaquatic, and prairie habitats. Wooded floodplain habitats that would have supported large deer populations may not have been abundant,

Table 4.1. NISP and %NISP for Major Faunal Classes
Recovered from Cahokia

	Emergent Mississippian			Mississippian			
	Loyd	Merrell	Edelhardt	Lohmann	Stirling 1	Stirling 2	Moorehead
Mammal	37	29	457	844	349	364	267
%	2.49	16.86	9.65	67.47	90.89	63.30	51.25
Deer	27	27	279	787	348	315	260
%	1.82	15.70	5.89	62.91	90.63	54.78	49.90
Fish	1409	131	3638	124	29	42	223
%	94.95	76.16	76.83	9.91	7.55	7.30	42.80
Bird	38	12	640	283	6	169	31
%	2.56	6.98	13.52	22.62	1.56	29.39	5.95
Total NISP	1484	172	4735	1251	384	575	521

but added destruction of deer habitat through agricultural practices and wood procurement may have put added pressures on deer populations, making it necessary for deer to be brought in from greater distances (Lopinot 1991). Once the field-dressed and reduced carcasses arrived at the site, further processing probably took place along with distribution along status lines.

The earliest Mississippian Lohmann-phase faunal assemblages are from the ICT-II and Tract 15A/Dunham Tract.[1] Both areas represent non-elite residential occupation at a time when social stratification was occurring at Cahokia. There is a dramatic change in the overall Mississippian Lohmann-phase faunal composition from the preceding Emergent Mississippian. Fish remains drop from about 77 percent NISP to 10 percent NISP, and mammal remains increase from 10 percent to 67 percent NISP. The increase in mammals is due to a concomitant increase in deer remains (table 4.2; figure 4.2). Bird remains continue to increase in the Lohmann phase (figure 4.2), and the composition remains heavily aquatic (figure 4.5).

Although deer remains, proportionately, increase dramatically, there is not much change in the body part representation (table 4.3; figure 4.6). The procurement pattern does not appear to change during this time except in volume. Deer were still being transported from a distance, but they were seemingly making a greater contribution to the faunal portion of the diet. This may indicate the elite had more control over outlying hunting territories or outlying communities so that more deer could be furnished to the growing central polity. This seems to go hand in hand with wood utilization at this

79

Table 4.2. Food Utility Indices for Cahokia Mounds

Location Phase	Emergent Mississippian				Mississippian							
	Palisade Loyd	Palisade Merrell	Palisade Edelhardt	Merrell Tract Edelhardt	Dunham Tract Lohmann	ICT-II* Lohmann	ICT-II* Stirling	J. Ramey Md.* Stirling	Tract 15A* Stirling	Kunnemann* Stirling	ICT-II Moorehead	Palisade Moorehead
LOW UTILITY												
Antler					2	1	4		1		1	
Skull	1		1	1							5	
Maxilla	1					1			2		1	
Mandible				1	1	3			1		6	
Teeth	2	3				8	1				4	
Axis/Atlas		3			1	5				1	2	
Phalanges			1	1		2			1	1		
Carpals			1			1		3			2	
Total Low NISP	4	6	3	3	4	21	8	4	3	2	19	0
%	17.39	18.75	1.64	6.82	5.56	12.88	7.55	3.33	3.80	3.85	26.76	0
MID UTILITY												
Vertebrae	2	14	28	9	11	22	17	27	14	7	7	
Pelvis+Sacrum	1	3	9	5	15	15	5	8	2	1		
Ribs	3	2	73		1	5	3	1	7	4	3	3
Scapula	1	3	17	6	4	10	8	2	3	4	5	1
Humerus	4	1	8	4	8	27	29	9	13	3	4	2
Radius/Ulna	1	1	11	4	6	13	22	19	8	12	5	2
Total Mid NISP	12	24	146	28	45	92	84	66	48	30	24	8
%	52.17	75	79.78	63.64	62.5	56.44	78.50	55	60.76	57.69	33.80	80
HIGH UTILITY												
Sternum					3	1			2	2	1	2
Femur	1		9	4	6	28	7	20	5	11	10	1
Tibia+Tarsals	6	2	25	9	14	21	8	28	21	8	16	1
Total High NISP	7	2	34	13	23	50	15	50	28	20	28	2
%	30.43	6.25	18.58	29.55	31.94	30.67	14.02	41.67	35.44	38.46	39.44	20
Total NISP	23	32	183	44	72	163	107	120	79	52	71	10

*Elite contexts: Tract 15A = House 209 + midden area, Kunnemann = Structure
**Early and Late Stirling communities combined

time. Lopinot and Woods (1993, 229) indicate that the use of nonlocal wood species was widespread at Cahokia and would be indicative of the elite having sufficient power to obtain tribute from great distances.

The subsequent Stirling phase at the non-elite residential area of the ICT-II shows this pattern to intensify with deer representing 91 percent of the recovered NISP (figure 4.2). This may be partly due to poor faunal preservation, which would adversely affect the recovery of the more fragile bird and fish

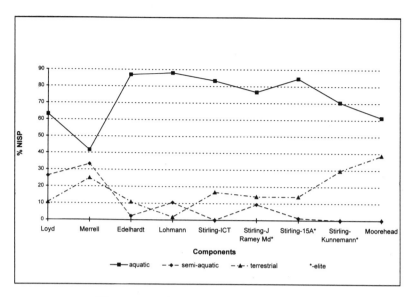

Figure 4.5. Birds Recovered from Cahokia

bones. However, the food utility indices probably are not greatly affected by preservation here. The denser bones are usually those that represent lower utility and should preserve over those that are less dense and of higher utility. As can be seen (table 4.3; figure 4.6), low utility elements remain low, even lower than in the Lohmann phase at ICT-II. The greatest difference is that high utility elements decrease. If better preservation had occurred the mid-utility elements would be even better represented.

As mentioned earlier, there are three assemblages that are from potential elite contexts for the Stirling phase. While all are small and have recovery or contextual problems, they are similar. The body-part representations are very close (table 4.3; figure 4.7). All three have very low low-utility percentages. Mid-utility elements are well represented, comprising slightly more than half the elements. The high-utility elements are represented in the highest proportions of any of the Cahokia assemblages, except for the Moorehead phase. It appears the hindquarters of the deer were more in demand by the elite. This is in contrast to Moundville where forequarters are represented more frequently in high-status deposits (Michals 1990, 1992). This corresponds to the low percentage of hindquarters found at the ICT-II (figure 4.7). This could indicate that once deer meat reached the site, it was further

Table 4.3. %NISP for Types of Birds and Vertebrates Recovered
from the Cahokia Site

Phase

	Loyd	Merrell	Edelhardt	Lohmann	Stirling ICT	J. Ramey Md.*	15A*	Kunnemann*	Moorehead
BIRDS									
aquatic	63.2	41.7	86.9	87.9	83.3	76.6	84.6	70.4	61.3
semiaquatic	26.3	33.3	2.3	10.5	0.0	9.4	1.3	0.0	0.0
terrestrial	10.5	25.0	10.8	1.7	16.7	14.1	14.1	29.6	38.7
VERTEBRATES									
aquatic	96.6	79.1	88.6	29.7	8.9	29.7	36.7	22.8	46.4
semiaquatic	0.7	2.3	0.3	2.2	0.0	2.1	0.5	0.0	0.0
terrestrial	2.7	18.6	11.1	68.1	91.1	68.2	62.8	77.2	53.6

*elite context

divided and distributed along status lines where more of the high-utility hindquarters were being provisioned to higher-status individuals.

It is difficult to predict how the distribution of other fauna would be affected by the social changes. It is possible a lower diversity of species might be represented, with species that are very abundant being targeted. A difference in species composition may be observed when looking at status divisions. Did higher-status individuals receive more deer and fewer fish, the larger fish and bird species, or the rarer species? Did they receive a portion of what everyone else was eating as tribute so that no difference in species composition is evident?

The Stirling-phase elite appear to be eating more birds than do their non-elite counterparts at the ICT-II (figure 4.2), but again this may be a factor of preservation. Because of the lack of birds in the Stirling phase ICT-II assemblage, the elite and non-elite assemblages cannot be compared for species representation. The main difference between the combined elite Stirling and the Lohmann ICT-II is that the use of terrestrial birds (turkey and prairie chicken) is higher in the elite contexts (table 4.4; figure 4.5; see also table 4.5). Prairie chicken is only present in the elite contexts during the Mississippian phases, although it is represented in each Emergent Mississippian phase assemblage (table 4.5). One might speculate that terrestrial birds were given more value by the Mississippian elite.

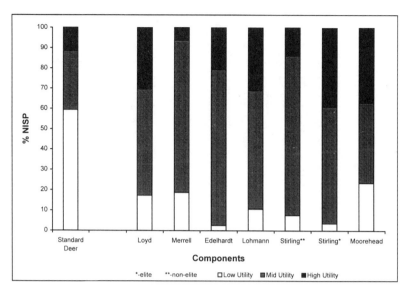

Figure 4.6. Food Utility Indices for Deer (Cahokia Mounds Site)

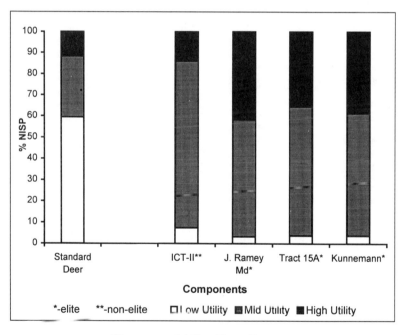

Figure 4.7. Stirling-Phase Deer FUI

83

Table 4.4. Species Diversity at Cahokia Mounds

	Emergent Mississippian				Mississippian						
Location Phase	Palisade Loyd	Palisade Merrell	Palisade Edelhardt	Merrell Tract Edelhardt	ICT-II Lohmann	ICT-II* Stirling	J. Ramey Md. Stirling	Tract 15A Stirling	Kunnemann Stirling	ICT-II Moorehead	Palisade Moorehead
MAMMALS											
Squirrel	3	1	148	16	37	1	19		11		1
Pocket gopher	1			1			1		2	4	
Muskrat	1			1							
Beaver								1			
Canid	5	1	2	1	8		1	5			1
Rabbit			8						5		
Mink				1							
Raccoon								2		1	
Deer	27	27	231	48	714	348	165	98	52	250	10
Elk								1			
Bison								1			
Total NISP	37	29	389	68	759	349	186	108	70	255	12
No. Taxa	5	3	4	6	3	2	4	6	4	3	3
BIRDS											
Grebe	3			2							
Swan			6	19	6	1	3	18	2	4	
Goose	2	1	42	3	40	1	6			2	
Snow/Blue goose		1		6	4	5			2	1	
Canada goose	1	3	18	9	23	2	12	2			
Mallard	8	1	27	50	88	1	13	18	7	1	3
Pintail				9	12		1	2			
Gadwall				12							
Widgeon				1				7			
Teal	5		65	114	23		11	12	4	9	
Surface-feeding	1		9	3	9				3		
Wood duck				4	2						
Ringneck/lesser				25	1						
Redhead				6				2			
Diving duck			10	6	1			2			
Goldeneye			16	46							
Ruddy			6				1				
Merganser			6	26			1				
Sandhill Crane	1	2	2	5	25		6				
Coot	3		1	3			1	1	2		
Sora	1	1									
Rail	7	1	1								
Willet	1										
Yellowlegs			1	5							
Plover			1						1		

(Continued next page)

Table 4.4. Species Diversity at Cahokia Mounds

Location Phase	Emergent Mississippian				Mississippian						
	Palisade Loyd	Palisade Merrell	Palisade Edelhardt	Merrell Tract Edelhardt	ICT-II Lohmann	ICT-II Stirling	J. Ramey Md. Stirling	Tract 15A Stirling	Kunnemann Stirling	ICT-II Moorehead	Palisade Moorehead
BIRDS (continued)											
Seagull				2							
Passenger Pigeon				4							
Turkey	1	2	17	20	1	1	7	11	2	11	
Prairie Chicken	3	1	21	7			2		6		
Bobwhite										1	
Hawk					3						
Total *NISP*	38	12	259	381	239	6	64	78	27	28	3
No. Taxa	11	6	18	22	11	4	11	12	7	6	1
FISH											
Sturgeon	1	1		7		1	1				
Gar	1	1	2	15	5		4			1	
Bowfin	98	8	8	109			2			3	9
Gizzard shad	12	1	9	46							
Pike	2			16						1	
Channel Catfish	3		17	5	2						
Black Bullhead	23	3	20	319	1		1			9	1
Brown Bullhead	6	1		144							
Yellow Bullhead	4		3	12			1			1	
Bullhead	419	38	202	296	19	9	2			116	3
Catfish	213	26	125	294	46	5	4	1	2	63	
Flathead Catfish										3	
Buffalo Sucker	99	16	218	350	30		9	1		2	1
Carpsucker	2	1	2	27	1						
Redhorse	3		1	3							
Chubsucker	2		2							1	
Sucker	63	12	64	379	18	2	9		1	2	
Bass	45	3	20	290							
Sunfish	212	6	13	124	1						
Rockbass	1			2							
Crappie				2							
Sunfish family	170	11	23	342		2	1			5	
White Bass	7		8	45							
Walleye	2	3	1	5							
Perch	13		1	1							
Drum	1		24	10		10	2		1	2	
Eel				2							
Minnow	7			30							
Total *NISP*	1409	131	763	2875	123	29	36	2	4	209	14
No. Taxa	22	11	17	23	7	5	8	2	3	10	3

Table 4.5. Emergent Mississippian FUIs from the Range and Cahokia Sites

	Cahokia EM	Range EM	Standard Deer*
Low FUI NISP	16	329	129
%	5.7	48.7	59.5
Mid FUI NISP	210	254	65
%	74.5	37.6	29.0
High FUI NISP	56	92	25
%	19.8	13.6	11.5
Total NISP	282	675	217

*Deer figures derived from Style and Purdue 1996, table 5.22

Fish cannot be compared because comparatively few remains were recovered from Stirling phase contexts (table 4.5). This could be a preservation problem for the ICT-II and a recovery problem for the elite contexts, since the latter were excavated prior to the implementation of flotation procedures. However, the lack of fish remains could be partly due to an environmental factor. It appears there was a drop in the water table during the Stirling phase. Stirling phase sites are located at lower levels on the floodplain than are the earlier Lohmann and later Moorehead phase sites (Emerson 1992). It is possible that there were less aquatic habitats from which to procure fish, or at least fish were not as abundant and were not able to be procured in such massive quantities.

During the Moorehead phase, the consolidation of population and power began to wane, and the sociopolitical structure of Cahokia again changed. The center's population decreased with movement to outlying areas (Pauketat and Lopinot, chapter 6; see also Koldehoff 1989; Koldehoff, Pauketat, and Kelly 1993; Woods and Holley 1991). With the dispersal of population during the Moorehead phase, do we see a reversion to patterns similar to the Emergent Mississippi Period? One might expect decreases in deer and a resurgence of aquatic species, or a diversity of species being exploited because more people are having to be self-sufficient, rather than relying on others for their food. If the hierarchy had lost some of its power, it would be harder to procure deer from great distances, making necessary a more localized exploitation strategy.

The evidence does indicate that the procurement of fauna during the

Moorehead phase was more localized. The Moorehead phase assemblages recovered from the ICT-II and the East Stockade show a decrease in mammal as well as bird procurement, but with an increase in fish (table 4.2; figure 4.2). The percentage of terrestrial birds (i.e., turkey) increases (table 4.4; figure 4.5). It is not known why waterfowl procurement would decrease since fish and waterfowl procurement would seem to compliment each other, especially if the water table was again higher allowing for more aquatic habitats. However, part of the assemblage recovered from the ICT-II may represent a more seasonally restricted deposition. Most of the turkey and many deer remains were recovered from a single pit feature that yielded few fish and waterfowl remains. This could indicate a late fall-winter deposition (L. Kelly 1991, 56).

For deer body-part representation, there is a marked increase in the percentage of low-utility elements and a marked decrease in mid-utility elements (table 4.3; figure 4.6). While it does not approach the expected percentage for a complete deer, it may indicate that the site was not being provisioned with as much deer meat; that deer were more scarce, requiring more of the carcass to be returned to the site; or that individuals may have been acquiring deer meat closer to the site.

The localization of faunal subsistence in the Moorehead phase correlates with wood utilization of the Moorehead phase on the ICT-II. Lopinot and Woods (1993, 226) state that greater localization in wood exploitation is clearly evident. This indicates that while not the most desirable, there were stands of trees in the vicinity of the site, which probably supported deer and turkey populations that could be exploited by the reduced Moorehead phase inhabitants of Cahokia. The increase in aquatic species taken, particularly fish, may be offsetting a decrease in deer procurement. Although more species of fish were identified for the Moorehead phase than for the preceding Mississippian phases, they are fewer than for the Emergent Mississippian phases. At this point, it is difficult to determine whether this is attributable to a decrease in the species available because of pollution of the waters from erosion, or whether it can be attributed to other factors.

Conclusion

This overview of the faunal assemblages analyzed from the Cahokia site indicates that changes in faunal subsistence did occur over time. The causes of these changes are multiple and complex. However, these subsistence changes do reflect social and political changes to some extent. The most dramatic changes are evident between the Emergent Mississippian phases and the early Mississippian phases when Cahokia was coalescing into a stratified, complex chiefdom. Significant changes are also evident between the Mississippian Stirling and Moorehead phases when Cahokia was beginning to decline as a major center. More subtle changes occur during the Lohmann and Stirling phases, which may reflect the formation of the social hierarchy and its elaboration. Although the evidence is merely suggestive at this time, it does indicate possible differentiation of access to certain foods between the elite and non-elite members of the population.

The most significant evidence is in the deer body-part representation. Beginning in the Emergent Mississippi Period and continuing through the Mississippian phases, deer were exploited at a distance from the site. Proportionately few extremity parts with lower food utilities have been recovered from the site. It is difficult to ascertain at this time whether the deer were provisioned by populations in the Cahokia hinterland or by Cahokia populations themselves. Did the populations at the top of the social hierarchy have differential access to fauna? It appears they may have. During the Stirling phase, deer meat brought to the site appears to have been further processed and redistributed along class lines. What factors were operative in the redistribution is not clear at this time. Was it tribute, ritual, nutritional, or a combination of these? Very detailed faunal analyses are needed before these questions can be addressed. More important, however, is the need for large faunal assemblages to be recovered from firm elite contexts. In their 1994 article, Smith and Williams discuss ways of identifying elite middens associated with mounds and techniques for their testing. Such research could be very useful in obtaining the needed elite faunal assemblages. Faunal analyses cannot always provide definitive data to test the social hypotheses put forth, but in conjunction with other data sets they can provide valuable information that increases our understanding of prehistoric social and political structures.

Rinita A. Dalan

5

The Construction of Mississippian Cahokia

A consideration of the landscape and how this landscape was modified over time provides information that is critical for understanding social and political change at Cahokia and the emergence of this premier mound center. Through effects on social cohesion, landscape-modification efforts were an important means of restructuring society across the Emergent Mississippian–Mississippian transition. Earth-moving activities were not an epiphenomenon of an already Mississippianized society; the creation of the cultural landscape played an integral role in the development of Mississippian culture within the American Bottom.

The cultural landscape at Cahokia, defined as that portion of the terrain that has been culturally modified, encompasses more than the mounds and open borrow pits. These features do provide a highly visible record of the extraordinary effort that went into sculpting and creating Cahokia, but, as the site's inhabitants filled and leveled large expanses of ground (Bareis 1975a; Dalan 1993a), we need also to consider subsurface expressions of earth-moving activities.

In order to approach landscapes as features worthy of study, a new kind of archaeology employing nontraditional methods is required (Deetz 1990). In my research at Cahokia, I have applied a number of geophysical methods as a relatively nondestructive and cost-effective means of investigating both surface and subsurface landscape expressions (Dalan 1993a; Dalan and Banerjee 1996). Combining these data with that arrived at using more traditional means provides a comprehensive and diachronic view of landscape alteration. It is this perspective of site formation that is useful in understanding the process of social and political change.

As a first step, surface geophysical methods, including electromagnetic conductivity (EM) and electrical resistivity surveys, were applied (Clark 1990; McNeill 1980; Scollar et al. 1990; Weymouth 1986). The geophysical surveys were employed to define broad-scale geomorphic and cultural features in order to arrive at a general understanding of the "natural" (i.e., pre-occupation) topography and how it was modified by the Cahokians (Dalan 1993b).

The surface geophysical surveys were followed by laboratory magnetic analyses of subsampled cores (Dalan and Banerjee 1996). Comparative plots of low-field susceptibility (X) and anhysteretic remanent magnetization (ARM) (Banerjee et al. 1981; King et al. 1982) allowed natural, undisturbed soils to be differentiated from areas of the site that had been culturally modified. The ARM versus X plots were supplemented by a number of other magnetic techniques (e.g., hysteresis loops, frequency dependence of X, low-temperature investigations, and Curie points) applied in the fields of Rock Magnetism (Banerjee 1981) and Environmental Magnetism (Thompson and Oldfield 1986). The laboratory magnetic methods provided increased control in defining the vertical and horizontal extent of natural and cultural features (Dalan 1993b). They also supplied information on the sediments involved in creating the cultural landscape, allowing fill components to be identified and sourced, and elucidating other construction details necessary for a robust interpretation of the process of landscape alteration.

The field and laboratory geophysical methods were supplemented by detailed topographic mapping and test excavations conducted as part of the Southern Illinois at Edwardsville–Cahokia Mounds Field School (SIUE-CMFS) (Holley, Lopinot, Dalan, and Woods 1990; Holley, Dalan, and Watters 1992; Holley, Dalan, and Smith 1993), and by various soil-chemical analyses. Previous archaeological research at the site was also evaluated for evidence concerning alterations of the natural landscape.

This combined approach was employed to detail the location, extent, and character of anthropogenically-modified terrain within an area known as the Grand Plaza (figure 5.1). Surrounding areas, both inside and outside of the "Central Precinct" (defined as the area enclosed by the central palisade [figure 5.2]) were also examined to assess whether the character and extent of earth moving in these areas differed markedly from that observed in the Grand Plaza.

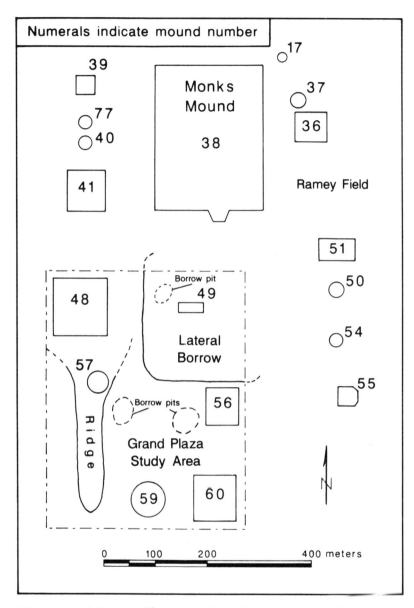

Figure 5.1. Schematic Map of the Central Precinct at Cahokia and Landscape Modification Features within the Grand Plaza

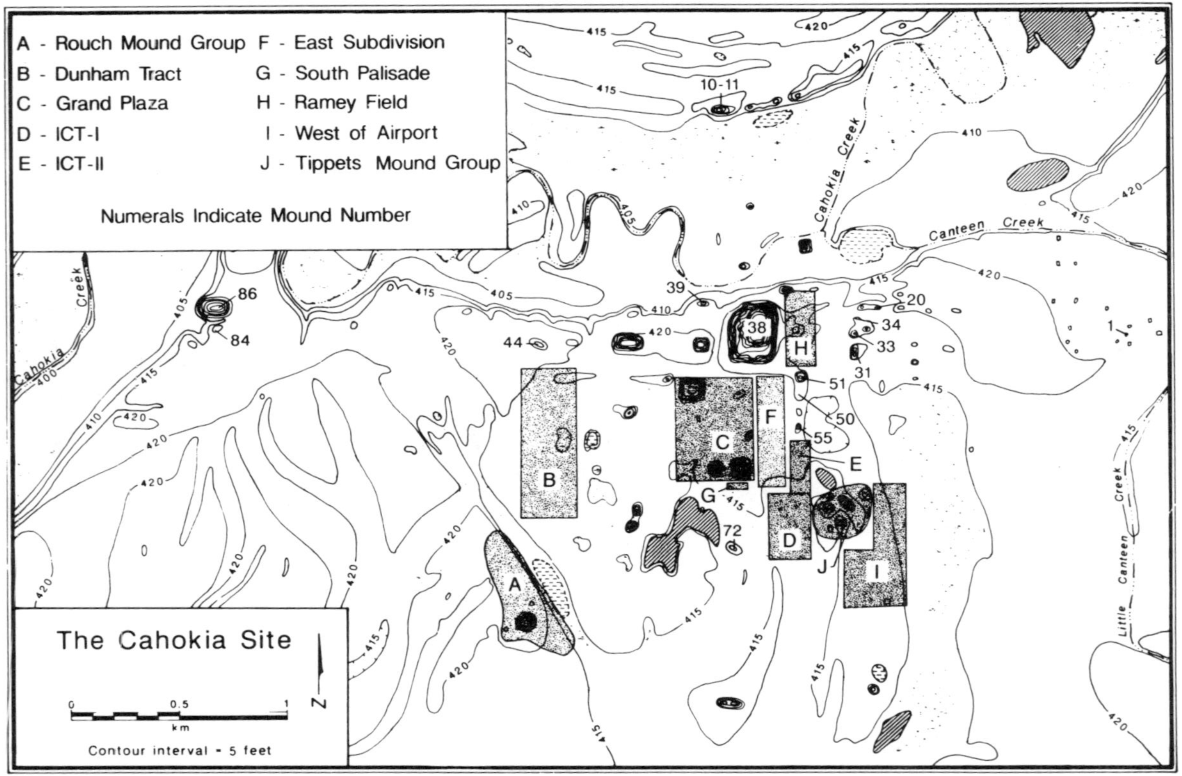
A - Rouch Mound Group
B - Dunham Tract
C - Grand Plaza
D - ICT-I
E - ICT-II
F - East Subdivision
G - South Palisade
H - Ramey Field
I - West of Airport
J - Tippets Mound Group
Numerals Indicate Mound Number
The Cahokia Site
0 0.5 1
km
Contour interval - 5 feet
N
Cahokia Creek
Canteen Creek
Little Canteen Creek
10-11
1
20
31
33
34
38
39
44
50
51
55
72
84
86

Figure 5.2. Select Mound Locations and Geophysical Study Areas at the Cahokia Site

Landscape Modification

Extensive subsurface evidence of anthropogenic earth-moving activities was encountered within the Grand Plaza where a complicated sequence of borrowing, leveling, reclamation, and mound construction was revealed. The pre-occupation surface consisted of ridge-swale topography overlain by nearly a meter of clayey sediments. A single sand ridge and abutting clay-filled swales were documented within the study area by EM surveys (figure 5.3). Buried northwest-southeast oriented ridge-swale topography is characteristic of the Cahokia site south of the Edelhardt Meander levee, between the Rouch Mound Group and the Spring Lake Meander scar (Dalan 1993a). Thus, the pre-occupation topography within the Grand Plaza was probably very similar to that documented by testing within the Dunham Tract and the Interpretive Center Tract-I (ICT-I) (Benchley 1977; Benchley and DePuydt 1982; Gladfelter, Nashold, and Hall 1979). It can be ascribed to the migration of the Spring Lake channel and subsequent backswamp deposition.

In a large-scale borrowing effort, the overlying clayey deposits were stripped from an extensive section of land (greater than 37,000 square meters) across the northern portion of the plaza (figure 5.1). Within the study area, this large lateral borrow is confined to the northern swale and adjoining sand ridge, but it also extends out of the area to the north and the east. The space covered merely by the portion of this borrow located within the Grand Plaza is greater than seventeen of the nineteen visible borrow pits that have been identified at the site by Fowler (1989, 178–88); thus it represents an earth-moving project of a massive scale.

The borrowing activities appear to have commenced late during the Emergent Mississippian period (Edelhardt phase) and were probably directed toward obtaining soil for the construction of Monks Mound (Mound 38; figure 5.2). The plaza would have provided a convenient, nearby source for fill, and the central 6.5-meter-high platform of black, organic clay documented for the base of Monks Mound (Reed, Bennett, and Porter 1968; Skele 1988) is the type of sediment that would have originally covered the study area.

The lateral borrow was then reclaimed, raising the surface to approximately the premodified level. Figure 5.4 provides a cross section through the borrowed area gained through test excavations (Holley, Dalan, Lopinot, and Smith 1990; Holley, Dalan, and Smith 1993), coring, and magnetic and soil-chemical analyses (Dalan 1993a). Key components of the fill include

93

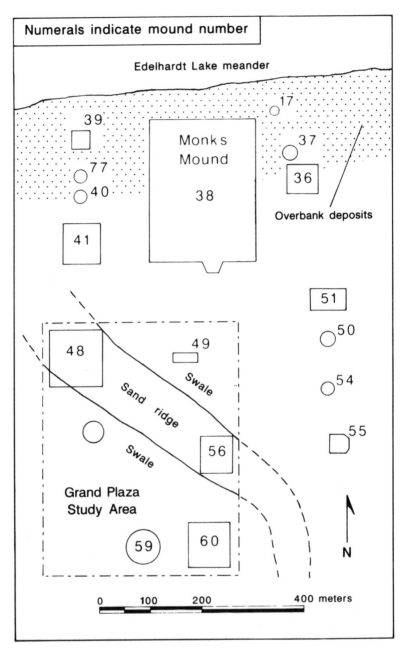

Figure 5.3. Select Geomorphic Features within the Grand Plaza and the Central Precinct

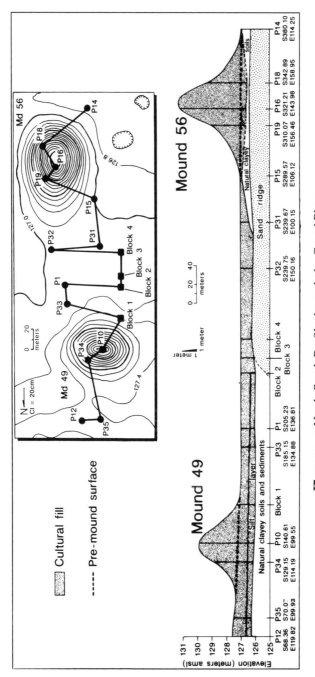

Figure 5.4. North-South Profile through the Grand Plaza

primary and secondary midden deposits derived from habitation areas situated on the natural levee along the Edelhardt Meander (figure 5.3) and clayey soils devoid of habitation debris. A mixing model, constructed using magnetic parameters, indicates that the natural clayey swale soils were added in amounts at least equal to, and probably greater than, amounts of soils obtained along with cultural debris from habitation areas. This indicates that the lateral borrow was not just a dumping ground but that it was actively being reclaimed. At first, the borrow may have served as a communal receptacle for trash; but as subsequent, upper fills were more uniform and contained less debris, they appear to have been actively directed toward creating a clean and level plaza surface. Reclamation of this area appears to have been rapid and was completed sometime during the Lohmann phase. A mound (Mound 49) was then built upon this surface, with soil for at least the initial stages of the mound mined from the reclaimed borrow (see Pauketat and Rees 1996).

Along the broadly sloping south face of the sand ridge, several other mounds were constructed (Mounds 56 and 57), with earth for these mounds at least partially derived from adjacent discrete borrows (Dalan 1993a). These borrows were then reclaimed. The documentation of what appear to be drainage features in the borrow located to the west of Mound 57 (Holley, Dalan, Lopinot, and Smith 1990; Holley, Dalan, and Smith 1993) indicates that considerable care was exercised in the filling of these smaller borrows.

The mounds and discrete borrows are located within an area of the plaza that is largely unmodified with the exception of a bank of habitation debris that runs along the western edge of the study area (figure 5.1). This ridge, which reaches a height of approximately 1 meter, may be part of an occupation area or it may represent a prehistorically constructed embankment similar to those recorded along plaza margins in ethnohistoric accounts (e.g., Lewis and Kneberg 1946).

The exact dating of these mounds, associated borrows, and the linear ridge feature is unknown, but we can at least say that they do not predate the lateral borrowing activities. A recent reexcavation of a portion of Warren K. Moorehead's trench into Mound 56 (as part of the 1992 SIUE-CMFS) indicates that construction of this mound was well under way by Stirling times if not earlier (Dalan, Holley, and Watters 1993).

In addition to the lateral borrow in the Grand Plaza, other large expanses of modified terrain have been identified in subsurface investigations within the Central Precinct (figure 5.2). University of Illinois excavations documented a filled borrow beneath Mound 51 that continued north into Ramey Field (a.k.a. East Plaza). Testing in Ramey Field indicated that this borrow was probably part of a much larger refilled area extending to the north (Bareis 1975a; Chmurny 1973; see J. Kelly, chapter 8). Built-up ground was identified within the South Palisade area by the 1989 SIUE-CMFS (Holley, Lopinot, Dalan, and Woods 1990). And finally, a consideration of estimated mound volumes for Monks Mound and other central mounds suggests that if the pattern of localized fill procurement documented for the mounds within the Grand Plaza holds we may yet find additional large tracts of reclaimed ground within the Central Precinct.

What is not certain is if and how these other reclaimed areas relate to the large lateral borrow documented in the Grand Plaza. In no case has the extent of these features been completely defined. Based on recovered artifacts, the sub–Mound 51 borrow appears to slightly postdate the borrow in the Grand Plaza, with reclamation of this area completed by the end of the Lohmann phase (Bareis 1975a; Chmurny 1973). A similar pattern of filling was recorded: cultural debris are concentrated in the lower layers and relatively "clean" soils were used for the upper portions of the borrow. In the South Palisade area, earth-moving activities occurred no later than late Stirling times.

Geophysical data, together with previous archaeological studies, indicate that the same degree of landscape modification is not found outside the Central Precinct. Evidence of large-scale stripping activities and land reclamation has generally not been identified in areas surrounding the site's core (figure 5.2). One exception is what appears to be a portion of an extensive borrow, identified during testing at the ICT-II (Woods 1985). As the earliest stage of the Central Palisade may have been constructed over this borrow, however, technically it may be located at the outer limits of the Central Precinct (Dalan, Holley, Fowler, and Iseminger 1989).

What is far more common in the surrounding areas is localized borrowing and mound construction amid unmodified terrain. And, in contrast to the Central Precinct where all borrows were carefully reclaimed, many of these borrows were left open. A few instances of reclaimed ground have been identified in outlying areas including a refuse pit below Mound 84 (Fowler 1989, 159 62; Griffin 1949; Titterington 1938), a refuse deposit north of Mound 34 (Perino 1957), and evidence of ground leveling beneath the Powell Mound (Mound 86), though these efforts generally were not on the same scale as those documented within the Grand Plaza (Ahler and DePuydt 1987). The ICT-II borrow may have filled in naturally, before or during the Lohmann phase (Woods 1985; Woods and Holley 1989).

Construction History

The contrast in patterns of landscape modification between the Central Precinct and surrounding areas becomes even more significant when time is factored in and the alteration of the landscape is viewed in relation to the rise, florescence, and decline of Cahokia. Mound construction will also be considered in this diachronic perspective of landscape modification, even though our dating of these mounds is nowhere near complete. Upwards of forty of the more than one hundred mounds at the site have been investigated, but we can tentatively date (using radiocarbon assays, the superpositioning of mounds over dated features, and ceramic inclusions in mounds), at least the initiation of construction for, perhaps only fifteen (figure 5.2). What becomes apparent in looking at dates for both these mounds and the central borrows is not so much a change in the tempo of mound construction (or a change in energy investment over time), but a marked change in the location and focus of construction efforts.

The lateral borrowing operations in the Grand Plaza and the earliest radiocarbon dates gained from Monks Mound provide evidence for the relatively sudden emergence of large-scale construction projects by the end of the Emergent Mississippi Period (Fowler 1989, 90–107; McGimsey and Wiant 1984; Reed, Bennett, and Porter 1968; Skele 1988). The raising of Monks Mound and the creation of the Grand Plaza dominated these early earth-moving efforts, and they formed the basis for a central precinct that was certainly functional by the end of the Lohmann phase. The main body of Monks Mound was largely completed by A.D. 1200, if not by the end of the Lohmann phase (Emerson and Woods 1990; Reed, Bennett, and Porter 1968; Skele 1988); the plaza was in place during the Lohmann phase; and the sub–Mound 51–Ramey Field borrow had been reclaimed.

Mounds on which construction began early during the Mississippian occupation (Lohmann and early Stirling phases) continued to focus on the community center as well as community boundaries. Mounds (50, 51, and 55) rose along the edges of the newly formed plaza (Gergen and Iseminger 1987; Chmurny 1973; J. Kelly, chapter 8; H. Smith 1973) and also at what we now define as the site's margins (Mounds 86, 10–11, and 1 [Ahler and DePuydt 1987; Pauketat 1993c, 1994a; J. Kelly, personal communication, 1992]). As mentioned above, we know that earth-moving efforts in the South Palisade area and at Mound 56 were completed at least by the Stirling phase. The ages of other mounds bounding and located within the Grand Plaza (Mounds 48, 49, 57, 59, and 60) are unknown. With the exception of one (Mound 86), all these early Mississippian mounds are relatively small in size.

In contrast, mound building during the late Stirling and Moorehead phases followed a much different pattern. During this period, construction was begun on Mounds 31, 33, 34, 44, and 84 (Fowler and Hall 1972; Griffin 1960; Griffin and Spaulding 1951; Wagner 1959; Wittry and Vogel 1962), and perhaps also on 20 and 39 (Moorehead 1929), thus focusing new construction efforts in intermediate areas of the site. As opposed to most of the earlier mounds (with the exception of Monks Mound and the Powell Mound), the relative size of these mounds also increased (Pauketat 1993c, 142).

Landscape Modification and Social Cohesion

Just as the construction of megalithic monuments in northwest Europe is seen to be an essential part of the transformation from forager to farmer (Sherratt 1990), mound construction and landscape modification within the American Bottom can be viewed as an integral component in the development of intensive agriculture and of stable nucleated communities. This relationship is advanced on the basis of concurrent developments within the American Bottom in the cultural landscape and in the agricultural and settlement systems, and also on links between Mississippian mound-and-plaza construction and agricultural concepts, rituals, and activities (Dalan 1993a).

Delayed returns associated with agriculture necessitate the establishment of a stable and cooperative labor pool (Ehrenberg 1989; Meillassoux 1973; Woodburn 1980). The communal construction and use of mounds, plazas, and other earthen features would have provided a means of creating and perpetuating social relations, and establishing and maintaining the labor force necessary for large-scale agricultural pursuits. The durability of this construction and its attendant message of group permanence would have assured a commitment to place and to the transformation, both social and ecological, of the landscape. An additional sense of community permanence was obtained by tying these works to the power of the ancestors (J. Kelly, chapter 8; Knight 1986, 1989a; Pauketat 1993c).

Early landscape modification efforts at Cahokia did not start out at a small scale but commenced with the construction of a huge mound, Monks Mound, and the Grand Plaza, features unequaled at any other Mississippian site. Together with other evidence of early planning, these features illustrate the scale of the community that was envisioned and represent a significant commitment by the site's inhabitants (Fowler 1974). Notably, these large-scale landscape alterations were initiated as early as the terminal Emergent Mississippi Period.

Monks Mound and the Grand Plaza were clearly critical in the definition and creation of a large integrated community. Their construction gave structure to this community, simultaneously emphasizing the importance of the ruling hierarchy and the masses. The large, accessible plaza, which appears to have been capable of accommodating the resident population and more, provided a centralized location for ritual activities and served as a collective representation of the group. In contrast, the mounds represented an intricate system in which the relationships of different community and polity groups were ordered. The power of the chief was manifested in a mound that stood above all others. The power of the center was expressed in the profusion of its mounds. Massive earth moving, which included the careful reclamation of large tracts of land within the Central Precinct, provided visualization of the superiority of Cahokia and created a community of a size previously unrealized in the American Bottom.

Mounds, other than principal mounds devoted to the chief and to the community temple, probably were tethered to different social units (i.e., clans and lineages), and most likely there were hierarchical implications in the size and positioning of mounds within a center (Holley 1992). Power and legitimacy would have been gained through construction and use, and actively employed to negotiate power relationships, symbolize the social ordering, and recruit groups into the community (Bradley 1984; Hodder 1990).

In contrast to the continuity represented by the plaza, there is a fluidity to mound construction—a fluidity in the number of mounds, in their arrangements, and in their sizes—reflecting the continual negotiation of the social system (J. Kelly, chapter 8). The scale of Monks Mound and the corresponding paucity of other Emergent Mississippian mounds is expressive of the overriding power of the chief and of the importance of the central hierarchy.

This is also manifest in the elaborate burials recovered from Mound 72 and in earth-moving efforts through the early portions of the Mississippi Period that functioned to support and emphasize the primacy of the center (Fowler 1991).

The erection of mounds in intermediate areas of the site during late Stirling and subsequent phases, together with a marked change in how much effort was directed toward refilling and reclaiming borrowed ground, stands in contrast to the earlier pattern of landscape modification. This shift in the pattern is interpreted to be the result of various groups jockeying for power and position (see Pauketat 1992, 1993c). An increase in the relative size of these mounds is perhaps indicative that they were beginning to challenge the power base represented by Monks Mound, which acquired only aprons and secondary mounds during the Moorehead phase. Other factors such as a reorganization of community structure (Holley et al. 1989), the increasing privatization of storage (Collins 1990; Holley et al. 1989), the return of public grounds to residential use (J. Kelly 1991d; Pauketat 1994a), and the construction of a palisade around the Central Precinct (J. Anderson 1973; Iseminger et al. 1990) also reflect a weakening of community-unifying central control and a protracted period of social decline (see Pauketat and Lopinot, chapter 6).

Mississippian Cultural Landscapes

Because Cahokia is the largest and most complex Mississippian mound center, perhaps it is unique in the degree to which the site's inhabitants impacted and altered the natural landscape. Research at other Mississippian sites, however, indicates that this is not the case. The largest of the plazas at Etowah was artificially elevated above the natural surface (Larson 1989, 136). At Chucalissa, an enormous amount of fill was used to level an ancient ravine, reshaping the plateau to provide additional land for mound construction (Nash 1972). The Ocmulgee site residents employed land filling within a previously borrowed area to increase the building surface prior to mound construction (A. Kelly 1938). The Snodgrass site also exhibits evidence of planned leveling and filling within its short period of occupation (Price and Griffin 1979). So if we want to understand Mississippian cultural landscapes in their entirety, then we have to study more than mounds and other surface features. If we want to look at the process of site formation, then we must also take into account subsurface evidence for earth-moving activities.

Cahokia also is not alone in the early formation of a stable community center. A plaza and attendant principal mounds were crucial elements in the creation of other large, integrated communities such as Wickliffe (Wesler 1989, 1991a, 1991b; Wesler and Neusius 1987), Kincaid (Cole et al. 1951), Hiwassee Island (Lewis and Kneberg 1946), and perhaps also Moundville (Welch 1990). The area selected as the community center provided a permanent focus for subsequent occupations.

Yet other Mississippian centers have provided evidence of quite different construction histories. For example, a marked change in the tempo of construction, not apparent at Cahokia, has been suggested for sites in the Yazoo basin region of the lower Mississippi valley (Brain 1978). Here, all major mound construction may have occurred within a relatively brief period of fifty to one hundred years. Differences such as these are important to investigate as a means of comprehending the development of individual Mississippian centers. Combined with more traditional data sources, this information can be used to provide a better understanding of local adaptations in the process of nucleation and consolidation.

Timothy R. Pauketat and Neal H. Lopinot

6

Cahokian Population Dynamics

The numbers of Native Americans who once lived at Cahokia, the primary center of the largest of Mississippian polities, has been pondered since Henry Brackenridge in 1814 concluded "that a very populous town had once existed" there (1962, 188). Maximum population estimates for the Cahokia site have varied from 500 to 50,000 people (cf. Gregg 1975a; Milner 1991, 34–35; Muller 1987, 12). In recent years, Cahokian demographics have been considered from two viewpoints. Some researchers see Cahokia as an urban center with a large nucleated population (e.g., Fowler 1974, 1975; O'Brien 1989, 1991). Others view Cahokia as a loosely knit, low-density aggregation of kin groups and ritual spaces (e.g., Muller 1987).[1]

This situation, where the perspectives of researchers loom larger in population estimates than actual archaeological data, is both unproductive and unnecessary. A numerical estimate of Cahokia's population is presented in the following pages that draws on architectural and community-organizational data only recently available. These estimates provide a basis for delineating diachronic demographic trends that inform an interpretation of Cahokia's demographic trajectory.

Previous Estimates

There are no direct historical means to reconstruct Cahokia's population size. Likewise, the demographic sizes and trajectories of other southeastern complexes provide little insight into Cahokian demography. Some southeastern polities visited by the de Soto expedition between A.D. 1539 and 1543, and others that predated contact, had dispersed populations, with towns consisting of at most a few hundred individuals (Anderson 1994a;

Blitz 1993; Clayton, Knight, and Moore 1993; Hally 1988; Muller 1978; Williams and Shapiro 1990). Other southeastern polities, including those south of the American Bottom in the vicinity of Memphis, had nucleated towns of one thousand or more individuals (Dye 1994; Morse 1990).

There is no reason to believe that the postcontact depopulated Southeast provides suitable analogs for precontact Cahokia (e.g., Swanton 1979, 12; cf. Muller 1987, 12). Nor is it necessary or reasonable to assume a homogeneous Mississippian population density across the Southeast prior to European contact. In fact, one might propose that, given the enormity of Cahokia proper, the site's support population was substantially larger than that of other southeastern polities. Such a presumption might have motivated Brackenridge (1962) to compare precontact Cahokia to Philadelphia at about 1814, which at the time had a population of about fifty thousand (Fowler 1991, 1). This, of course, was nothing more than a guess, but then, most other estimates have also been impressionistic guesses.

Population estimates based on quantified archaeological data have been few in number. Thomas (1907) estimated a population of around ten thousand individuals for the Cahokia site based on mound fill volume and labor constraints. Reed, Bennett, and Porter (1968, 146) estimated that a "sustaining population" of about ten thousand would have been needed to build Monks Mound, the largest of earthen mounds at Cahokia (cf. Muller 1987, 12). In a similar vein, Iseminger (1990, 37) has estimated that the two thousand to four thousand people necessary to construct each of Cahokia's central palisade walls would have been drawn from a sustaining population of eight thousand to twenty thousand people.[2]

Gregg's Estimate

Unlike previous researchers, Michael Gregg (1975b) estimated Cahokia's population based on architectural data. His estimate, derived from an interpretation of the Tract 15A and Powell Tract community plans, consisted of a density figure of 5,000 people per square mile (2.5 square kilometers), or 2,000 people per square kilometer. Given this density, he estimated that 25,500 Stirling-phase people lived at the Cahokia site as he defined it (Gregg 1975b, 134). This estimate was based on a diamond-shaped quadrilateral area bounded by Mound 1 to the east, Kunnemann Mound to the north, Powell Mound to the west, and Harding Mound to the south. The area within this quadrilateral encompasses 13.2 square kilometers. Gregg (1975b, 131–32) eliminated the estimated total area occupied by mounds (75 acres) and the enclosed part of the quadrilateral below an elevation of 127 meters amsl, leaving 6.9 square kilometers (1,725 acres) of the original 13.2 square kilometers (3,300 acres) as inhabited area.

Using house density data from Tract 15A and the Powell Tract, Gregg (1975b) derived a density figure of eight houses per acre for the Stirling phase. By applying Narroll's (1962) ratio of 10 square meters per person, he derived estimates of 1.86 persons per building and 14.8 persons per acre. Projected for the 1,725 acres of estimated habitable space within the site, the resulting site population was 25,530. An editor's footnote added that 42,780 people might be a "maximal" estimate of the Stirling-phase population of Cahokia using Casselberry's (1974) formula of 6 square meters of floor area per person (Gregg 1975b, 134n). A number of archaeologists have deemed this population figure to be overinflated (Ford 1974b, 406; Griffin 1983, 282; Milner 1990, 11, 1991, 34).

Gregg's (1975b) population estimates should be revised for several reasons. Gregg did not exclude from his estimate plazas, woodhenges, or other uninhabited or sparsely occupied portions of central Cahokia. Furthermore, he did not exclude those portions of the quadrilateral base area (13.2 square kilometers) that were not home to many people. The quadrilateral boundary does not adequately circumscribe Cahokia as an agglomeration of mound-plaza-residence clusters (Kelly 1991b). Cahokia's high-density occupation area does not correspond precisely with the 127 meters amsl contour line. Excavations at the Interpretive Center Tract II (ICT-II), for instance, revealed that intensive residential occupation occurred below the minimum occupational elevation set by Gregg (1975b), between 126.4 and 127.2 meters amsl (Collins 1990; Fowler 1991, 24). This problematic assumption is compounded by the use of Narroll's household population formula (i.e., 10 square meters of floor area/person) and Gregg's assumption that certain buildings were occupied for the century-long Stirling phase.[3]

Domiciles, Households, and Community Sampling Error

Some of the problems of the previous population estimates were corrected by Milner (1986) in his estimate of a segment of the rural population south of Cahokia. Milner's (1986, tables 3–5) estimates were based on a range of plausible projections of rural domicile longevity (three to ten years) and phase-specific domestic-group sizes (cf. Pauketat 1989). Milner's rural population density estimates, of course, are not applicable to Cahokia proper. The occupation spans of domestic zones or household clusters at Cahokia and other central communities probably exceeded those of many rural sites. The spatial distribution and functions of buildings at Cahokia undoubtedly were unlike rural building distributions or functions.

With limited structural renovations, buildings at Cahokia were occupied by households for up to three decades (see Pauketat 1989, 290, chapter 2). That Cahokian domiciles were occupied for decades is borne out by the evidence of building reconstruction and the additional accumulations of refuse (Pauketat 1994a, 85–86). Many Cahokian buildings unearthed by excavations at Tract 15A, the Dunham Tract, the Falcon Drive-In, and the ICT-II were rebuilt in the same place over and over (Collins 1990; Gums and Holley 1991; Pauketat 1994a, figure 4.7, 1996).

Any given household cluster at Cahokia might have included one or two (and rarely three or more) buildings. At several rural sites and at the Lohmann site to the south, household clusters include two structures, each perhaps serving a distinct function within the daily or seasonal lives of the household (Emerson, chapter 9; see also Mehrer 1995; Mehrer and Collins 1995; Prentice and Mehrer 1981; Milner 1986, 230; Pauketat 1989, 295). Unfortunately, the archaeological complexity of excavated residential tracts at Cahokia usually precludes the simple isolation of individual domestic zones there. It is possible that a single household might have used one or two structures at any given time, although the number of houses used by a household might have been a function of household size, eliminating any problematic effects the numbers of houses per household would have on a population estimate.

Beyond the problem of the number of structures per household, there probably was not a simple linear correlation between the number of people making up a household and house size (see Milner 1986, 231). At Cahokia, a general pattern of increasing structure size through time was suggested by Gregg (1975b, 132) to indicate ever-larger households. However, diachronic changes in domicile floor area, especially subtle changes, might also be a reflection of the changing uses to which internal space was put, the differential social status of the occupants, or the construction methods or cultural meanings of the buildings themselves (Collins 1990, 228–30; Mehrer 1988, 149–

61; Pauketat 1994a, 139–40). At least two building size modes are evident in the Lohmann and Stirling phase architectural data at Tract 15A (Pauketat 1996), the large building mode perhaps being the homes of higher-status households (which may have included more people than lower-status domestic groups).

While problems persist surrounding domestic-zone isolation and the relationship between house and household size, a better grasp of Cahokia's community dynamics has been attained since 1975. Residential areas were not uniformly distributed about the landscape irrespective of the locations of mounds, plazas, or cemeteries, and Cahokia's boundaries undoubtedly fluctuated through time, probably never conforming to the quadrilateral depicted by Fowler (1975, 96–97) and Gregg (1975b, figure 73). Cahokians did not live in all parts of this area, although they did reside in areas not even considered by Gregg (1975b). For instance, investigations in the western part of the site have demonstrated the existence of Mississippian occupations outside of the quadrilateral considered by Fowler (1975) and Gregg (1975b) to define Cahokia (see Gums et al. 1989; Keller, Kelly, and Witty 1994; Lopinot, Brown, and Holley 1989). Closer to the very core of the Cahokia site, the bases of the "Creek Bottom Group," five mounds around a northern plaza (immediately north of Monks Mound), are elevated between 125.0 and 126.0 meters amsl and presumably would have been surrounded by buildings, as typical of mound-and-plaza clusters at Cahokia (Fowler 1989, 203; see J. Kelly, chapter 8; Pauketat and Emerson, chapter 1).

Calculating Cahokia's Habitable Area

Cahokia, as an aggregation of mounds, plazas, and residential loci, may be bounded best by a circular catchment within which an irregular zone of high-density occupation may be delineated. A catchment 3.25 kilometers in diameter and covering an area of 8.3 square kilometers circumscribes most mounds and plazas of the Cahokia group. Within this area lie expansive plazas devoid of residences and high-density occupation areas. The Powell Mound and other isolated mounds and residential areas may be circumscribed by smaller catchments (figure 6.1).

Based on surface surveys and more recent excavations within the Cahokia and Powell Mound Group catchments, we possess some knowledge of where intense residential occupation was and where it was not (J. Anderson

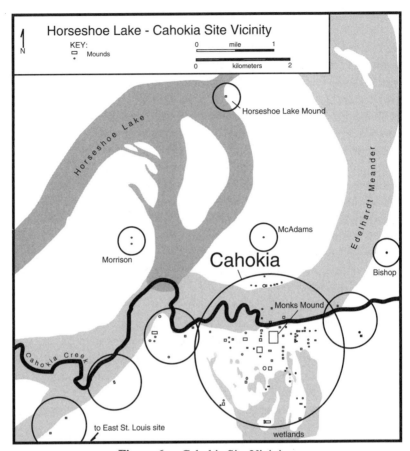

Figure 6.1. Cahokia Site Vicinity

1977; Bareis 1963; Bareis and Lathrap 1962; Gums et al. 1989; Holley 1990; Iseminger et al. 1990; Keller, Kelly, and Witty 1994; J. Kelly, chapter 8; Lopinot, Brown, and Holley 1989; Moorehead 1929; O'Brien 1972a; Pauketat 1996; Wittry 1960, 1961; Woods and Holley 1989). While we do not have precise dates on the construction of most plazas at Cahokia, the construction of the Grand Plaza is thought to have been initiated near the beginning of the Lohmann phase (Dalan, chapter 5; Holley, Dalan, Lopinot, and Smith 1990; Holley, Dalan, and Smith 1993). The West Plaza also lacks evidence of significant Lohmann- and Stirling-phase residential occupation (J. Kelly 1980, 1991b, chapter 8; Salzer 1975). The East Plaza is not well understood, having been relocated through time, but will be considered here as well (Kelly 1991b, chapter 8).

The areas enclosed by the Grand Plaza (19 hectares), the western plaza (9 hectares), and the eastern plaza (ca. 9 hectares) are eliminated from the total occupation area, as is the surface area covered by mounds and borrow pits. Excluding the three large plazas and all mounds, the high-density residential area covers 1.5 square kilometers of the Cahokia catchment and 0.3 square kilometers of the Powell Group catchment, or a total of 1.8 square kilometers (figure 6.2). Other smaller plazas undoubtedly existed within occupation areas, and these are represented in the building-density data used here.

The 1.8 square kilometer, high-density occupation area corresponds for the most part to the well-drained land above 126.5 meters amsl south of the Edelhardt Meander scar and north of a series of Mississippian borrow pits (southeast and southwest of the Grand Plaza). The Kunnemann Tract north of the Edelhardt Meander and a ridge near the "Rouch Mound Group" also comprise high-density residential areas of the Cahokia site (Holley 1990; Moorehead 1929, figure I). The low-lying "South Group" does not exhibit evidence of the kind of continuous residential occupation common to other parts of the site. Several low rises around the Harding Mound, a communal mortuary facility, may be small house mounds surmounted by the few domiciles or special buildings in that locality (Fowler 1991; J. Kelly 1991b). Whether a substantial residential occupation was associated with the Creek Bottom Group is not known, because modern alluviation in the Edelhardt Meander scar has obscured the Mississippian occupation surface and no excavations have been conducted there. There certainly are low-density occupation areas in other portions of the Cahokia catchment and south of the Powell Mound catchment (e.g., Keller, Kelly, and Witty 1994), but these are not included in the present consideration.

Emergent Mississippian and Mississippian domestic remains are commonly found within the high-density occupation zone of the Cahokia and Powell catchments. Importantly, Lohmann-phase remains are ubiquitous in all portions of the high-density occupation area outside the large plazas. Stirling-phase remains are almost as ubiquitous, although central portions of Cahokia may have been reserved for nondomestic uses at that time (Fowler and Hall 1975, 5). Edelhardt- and Moorehead-phase remains are not as widespread and Loyd-, Merrell-, and Sand Prairie–phase remains are even less common (J. Kelly 1991b).

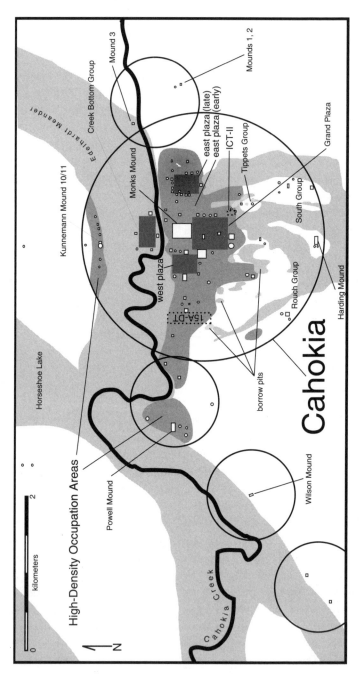

Figure 6.2. Cahokia Site Mounds, Plazas, and Residential Areas

Emergent Mississippian remains seem largely restricted to the ridge south of the Edelhardt Meander scar that extends from the Powell Mound east under Monks Mound. Emergent Mississippian remains are seldom found more than a couple of hundred meters south of this ridge crest bordering the meander scar (cf. Collins 1990; Holley, Lopinot, Woods, and Kelly 1989; J. Kelly 1980; Pauketat 1994a, 1994b, 1996). This probably reflects the structure of community organization, groups of courtyards strung out along the ridge, that predates the planned Mississippian center featuring the Grand Plaza. Likewise, the fewer Moorehead-phase remains are indicative of a decline in the numbers of people concentrated at Cahokia or the insignificance of certain areas as residential locations.

Architectural Data from Cahokia

Two analyzed sets of architectural data from the Cahokia site for which the extent of excavations and phase affiliation of buildings are known can be used to estimate population. The first is the Tract 15A and Dunham Tract (15A-DT) excavations and the second is the Interpretive Center Tract-II (ICT-II) excavations (Collins 1990; Pauketat 1996). Only rectangular buildings in the 15A-DT and ICT-II samples are included in the calculations of building density. In cases where a building was reconstructed or substantially repaired (represented by at least two new wall trenches or rows of posts), each reconstruction or reparation is counted as a separate building. The Powell Tract excavations used in Gregg's (1975b) estimate revealed an intense domestic occupation, similar to the 15A-DT and ICT-II samples, but the uncertainties regarding the limits of the excavations and the phase affiliations of some buildings make these excavations of less use in the estimation procedure.

The 15A-DT Sample

A total of 15,613 square meters of surface area was exposed in the Tract 15A and the Dunham Tract excavations. These contiguous tracts witnessed a series of different uses over the Emergent Mississippi and Mississippi Periods (Pauketat 1994a, 1996). This included a residential use during the Edelhardt phase (A.D. 1000–1050), continued and intensified residential occupation during the Lohmann phase (A.D. 1050–1100), subsequent construction of the

Table 6.1. Cahokia Building Density Data

	15A-DT (15,613 m²)				ICT-II (5,289 m²)		
Phase	N of Bldgs.	m²	N/km²	m²/km²	N of Bldgs.	m²	N/km²	m²/km²
	(x 64.05)				(x 189.07)			
Merrell	0	0	0	0	0	0	0	0
Edelhardt	63	362	4035	23186	0	0	0	0
Lohmann	111	1083	7110	69366	18	252	3403	47646
Stirling	33	726	2114	46500	52	851	9832	160899
Moorehead	26	627	1665	40159	11	224	2080	42352
Sand Prairie	0	0	0	0	0	0	0	0
Total	233	2798	14924	179212	81	1327	15315	250896

Post-Circle Monument (a.k.a. "woodhenge") and more restricted residential occupation during the Stirling phase (A.D. 1100–1200), and residential use again during the Moorehead phase (A.D. 1200–1275). During the Edelhardt phase, single-post-wall structures having floor areas ranging from 4 to 14 square meters were arranged around courtyards in groups much like the pattern John Kelly (1990b) has documented at the Range site. In contrast, wall-trench buildings (in two size modes) dating to the Lohmann phase appear to have been arranged around a small plaza. Lohmann-phase evidence of structure renovation and rebuilding is common, and the numbers and area covered by Lohmann-phase buildings is significantly greater than the preceding Edelhardt-phase sums (table 6.1). For the excavated portions of the Dunham Tract to the south of Tract 15A, Lohmann- and Stirling-phase buildings are numerous, but there is no evidence of Edelhardt- or Moorehead-phase structures (Pauketat 1994a, 1996).

Two of the Stirling-phase buildings in the 15A-DT sample are quite large (94 and 229 square meters), probably due in part to their association with the Post-Circle Monument, yet did contain domestic garbage (Pauketat 1996). The presence of this monument prevented domestic occupation of this portion of the site and resulted in an overall reduced density of buildings and floor area compared to the Lohmann phase (table 6.1). Other Stirling-phase buildings to the south of the Post-Circle Monument on the Dunham Tract are found in numbers comparable to the Lohmann phase and are smaller, like their Lohmann-phase antecedents. The fewer Moorehead-phase buildings, none located on the Dunham Tract, are larger than the ordinary Lohmann-

Table 6.1. Cahokia Building Density Data

Phase	Combined Tracts (20,902 m²)				Adjusted Bldg. Data*		Mean Floor Area (m²)
	N of Bldgs.	m²	N/km²	m²/km²	N/km²	m²/km²	
		(x 47.84)					
Merrell	0	0	0	0	0	0	0.00
Edelhardt	63	362	3013.9	17318.1	60.28	346.36	5.75
Lohmann	129	1335	6171.4	63866.4	123.42	1277.32	10.35
Stirling	85	1577	4066.4	75443.7	40.66	754.44	18.55
Moorehead	37	851	1770.1	40711.8	23.60	542.83	23.00
Sand Prairie	0	0	0	0	0	0	0.00
Total	314	4125	15022.0	197340.0	247.96	2920.95	

*Combined tract figures divided by duration of phase to obtain building N and M² per km³ per year

and Stirling-phase buildings but, with average floor areas less than 35 square meters, cover almost as much area as the Stirling-phase total (Pauketat 1996, table 6.11). Some of these Moorehead-phase buildings appear to have been clustered in groups of two or three and were scattered across the northern portion of the excavated area where the Post-Circle Monument had stood.

The ICT-II Sample

A total of 5,289 square kilometers of surface area was exposed in the Interpretive Center Tract-II excavations, near the southeast corner of the Grand Plaza, and it included Lohmann-, Stirling-, and Moorehead-phase residential occupations (Collins, chapter 7). The earliest occupation of the tract seems to have been a series of late Lohmann-phase buildings, all constructed using wall trenches and arranged around a plaza partially exposed in the excavated area. That the ICT-II Lohmann-phase building density figures are less than the 15A-DT figures is due in part to the lack of an early Lohmann occupation of the area and is reflected in the building density calculations (table 6.1).

The relatively dense stand of late Lohmann-phase buildings in the ICT-II sample was replaced by sparser numbers of Stirling-phase occupations, perhaps following a brief hiatus (J. Kelly 1991b). The Stirling-phase residential occupation was comprised of discrete domestic units with houses repeatedly reconstructed or repaired, making the Stirling-phase building density figures exceed significantly those of the 15A-DT sample (table 6.1). The ICT-II Moorehead-phase occupation also consists of discrete household clusters with lengthy occupation spans, although the ICT-II Moorehead-phase occupation may not have covered the entire seventy-five years alotted that phase.

None of the Stirling- and Moorehead-phase buildings at the ICT-II were as large as the largest 15A-DT buildings, perhaps because they were typical domiciles or special-purpose buildings for a non-elite subcommunity. Average ICT-II building size did increase through time, as seen in the 15A-DT sample, and the Moorehead-phase building density figures from the ICT-II are similar to the 15A-DT figures.

Population Estimates

The occupations of Tract 15A, the Dunham Tract, and the Interpretive Center Tract II are comparable, taking into account the late Lohmann-phase initation of the ICT-II occupation and 15A-DT's Post-Circle Monument. It is likely that these occupational patterns and monumental interruptions characterize Lohmann- and Stirling-phase Cahokia in general, as noted in general summaries of Cahokia's occupational history (Fowler and Hall 1975). Thus, an average number of buildings and floor area per square kilometer may be derived for the combined 15A-DT and ICT-II sample. This is accomplished by multiplying the numbers of buildings and floor area totals per 20,902-square-meter area (the total excavation area) by a factor (of 47.84) that adjusts building density per excavated area (square meters) upward to reflect building density per square kilometer. It is necessary, however, to adjust for the variable lengths of phases by dividing the combined-tract-density figures by the phase length (between fifty and one hundred years). This adjustment gives us the building numbers and floor area (square meters) per square kilometers per year (table 6.1).

Calculating Population Density

The adjusted building data (quantity/square kilometer/year) serves as the basis for population estimates. These estimates may be derived by multiplying the adjusted building data by average building longevity (years) and average numbers of persons per building. Average building longevity probably was not less than five years, although lightweight single-post buildings of the Edelhardt phase might not have lasted as long as later Mississippian wall-trench buildings. The occupation spans of rural domestic zones might have

114

been less than this given other physical and social environmental factors (Milner 1986; Pauketat 1989). At Cahokia and other towns, the evidence of lengthy domestic-zone occupation spans and building repair or reconstruction is indicative of building longevities of ten years or more (see Pauketat, chapter 2).

Average numbers of persons per building will be calculated to be consistent with Milner's (1986) calculations for rural population density. This entails allowing 2.25 square meters for each of the first 6 householders and 9 square meters for each subsequent building occupant (S. Cook 1972 cited by Milner 1986, 231). Given the mean floor areas of 15A-DT and ICT-II buildings (table 6.1), an average of 2.55, 4.60, 6.56, and 7.06 people resided in Edelhardt-, Lohmann-, Stirling-, and Moorehead-phase buildings at Cahokia, respectively. A range of persons per square kilometer may be derived from the Cahokian data given variable building longevity and household size estimates (table 6.2). Persons per square kilometer should be multiplied by the total size of Cahokia's high-density occupation area to arrive at the final population estimate for each phase (table 6.3).

High-Density Occupation Estimates

Sufficient data are lacking to estimate the population of the early Emergent Mississippian occupation of the Cahokia site, although we can assume that it was smaller than that of the Edelhardt phase. Extrapolating from the combined 15A-DT and ICT-II sample, the Edelhardt-phase occupation of Cahokia probably ranged from almost 1,400 to nearly 2,800 people, given building longevity estimates of five to ten years (see tables 6.2–6.3). Another way of calculating the Edelhardt-phase population is to use only the 15A-DT data but restrict the high-density area to half (0.9 square kilometers) its Mississippian dimensions. Estimates of the Edelhardt-phase population using this method range from 926 to 1,852 people.

The Lohmann-phase population estimates constitute a dramatic increase over the Edelhardt-phase estimates. Given reasonable longevity estimates of ten to fifteen years per building and 4.6 persons per building, the total population of Cahokia from A.D. 1050–1100 was about 10,200 to 15,300 people (table 6.3). Lower estimates can be derived if the high-density occupation area is reduced or if other variables are altered. Higher estimates would result if average building longevity exceeded fifteen years or if the high-

Table 6.2. Building Density and Persons per Kilometer Squared

| | N of Buildings/km² | | | | Persons/km² | | | |
| | by Longevity Estimate | | | | At 2.55 persons/Bldg. | | | |
Phase	5 yrs	10 yrs	15 yrs	20 yrs	5 yrs	10 yrs	15 yrs	20 yrs
Edelhardt	301	603	904	1206	**767.6**	**1538.0**	2305.2	3075.3
Lohmann	617	1234	1851	2468	1573.0	3147.0	4720.1	6293.4
Stirling	203	407	610	813	517.7	1038.0	1555.5	2073.2
Moorehead	118	236	354	472	300.9	601.8	902.7	1203.6

Note: The numbers set in bold face are considered to represent the most reasonable estimates

density area spilled out into portions of the Cahokia catchment not considered here.

The Stirling-phase population—given the combined data set, an average of 6.56 persons per building, and a ten-to-fifteen-year average building longevity—is less than the Lohmann-phase maximum. The combined-tract figure ranges from nearly 5,200 to 7,200 people. This figure, a reduction of the Lohmann-phase figures, is skewed by the absence of occupation on Tract 15A (because of the nonresidential usage of the tract between A.D. 1100 and 1200). The combined-tract figures, however, may accurately reflect a reduced domestic occupation and the increased elite-ritual usage of the central portion of Cahokia, as noted by others (e.g., Fowler and Hall 1975, 5; Holley 1990, 28).[4] If we use only the ICT-II data set to estimate population density, estimates would be skewed beyond the Lohmann-phase levels.

The Moorehead-phase population constitutes a clear decline or constriction of Cahokia's population. Both the 15A-DT and ICT-II data sets indicate this pattern. Even allowing 7.06 persons per building and building use lives of ten to fifteen years, the total population of Cahokia would have ranged from 3,000 to 4,500 individuals. The population of Cahokia during the subsequent Sand Prairie-phase must have dropped considerably, given the lack of remains in the 15A-DT and ICT-II samples, but we are not able to provide an estimate given this sampling situation.

Regional Population Dynamics

The estimates of Cahokia's population do not in and of themselves provide a model of the population dynamics of the American Bottom region. The re-

Table 6.2. Building Density and Persons per Kilometer Squared

Persons/km²

Phase	At 4.6 persons/bldg				At 6.56 persons/bldg				At 7.06 persons/bldg				Mean
	5 yrs	10 yrs	15 yrs	20 yrs	5 yrs	10 yrs	15 yrs	20 yrs	5 yrs	10 yrs	15 yrs	20 yrs	20 yrs
Edelhardt	1385	2773.8	4158	3075	1975	3956	5930	7911	2125.0	4257	6382	8514.4	3157.1
Lohmann	2838	**5676.4**	**8515**	6293	4048	8095	12143	16190	4356.0	8712	13068	17424.0	6463.1
Stirling	934	1872.2	2806	2073	1332	**2670**	**4002**	533	1433.0	2873	4307	5739.8	2129.6
Moorehead	543	1085.6	1628	1204	774	1548	2322	3096	833.1	**1666**	**2499**	3332.3	1236.1

Note: The numbers set in bold face are considered to represent the most reasonable estimates

gional distribution of people and the rate and scale of population centralization and decentralization should be taken into account alongside the population estimates in order to understand Cahokian development.

Centralization and Decentralization

The present estimates of Cahokia's population do not comprise an adequate
description of the demographic dynamism thought to have been an integral
component of Cahokian community development. There were other major
towns or minor mound-residence clusters within the Central Political-
Administrative Complex (see Pauketat 1994a; Pauketat and Emerson, chapter 1). The East St. Louis site, itself a large Mississippian center with some
fifty mounds, was located only a few kilometers southwest of Cahokia
(J. Kelly, chapter 8). The St. Louis site, with its twenty-two mounds, was
located just across the Mississippi River.

Episodic movements of people and administrative functions from Cahokia to East St. Louis or St. Louis and back again over the duration of the
Mississippi Period were probably common, similar to other southeastern
chiefdoms (Anderson 1994a; M. Williams and Shapiro 1990). Population
fluctuations within the region would have accompanied the dynamic social
and political landscape of the American Bottom (in the sense of Milner
1990). Households would have detached and reattached themselves to various chiefly patrons as these patrons lost or gained political power, or as local
political domains waxed and waned. In addition to politically inspired population movements, Cahokia probably had some part-time or seasonal resi-

Table 6.3. Cahokian Population Estimates

| Phase | Population Density Estimates | | Total Cahokian Population | |
| | persons/km² | | persons/km² x total site area* | |
	low	high	low	high
Edelhardt	768	1538	1382	2768
Lohmann	5676	8515	10218	15327
Stirling	2870	4002	5266	7204
Moorehead	1666	2499	2999	4498

*This area is 1.8 square kilometers

dents. Seasonal population fluctuations may have correlated with the agricultural cycle or annual centralized rites.

While inter-center population realignments likely occurred between A.D. 1000 and 1300, complete occupational hiatuses of the large Mississippian centers—Cahokia, East St. Louis, and St. Louis—seem unlikely. For some parts of Cahokia, continuous domestic occupation is evident, at least for decades if not centuries (e.g., Pauketat 1994a, 1996). Given that Lohmann-, Stirling-, and Moorehead-phase components are currently alotted only 225 years yet known from the Cahokia and East St. Louis sites, and likely for the St. Louis center, we may infer that the Central Political-Administrative Complex was home to more people than represented only by the Cahokia population estimates (see J. Kelly, chapter 8).

Regardless of the occupational uncertainties, the Central Political-Administrative Complex did witness a dramatic nucleation of people within the century-long span covered by the Edelhardt-to-Lohmann phase. Based on the 15A-DT data alone, Pauketat (1993b; 1994a) elsewhere estimated a three- to fourfold increase in Cahokia's resident population. The current population estimates indicate that the Lohmann-phase population of Cahokia constitutes a five- to tenfold increase in numbers over the preceding Edelhardt phase (figure 6.3).

The subsequent Stirling-phase population represents either a stabilization of the population or a decline in the numbers of people living at Cahokia, as defined by the 3.25-kilometer-diameter catchment. If there was a decline in Cahokia's population, it would seem to have been in part a result of the construction of large monuments, like mounds or the Post Circles on Tract 15A,

118

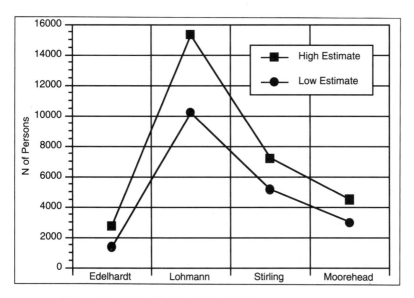

Figure 6.3. Cahokia Population Estimates through Time

in places where people had once resided. Displaced Cahokians presumably would have moved outside the Cahokia site proper.

Rural Population Density and Productive Potential

While rural population density data are uneven in quality at present, important points emerge from comparisons with the Cahokian estimates. First are the corroborative patterns of rural-locality depopulation and possible repopulation. Second, Cahokia at the climax of population nucleation may have relied on rural areas to some extent for necessary foodstuffs and material objects.

We have elsewhere noted a significant decrease in rural-site density from the Edelhardt phase to the Lohmann phase (Lopinot 1993; T. R. Pauketat, Rees, and S. L. Pauketat 1996). These observations are based on pedestrian surveys of a total of 674 hectares around Horseshoe Lake (figure 6.1) and a 270-hectare parcel 10 kilometers northwest of Cahokia (Pulcher 1985). In one survey sample, there was only one Mississippian site for every twelve Emergent Mississippian sites, while in others the ratio was about 1:1.5 (T. R. Pauketat, Rees, and S. L. Pauketat 1996).[5] A reduction in the rural population density seems to have occurred. This reduction may have occurred as a general abandonment of some Emergent Mississippian villages around A.D. 1050. Excavations at a small Edelhardt-phase center in the Horseshoe Lake peninsula have been used to argue for a short-term political and administrative center that was abandoned near the end of the Edelhardt phase (T. R. Pauketat, Rees, and S. L. Pauketat 1996). Such abandonment and rural depopulation in general may correspond to the regional centralization of population at Lohmann-phase Cahokia.

Milner (1986) estimated a Lohmann-phase rural population density of between nine and forty-five persons per square kilometer for a portion of the American Bottom 5 to 20 kilometers south of Cahokia. This rural population was composed of small homesteads that were probably subsistence sufficient yet tightly integrated into a Cahokia-centric sociopolitical network (Emerson, chapter 9). It is possible that Cahokia's Lohmann-phase population of around 10,000 individuals may have exceeded the productive potential of the Cahokia vicinity,[6] making rural production by these dispersed households integral to a Cahokian economy (cf. L. Kelly, chapter 4; Lopinot, chapter 3).[7]

The rural population of the floodplain seems to have increased by the Stirling phase, when between fourteen and forty-seven persons per square kilometer resided outside of towns in the floodplain (Milner 1986, tables 3–5). This increased rural density, as it corresponds to the decreased Cahokian figure, might suggest a population movement out of Cahokia and into the immediate rural countryside. However, as the rural population density of the subsequent Moorehead phase also dropped to about five to eighteen persons per square kilometer (Milner 1986, 234), an overall decline or reconfiguration of the Cahokia polity might be postulated. By the Sand Prairie phase, the population density of both Cahokia and the rural floodplain had decreased markedly, while the surrounding uplands had experienced a population surge (Koldehoff 1989, 61; Koldehoff, Pauketat, and Kelly 1993; Woods and Holley 1991).

The projected centralization-decentralization trajectory need in no way convey a continuous or unidirectional political-economic and demographic coalescence and fragmentation. Minor, episodic recentralizations or stabilizations of population levels that are difficult to detect archaeologically might have occurred during the Stirling and Moorehead phases. Stirling-phase population decentralization, albeit a precursor to later depopulation,

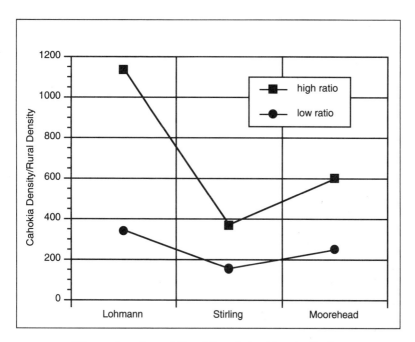

Figure 6.4. Central-Rural Population Density Ratios

may not correspond in a one-to-one fashion with social or political disintegration (see Pauketat 1994a). In fact, the ratio of Cahokia population density to rural population density by phase illustrates that the regional Moorehead-phase population distribution is perhaps more similar to the Lohmann phase, being more highly centralized, than to the Stirling phase (figure 6.4).

Conclusion

Previous estimates of Cahokia's peak population of around ten thousand individuals are probably not far off from the Lohmann-phase maximum. Gregg's (1975b) estimate of more than twenty thousand individuals at Stirling-phase Cahokia proper is too large. Instead, there appears to have been a large-scale nucleation of people from surrounding rural lands, and perhaps uplands, to Cahokia at around A.D. 1050. This nucleation was followed by a decentralizing pattern that might be related to the movement of people out of central Cahokia to its fringes (figure 6.5). By the Moorehead phase, Ca-

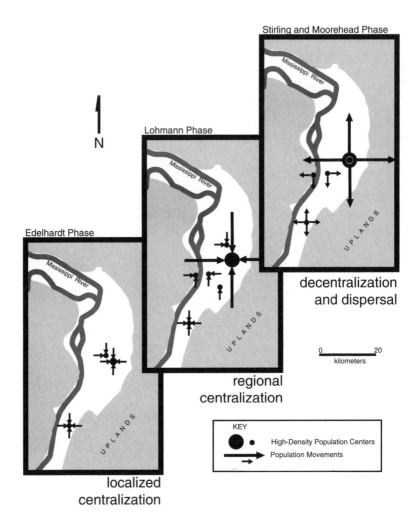

Figure 6.5. Population Dynamics in the Northern Bottom Expanse

hokia's population, while substantial relative to other southeastern polities, was less than it had been decades earlier. The reduced magnitude of Moorehead-phase Cahokia finally gave way to the dramatically dwindled population of the region by A.D. 1300.

The present population estimates provide a means by which other considerations of Cahokian community development and Cahokia's place in the

Southeast may be gauged. The estimates are well founded but subject to revision pending additional archaeological knowledge. They should not be viewed as absolutes or as indicators of a static urban population. Rather, they are averages that undoubtedly obscure within-phase demographic dynamics that were part and parcel of Cahokian social and political history.

James M. Collins

7

Cahokia Settlement and Social Structures as Viewed from the ICT-II

Archaeologists can conceive profitably of settlement patterns in terms of three levels. The first and most basic of these is the individual building or structure; the second, the manner in which these structures are arranged within a single community; and the third, the manner in which communities are distributed over the landscape.

Bruce G. Trigger, in *Settlement Archaeology*

In 1985 and 1986, more than one-half hectare of the Cahokia site was excavated in an area just southeast of the Central Ceremonial Precinct prior to the construction of the modern site interpretive center.[1] This area has come to be known as the Interpretive Center Tract-Location II, or more commonly the ICT-II (figure 7.1). More than five hundred features, including more than seventy domestic structures inferred to represent the remains of eighteen individual "archaeological households," comprise the database for the following discussion. Elsewhere, a functional classification for features at the ICT-II has been explicitly defined (Collins 1990, 46–102). This classification includes seven categories: (1) pits of indeterminate function; (2) cache and storage pits; (3) fire-related features; (4) postmolds and post-pits: (5) enclosed wall-trench structures; (6) other structures; and (7) miscellaneous other features (butchering stations, borrow areas, etc). These seven major classes were further divided into twenty-seven subclasses.

Recently, feature-pattern interpretations equivalent to Winter's (1976) concept of the "household cluster" have found broad acceptance by archae-

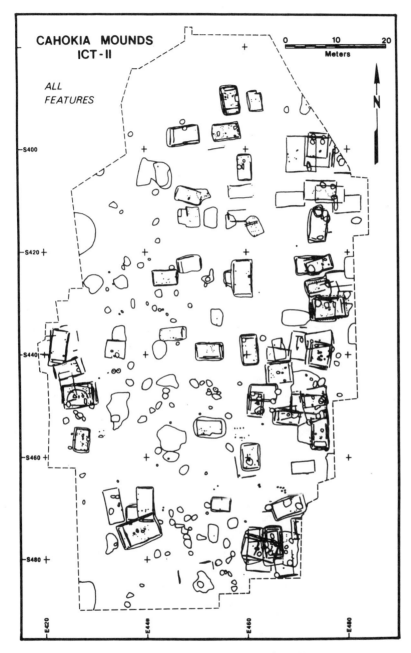

Figure 7.1. The ICT-II Showing Excavated Features

125

ologists who study Mississippian settlements (Collins 1990; Emerson and Milner 1982; Mehrer and Collins 1995; Milner et al. 1984; Rogers and Smith 1995). Discrete feature clusters, comprised of combinations of distinct feature classes and subclasses, can be viewed as archaeological domestic zones in the sense of Winter's household cluster. As such they are inferred to represent the archaeological remains left by culturally circumscribed domestic groups that were probably households and perhaps families (Collins 1990, 103–4). The analysis of archaeological households allows for interpretation of diachronic patterns of household demography and economy vis-à-vis the local community and the Cahokia elite during the period of occupation between about A.D. 1050 and 1275.

ICT-II Components

Lohmann-, Stirling-, and Moorehead-phase communities have been identified at the ICT-II based on structural and ceramic data (Collins 1990; Holley 1989). Details of the community arrangements for the three phases have been presented elsewhere and are summarized here (Collins 1990; Mehrer and Collins 1995).

During the Lohmann phase, areas of the Cahokia site formerly in residential use were usurped for ceremonial and other elite related purposes (Holley, Lopinot, Woods, and Kelly 1989, 345; Wittry and Vogel 1962, 27–28). The occupation of the ICT-II at that time reflects a rapid increase in site population and the massive restructuring of the existing site (Mehrer and Collins 1995). The Lohmann community at the ICT-II also represents the original occupation of the tract and therefore documents the preferred organization of a residential community at that particular time.

The orientation of the ICT-II Lohmann community is generally linear along a north-south line that approximates the E460 baseline (figure 7.2). It appears that Lohmann household clusters developed along this axis. All individual structures associated with the Lohmann component exhibit long-axis orientations within a few degrees of the cardinal directions. Such a structured configuration is evidence that the planning of the new Lohmann community at the ICT-II was tied to a pan-Cahokia pattern. The local community, along with the placement of many mounds and other features of the site during the Lohmann phase, was organized on a systematic plan lending support to Fowler's (1969b, 1989) theory of a Cahokia Grid or Axis. The conclu-

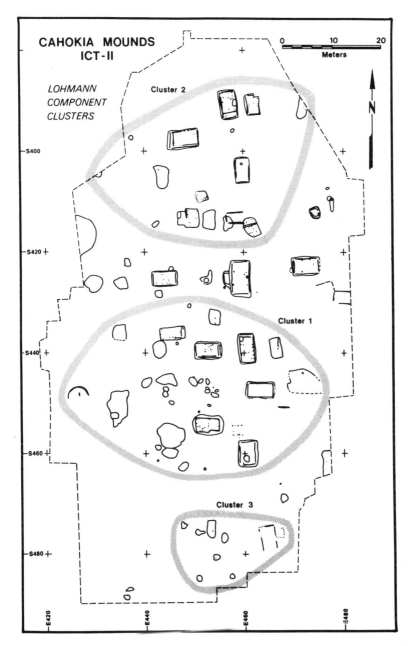

Figure 7.2. The ICT-II Showing Excavated Lohmann-Phase Features and Defined Household Clusters

127

sion that the development of the Cahokia site during the Lohmann phase, including residential development, was planned by a central authority seems warranted.

The settlement pattern changed markedly during the subsequent Stirling phase (figure 7.3). There was evolutionary continuity from the Lohmann to Stirling community as evidenced by the fact that initial Stirling development surrounded, rather than overlapped, the Lohmann settlement. The Cahokia Grid was no longer a primary criteria for community development or individual structure orientation. After the initial development of the early Stirling community, Stirling household clusters were typified by considerable spatial continuity. The area formerly occupied by the Lohmann community became an open plaza. Stirling-phase households continued to develop around this local plaza. Many Stirling household structures were rebuilt as many as six times, on the same spots occupied by earlier structures. This spatial continuity is suggestive of a pattern of long-term, household-based domestic tenure during the Stirling phase.

Another significant factor in the orientation of the Stirling community was the construction of a large, low-profile mound (Mound 107) located immediately to the south of the neighborhood plaza. This mound is clearly the reason for the orientation of at least two late-Stirling household structures (figure 7.4). Evidence of a large late-Stirling-phase building was recovered from the south-central summit of Mound 107. It is assumed the occupant or occupants of the structure on the mound held an elevated social, as well as physical, status within the local late-Stirling-phase community. Another bit of evidence relating to the incorporation of status distinctions into the local social sphere at the ICT-II during the late-Stirling subphase is a small ceramic anthromorphic masquette recovered from the disturbed surface of Mound 107. This broken piece of art can be interpreted as a nonexotic representation of a short-nosed god, and thus perhaps a local or vernacular expression of a widespread Mississippian ritual artifact (see Hall 1991). Its presence can be taken as another indication of the elevated status of the individual or individuals occupying the mound. In short, by the late-Stirling subphase, the orientation of household clusters within the local ICT-II community was related to the development of a local mound and plaza complex and local social hierarchy rather than being dictated by a sitewide central authority.

At the ICT-II, there is no identifiable continuity apparent between the late-Stirling- and Moorehead-phase settlement patterns, and the possibility exists

128

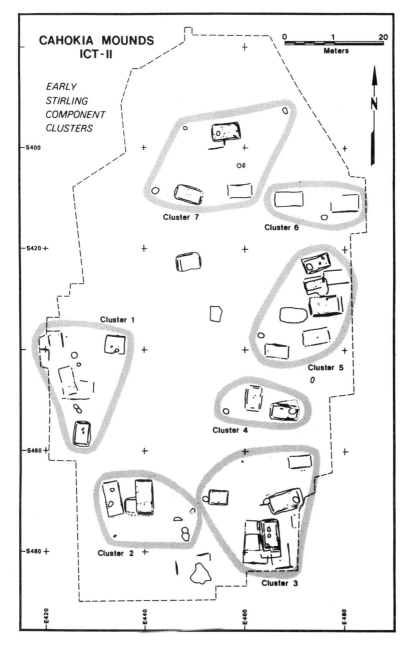

Figure 7.3. The ICT-II Early Stirling Component Showing Defined Household Clusters

129

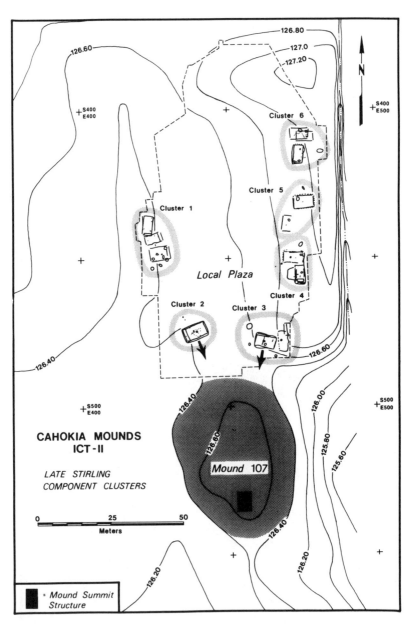

Figure 7.4. The ICT-II Showing Late Stirling Component Features, Defined Household Clusters, and the Relationship of Households to Mound 107 and the Local Community Plaza

130

of an occupational hiatus between the two occupations. The Moorehead pattern (figure 7.5) consists of household clusters that occupy the higher elevations of the tract. With the apparent decline in Cahokia population and political authority during the Moorehead phase, households apparently selected residential locations for environmental rather than cultural reasons. The residual population of the site was free to occupy any convenient, preferably topographically high, location, without either authoritative sitewide influence or the constraints of a local mound-and-plaza-oriented settlement structure, as was the case previously.

Household Composition and Home Economics

Some structural variables pertinent to the analysis of household clusters include (1) the number of households per component; (2) relative household area; (3) relative number of features per household; and (4) relative number of feature classes and subclasses represented per household. Due to the configuration of the ICT-II excavation block, many of the feature clusters represent only portions of larger patterns. In the discussion that follows, all clusters are accorded equal weight despite the possibility that some may be more complete than others, because all components are affected more or less equally by the same bias. All metric and formal data pertinent to the aforementioned variables are available elsewhere (Collins 1990). The following presents the data in synthesized form (see figures 7.6–7.10).

Mean data for each household cluster variable, based on all clusters from all components, provide a baseline from which individual components can be assessed. Given four components, the mean number of household clusters per component is 4.5, with an average household area for all components equal to 377 square meters. Household area was determined by multiplying the maximum east-west by maximum north-south distances between features within individual household clusters. An average of seventeen features per defined household cluster are present, representing an average of five feature classes and eight subclasses per household.

The Lohmann component includes three household clusters (figure 7.2). Cluster 1 features are distributed in a pattern that can be easily interpreted as reflecting prehistoric household activities. At the center of the cluster are a number of fire-related features. These are surrounded by a series of house structures. Along the cluster periphery are auxiliary storage features—

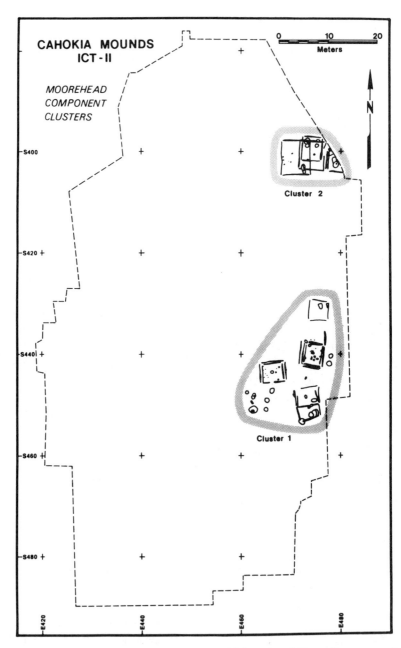

Figure 7.5. The ICT-II Showing Excavated Moorehead-Phase Features and Defined Household Clusters

132

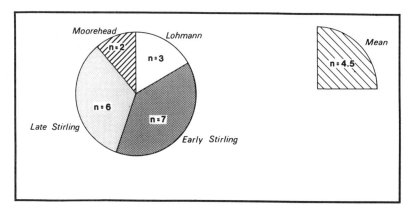

Figure 7.6. Number of ICT-II Households per Component

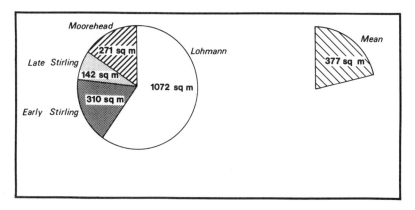

Figure 7.7. Average Area of ICT-II Households per Component

butchering and processing areas, borrow areas, and a sweat lodge. Lohmann clusters 1 and 2 are separated by a unique T-shaped structure that presumably served an integrating function between the two households (see Mehrer and Collins 1995). Cluster 2 reflects a feature pattern similar to cluster 1, but it is smaller in areal extent and has fewer features, and types of features, than its southern neighbor. These data may indicate a smaller, less mature, or at-rophied household. Only a portion of cluster 3 is situated within the exca-vated tract, and it is, therefore, the smallest of the Lohmann clusters in areal extent and contains the fewest features and types of features.

Despite the fact that Lohmann cluster 3 fell only partially within the tract,

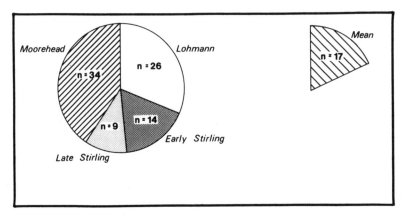

Figure 7.8. Average Number of Features per Household
for ICT-II Components

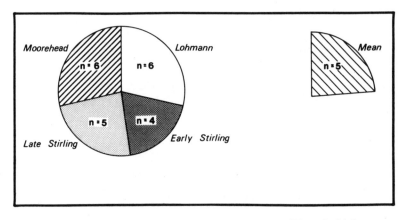

Figure 7.9. Average Number of Feature Classes per Household for ICT-II
Components

the Lohmann household area mean is the largest for any component and is
2.8 times the mean for all household clusters (figure 7.7). The Lohmann
component means for number of features, number of feature classes, and
number of feature subclasses represented per household are also above the
comparable means for all households (figures 7.8–7.10).

Stirling component data, in both its early and late facets, are significantly
different from the Lohmann data. Stirling-phase household clusters gener-

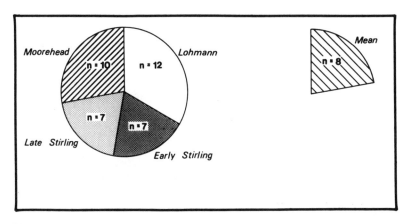

Figure 7.10. Average Number of Feature Subclasses per Household for ICT-II Components

ally consist of one or two structures (superimposed rebuilding episodes not included) and only a few ancillary features that predominantly serve cooking and storage functions. With the exception of cluster 7, which may represent an atrophied household, the feature clusters defined for the early Stirling component (figure 7.3) persisted into the late Stirling occupation of the tract (figure 7.4). While the composition of these clusters changed in terms of their constituent elements, the spatial configuration of the clusters on the landscape did not.

Mean values for all Stirling-component household variables fall below the comparable means for all tract household clusters (figures 7.6–7.10). An obvious trend during the Stirling phase is toward a greater number of definable household clusters, clusters that individually cover less area and are represented by fewer features, feature classes, and feature subclasses per household.

The Moorehead household sample is more limited, but the trend toward smaller household areas, represented by fewer features and types of features, is reversed (figure 7.5). Cluster 1 in the Moorehead-component feature pattern is useful for illustrating this point. This household cluster included three functionally distinct buildings surrounding a small courtyard that included a central hearth. Another building with morphological characteristics similar to ethnohistoric descriptions of smokehouses or hide-processing facilities was situated to the north of the other buildings. A complex of storage, processing, and cooking facilities was situated at the southwest margin of the household cluster. Cluster 2 lies at the margin of the excavation tract, is incomplete, and therefore difficult to interpret. Nevertheless, the mean Moorehead household area is below the mean area for all households; however, the mean number of features per household, mean number of feature classes, and the mean number of feature subclasses represented per household are all above the respective tract averages (figures 7.6–7.10).

What is the significance of all this? Given the discrete household clusters defined for the ICT-II components are the archaeological representations of discrete domestic groups that lived at the tract, then the diachronic changes noted for household cluster variables probably are reflective of changes in the social patterns of those domestic groups. Changes in the size and composition of household clusters through time infer changes in the social dimension.

Most basically, the proposition here is that the relative area of household clusters reflects the relative size of the domestic groups that produced them. For instance, based on the data presented, the Lohmann household clusters reflect supra-family domestic units, while the Stirling household clusters represent smaller domestic units, perhaps nuclear families. Observed patterns of storage and cooking behavior support such an inference (Collins 1990).

For instance, the percentage of exterior pits and small cache pits per component increased through time at the ICT-II; however interior cache and storage pits were most numerous during late Stirling times. While exterior cache and storage pits occurred less frequently during the Lohmann phase, their mean volume was far greater than cache and storage pits in other components. This fact, and clear evidence for commonly held, above-ground, granary-type storage features during the Lohmann phase, suggest that storage patterns during Lohmann times were communal in nature, reminiscent of the Emergent Mississippian pattern (cf. Kelly et al. 1984). The progressively more numerous and smaller cache and storage pits of Stirling and later Moorehead times may argue, in turn, for increased privatization of storage practices. Similar trends have been noted at other Mississippian sites in the American Bottom (Mehrer and Collins 1995).

If interior cache and storage pits are viewed as the most private type of storage facilities, the late Stirling subphase represents a time of intense privatization in storage behavior. Fifteen percent of all late Stirling features were large, interior cache and storage pits. The lowest ratio, per component, of external to internal pits is also found in the late Stirling component.

Many researchers are inclined to view subsurface storage facilities as true caches, places where goods are stored and perhaps hidden during temporary abandonment of a site. Pursuing this line, it could be argued that during periods of settlement abandonment, exterior cache and storage pits would have been more secure than interior pits—it being easier to camouflage the location of exterior pits. Based on acceptance, ICT-II storage-pit data suggest that such abandonment would have been most likely during Moorehead times. The Moorehead phase had the largest ratio of external cache and storage pits to structures of any Mississippian component at the ICT-II.

There are similar trends apparent when the distribution of cooking facilities at the ICT-II is examined. Exterior fire pits were more common during the Lohmann phase than during subsequent phases. The Lohmann fire pits were also less scattered in their distribution than those of later phases. Like storage behavior, cooking may have been more of a communal or group activity in Lohmann times than it was later. The frequency and distribution of pit ovens, and roasting and steaming facilities, reinforces the notion of Lohmann-phase communalism vis-à-vis cooking and food storage. The locations of these features among and within the three defined Lohmann clusters suggest that these large cooking facilities were shared by the members of the households represented. The use of these large, apparently communal facilities persisted into the early Stirling subphase, perhaps for feast or ritual purposes, but they were absent in later assemblages.

In summary, Lohmann-phase storage and cooking facilities were used by larger domestic groups and exhibit a distinctly communal orientation at the ICT-II, while Stirling households were smaller, and storage and cooking patterns are noted to have become increasingly more private (Collins 1990). The Moorehead data may suggest periods of site abandonment.

Numerous studies have indicated positive correlations between the size of household compounds and the relative wealth and number of their inhabitants (e.g., Kramer 1982; Netting 1982). Given this, I propose that the occupants of the ICT-II Lohmann households were both more numerous and more materially advantaged overall than their Stirling and Moorehead counterparts.

The variety and composition of household clusters per component are suggestive of certain other social correlates. Greater numbers of features and feature types are evident among the household clusters associated with the Lohmann and Moorehead components than among the Stirling household clusters (figures 7.8–7.10). From this, therefore, a greater variety of domestic and subsistence activities were carried out within the confines of the Lohmann and Moorehead household clusters than within the Stirling household clusters. This evidence leads to speculation that certain domestic and subsistence activities were performed elsewhere for the Stirling inhabitants of the tract.

Social Structure

Cross-cultural statistical studies of structure shape and size lend support for certain archaeological inferences pertinent to the various occupations of the ICT-II. These studies are based on ethnographic rather than archaeological societies and such inferences are, therefore, somewhat qualified; nevertheless they are interesting.

Whiting and Ayres (1968) demonstrate a significant correlation between the use of rectilinear structures and societies that lived in sedentary settlements. In the same article, they note a high correlation between rectilinear structure shapes and societies that tended to be monogamous. Similar cross-cultural studies by Ember (1973) and Divale (1977) suggest that mean structure area of a given society is a strong indication of that society's residence rules. Both studies found that matrilocal societies almost always have houses with larger floor areas than patrilocal societies. Patrilocal residence is indicated for households with floor areas of less than 42.7 square meters. A number of excavated Upper Mississippian sites were recently seriated by this technique, and the method was useful for characterizing the evolution of Oneota residence rules from the Developmental through Classic and Historic horizons (Hollinger 1993). Based on these studies, structural data from the ICT-II may support a pattern of sedentary, monogamous, and patrilocal households.

Along similar lines, Whiting and Ayres's data (1968) suggest that societies using dwellings larger than 18.6 square meters are characterized by status distinctions, extended families, or both. This inference is less compelling considering that multiple dwellings were probably used by Mississippian households. Nevertheless, at the ICT-II, both the Lohmann-phase (13.08 square meters) and early Stirling subphase (16.71 square meters) structure area means fall well below 18.6 square meters. By contrast, the structure area mean for both the late Stirling subphase (22.98 square meters) and Moorehead-phase (25.73 square meters) components are in the range that suggests status distinctions. This ties in well with the other trends that suggest a pattern of communally oriented behavior during the Lohmann phase, breaking down later into patterns that became increasingly more private and class-oriented during the Stirling phase.

Conclusion

What emerges from these data is a pattern reflective of large Lohmann-phase domestic groups that were well integrated into a somewhat rigid Cahokian order. Lohmann-phase households carried over communal patterns of domestic activities such as storage and cooking practices from Emergent Mississippian forebears. This order was supplanted during the later occupations of the tract when, by all indications, status distinctions, subgroup solidarity, and household autonomy became increasingly important at the local level. The most basic indication of this new arrangement was the emergence of a local mound-and-plaza complex and local social hierarchy. Supplementary evidence in support of this inference includes the increasing tendency toward private storage and cooking practices through time, and cross-cultural data concerning dwelling size.

Status distinctions among the occupants of the ICT-II became progressively greater, at least through the late Stirling component. A correlate would hold that, during the Lohmann phase, overall status distinctions between Cahokia's elite and the site's resident population were most pronounced (see Fowler 1969b, 1991). During the subsequent Stirling phase, status differentiation increased among the populace as elite subgroups developed at the site (Pauketat 1992). Local elites may have developed from what had been an essentially egalitarian residential population. At that time, the polarization between the paramount Cahokia elite and the local "lords" of elite subgroups may have diminished (see Barker and Pauketat 1992). The local elites are here seen as intermediaries between the paramount chiefs and the members of the elite subgroup. Assuming a lineage-based development of the elite subgroups, the status of all individuals comprising a local lineage probably was raised correspondingly. Competition among the rising elite subgroups may have led to either the enfranchisement or disenfranchisement of social power, resulting in either the satisfaction or disillusionment of certain groups. It seems likely that the enfranchised subgroups would have accrued wealth and prestige while other groups fell away, effectively losing the struggle for social power.

Whether or not this condition was amelioratory in the long run is probably a matter of perspective. The proposed depolarization of status distinctions between the paramount elites and the newly empowered local elites was probably necessary to extend the Cahokia polity. However, the progressive disenfranchisement of those subgroups without social power may have led to the disillusionment of large segments of Cahokia society. Eventually, the disillusioned and disenfranchised may have simply moved away. Precisely this type of social disenfranchisement is what Emerson (1991a) has suggested as a driving force behind Middle Mississippian expansion into the northern hinterlands (Emerson and Lewis, eds., 1991).

The huge status distinctions characteristic of early Cahokian society were likely acceptable so long as the greater populace shared a lower, but more or less egalitarian, social position. Yet ironically, the rise of competing elite subgroups and the concomitant infiltration of status distinctions into the lower order of Cahokia society may have been factors presaging the demise of the great Cahokia center.

John E. Kelly

8

Stirling-Phase Sociopolitical Activity at East St. Louis and Cahokia

Any understanding of social organization and sociopolitical change at Cahokia is embedded in certain assumptions regarding the level and degree of sociopolitical integration and its subsidiary centers (figure 8.1).[1] Most Mississippian centers including Cahokia and others in the American Bottom consist of large earthen mounds organized around a central plaza. The mounds and plazas are embued with various symbolic messages (Knight 1986, 1989a). The size of such monuments is a measure of human labor and a barometer of the amount of centralized control exerted by the elite upon the populace (Drennan 1991, 282–83; Earle 1991b, 85). Furthermore, this basic configuration was the *arena* of Mississippian sociopolitical organization. Within this arena the elite conducted their business through a variety of ceremonies, as attested by Cahokian monuments and, most recently, by detailed excavations at the East St. Louis site.

Cahokia's Configuration and the Stirling Phase

The Stirling phase is generally perceived as Cahokia's cultural climax (Emerson 1991a; Pauketat 1992). Most of Monks Mound was presumably completed by the Stirling phase, including the construction of the largest building identified to date on the uppermost terrace. The Grand Plaza, around which the lives of the most powerful were presumably organized, extended to the south (figure 8.2). The abode of the living paramount chief may have been atop Monks Mound.[2] On the opposite side of the Grand Plaza were a pair of large mounds, Fox (rectangular) and Round Top (circular).

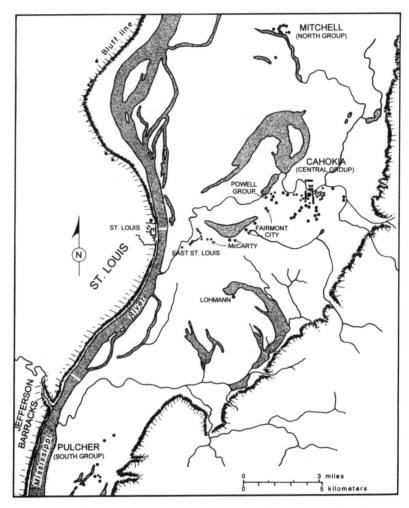

Figure 8.1. Mississippian Mound Centers in the Northern American Bottom (adapted from Bushnell 1921, figure 99).

Mounds flanking the east and west sides of the Grand Plaza served to further delimit this large public arena and, in turn, the different social components affiliated with this segment of the community (J. Kelly 1993c, 1994c).

Of note is the distinct dichotomy evident between those mounds on the west and those on the east of the Grand Plaza. Four small mounds are aligned along the eastern margin (e.g., figure 8.3). On the west, the Castle Mound

142

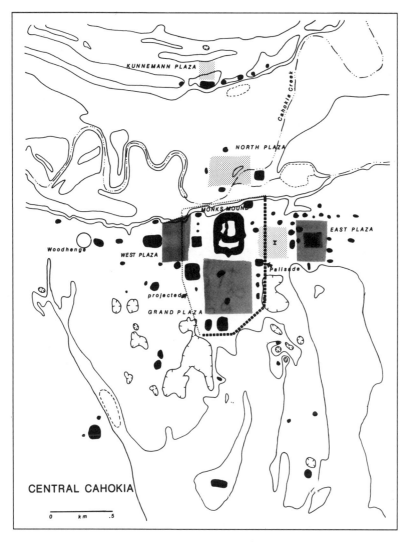

Figure 8.2. Central Cahokia

(Mound 48), the second largest platform mound at Cahokia, is paired with the smallest mound (Mound 57) in the Grand Plaza complex. This asymmetrical opposition was expanded to the plazas on the east and west of Monks Mound. The existence of East and West Plazas are affirmed by mound arrangements and the abandonment of the Merrell Tract and Tract 15B as resi-

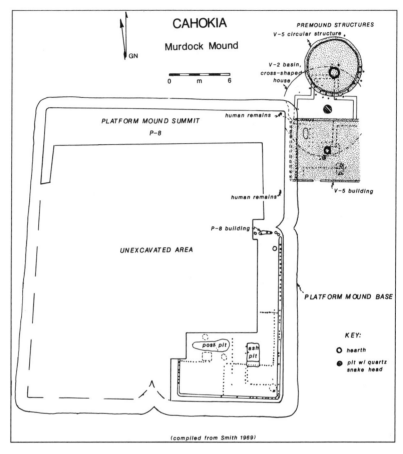

Figure 8.3. Cahokia, Murdock Mound

dential areas during the Lohmann phase (Salzer 1975; Wittry and Vogel 1962). Large post-pits were erected in the West Plaza (figure 8.4) and perhaps in the area east of Monks Mound, if the lack of Lohmann-phase activity is any measure (Iseminger et al. 1990).

The mounds associated with a later East Plaza, removed just to the east of the early plaza, are more numerous (at least fourteen) and small, while those around the West Plaza are less numerous (eight) and exhibit extremes (figures 8.4–8.5). A small plaza complex, the North Plaza or "Creek Bottom" group of five mounds, lies to the north of Monks Mound in the ancient Edelhardt channel scar (Fowler 1989). The large Kunnemann Mound, 900

144

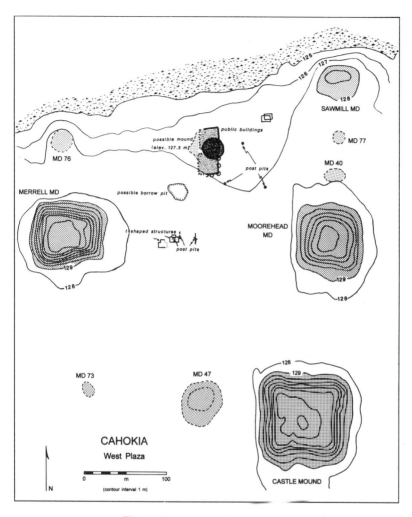

Figure 8.4. Cahokia, West Plaza

meters to the north of Monks Mound, was a complex Stirling-phase tumulus (Pauketat 1993c). It was surrounded by an extensive Stirling-phase occupation with a possible plaza to the north of the Kunnemann Mound (Holley 1990, 1995). The quadripartite configuration of plazas with Monks Mound at the center essentially depicts a cross, whose arms define the four directions. There is, on one hand, a clear dichotomy that suggests symmetry, yet in the

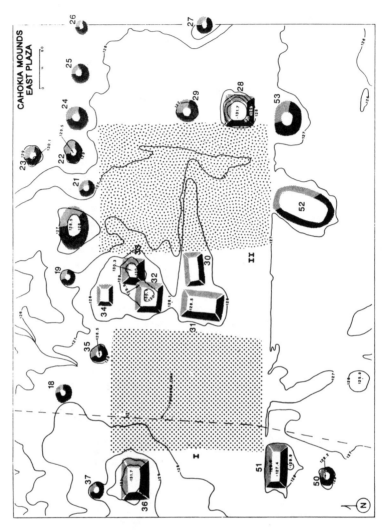

Figure 8.5. Cahokia, East Plaza

146

details an asymmetry is prevalent throughout, big versus small, and few versus many.[3]

As evidenced from archaeological excavations southeast of the Grand Plaza and along the site's western edge, residential areas were peripherally placed (Collins 1990; Pauketat 1996). Moving beyond the western periphery, surface materials and limited excavations indicate an extensive Stirling-phase residential area (Bareis 1963; Holley, Dalan, and Watters 1992; Lopinot, Brown, and Holley 1989, 1993). On the basis of surface materials, a smaller residential Stirling-phase component was distributed to the southeast at the Rouch Mound Group (Holley, Dalan, and Watters 1992). For the Powell group, excavations and surface collections have verified an extensive Stirling-phase residential area (figure 8.6) (A. Hall, Kelly, and Koldehoff 1995; Keller, Kelly, and Witty 1994; J. Kelly 1991d; O'Brien 1972a).

Much of the material collected by Moorehead (1922, 1923, 1929) from the East Plaza (a.k.a. Ramey Tract) dates to the late Stirling and Moorehead phases (J. Kelly 1991d, 1993c; R. Wagner 1959). A late Stirling residence was superimposed by one of the palisade walls in this area east of Monks Mound (Pauketat 1987a, 1987b). In fact, a central palisade was erected around the central part of the site during the latter half of this phase (figure 8.2). The palisade was rebuilt at least three times and lasted into the subsequent Moorehead phase (Iseminger et al. 1990). Of particular interest and of extreme significance is the presence of the late East Plaza complex *outside* the palisade (Iseminger and Kelly 1995). Although this does not necessarily preclude the palisade's defensive role, it does symbolically delineate the central precinct for at least another century.

East St. Louis Mound Center

The mound center at East St. Louis was also occupied during the Stirling phase (J. Kelly 1994a). In many respects the history of occupation as now envisioned at East St. Louis may parallel central Cahokia and the Powell group. The East St. Louis center was the first group described among the prairies adjacent to Cahokia Creek by Brackenridge as he crossed the Mississippi River. He characterized this group as a semicircle of forty-five mounds a mile in extent and facing the Mississippi River. By the time they were mapped by Patrick more than fifty years later, the number had been reduced by two-thirds, but the semicircular pattern remained (figure 8.7). This pat-

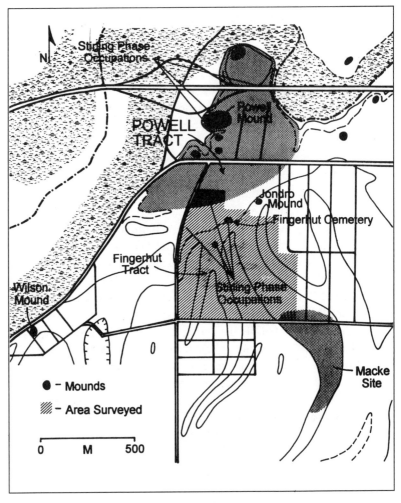

Figure 8.6. Cahokia, Western Periphery, Stirling-Phase Occupations

tern is attributable to the local landscape. Some mounds to the north were dispersed along a north-south ridge, while a western group extended along an east-west terrace. Recent excavations produced little evidence to indicate that East St. Louis was an integrated group of mounds.

The sudden growth of the city of East St. Louis after the Civil War resulted in the destruction, or at least leveling, of the mounds in this group.

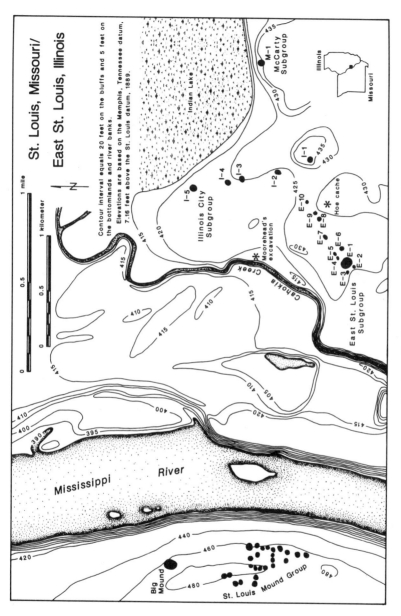

Figure 8.7. The East St. Louis and St. Louis Mound Groups

149

The largest mound, the "Cemetery Mound," was destroyed in late 1870, a year after the Big Mound in St. Louis had been removed. This elongated earthen edifice was a major mortuary monument, comparable in size to the Big Mound, the Powell and Rattlesnake mounds at Cahokia, and the Great Mound at Mitchell. The Cemetery Mound covered two large mortuary pits and concealed the presence of several large cedar posts (J. Kelly 1994a). These facilities were capped by more than thirty feet of fill, perhaps representing a ritual burial of the East St. Louis (ESL) group's ruling lineage.

Recent excavations into this area of the site provide a unique and insightful look of the core of a Mississippian center outside Cahokia (J. Kelly 1994a). Although the Cemetery Mound (E-I in figure 8.8) was removed, a series of large architectural features were mapped and excavated beneath this mound. In addition to these features, one previously unrecorded mound (E-II) was identified along with the base of another previously recorded mound (E-6). Contiguous to these mounds were other large structural features and at least two borrow pit areas. Investigations in the rail yards approximately 125 meters to the north also yielded a similar suite of large architectural features. Each of these seven areas will be described and then discussed in terms of Cahokia.

Mound E-II

Located at the western end of the area investigated, Mound E-II was not present on Patrick's earlier map of the East St. Louis group (figures 8.8–8.9). On the basis of the orientation of the fills and the structures, this rectilinear mound is positioned to the cardinal directions. It is about 32 meters east-west at the base and is approximately 80 centimeters in height. Six Patrick-phase pits and Lohmann- or early Stirling-phase structures predate the mound's construction. An L-shaped structure and a small (ca. 3 meters in diameter), circular sweat lodge were erected on the ridge at the western edge of the project area (figure 8.9).

Following this occupation, there was some borrowing on top of the ridge with more extensive borrowing extending to the north and east of the ridge's backslope. This borrowing in places extended to a depth of 1.5 meters. The edges of this borrow area are quite irregular due in part to extensive gullying. The borrow area was filled, and mound construction began shortly thereafter. The borrowing and the subsequent mound construction appear to date to the early Stirling phase. The mound consists of a single platform 40 to 60

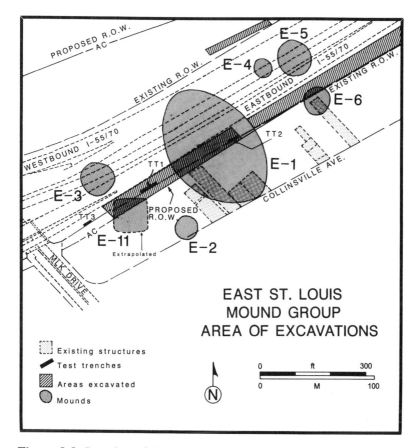

Figure 8.8. Location of Test Trenches and Excavations in the Cemetery Mound Area

centimeters in height. This first stage is capped by approximately 20 to 40 centimeters of fill. The mound was constructed so that it tied into the ridge, with the depth of mound fill only about 30 centimeters. A later burned Moorehead-phase house was superimposed on this unit.

Minimally, seven rectilinear structures are evident in the excavated area, along with at least four single-post screens. One large hearth was located within one of the buildings. A comparable superimposed sequence of nine circular buildings 8 meters in diameter was constructed contiguous to the rectilinear buildings on the east. They were placed on the ridge side of the

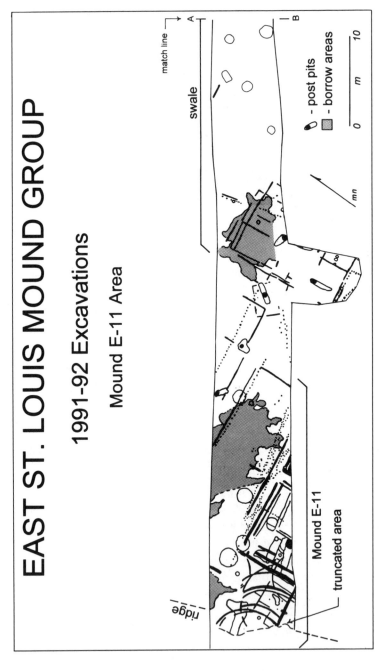

Figure 8.9. East St. Louis Excavations, Mound E-II Area

platform overlooking the slough to the west. In addition to these buildings, there are at least three large post-pits that appear to predate these buildings and, another large post-pit with a depth of 3 meters that postdates the other three structures.

Area between Mound E-II and the Cemetery Mound

The area between Mound E-II and the Cemetery Mound is a 45-meter-wide swale (figure 8.9). The Late Woodland occupation beneath Mound E-II extends into this area with an additional ten Patrick-phase features. The initial Mississippian use of this area consists of a complex series of superimposed rectilinear, wall-trench and single-post structures. A small (ca. 8–9 meters in extent), shallow (60 centimeters), irregular borrow area was then excavated in this area. At least three smaller post-pits were located along with a line of deep (50–60 centimeters) posts that extend beneath the north edge of Mound E-II. This line may represent a palisade or screen associated with the mound. The post-pits are aligned equidistant (ca. 6 meters) from one another in an east-west direction. Two other post-pits were associated with two of the buildings. A possible fourth post-pit is aligned to the west beneath Mound E-II. The materials from the borrow area are indicative of early Stirling-phase activity.

Area beneath the Cemetery Mound (E-I)

The Cemetery Mound as described in two nineteenth-century newspaper accounts was approximately 100 meters long and 75 meters wide, with a height between 10 and 12 meters (J. Kelly 1994a). The mound was removed in December 1870 for levee and dike fill near the river. Although no mound fill was encountered during the recent investigations, a large, oval post structure (ca. 24 meters in diameter) with a central post-pit was identified beneath the center of the mound, as well as a sequence of buildings immediately west of this large structure (figure 8.10). Another building sequence was evident along the eastern margins of this mound.

A large circular post structure 15 meters in diameter is the earliest construction in this sequence. This structure was rebuilt twice, and the decreasing depth of the rectangular posts suggests that a sequence of small platforms was being established. It is superimposed by a complex of features includ-

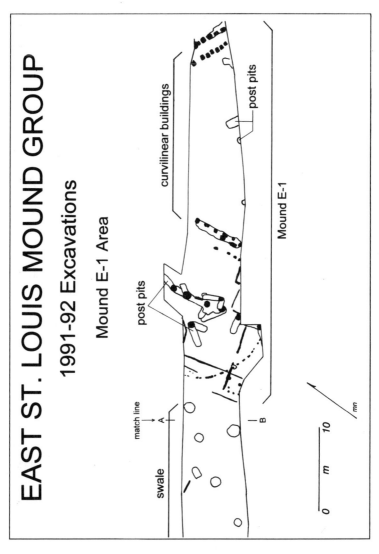

Figure 8.10. East St. Louis Excavations, Mound E-1 Area

ing at least eight post-pits with associated insertion and extraction ramps. In seven of these pits, the posts were placed to depths that exceeded 2 meters. Six of the deep posts were spaced equidistantly (2 meters) in a north-south alignment. These, in turn, were superimposed by a series of rectilinear wall-trench buildings. Again the depth of the building wall trenches suggests that these were being placed on an earthen platform. Although a number of wall trenches were involved, a minimum of three buildings could be identified. An occasional human bone suggests that this area may have been established as a mortuary early in the mound's history.

The large curvilinear enclosure consists of square posts 50 to 60 centimeters in diameter, arranged in two lines that form an acute angle. The "walls" of this structure were replaced at least three times. Two separate walls lie to the east with rebuilding evident on each. It appears that each time a wall was rebuilt, the depth of the "post" decreased, suggesting that successive structures on each subsequent platform stage were less able to penetrate the sub-mound zone.

Area East of the Cemetery Mound and West of Mound E-6

The area east of the Cemetery Mound consisted of a modern alley way (approximately 4 to 5 meters in width) that extended for a distance of about 75 meters. At the end of this alley way was located Mound E-6 (figure 8.11). The area on the eastern edge of the Cemetery Mound consisted of another sequence of buildings. Three post-pits were located along with two superimposed rectangular wall-trench structures with basins. On the basis of size these appear to be residential dwellings, although the wall trenches were 70 to 80 centimeters in depth. Except for a few scattered sherds and flakes, little debris was recovered from this area. A portion of a small, circular wall-trench structure was also mapped and excavated. The shallow depth of the wall trenches suggests it may have been placed on a low platform. Farther east, another series of circular post buildings and long linear wall trenches and posts were encountered. These appear to represent screens or walls immediately west of Mound E-6. As such, they form a corner that might represent the southeast corner of a plaza area that, unfortunately, extends underneath the interstate highway to the north. In addition to these walls an 8-meter, circular wall-trench building was located on the western edge of a swale extending 80 meters.

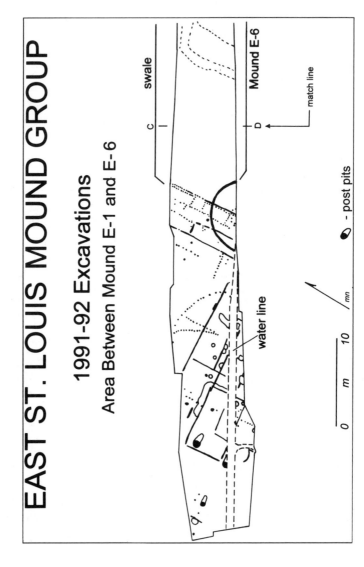

Figure 8.II. East St. Louis Excavations, Area between Mounds E-I and E-6

The Mound E-6 Area

Mound E-6 was built on a series of flood deposits that filled in the swale to a depth of approximately 30 centimeters (figure 8.12). Also located beneath the mound and the slough fill was a 10-centimeter-thick extensive area of Lohmann-phase cultural refuse. This debris appears to have been thrown into the swale from the south and east, and it was composed primarily of residential garbage that might be associated with a community located on a ridge farther to the east of this swale. It is also possible that it might be occupational debris associated with the initial use of Mound E-6. In places beneath this deposit was a thin deposit of limonite-stained fine sands or silts (2–3 centimeters) that might indicate some initial erosion from the mound.

The source of the remaining natural fill above Feature 418 was probably derived from a series of massive floods associated with the Mississippi River and its tributary Cahokia Creek. Turbidized deposits beneath and in close proximity to Mound E-6 suggest episodes of erosion perhaps associated with the initial stages of the mound. These hypothetical stages do not show in our profiles but instead are located to the southeast, outside the limits of excavation.

Only the basal portion of Mound E-6 was evident in the excavations. As in Mound E-11, it was possible to delineate a series of horizontal fill units that indicated that the mound was rectilinear in form and oriented with the cardinal directions. Unlike Mound E-11, Mound E-6 did not exhibit any evidence of structures; however, only a small portion of the northwest corner of the mound was exposed. It also was possible to delineate at least seven additions to the mound in profile and plan that extend to the west. Of interest was the lack of any significant additions to the north. Only three additions were identified. Instead, it appears that a large rectilinear wall-trench structure was placed to the north of the mound. Each time there was a new mound addition, another structure was built. Several irregular basin pits were excavated into the north edge of the mound as well. One of these may represent a rectangular basin structure.

The debris recovered from the mound fill is suggestive of an early Stirling-phase construction. In addition to the cultural debris, the remains of several incomplete but partially articulated individuals were recovered from the western edge of the mound. One individual had an associated conch shell. It appears from the position of the various elements and the incomplete nature of the skeletons that these individuals had been redeposited, perhaps

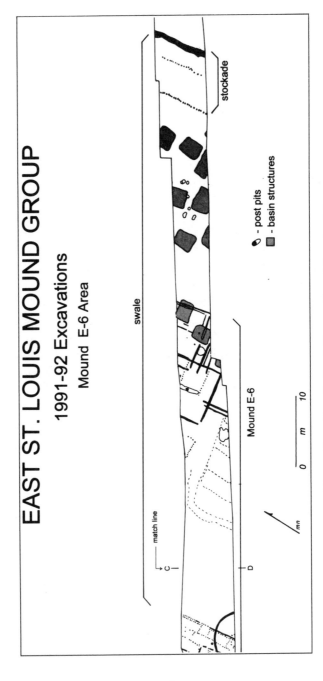

Figure 8.12. East St. Louis Excavations, Mound E-6 Area

158

from a charnel structure on the summit of this mound. It appears that this individual had been disinterred rather than reinterred.

Area North and East of Mound e-6

A series of eleven small basin "structures" superimposed on the slough deposits were distributed in two clusters to the north and east of Mound e-6. Of the eleven structures, only two had wall trenches. The three "houses" in the western cluster are directly north of Mound e-6 with at least two of these facilities extending up on the edge of the mound. The eastern cluster of eight structures is separated from the western cluster by a space of 7 meters. These structures were located within 5 meters of two parallel lines of posts to the east, which we will call "fences." These fences were north-south oriented and extended outside the limits of excavation. A wide, relatively deep trench 80 centimeters deep parallels these two walls on the east and is suggestive of a ditch. This ditch also delineates the eastern edge of the swale.

The structures were burned to varying degrees and in most instances contained rather large, if not complete, sections of late Stirling-phase vessels. Most of the structures also contained an occasional complete tool such as a hoe, knife, celt, or an adze. Large masses of carbonized maize found along with the other items in several of the structures may suggest their use as storage sheds rather than as domiciles.

Rail Yard Area

On the north side of the interstate highway a series of six backhoe trenches was placed through nearly 1.5 meters of railroad fill to determine the presence of any intact prehistoric cultural deposits (figure 8.13). Trench 2 contained the northeast corner to a large, wall-trench structure. Trench 4 contained seven superimposed post-pits that clustered in a small area. These might represent the center of a plaza or other central area. These post-pits were in part superimposed by a small basin structure similar to those on the south side at the east end of the excavations. This structure had burned and was found to contain a complete Ramey Incised vessel along with portions of two other ceramic vessels. A large mass of carbonized maize kernels was recovered along with a serrated and notched Cahokia-style point. Another burned structure was located farther to the west, superimposed on a large

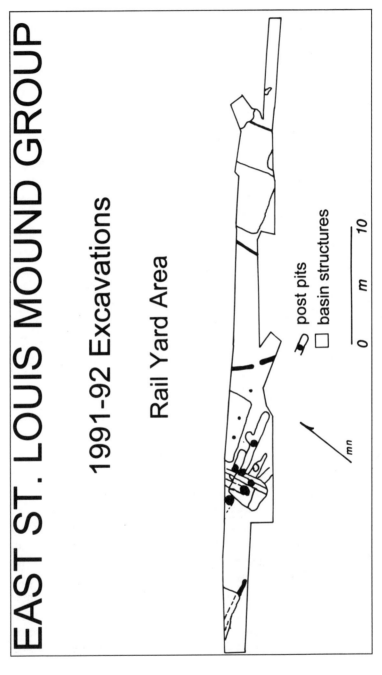

Figure 8.13. East St. Louis Excavations, Rail Yard Area

wall trench that extended outside the limits of excavation to the north. Yet another wall-trench structure was located north of the post-pits, and another three basin structures were found to the east. The materials from these structures are indicative of a Stirling-phase occupation. Several of the smaller basin structures indicate a continuation of the late Stirling-phase residential area on the south side.

Summary

The recent investigations of the East St. Louis mound center have resulted in the identification of occupational remains and the basal portions of three mounds. The area investigated is restricted to the west end of the East St. Louis mound group and represents a community that primarily dates to the early Stirling phase. These mounds and associated structures form what appears to be the southern edge of a plaza. This plaza would measure approximately 150 meters east-west if Mounds E-11 and E-6 delimit the west and east ends of this area, respectively. If the aforementioned plaza dimension is correct, it corresponds in size to the apparent plaza areas of the St. Louis (150 meters by 180 meters) and Mitchell (150 meters by 150 meters) mound centers. These areas, however, are dwarfed by plaza dimensions at Cahokia. Cahokia's are two to three times as large as the St. Louis and Mitchell plazas, with areas that range between three and nine times in total extent.

The other mounds in the East St. Louis group outside the investigated area may indicate other activities or centers separate from this community in time or space. Although the primary mound construction and building activity dates to the early Stirling phase, there are indications of an even earlier Lohmann-phase occupation and later Stirling- and Moorehead-phase occupations.

Discussion

The East St. Louis excavations are a fortuitous transect through the ceremonial heart of a Mississippian center coeval with, and undoubtedly subservient to, Cahokia. From this rather focused, yet narrow glimpse, the history of East St. Louis—particularly its climax—coincides neatly with that of the Powell Mound group and the Cahokia site, except that Cahokia persisted for another century. When considered in a historical perspective, these congruities can be briefly summarized as follows.

It is unclear whether East St. Louis did, in fact, emerge as a mound center during the Lohmann phase, although the circular and L-shaped structures, and the array of exotics recovered from the sealed deposit beneath Mound E-6 are suggestive of such an emergence. This Lohmann-phase occupation at East St. Louis stands in marked contrast with the flurry of activity of Cahokia, characterized by Pauketat (1993a, chapter 2) as the "Big Bang." As originally stressed by Fowler (1974, 1989), the basic plan for Cahokia appears to have been carefully conceived and executed by A.D. 1050.

The Stirling phase epitomizes the construction of sociopolitical power at Cahokia and at the East St. Louis mound center. The enormous amount of nonresidential construction during the subsequent Stirling phase is particularly dramatic (J. Kelly 1990c; Pauketat 1992). This is true of Cahokia, the Powell Group, the Kunnemann Tract, and the East St. Louis site. For example, from Stirling-phase mound context we have Pauketat's (1993c) description of Holder's excavation at the Kunnemann Mound, where numerous small platforms were established and built upon. This pattern is replicated at the Murdock Mound by Harriet Smith (1969). Again, a series of specialized buildings was followed by the construction of a series of small platforms with buildings (figure 8.3). In off-mound plaza areas we have the construction of a series of large enclosures, first documented by Wittry at the north end of West Plaza, where at least five construction episodes are evident (figure 8.4). A sequence of large, circular Post-Circle Monuments or woodhenges were erected west of Monks Mound (see Pauketat 1994a). Large buildings and specialized structures were placed to the north of the monuments and woodhenges, along the levee bank. A large building topped Monks Mound. On the Powell Tract, an extensive Stirling-phase residential area was identified, and a large building was erected in the midst of this area along with peripherally positioned circular structures or sweat lodges (figure 8.14). Large post-pits were located beneath Powell Mound 2, and the presupposition is that the large Powell Mound was constructed during the Stirling phase.

At Cahokia and East St. Louis, we observe two patterns in the realm of monumental architecture—labor mobilization and monument reconstruction. Large buildings were located atop mounds as well as at the base of mounds along and in the vicinity of plazas. The fabrication of these large buildings involved the expenditure of a considerable amount of labor relative to the construction of a typical residence. What this suggests is the ability of an elite group of individuals to command a labor force of unknown di-

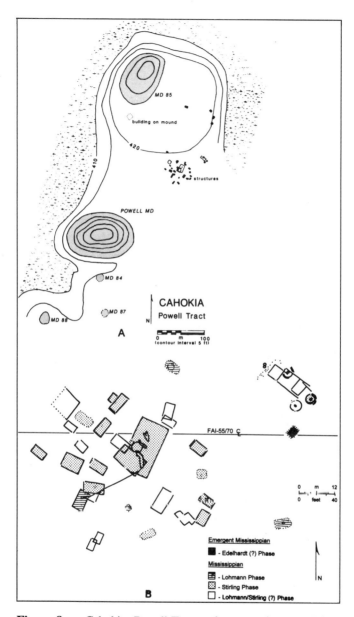

Figure 8.14. Cahokia, Powell Tract 1960 excavations: A, Distribution of Mounds and Excavations (based on Fowler 1989); B, Detail of Excavations (based on O'Brien 1972, figure 13)

mension. Webster (1990) has recently proposed that the command of labor was an important element in the evolution of social stratification (see also Trigger 1990, 127). Such was undoubtedly the case at Cahokia where the social organization was presumably reflected in the site's overall configuration. In many respects the hierarchical arrangement of kin groups or lineages about specific plazas is, at face value, indicative of a "conical clan" or a ranked hierarchy of clans (Kirchoff 1955; Knight 1990).[4]

The impact of the late eleventh-century nucleation was to draw kin groups into Cahokia and its subsidiary centers at Powell and East St. Louis. Those individuals drawn into the Stirling-phase orbit may have provided the necessary labor force, one based on kin obligations. It is clear that the amount of labor was compounded as one moved from the outer centers inward and from the outer limits of Cahokia toward Monks Mound. One measure, structure size, decreases from Monks Mound out where the structure atop Monks Mound measures between 400 and 800 square meters, while the enclosures on Tract 15B vary from 200 to 600 square meters, and those on Tract 15A are reduced to 250 square meters or fewer. A similar decrease is evident as one moves from Cahokia outward toward the Powell Mound Group, where a large building covers approximately 150 square meters. However, at East St. Louis, at least four of the structures that were measurable had internal areas encompassing between 100 and 500 square meters. The largest were centered beneath or in the lower stages of the Cemetery Mound.

Rebuilding at a single locus was quite common, both in the case of mound additions and the replacement of structures both on and off the mound. In addressing this pattern of rebuilding, one must also consider the inherent symbolism of renewal and rebirth, as well as those mechanisms that in effect govern such replacement. On the surface, rebuilding is perhaps attributable to simple maintenance due to the ravages of time. It is has also been suggested by Porter (1974) in his analysis of the Mitchell site data that such changes were perhaps part of an annual ritual associated with such ceremonies as the Green Corn ceremony. At the other extreme are those events associated with the death of an elite personage that required ritual burial and renewal. While no specific interval may have been involved, ritual purification was certainly linked to this pattern of renewal. The numerous large, circular buildings at East St. Louis and in certain locations of Cahokia may represent sweat lodges in which individuals were ceremoniously purified.

Knight's (1986, 1989a) discussion provides an important insight into the nature of Mississippian religion. The mound is a metaphor for earth and in turn is associated with rites of intensification. The cycle of birth, death, and rebirth are linked to earth, the ultimate source of fertility. One must note, however that these are *raised* platforms of earth. Although there is the ultimate idea of burial and subsequent rebirth with a new blanket of earth, the platforms are nonetheless raised upward toward the sky, and their orientation toward the four quarters reinforces the earthly manifestation of these quarters. This quadripartite arrangement represents the earthly counterpart of the sun. Thus, an opposing metaphor is hidden in the erection of mounds, especially one such as Mound E-11 in which there is no ritual of renewal with regard to the mound; instead, this renewal is confined to the multiple rebuildings. The manner in which such rituals were conveyed through the careful addition of minute mound stages is quite interesting (see Pauketat 1993c). Clearly, each mound module was able to assemble the necessary labor to carry out such activity.

Conclusions

The recent investigations at East St. Louis serve to document an intense area of Stirling-phase activity along the edge of a plaza. Such activity parallels similar but more massive and extensive construction projects at Cahokia. This monumental architecture reinforces the role of kin groups in the construction and maintenance of the mounds and structures. At East St. Louis, that various large structures were located on mounds and contiguous to mounds with reconstruction was a common occurrence. While patterns of renewal and purification are endemic to Native American societies, these expressions are manifested in different ways and forms. One can readily see the varied yet redundant way in which renewal and purification were conducted during the Stirling phase.

However, by the end of the Stirling phase and into the Moorehead phase, the rituals and purification were conducted and portrayed in slightly different ways and on a less frequent basis. No longer do we see the thin multiple and incremental episodes of mound additions. Instead, more massive additions were established, perhaps for longer periods of time (Pauketat 1993c, 142). The pool of labor also was focused on more massive construction projects such as the central palisade. This would certainly have siphoned away the labor that had once been devoted and dispersed throughout the site to the numerous societal segments. In essence, ritual behavior became more focused and hence less costly in the long run, yet such rites continued to be performed under a different and reconstituted hegemony. Saitta (1994, 212) has argued, in fact, as one of his points regarding the Cahokian political economy that the "long-term dynamics culminated not in organizational collapse but in a reorganization of communal political economy in the American Bottom." What is not clear at this time is what forces may have reversed the status quo at Cahokia and its satellites. The construction of palisades there and at East St. Louis, and the corresponding emergence of the Mitchell center, suggest the emergence of pressures from within.

Thomas E. Emerson

9

Reflections from the Countryside on Cahokian Hegemony

The sociopolitical structure of prehistoric Cahokia has been the subject of intermittent debate among regional researchers. For a number of years this debate was sporadic and generally unfocused. However, in 1974, papers by Guy Gibbon and Melvin Fowler directly confronted the problem of Cahokian sociopolitical structure. Gibbon (1974) proposed, in a tightly constructed model with testable attributes, that Cahokia was the urban center of a theocratic state that may have dominated much of the Midwest for several centuries. Fowler's (1974, 1978) more widely known model describes four hierarchical layers of sites ranging from an urban Cahokia to rural farmsteads with a proposed sociopolitical structure emphasizing centralized economic control and redistribution (in the sense of Service 1975). Pat O'Brien, in a flurry of articles (1972a, 1972b, 1989, 1991, 1992, 1993), has been in the forefront of those arguing for the existence of a Ramey state. In general, those advocates of state-level organization have emphasized the evidence for monumental architectural construction, settlement planning, a socially hierarchical society, sizeable population concentrations, centralized economic control and redistribution, and regional trade and interaction. They often refer to the state-level societies of Mesoamerica and the Near East for analogues.

More recently, however, another perspective has emerged among active American Bottom researchers that argues for a much less cohesive sociopolitical organization about Cahokia —as portrayed in various works by Milner (1990, 1991), Pauketat (1989, 1991, 1994a), and myself (1991a, 1995). In this scenario, the American Bottom is home to moderately dense populations organized into a number of competing polities that display a diachronic flux of political coalescence and dissolution. While recognizing the presence of many of the same attributes that advocates of the Ramey state use as evidence, this model questions the assumptions made and conclusions drawn from that evidence. Instead, our model relies on placing Cahokia within its southeastern United States historical context and within the worldwide pattern of complex chiefdoms (cf. Anderson 1990b, 1994a; DePratter 1983; Drennan and Uribe 1987; Earle 1987).

None of those involved in the debate would deny the essential fact that ancient Cahokian society involved a complex sociopolitical structure—the question is the specific degree and organizational form of that complexity. Until recently (i.e., Mehrer 1988; Pauketat 1989, 1991), little effort had been focused on addressing the issue through a systematic, detailed examination of the archaeological record. This chapter examines one small manifestation of Cahokia's political power as reflected in the ability of the Cahokian elite to exert hegemonic control over the smallest population segment within the settlement hierarchy—the scattered rural population living outside the highly organized towns and villages.

Conceptual Approach

Directed study of Cahokian political structure has been hampered and the goals obscured by many researchers' adherence to a typological approach in the classification of societies. De Montmollin (1989, 11–16), in a useful critique of the misguided thinking that social typologies generate in the characterization of ancient political organization and structure, demonstrates how such approaches operate at a high level of abstraction that obscures critical synchronic and diachronic variability within societies. Such abstractions often reify society and eliminate from consideration intragroup diversity, cooperation, and conflict—surely critical factors in understanding political structure. Most distressing, however, is the tendency in such approaches for the identification and "typing" of ancient societies to become an end in itself. Such a goal may be based upon the unsubstantiated belief that variables used to distinguish social types are causally related and covary. Consequently, such research assumes that if the presence of one variable can be documented, the presence of the inferred variables can be assumed. Examples of such presumptions abound in Cahokian interpretations. However, there is extensive documentation indicating that the variables used to define societal types, for example, chiefdoms or states, do not necessarily covary (cf. De Montmollin 1989, 14–15; Feinman and Neitzel 1984; Spencer 1987; Upham 1987). The search to identify ancient Cahokian political structure and organization through the identification of its societal type is rejected here as a viable or fruitful research strategy.

An alternative approach for the study of past political structure does exist in the form of *bundled continua of variation* as defined by Easton (1959) and implemented in an archaeological context by De Montmollin (1989). This approach involves studying single variables, each as a continua between polar extremes, and it allows the independent investigation of covariation among variables (rather than its simple assumption). The definition of variables and continua are specific to the research goals of the particular study being undertaken. In this case, I am interested in examining the evidence bearing on the relative complexity of political organization at Cahokia, within a diachronic framework, using a specific set of rural architectural data.

How do we examine this issue? Our understanding of hierarchical sociopolitical organizations and their posited relationships to settlement hierarchies has been greatly expanded by the application of informational and organizational theory to archaeological data sets by Gregory Johnson (1973, 1978) and Henry Wright (1977, 1984), and jointly (Wright and Johnson 1975). Essentially, these models demonstrate the correlation of increasing variation and levels of settlement hierarchies with increasing sociopolitical complexity. This broad correlation provides our settlement studies with strong sociopolitical postulates relating to Mississippian administrative, decision-making, and overall hierarchical organization.

Moreover, the recognition of the settlement-hierarchy relationship allows us to track variations in the sociopolitical realm through shifting modes of settlement articulation. To accomplish this, Lightfoot and Upham (1989, 20) utilize three axes to characterize variation in political systems including (1) a vertical axis that consists of "the number of vertical tiers in the decision-making organization"; (2) a horizontal axis that describes "the structure of decision-making at any specific tier in the hierarchy"; and (3) the power axis that "refers to the power and authority that are manifest in any specific tier of the decision-making." In this last axis, authority is measured in the ability of the elite to make decisions for and manipulate those of lower status, often with mechanisms such as ritualism and economic control, while power is the ability of elites to enforce their decisions.

The question, of course, is how does the archaeologist translate this organizational management model and these political characteristics into continua of variation readable in the material record. This issue has been addressed in some detail by those attempting to distinguish egalitarian from hierarchical societies in the southwestern United States (Lightfoot 1984, 42–49; Lightfoot and Upham 1989, 22–29; Upham, Lightfoot, and Jewett 1989). Specifically addressing archaeological evidence of hierarchical organization present within the settlement system, Lightfoot notes that hierarchical systems should be characterized by clear hierarchical variation in settlement sizes, locational centrality for centers of power, functional variation among the tiers of the settlement hierarchy, and variations of burial treatment (1984, 43–47). Within the Cahokian polity the conditions allowing for the recognition of a hierarchical organization have been satisfied by the evidence of the archaeological record (e.g., Fowler 1978). This evidence confirms the existence of a number of large temple mound centers that may have been contemporaneous and that likely interacted at a number of levels. However, it must be recognized that little direct evidence is available on the nature of polity interaction in the American Bottom. What I am seeking to present here is evidence of variation within specific hierarchical levels of that broader organizational structure and its reflections on the power of the Cahokian polity.

Since this study is focused on the lowest levels of the Cahokian settlement system, it is on this aspect that I will concentrate my attention. Again, Lightfoot's model (1984) for the study of sociopolitical change provides a guide for my examination of the Cahokian polity's hierarchial system. He provides an outline of sociopolitical assumptions about power and leadership that should have measurable archaeological manifestations at each tier in the political hierarchy (Lightfoot 1984, 46–47). Lightfoot uses identified differences between settlement tiers to demonstrate the existence of a hierarchical sociopolitical system within certain prehistoric southwestern native groups.

Adapting from Lightfoot's arguments, such archaeological markers should also be valid in identifying both synchronic and diachronic sociopolitical variation within a hierarchical tier. These archaeological manifestations focus on markers within a settlement tier that reflect stopping points on the continua that are thought to be indicative of different levels of political structure. The markers include (1) variation in access to and accumulation of valued goods such as are often associated with elite prestige economies; (2) variations in facilities for the accumulation and storage of both valued goods and comestibles; (3) variations in spatial location with regard to other group members; (4) the presence or absence of an "architecture of power;" (5) "artifacts of power" (i.e., badges of office that are limited to religious or political positions); and, finally, (6) variation in differential postmortem treatment of individuals within the tier.

At one end of the continua we should see evidence for the accumulation of valued goods, greater storage facilities, the occupation of centralized locations, the presence of artifacts and architecture of power, and differential mortuary practices. In opposition, one should recognize a lack of accumulated goods of all kinds, a noncentral spatial location, the absence of specialized artifacts and architecture of power, and an undifferentiated mortuary pattern. The social and political implications of these continua are related to a number of factors but appear to be heavily correlated with the differences apparent in societies typically viewed as unitary, centralized, contractually organized, stratified, and hierarchically structured as opposed to those that are segmentary in nature, featuring a decentralized organization and kinship and ascriptive relations (cf. De Montmollin 1989, 16–29). I would especially like to emphasize the importance of one of these continua—the recognition of the "architecture of power." I believe it is one of the strongest measures of hierarchical variation and political power. I find this concept additionally supported by Susan Kent's (1990) extensive ethnohistoric and ethnographic study documenting that sociopolitical complexity in a society "determines the organization of space and the built environment, particularly with respect to partitioning or segmentation," and that a society's sociopolitical complexity is shown in the increasing segmentation of space, material culture, and architecture. Obviously, the reverse should also be true, and the record should reflect the decreasing segmentation and partitioning of space as societies simplify their sociopolitical systems.

Rural Settlement Complexity of Regional Polities

To situate Cahokian settlement complexity within a relevant framework, it is necessary to examine the evidence for settlement organization of other contemporaneous regional polities. Unfortunately, the record is scant. Within the immediate Cahokian sphere of the upper Mississippi River valley there are no Middle Mississippian polities that are even remotely similar in their manifested complexity of large-scale public construction (i.e., mounds, plazas, palisades, post alignments), nucleated settlements, or population density. As Bruce Smith (1978, 494ff.) has noted in his survey of Mississippian settlement patterns and systems, research on the lower levels of Mississippian settlement hierarchies has been sadly lacking. Few excavations have been done in small villages, hamlets, farmsteads, or other small sites that would provide evidence for functional variation. Generally, reconstructions of Mississippian site hierarchies and site types are based on surficial evidence and molded to fit preconceived models.

Limited reliable settlement data do exist for three local Middle Mississippian enclaves in the Midwest; these include the Spoon River peoples of the central Illinois River valley (Conrad 1991), the Powers Phase peoples of the Missouri Western Lowlands (Price 1978), and Kincaid peoples of the Ohio River Black Bottoms (Muller 1978). In each example, there is some documented variation among the settlement forms of the rural populations; however, none display the specialization of the small site hierarchies at Cahokia.

The Powers-phase settlement hierarchy is thought to include four levels, consisting of a central civic-ceremonial site, villages, hamlets, and limited-activity (i.e., farmsteads) sites. The civic-ceremonial center and the village sites are considered to have multiple religious and administrative functions while hamlets and limited-activity sites are viewed as generalized residential subsistence loci (although a limited amount of variation was noted at several limited-activity sites [Price 1978, 227]). The Black Bottom Mississippians appear to have possessed a system with more affinity to that of the American Bottom. Butler (1977) and Muller (1978) describe a rural system that includes a hamlet surrounded by dependent farmsteads linked to form a "dispersed village." These small hamlets may have controlled the attached farmsteads and contained the residence of a local headman. While exotics, fineware, and cemeteries were present in some hamlets (Riordan 1975), Muller (1978, 285–86) has argued that such hamlets were primarily the residences of subsistence farmers with little or no political or religious functions.

The Spoon River Mississippian settlements of the central Illinois River valley are presumed to follow the traditional model of central temple towns surrounded by dependent hamlets and farmsteads. Although his terminology varies from other Mississippian researchers, Harn (1978) sees the temple towns and hamlets (re, villages of other researchers) as having ceremonial and political functions. The smaller sites are subsistence-oriented residences. Conrad (1991), on the other hand, has argued that the initial settlement of the valley is represented by the direct importation of a "foreign" settlement type from the Cahokia area. He presents data indicating the earliest Middle Mississippian site known, the Eveland site, is an example of an American Bottom civic center and that only later did the system of centralized temple towns and associated farmsteads arise in the area.[1]

It is also important to consider the evidence from other Southeastern polities of a roughly comparable scale of size and complexity. Sites in this category would certainly include Etowah and Moundville. Unfortunately, comparable data are virtually absent from such large polities. Research has primarily focused on the major ceremonial center or associated small-mound centers. This is true even of the Moundville polity (cf. Peebles 1978; Steponaitis 1983; Welch 1991a, 1991b) that is among the most investigated large centers in the Southeast. The single exception to this pattern is the work conducted at the Lubbub Creek single mound center and some of its associated small sites on the Tombigbee River (Blitz 1993; Peebles 1983).

Four examples of what Blitz (1993, 59–68) classifies as dispersed small sites and interprets as traditional "farmsteads" were excavated in the Lubbub Creek settlement system. While the sample size from this secondary mound-center system is limited, the variation in small sites is intriguing. One of the farmsteads, 22Lo600, contained two structures, one circular and one rectangular, a small cemetery, and a dozen or so pit features. Excavations at 22Cl527 revealed two circular to oval residences, a possible sweat house, a large cemetery, and pit features. A single residence was present at 22Cl814 while 1Gr2 includes a cemetery, several possible structures, and pits. Even this limited sample bespeaks a dramatically different social, religious, and political organization operating within the Lubbub Creek polity from that which is found in the northern Middle Mississippian sites discussed above.[2]

This brief examination of the rural settlement forms of regional Mississippian polities has demonstrated that there is variation within the lower levels of the Mississippian settlement hierarchies, but none achieved the social and political complexity displayed within the Cahokian countryside. This is to be expected, given the difference in the magnitude of scale between Cahokia and the smaller regional polities (see chapter 1).

A Model for Cahokian Rural Settlement

In a detailed study of Middle Mississippian settlement form, I have argued (Emerson 1995, 116–40) that essentially two patterns of rural settlement articulation can be documented—direct and sequential. In systems of direct articulation, small rural sites, such as farmsteads, hamlets, and small villages, are directly linked to mound centers. While such sites may vary in size, they are virtually interchangeable in function (usually food production), they lack any evidence of internal hierarchy, and they played no specific political, religious, or community roles within the settlement system. In a sequential pattern of articulation, however, rural sites were internally differentiated in regard to function. They showed clear evidence of lateral integration through rural ceremonial or civic nodal sites into dispersed villages and, through such nodes, vertical integration with mound centers. I have suggested that both forms of articulation are present in the Cahokia region during different time periods.

During the Mississippi Period, the countryside around major mound centers was filled with numerous rural settlements. For the most part, these small sites consisted of small family residences of subsistence farmers. Archaeologically, these sites are represented by one or two rectangular structures and surrounding storage pits (figure 9.1). They have been well documented through recent investigations (e.g., Jackson and Hannenberger 1990; Milner 1983a, 1984a). There are also a number of small sites that consist of single structures with little debris and few, if any, pits, which probably represent agricultural "field" houses (Finney 1993).

My ongoing research (Emerson 1992, 1995, 272–99; Emerson and Milner 1981) has demonstrated that a number of rural nodal settlement types can be defined in the American Bottom. These include nodal households, civic nodes, and ceremonial nodes. Nodal households appear to represent a family residence but with the important presence of artifactual and architectural evidence indicating the occurrence there of suprafamily-level activities and possible community functions. Such evidence might include large numbers of bowls suggesting communal feasting, granaries, or other storage facilities, or prestige artifacts. Civic nodes reflect the specialized material expressions of community or centralized political and social power. Such nodes may include multiple, functionally differentiated buildings, have a high content of ritual or prestige artifacts or both, specialized architecture (e.g.,

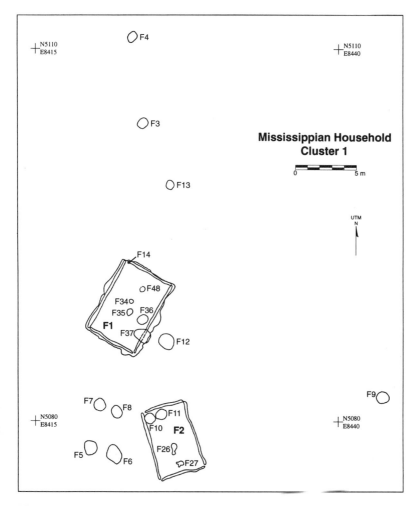

Figure 9.1. Robert Schneider Stirling-Phase Farmstead (after Fortier 1985, figure 6)

sweat houses), or large-scale storage facilities. Such nodes are also reflected in buildings that might have functioned as mens' houses or served for communal gatherings. The final nodal settlement forms are ceremonial. These sites are involved in ritual and mortuary activities. They are notable for their exotic ceramic assemblages, stone figurines, burials, ritual plants, and specialized architecture (e.g., temples, sacred fire enclosures, store houses).

175

The appearance and disappearance of these settlement forms, and their variance through time, provide insights into Cahokian centralized political integration and domination. The settlement of the Mississippian rural landscape is, in effect, a measure of the integration of the Cahokian polity. We might postulate that if the Cahokian polity is actually dominant over the surrounding countryside that variations in rural settlements should closely correlate chronologically and functionally with changes at Cahokia. Conversely, rural autonomy should be reflected in little or no correlations between changes at Cahokia and in the countryside. In the following pages I will explore this issue.

Cahokian Archaeological Evidence

Here I will examine the evident sociopolitical patterns revealed in a brief diachronic survey of the archaeological evidence from the American Bottom rural settlements, beginning with the last vestiges of the Emergent Mississippi Period. (The following summaries are based on the longer discussions and more detailed evidence presented in Emerson 1995.) Evidence from the American Bottom indicates that late Emergent Mississippian centers had attained the status of formalized towns with a structured organization including central plazas, high-status and commoner residences, and sizeable population clusters. While it is likely that temple mound construction was initiated during this period, as yet no such early mounds have been discovered. Pre-Mississippian rural settlement consisted entirely of isolated farmsteads and hamlets, apparently serving simply as residential sites, with no evidence of internal status differentiation, ranking, communal activities, or political specialization apparent (cf. J. Kelly 1990a; J. Kelly et al. 1984). Such sites conform to our conception of an unorganized rural population of subsistence farmers linked directly to and controlled by the central towns.

The onset of the Lohmann phase sees the first changes in the organizational structure of the rural landscape with the appearance of status differentiation and communal facilities (see Emerson 1995). At the Julien site, a Lohmann-phase nodal household included a single residential building with two adjacent, specialized, limestone-floored, circular storage facilities (presumably for food); a marker post; caches of tools and exotic items; and a large number of bowls. The presence of these large-volume storage facilities indicates control of foodstuffs in excess of the needs of a single family and indicates gathered surplus for either communal use or elite control.

The Lohmann-phase ceremonial ML-2 and civic ML-1 settlements at the Range site (Hanenberger and Mehrer n.d.) may represent the first appearance of specialized architectural facilities and communal ceremonial activities in the countryside. ML-2 contains two buildings, one of which was relatively small and may have had some specialized use, and a massive rectangular pit. The small building and pit contained an extensive amount of debris with more than seventy vessels of various types (some of which had been ceremonially killed), exotic minerals, beads, a stone (marble?) discoidal, and other artifacts. Most indicative of ritual activity was the presence of red cedar and tobacco remains. The complex provides extensive evidence of use in communal activities with overtones suggesting its association with some form of religious renewal ceremony. Traditionally, such renewal ceremonies have been linked to Green Corn or Busk ceremonialism, and this feature complex may represent an early form of the practice we see so well developed at later Stirling-phase sites such as BBB Motor (Emerson 1989, 1995; Emerson and Jackson 1984) and Sponemann (Fortier 1991c).

The contemporaneous civic node, ML-1, just to the north of ML-2 continues the communal theme of Lohmann nodal facilities with the presence of a massive 60-square-meter, square, single-post, open-sided, roofed communal building containing benches and cooking facilities (Hannenberger and Mehrer n.d.). In this case, the emphasis is on the civic and political aspects of communal life. Such meeting places were commonly referenced in the southeastern ethnohistoric record as facilities for daily meetings of adult males to take "council" on important social and political questions, to gossip, imbibe "black drink," or the local equivalent, and generally socialize (e.g., Hudson 1976). Two associated structures show evidence of some longevity through rebuilding and may represent a set of paired residential and increasingly larger, expanded storage buildings. Despite the "communal" appearance of ML-1, there were not extensive debris—reinforcing the concept of the co-use of this complex with ML-2 that has extensive debris but no real communal architecture. ML-2 represents the ceremonial- and religious-activity area balanced against the civic nature of ML-1 to create a unified complex.

The Lohmann burial complex expressed at the BBB Motor site (Emerson 1995) reinforces the perception that status and rank differences are becoming prevalent within Lohmann society. This isolated mortuary complex contains the remains of at least eight (and probably more) individuals buried in two recognizable groups (moiety or status divisions?). Although lacking any obvious distinctions or markings with high-status mortuary accompaniments, the placement of these individuals within a specialized facility connotes a noncommoner status. The inclusion of both adults and children reinforces the concept of an ascribed status for these individuals. The two buildings present probably represent a domicile (for a guardian) and a building with benches, perhaps for ceremonial use or storage of goods. This ceremonial node appears to represent a low-level, elite mortuary repository, given its specialized nature and the relatively restricted number of burials, perhaps for members of the ranking lineage in a dispersed village system. The absence of blatantly high-status burials may reflect the movement of lead elites to hierarchically superior centers for burial (e.g., the elite Lohmann mortuary complex at Mound 72? [Fowler 1991]). Likewise, commoners must have been interred in other less specialized locations (Milner 1984c).

During the Lohmann phase, the countryside provides the first evidence of status differentiation among the rural populations. No longer are rural settlements simply the uniform residences of egalitarian subsistence horticulturalists; rather, we see evidence of wealth and power variation expressed in control over maize storage facilities, exotic artifacts, and general high densities of material goods. This phase is also defined by the introduction of specialized architecture and marker posts to designate differentiations in spatial areas and functional activities. Communal activities are recognized in rural settlements with the appearance of "community houses," "renewal" and "fertility" ceremonials, as well as low-level elite mortuary facilities. Such activities may have established the basis for the later Stirling-phase specialized functionaries, although recognition is difficult via the usual residential or artifactual patterns. The creation of the Range communal civic and ceremonial area and the mortuary complex at the BBB Motor site is not simply the grafting on of specialized facilities to some preexisting residential complex but rather the development of an entirely new functional type of architectural complex.

Beginning about A.D. 1100, the Stirling-phase archaeological record marks the greatest expression of Cahokian local and regional power and influence (Emerson 1991a; Milner 1990; Pauketat 1992). The Stirling florescence is reflected in the countryside as well as in the major mound centers and at the regional level. This phase is marked by the creation of numerous specialized facilities and evidence of the appearance of their attendant functionaries throughout the rural areas. Since our original recognition of dispersed villages with their farmsteads, nodal hamlets, and temple and mortuary facilities, additional excavations and analysis have refined our understanding and revealed the variation that was concealed within these simple forms of settlement (Emerson and Milner 1981, 1982, 1988; Milner and Emerson 1981). There are now multiple excavated farmsteads (e.g., Jackson and Hannenberger 1990; J. Kelly 1994b;, Milner 1983a, 1984a), three distinct examples of Stirling-phase civic nodal sites and two ceremonial complexes that are analyzed in reports and that I have had the opportunity to reexamine (cf. Emerson 1992, 1995). These nodal sites include the Labras Lake (Yerkes 1980, 1987), Range (Hannenberger and Mehrer n.d.), and Julien (Milner 1984a) civic nodes, the temple and mortuary ceremonial node at BBB Motor (Emerson 1984, 1995), and the ceremonial node at Sponemann (D. Jackson, Fortier, and Williams 1992).

Labras Lake is an early-to-middle Stirling-phase civic node that includes three rectangular wall-trench structures clustered about a small courtyard with two sweat lodges (figure 9.2). House 2 had many interior posts, indicating its possible division into at least three sections either as storage areas or to isolate activities within chambers of the structure. An area off the southeast corner of the courtyard is marked by the presence of numerous pits, marker posts, and an isolated wall trench. Structure rebuilding indicates considerable occupation longevity and utilization. Potential status items include a Ramey knife, several beakers, an effigy, and decorated fineware bowl and jar, a squash-effigy jar, a Ramey-Incised jar, a red-filmed water bottle, and exotic minerals.

Another comparable contemporaneous node was found at Julien and includes five rectangular structures and two circular buildings arranged about a courtyard. On the western side of the courtyard were two wall trench buildings and an earlier, smaller building. The small building may represent a storage facility paired with a residence. In the eastern cluster, two paired wall-trench structures are associated with a circular single-post sweat house. One of the wall-trench structures was unusual with a prepared floor, a pit with multiple re-uses, and a cached vessel in the floor. These structures contained Ramey-Incised vessels, exotic minerals, a plain and hooded water bottle, and a trailed plate. This cluster also had two isolated wall trenches and a large marker post associated with it.

One of the rectangular structures is superimposed over a circular wall-

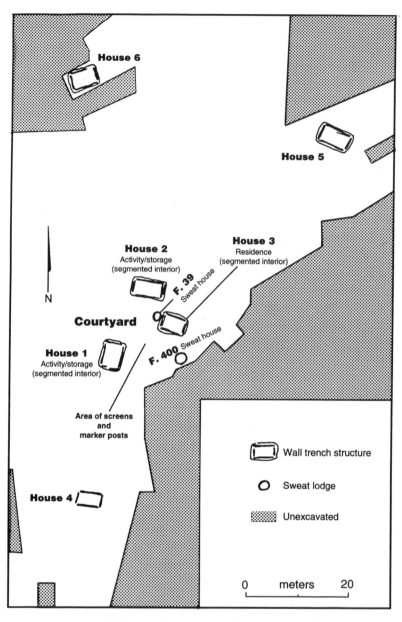

Figure 9.2. Stirling-Phase Labras Lake Civic Node (after Emerson 1992, figure 7.2)

trench facility that contains no internal features.[3] This facility is roughly equivalent in size to the limestone-floored storage areas associated with the Lohmann-phase nodal household at the Julien site mentioned earlier. The lack of any internal evidence of fires or hearths argues against its being a sweat house, and Milner's original identification (1984a, 30) of this as a possible communal storage building seems reasonable.

This identification as an early Stirling storage facility suggests a possible transition of nodal authority from a Lohmann-phase base of stored comestibles or seed for planting (i.e., civic or economic power or both) to one emphasizing ceremonial and religious authority marked by the appearances of Stirling-phase sweat houses. In the Julien civic node, the storage facility was an earlier construction that was abandoned and later covered by a large wall-trench structure. This may mark an important transition of the nature of the rural power base near the beginning of the Stirling phase.

The most complexly organized early-to-middle Stirling civic node was MS-1, excavated at the Range site (Hannenberger and Mehrer n.d.) and consisting of northern and southern clusters of structures and associated features. The southern cluster included three rectangular buildings arranged around a courtyard; two had wall trenches, and one small, flimsy, single-post structure may have served as a cooking facility. One large structure had innumerable interior posts, suggesting either an internally segmented storage or activity space, or benches for communal activities. Rebuilding was minimal in this cluster, and status items were limited to exotic minerals, Ramey-Incised vessels, and quartz crystals.

Separated to the north was a second cluster with three rectangular wall-trench structures and four sweat houses. The wall-trench buildings include a very small example with a single intensely fired hearth. I believe it is an ancillary building functioning, perhaps, as a cooking area. It is superimposed by a very large (the largest at the Range site) and very "empty" (only two central posts) building containing a single specialized limestone-floored interior pit. The structure may have served some communal function, perhaps large-scale storage since numerous food remains were preserved when the building burned. The remaining wall-trench structure shows rebuilding and again has internal divisions, perhaps into thirds. Such interior spatial segmentation seems commonly associated with certain buildings in Stirling-phase nodes. A heavy concentration of status items was recovered from this building. The cluster also contains isolated pits, post screens, and four sweat houses that may represent two pairs of contemporaneous buildings. Status items from the area include quartz crystals, exotic minerals, copper, modelled clay objects, Ramey-Incised lip-notched jars, bottles, and pinch pots.

The Range site, ML-I, component seems to represent the Stirling civic node played out on a grand scale with several possible residential units, multiple cooking facilities, a large communal storage or meeting structure, and possible paired sweat houses. This structural pattern, however, does not differ dramatically from what has been observed at the other nodal sites. Labras Lake is the simplest form with a single group of sweat houses and structures organized about a single courtyard; Julien is slightly more complex with two groups of structures around a courtyard, with Range being the most complex version of the pattern.

A key marker for Stirling civic nodes is the presence of one or more sweat houses.[4] The introduction of this ritual phenomenon into the nodes represents a significant shift in both the definition and role of local leadership toward an alignment with sacred power. Up to this point in time, Lohmann-phase leader-commoner distinctions seem to be marked by a limited differential access to stored and exotic goods as signified at the Julien nodal household. Rural leadership appears to have maintained some power through the control of granaries as presumably communal maize storage facilities. Whether this storage was for coercive or humanitarian goals is irrelevant since its function would have been the same: control over the subsistence future of members of the rural community. Lohmann religious activities were communal and fertility-related as represented at the ML-2 "renewal" facilities. Civic power, too, appears to be shared with an emphasis placed on group gatherings, presumably to make consensus decisions on local issues. The presence of any local leader with a drastically distinctive lifestyle is missing in the archaeological evidence from the rural Lohmann phase.

The most striking developments in rural organization, that is, temple-mortuary ceremonial nodes, appear and reach their apogee during the Stirling phase. Two excellent examples of rural temples are recorded at the BBB Motor (Emerson and Jackson 1984; Emerson 1989, 1995) and the Sponemann sites (D. Jackson, Fortier, and Williams 1992). The BBB Motor site (figure 9.3) contains a temple building, a sacred fire enclosure, a ceremonial courtyard, and a large number of exotic items including fire-clay fertility figurines (cf. Emerson 1982, 1989, 1995), crystals, Ramey-Incised and effigy jars, mica, sacred red cedar, and evidence for the use of a hallucinogen,

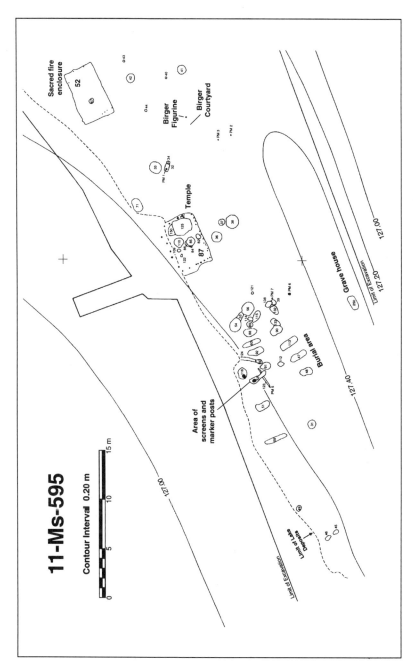

Figure 9.3. BBB Motor Site Stirling-Phase Temple-Mortuary Ceremonial Node (after Emerson 1984, figure 45)

183

Datura. Also associated with the temple was a burial area with twelve burials, eleven burial processing pits, and a grave house. As in the earlier Lohmann mortuary complex, the graves contained the processed remains of adults and children, suggesting its use by a restricted segment of the broader population—perhaps by a prominent lineage.

At the late Stirling Sponemann site, the temple complex theme is played out on a grand scale (D. Jackson, Fortier, and Williams 1992; Fortier 1992a–c; Emerson 1995). Here eight structures, including a temple, storehouses, a sacred-fire enclosure, food preparation area, and possible residences, are located on three sides of a large courtyard. The complex also contained a large renewal pit with extensive exotic debris, numerous marker posts, and isolated wall screens. The artifact assemblage includes such exotic items as several fireclay figurines, Ramey-Incised and effigy pots, crystals, red cedar, and other possible ceremonial plants. The evidence for the interpretation of the area as a fertility-related temple complex similar to BBB Motor seems adequate, but it differs drastically in size and scope. While BBB Motor appears to have been used by a fairly small group in an isolated locality, Sponemann is at the edge of a sizeable Stirling-phase village and may have been the focus for large ceremonies. Also, noticeably missing is any evidence of mortuary-related activities.

The presence of the Stirling civic nodes strongly indicates the existence of specialized political leaders with power bases linked to the religious realms of ritual purity, while the rural temple, mortuary, and fertility ceremonial nodes argue emphatically for the appearance of religious and mortuary specialists. If I have correctly interpreted the coexistence of "renewal" symbolism (i.e., fertility activities) and civic authority in the Lohmann-phase nodes, then the Stirling phase marks the emergence of specialization in leadership roles and the exercise of power. In fact, perhaps the single most defining attribute of the Stirling rural landscape is the elaboration of leadership roles into at least three recognizable categories as political, religious, and mortuary specialists. Given the nature of the occupancy and utilization patterns at sites I have examined, I would also argue that these are separate "roles" filled by different individuals. This social complexity as reflected in architectural, material culture, and symbolism is unmatched in either previous or subsequent phases. The dominant theme of Stirling-phase symbolism bespeaks the importance of the spiritual realm of fertility and life, *and* the importance of its representatives on earth.

The subsequent Moorehead and Sand Prairie phases are poorly represented in the rural areas; however, there is sufficient information to suggest
some possible trends in the development of Cahokia's political hegemony in
the countryside (cf. Emerson 1995). The only example of community organization available from the Moorehead countryside is from the Julien site
(Milner 1984a) and reflects the shift from a sacred and religious organization
to one again emphasizing a secular, communal base. The Moorehead community at Julien contains a number of residential and ancillary structures associated with what appears to be a communal "men's house." The structure,
with 42 square meters of interior space, with benches along two walls, multiple hearths, and extensive material debris such as exotic minerals, arrow-
head caches, chipped-stone tools, abraders, and domestic ceramic vessels,
provides a convincing picture of a communally used building. Its ancillary
building may have served a more restricted use for storage or special activities, although it contains a debris assemblage similar to the communal
structure. Although I have not attempted to disentangle the Moorehead residential compounds, the extensive reuse of a building site, multiple and functionally differentiated contemporaneous structures, and a large number of
exotic artifacts may indicate the presence of high-status individuals near the
communal building. The disappearance of the specialized architecture of the
previous Stirling-phase sweat lodges and temple and mortuary complexes is
striking, and it denotes the dramatic organizational shift that swept the rural
areas at this time. The reappearance of community structures at small rural
nodes, coinciding as it does with the disappearance of the religious architecture, indicates the decline of the sacral and religious power base evident in
the previous phase (emanating from the centers) and the reemergence, or,
perhaps, simply renewed dominance, of local communal political and social
forms of power.

The final dissolution of centralized power over the countryside is reflected in archaeological evidence from the terminal Moorehead or early
Sand Prairie phase (Emerson et al. 1996). During this phase, there appear to
be no obvious central nodes of political power in the rural areas. Missing
from the Sand Prairie–phase archaeological record are features such as sweat
houses or communal structures. Evidence, however, of communal activities
is not absent but rather refocused on communal, rural mortuary facilities
such as the Florence Street (Emerson, Milner, and Jackson 1983) and East
St. Louis (Milner 1983b) sites' charnel structures and cemeteries. These

cemeteries may have some associated ancillary structures (e.g., structures 60 and 61 at Florence Street), but the evidence for such a phenomenon is unclear at present. These isolated communal cemeteries substantiate the premise that significant organizational changes have occurred in Mississippian society. Not only have the attributes of hierarchical political and religious domination been severely diminished, but the evidence for differentiated, ascribed social status as reflected in mortuary patterns seems much reduced. Such a behavioral pattern may be reflected in what appears to be the increasing "wealth" of later Mississippian rural folks at the expense of any centralized elite (cf. Emerson 1995).

Discussion

I have argued in this chapter that traditional typological approaches to understanding Cahokia's prehistoric political structure have not been fruitful because they obscure the very phenomena that are being studied. The identification of the diversity and variation within such hierarchial societies provides the basis for understanding their development. A more focused alternative employed here has been the investigation of change and stability within specific variables (see Easton's [1959] bundled continua of variation). Using this approach I have examined the evidence from the surrounding rural countryside to gain a perspective on fluctuations in the power of the central Cahokian elites between A.D. 1050 and 1300. Specifically, I have touched on, in a very summary manner, the evidence of elite power as indicated by diachronic variations in wealth storage, centralized locations, an architecture of power, artifacts of power, rural prestige goods, and differential mortuary practices. In addition, I have observed the appearance of spatial markers of power (after Kent 1990).

The information from the rural sites supports the long-known, general, chronological sequence and assumptions concerning broad trends in Cahokian political power (Emerson 1991a; Fowler and Hall 1975; Milner 1990). Critically, it demonstrates the synchronism of political and social change in the countryside and at Cahokia. In a recent landmark study, Pauketat (1991, 302–30; 1994a) has constructed an elegant scenario portraying the consolidation, sacralization, and dissolution of elite power at Cahokia. His work is the first major attempt by a scholar to comprehend the internal development of the polity in terms of integrated social, political, and economic factors based on extensive analysis of Cahokian archaeological data and, consequently, is of great utility in analyzing rural events (cf. Emerson 1995, 457–69).

Both Cahokia and the countryside demonstrate a gradualist evolution of Emergent Mississippian lifeways during the period from about A.D. 800 to 1050 that probably involve the first appearance of simple chiefdoms. The countryside is marked by the presence of small farmsteads and hamlets that are likely linked to the emerging, large, plaza-oriented but moundless towns. However, the shift at A.D. 1050 to the Lohmann phase is dramatic. In the rural areas, the clustered Emergent Mississippian villages are replaced by dispersed farmsteads, nodal households, and small nodal communally oriented civic and ceremonial centers.

A similar transition is noted at Cahokia, which Pauketat sees as signaling the "physical and social transformation of Cahokia" (1991, 310–11) and as "a qualitative political-economic shift and restructuring of social organization . . . [that] is inferred to be the political consolidation of a complex chiefdom" (1991, 307). Lohmann-phase Cahokia shows significantly increased population densities, the appearance of large-scale public constructions, blatant evidence in the Mound 72 elite burials and retainer sacrifices of elite control over resources and lives, shifts in architectural and household patterns, and a large increase in the material wealth of the population (see Fowler 1991; Pauketat and Lopinot, chapter 6).

The Stirling phase, Pauketat (1991, 323–24) argues, is denoted by the appearance of centralized ritual and sacralized power associated with a divine paramount chiefdom at Cahokia. Archaeologically, this chiefly power is symbolized in Ramey iconography, woodhenge construction, and mound construction and reconstruction. An especially critical and intrinsic part of this hierarchical control is the elaboration and proliferation of fertility symbolism and "rites of intensification" by the elite. In the countryside, Cahokia's power is expressed through the presence of specialized civic and ceremonial nodes, and mortuary facilities that reflect a dramatic increase in rural hierarchical elaboration with the development of specialized religious and civic offices.

Pauketat (1991, 326–27) provides a scenario of Cahokian decline that emphasizes political decline leading down a slow path to polity morbidity. Evidence he has gathered from Cahokia indicates the decrease in the Moorehead phase populations, integration, structure diversity and exotics although, conversely, one can trace continuance of the elite "symbols" through most of this phase. The final Cahokian decline, when it finally comes in the late Moorehead phase, is total (Pauketat and Emerson, chapter 13).

The countryside mirrors this pattern of decline, but as always the transitions are more abrupt given the restricted database. The break with the complex, rural Stirling-phase hierarchical structure is total and complete—in an archaeological instance all the specialized civic and ceremonial facilities disappear. The rural Moorehead pattern suggests a return to a simpler way—that of communal leadership lacking any obvious political or religious specialists.

For most researchers, the Sand Prairie phase within the American Bottom represents the aftermath of Cahokian decline. Within the rural areas, archaeological evidence is limited to the isolated households and associated complex community cemeteries. Mortuary ceremonialism has become the central organizing premise in the Sand Prairie "community," while evidence of even communal forms of political organization is missing.

At the height of Cahokian elite power, the Lohmann and Stirling rural settlements reflect a pattern indicative of a society that might be characterized as unitary, centralized, hierarchically structured, stratified, and, perhaps, even contractually organized. At these sites we find evidence for the placement of civic nodes in centralized areas, the practice of wealth accumulation, the creation of a specialized architecture of power, the accumulation of prestige artifacts, and differentiated mortuary patterns. Also, during these phases the greatest differentiation and segmentation of space can be found in site organization, marked spatial boundaries, and architectural patterns.

The Moorehead- and Sand Prairie–phase rural sites clearly reflect the shift from previous patterns of social and political unity and hierarchy to one characterized by a decentralized organization, kinship and ascriptive focuses, and community emphasis. This is illustrated in the disappearance of many previous markers such as the architecture of power, a decrease in prestige goods and wealth accumulation, the introduction of an egalitarian mortuary framework, a change in the sacralization of space, and the removal of many spatial boundaries as previously defined by architectural segmentation, marker posts, screens, and structured site organization.

To some extent this study has reaffirmed general perceptions concerning the rise and fall of the Cahokian polity. It has especially supported the model of Cahokian political history proposed most recently by Pauketat (1991, 1992, 1994a). This affirmation has been based on an independent body of data that has previously been downplayed or ignored in research on Cahokian political power. Specifically, it has been argued that the Mississippian rural settlements can be seen as an independent measure of the integrative strength of the Cahokian polity. Such a data set strengthens our understanding of Cahokian political domination. This study has also shown that taxonomic approaches to the study of Cahokian political power disguise a wealth of critical variation that is essential to our fuller understanding of prehistoric sociopolitical structure.

In this chapter, I have demonstrated patterned shifts in the rural organizational structure about Cahokia between A.D. 1050 and 1350. Furthermore, these shifts have been demonstrated to be synchronized with changes observable within the political history of the Cahokian paramount center. Going beyond simply the identification of these organizational structures, I have tried to present an interpretive context, within reasonable social and political parameters, that can be derived from the data. I have argued that instead of an undifferentiated plane of rural settlement one has an extremely complex political, social, and religious infrastructure. The variations in this rural infrastructure can be seen as a direct reflection of variations in the level of Cahokian domination. Furthermore, the understanding of this complex rural organizational structure can and has provided and can continue to provide political, social, religious, and economic insights into the internal organization and functioning of Cahokia itself. Only by adopting appropriate theoretical and methodological approaches, such as those employed here, can we explore such questions.

Thomas E. Emerson

10

Cahokian Elite Ideology and the Mississippian Cosmos

de materialibus ad immaterialia

Twelfth-century comment by Abbot Sugar on his reconstruction of

the Abbey Church of St. Denis

In this chapter I intend to explore the realms of Mississippian cosmology and ideology within a framework of elite hierarchical power. Toward this end I will provide an interpretation of aspects of Cahokian cosmology, iconography, and symbolism as they are materialized in the world. Such a reading is made possible by examining Cahokian cosmology within the context of Eastern Woodlands native ethnohistory and ethnography and within the broader perspective of hierarchical societies. Furthermore, I propose that the manipulation of the cosmos by the Cahokian elite to stabilize and enhance their hierarchical position can be traced in that same material record. To examine that process, I will utilize the architectural, artifactual, settlement, and contextual archaeological evidence from the rural areas surrounding Cahokia.

Theoretical Position

In this study I have deliberately separated two concepts, that is, religion and ideology, that have become so intertwined in much anthropological research as to often be conceived of as synonymous (e.g., various papers in Demarest and Conrad 1992). Such a synonymy is detrimental to my goal of exploring the interactions of symbolism, cosmology, and world view within the hierarchical world of social and power relationships. Consequently, in this discussion I will use religion and ideology to refer to two very different relationships. In regard to "religion," I have chosen to follow those who see it in the broader sense of a culture's perception of cosmological order in the real and supernatural world. Geertz (1973) has succinctly expressed this perspective in viewing religion as a symbolic system that creates a society's conception and interpretations of their interactions with the world. A very pointed, yet expressive, aspect of religion is encapsulated in the concept of "world view," which is a society's "picture of the way things in sheer actuality are, their concept of nature, of self, of society. It contains their most comprehensive ideas of order" (Geertz 1973, 127). An essential part of this interpretive approach is the specific correlation of an idealist cosmological universe with its materialistic expression in the real world through multitudinous material symbols, that is, the material "containers" of the cosmos.

Ideology, because of renewed interest in "postprocessual" paradigms, has been subject to extensive redefinition and reinterpretation, ranging from its conception as "the belief and value system of a society" (Sharer and Ashmore 1987, 406) to its use to describe a political agenda of prejudice, emotion, and bias (e.g., in Geertz 1973). However, the majority of discussions and elaborations of ideology spring from a Marxian base (Abercrombie, Hill, and Turner 1980, 7–29; Giddens 1979, 165–97; Larrain 1979, 13–34; Sumner 1979, 1–56). For Marx and Engels, a precept of ideology was the "false consciousness" of a dominant ideology, a creation of the ruling classes, arising from the inequality of economic relations in order to mystify the masses, serving to naturalize inequality, to engage the masses in their own domination (Marx and Engels 1989; Larrain 1979, 35–67).

Today few theorists would advocate the idea of a social wholeness encapsulated within a dominant ideology but would speak rather of multiple ideologies within a society (e.g., Abercrombie, Hill, and Turner 1980; Bloch 1989; Giddens 1979). Subordinate groups often preserve ideologies that clearly differ, or may even be in conflict with, the dominate ideology espoused by the ruling elite; yet this does not denigrate the importance of the dominate ideology. Ideology creates the social and natural world for humans, explaining and naturalizing it—no member of a society can escape the influence of its dominate ideology. As Pauketat (1991a, 19) neatly summarized it, the "dominant ideology appropriates the consciousness of individuals," yet the elite cannot totally suppress subaltern ideologies. Consequently, the role of a dominant ideology in "managing" subordinate groups is one fraught with potential problems, conflict, and contradictions.

I am specifically interested in the manifestation of ideology as elite power in its more traditional Marxian aspects in Mississippian society. For that approach, it is appropriate to follow Giddens (1979, 187) who argues that the primary value of the ideological concept is as a "critique of domination." In a similar vein, Shanks and Tilley (1982, 131) regard ideology "as a mode(s) of intervention in social relations, carried on through practice, which secures the *reproduction* rather than the *transformation* of the social formation in the presence of contradictions between structural principles at the level of structure, and of clashes of interest between actors and groups at the level of system." Such definitions are in keeping with the view that ideology involves the manipulation of ideas and material, and "provides the framework within which, from a particular standpoint, resources are given value, inequalities are defined, and power is legitimated" (Hodder 1991, 72).

Inclusive in the above discussion is the implication that the ideology of domination "functions" within social formations—these functions have been delineated by Giddens (1979, 193–96) as the (1) representation of a specific group's interest as those of all society's members; (2) denial or shift to a different social sphere of contradictions within a social system; and (3) reification or naturalization of the status quo to support its permanence and durability and disguise its susceptibility to change. These aspects of ideological functions intermesh in the complex weave of society. Within such a context ideology interacts with power through practice and is manifested in the material world.

The role of ideology has come to the fore in studies chiefly of hierarchical societies as a recognized and formidable interpretive base when operationalized in conjunction with the more traditional areas of economic and military control (Earle 1989, 86). Often derived from a Marxist orientation, such new studies of inequality focus on points of conflict and stress within societies, points such as elite-commoner friction and elite and intercommunity competition.

Ideology may be manifested in a number of ways (Earle 1987, 298–300; 1991a, 6–10), two of which are important here. Foremost are "ceremonies of place associated with the creation of a sacred landscape." Such communally constructed landscapes are the homes of the elites who mediate society's relationship with the cosmos and serve, in addition, as a spatial materialization of that cosmos. Secondly, "symbols of . . . power" encompass the exotic, ritual objects associated with elite positions and are often part of an extensive trade and exchange network involving distant places and foreign elite interaction. Such objects, categorized as part of an "international style," symbolize social distance and esoteric power indicating the elites' participation in the wider world (cf. Helms 1979; Pauketat, chapter 2).

This brings us to the issue of comprehending the link between the material world and the cosmos. Here I will follow the lead of certain researchers in emphasizing the material world as "constituting a symbolic, active communicative field" (Shanks and Tilley 1987, 95; see also Douglas and Isherwood 1979). In such an approach, assemblages of goods present a set of coherent, intentional meanings aimed at knowledgeable actors who are able to read those messages (Douglas and Isherwood 1979, 5). If we perceive material items in this light, then we must step back from understanding "[m]aterial culture . . . as . . . merely a *reflection* of cognitive systems and social practices but [see it as] actively involved in the formation and structuring of such practices" (Shanks and Tilley 1987, 85). Goods are mediators in social practice—not simply "objectified thoughts."

The implications of this concept are twofold (Hodder 1992). First, this concept strongly emphasizes the cultural and *contextual* aspect of "material culture," thus redirecting our approach from functional and physical form. More importantly, it brings to the fore the often weak relationship between an object's meaning and its physical properties within and between societies. When objects are perceived as active, flexible social mediators, the perception necessitates an awareness of the multivocality of meaning in their interpretation. A second implication of this concept is that it correctly stresses the importance of cultural, social, and historical context within the archaeological interpretation of meaning.

Like society, material culture is structured, and this structure is discernible through the patterning in the archaeological record. It is a "structured record, structured in relation to the social construction of reality and in relation to social strategies of interest and power and ideology as a form of power" (Shanks and Tilley 1987, 98). This allows goods to act as "a structured sign system" and mandates that the material world be treated as a meaningfully structured mediator within the realm of social relationships. In such an active role, material goods have value in understanding the formation and continuance of social relations, especially in the context of inequality, power, and ideology. This is especially apparent in the social consumption of material goods. The "partitioning among goods" reflected in the archaeological record should be related to the "underlying partitioning in society," and such distinctions of inequality or status should be emphasized even more by sets of material goods (Douglas and Isherwood 1979, 97, 118). Douglas and Isherwood (1979, 88ff., 131–46) have focused on delineating the importance of material goods as communicative devices of "exclusion" by those in power to establish material boundaries of status. In this context they stress "luxuries as weapons of exclusion" within a status-consumptive information system.

Returning now to the original theme of this section, I will briefly summarize the relationship of religion and ideology as I perceive it. Religion as encapsulated in a society's "world view" provides the basic structuring and organization of that society and its cosmos. It is both within and against this structure and "vision" that ideological forces operate to manipulate it in a way beneficial to a social or political faction. If a religious world view provides the framework for the cosmos, ideology is one of the forces that seeks to act upon that structure, either to transform or maintain it. Archaeologists can now identify and interpret religion and ideology with some assurity through their material manifestations (cf. Emerson, 1989, 1995; Pauketat and Emerson 1991). There is an increasing acceptance of idealist concepts such as cosmology, symbolism, and ideology as important factors in understanding hierarchical societies. In this chapter, I will explore some of these variables for the prehistoric polity of Cahokia in the four centuries between A.D. 900 and 1300.

Contextual Setting

The prehistoric polity of Cahokia must be considered within its appropriate context as one of the preeminent religious and political centers of the Mississippian world. The center of that Mississippian world was the southeastern United States. It is in those cultures, with their complex political and social organization, religious beliefs, and horticultural basis, documented most closely in the sixteenth- and seventeenth-century chiefdoms encountered by Europeans, that we must seek an understanding of the Cahokian cosmos. A rich world of documentation from early Eastern Woodland native inhabitants promises to enrich and expand our understanding of the Cahokian symbolic repertoire. An essential bulwark of my arguments and interpretations in this work lies in accepting the validity of the ethnohistoric and ethnographic data from Southeast, Prairie, and Plains native cultures as a source of insight into

Mississippian iconography and religion. I am confident that it is a valid approach and one that has a long history of success in Eastern U.S. archaeology. As Vernon J. Knight Jr. (1981, 127) states:

> Within an historical perspective, the theme of previous investigations of these issues by Swanton [numerous works], Waring [1968, Waring and Holder 1945], and Howard [1968] was a demonstration of the importance of the diachronic link from Mississippian archaeology to the ethnohistorical record of the Southeastern Indians. These investigators found positive links between historically recorded ritual, icons, and myths on the one hand, and Mississippian ritual features and icons on the other. They concluded, from different perspectives and attending to different data, that historical Southeastern aboriginal religion was in essence a debased form of a uniform religious complex which reached its peak in Mississippian times, and that historical manifestations could therefore be used to make inferences about the ancestral forms known to archaeology.

More recent scholars have elaborated and refined the earlier approaches to provide a greater depth of interpretation of Mississippian iconography and ritual. In this regard I would cite as examples the research of Robert L. Hall (e.g., 1976, 1977, 1979, 1985, and especially 1989 and 1991), Knight (1981, 1986, 1989a, 1989b), Prentice (1986), Brown (1976a, 1985), Phillips and Brown (1978), Emerson (1982, 1983, 1989, 1995), and Pauketat and Emerson (1991). These more detailed studies have not only served to validate the relationship between the archaeological and ethnohistoric records but have shown the widespread nature and historical persistence of many of the involved iconographic ritual and belief systems.

In dealing with uneven and diverse recorded ethnohistoric data, a concern lies in identifying the shared core iconographic structure. Confusion of regional details and variation with broader patterns of meaningful structuration can seriously hamper our understanding of Mississippian symbolic patterning. Useful sources to direct one from the idiosyncratic particulars to the broader patterns include now classic studies of southeastern Indians by Hudson (1976), in which he presents a synthetic overview of the cosmological system of the native tribes (albeit with strong Cherokee overtones), and Howard's (1968) and Waring's (1968) examinations of the Southeastern Ceremonial Complex. Such a perspective is important in dealing with the recognition of symbolic patterning in archaeological assemblages. The recent excavations of the BBB Motor, Sponemann, and other comparable American Bottom Mississippian sites, because of their unique combinations of ceramics, burials, figurines, and exotic items, have presented rare opportunities to seek themes based on symbolic expressions in many media that are associated within an integrated system (e.g., Emerson 1982, 1989; Fortier 1991b, 1991c; Pauketat and Emerson 1991; Prentice 1986).

Mississippian World Structuring

If there was a single overriding theme in the cosmology of the southeastern Indian groups, it was the organization of the natural and supernatural worlds into dualistic categories expressed as sets of oppositions, such as the opposition of the Upper and Lower World. As Hudson (1976) has noted, much of the concern among these groups focused on maintaining the separation of the Upper and Lower Worlds and avoiding the resulting pollution if they became mixed. Although humans could not affect the intrinsic powers of the Upper and Lower Worlds, it was possible to mitigate their impact in this world. This symbolic system can be seen as embodying a triadic structure that included the Upper and Lower Worlds and the world of people. The world of the Mississippian peoples was very similar to that of the historic southeastern tribes.

The structuration of the Mississippian world in dualistic sets involves wider parameters for comprehending the cultural milieu that we are investigating—these parameters involve the four-cornered world and the critical importance of the directional symbolism. The quadripartite cosmos is quite literally all-pervasive both specifically in "Middle Mississippian" and generally in North American Indian symbolism (see Griffin 1952, 1967, 1985). Recognizing that Mississippian peoples and the historic southeastern groups appear to have organized their world (at least in some aspects) within a framework of oppositions and quadripartition allows one to use that framework as a descriptive and a device.

A centered quadripartite world view was hardly an original perspective to the Middle Mississippian American Bottom. At least four centuries earlier such patterns are recognizable. Local villages had attained a four-sided organization, that is, laid out about a central courtyard, by the Late Woodland

Patrick phase (A.D. 600–800). In the subsequent Dohack phase (A.D. 800–850), however, we first see the classic expression of quadripartitioning in the creation of a community square, consisting of four rectangular pits arranged in a square around a central post. Kelly (1990b, 92) argues that "[t]he overall configuration of Dohack phase communities and their central corporate facilities also appears to embody certain symbolic elements that underlie Mississippian belief systems. The central fourfold pit complexes, often accompanied by a central post, could well reflect the initial emergence of the cross-in-circle complexes." He further relates the presence of elite structures, fire, and above- and below-ground facilities to the historic "fire-sun-deity" and "upperworld-lowerworld" dichotomy.

This quadripartite pattern continues in various forms to emerge full bloom with the appearance of Mississippianism at A.D. 1050. The emergence of the rectangular plaza surrounded by mounds reflects a large-scale reenactment of this pattern. While the mound-and-plaza organization complex has been linked to the cross and circle, it can also clearly be seen as a spatial representation of the four cornered cosmos (see J. Kelly, chapter 8). In fact, the four-sided platform mounds may have graphically portrayed the cosmos as "earth-islands" as imaged in Muskogean belief of the world as flat-topped and four-sided (Knight 1989a, 287). Knight (1989a) has further tied the mound icon to earth symbolism involving the earth "navel," Green Corn ritualism and fertility, and world renewal, effectively linking it to the central focus of Cahokian belief systems.

John Douglas (1976, 257–69), using extensive ethnographic and ethnohistoric data, argues further that the late prehistoric native world view conceived of a four-quartered world in which the primary axis ran northwest to southeast with a second divisor running northeast to southwest. This created four diamond-shaped quarters to the north, east, west, and south. In such a world north is linked to east and south to west, spiritually. A semicardinal orientation of many of the religious and political sites in the American Bottom is apparent. At the same time, however, the primary center at Cahokia reflects a different organizational plan keyed to the cardinal directions (cf. Fowler 1989; J. Kelly, chapter 8). Regardless of minor variation, the organization and contents of these sites portray the Mississippian world view in a microcosm and suggest adherence to an overall plan reflecting the dualistic quadripartite nature in the cosmology of the builders.

Red Goddesses and Cosmic Containers

One of the major turning points in comprehending Cahokian religious symbolism occurred with the excavation of a small, rural, Stirling-phase temple, complete with its ritual paraphernalia, at the BBB Motor site near Cahokia. The discovery of female stone figurines, Ramey-Incised vessels, burials, crystals, galena, mica, and other exotica provided an opportunity to analyze such material within its appropriate cultural context (Emerson 1982, 1984, 1989, 1995). Our understanding was further enhanced by later excavations of an even larger Stirling-phase rural ceremonial complex at the nearby Sponemann site (D. Jackson, Fortier, and Williams 1992). It is these materials that form much of the basis for our current understanding of Cahokian religious symbolism.

Red Goddesses

The Stirling-phase BBB Motor and Sponemann sites have produced some of the few contextually certain examples of the highly artistic Cahokia-style (cf. Emerson 1983) stone figurines known from the American Bottom. These figurines are unmatched in their symbolic content and their potential value in exploring the Cahokian religious world and have aided in interpreting previously discovered figurines, pipes, and other symbolic materials (Emerson 1982, 1989, 1995; Farnsworth and Emerson 1989).

The spectacular BBB Motor and Sponemann figurines are made of a soft red stone. Early descriptions of similar red stone figurines in the American Bottom area referred to the raw material involved as "fireclay."[1] Fireclay, or "flint clay" as it is properly known, is a local material in southeastern Missouri that closely resembles bauxite in color, texture, and workability (Hughes and Emerson 1995). Likely use of this source for the manufacture of American Bottom figurines is reinforced by the fact that Mississippian trade in the American Bottom with this area is known to have occurred in galena (Walthall 1981), Crescent Quarry cherts (McElrath 1983), and ceramics (Milner et al. 1984). Although specific sources have not been identified, I would credit the local fireclay or flint-clay source as providing the raw material for the Cahokia craftsmen to produce figurines (Hughes and Emerson 1995).

Two figurines, Birger and Keller, are associated with the Stirling temple area of the BBB Motor Site. The Birger figurine depicts a supernatural event, implying that the imaged individual belongs to the realm of the mythological rather than the natural world. The sculpture (figure 10.1) depicts a kneeling or squatting female on a circular base (described in detail in Emerson 1982). Her left hand rests on the head of a feline-headed serpent, and her right hand holds a hoe with which she strokes or tills the serpent's back. The feline-headed serpent motif is widespread throughout the Southeast during the Mississippi Period and later periods, with many of the depictions bearing a resemblance to the Birger figurine. On the woman's back is a flat, square pack, held in place by a strap wrapped around her shoulders.

At the woman's left side, the serpent's body bifurcates and is transformed into vines. One vine with three fruits runs along the woman's feet and around her left side, while the second vine with three fruits crosses diagonally up her back and over her left shoulder. While the fruits are clearly gourds or squash, the artistic rendering makes the botanical identification ambiguous. They have been variously identified as bottle gourds (*Lagenaria siceraria [Mol.]* Standl) by Donald Lathrap (personal communication, 1981), the yellow-flowered gourd (*Cucurbita pepo* var. *ovifera*) by Thomas Whitaker (personal communication, 1981) and, more recently, as the hitherto unrecognized *Cucurbita argyrosperma* by Gayle Fritz (personal communication, 1992).

The Keller figurine (described in detail in Emerson 1982) represents a female kneeling on a rectangular base (figure 10.2). The carving is not as detailed as is the Birger figurine and differs stylistically. The forehead slopes back and appears to portray cranial deformation. The individual has long, straight hair pulled back behind the ears and hanging down her back to below the waist. The lower portions of her body are covered with a short wrap-around skirt, ending just above the knees.

The figure is depicted as kneeling on a base formed by ears of corn or bundled reeds woven into a mat. In front of the woman is a rectangular, boxlike object, which appears to be a basket. Although broken now, at one time a plant stalk, possibly maize, emerged from the base, rose through the right hand of the figure, to sweep back to attach to the side of the head, just above the ear. A similar motif was observed in the McGehee figure pipe, recovered near the mouth of the Arkansas River in 1969 (Perino 1971, 117; author's personal observation).

The Sponemann site component contained the shattered remains of at least three deliberately destroyed figurines. Unlike other figurines from the American Bottom, the Sponemann-site figurines had been smashed into

Figure 10.1. Birger Figurine (after Emerson 1984, plate 5)

more than five hundred small fragments, virtually all of which were recovered from a rural temple structure. Despite the prehistoric burning and fragmentation of the specimens, it has been possible to reconstruct major portions of three figurines labeled the Sponemann, Willoughby, and West figurines. The following discussion is based on information from Fortier's detailed descriptions (1991b) and my personal examination of both photographs and the actual figurines.

The Sponemann figurine (figure 10.3) represents the head, upper torso, and arms of a female with various additional motifs including ears without ornaments, a necklace, breasts with nipples, possible gourds or pack on the back, and a headband or turban (or more likely a tumpline?). The individual's arms are outstretched with palms up. From each palm a plant stalk arches upward to the side of the figure's head (ala the McGehee figurine discussed above). While the specific plant species are uncertain, they may represent sunflowers or corn.

The most complex specimen recovered is the Willoughby figurine (figure 10.4). It also represents a highly fragmented and incomplete female with only portions of the head, upper torso, and lower body present. The upper torso includes breasts, detailed facial features, and an unornamented ear,

200

Figure 10.2. Keller Figurine (after Emerson 1984, plate 8)

Figure 10.3. Sponemann Figurine (after Jackson et al. 1992, plate 9.3)

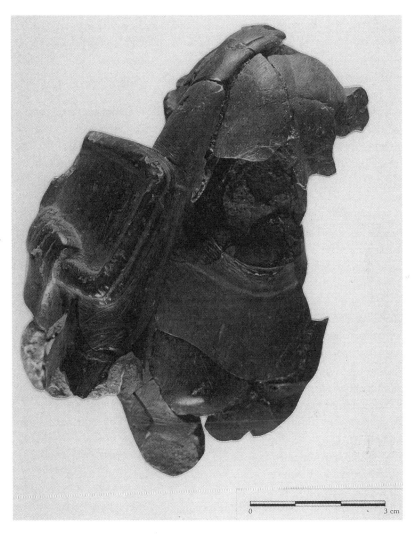

Figure 10.4. Willoughby Figurine (after Jackson et al. 1992, plate 9.7)

hands holding rectangular "vessels," and branching plant vines. Fortier (1991b, 285) assesses the evidence and presents a reasonable argument for the rectangular hand-held objects being dishes associated with ethnohistorically reported Green Corn ceremonialism. The only other possibility that may be represented in the figurine is rectangular stone "paint" palettes similar to those recovered from Moundville and surrounding sites. The lower torso depicts a rectangular basket and lower-leg portions wrapped in a skirt. In the Willoughby basket the engraved panels are horizontal and vertical, strongly suggesting a woven-cane (?) construction.

The snake motif plays a dominant role in the West figurine fragments (figure 10.5) that have been assembled. The figurine segments depict a female with a rattlesnake coiled on her head, a partial torso with small right breast, perhaps a portion of backpack, and several snake heads and a tail rattle. The snake depicted is not the feline-headed serpent of the Birger figurine but a specific portrayal of the rattlesnake including its triangular shaped head and rattles.

Because of the fragmented condition of the specimens, more than 120 worked pieces could not be associated with a specific figurine but could be separated into groups containing recognizable pieces of vines, baskets, torsos, snake-gourds, and other miscellaneous items. At least two other basket forms similar to that depicted on the Keller figurine were present. Two fragments may be decorated gourd or backpack motifs. The most intriguing piece recovered, however, is a small fragment showing the lashings on a stone hoe virtually identical to the Birger figurine hoe. Few other Cahokia area figurines (cf. Emerson 1982, 1983) show any demonstrable thematic relationship to the BBB Motor and Sponemann site figurines, with the exception of the more abstract Schild site pipe (Perino 1971, 119) and Macoupin Creek Figure pipe (Emerson 1982, 13–15; Farnsworth and Emerson 1989) from the lower Illinois River valley and the Svehla effigy elbow pipe (Emerson n.d.a). The stone effigy of some interest is a fireclay pipe recovered with a Mississippian burial (in association with a Ramey-Incised jar and an effigy hooded water bottle) at the Schild site, Greene County, Illinois, in the lower Illinois River valley (Perino 1971, 117–18). This effigy is highly schematic (figure 10.6). The effigy figure sits on a long rectangular base. Behind it is a round pipe bowl, about which is coiled a serpent with its tail on the right and its head on the left. The serpent's head is large, bulbous, and devoid of features. The main figure is a kneeling human wearing a short wraparound skirt. The sex of the figure, based on the skirt and the lack of ear ornaments (both of which appear to be limited to females), is probably female. Ears are faintly portrayed on the sides of the head, and the hair is described as hanging "vertically in a rectangular pack located between the shoulder blades" (Perino 1971, 117). The figure has her left hand raised to her breast while her

Figure 10.5. West Figurine (after Jackson et al. 1992, plate 9.10)

right arm runs down her body and ends in a large bulbous protrusion that may be a pouch or a fruit. There is a hoe over her right shoulder.

Another fascinating effigy is the Macoupin Creek Figure pipe (formerly called the Piasa Creek Figure pipe [Emerson 1982, 13–15, 1995; Farnsworth and Emerson 1989], which appears to represent a kneeling male shaman with a gourd rattle in one hand and a snake or snakeskin around his neck. Another representation of the snake-person association has been discovered recently by the author (Emerson n.d.a, 1995) in a specimen from a private collection and most likely from the Cahokia site. The specimen, the Svehla effigy elbow pipe (figure 10.7), is made of a pinkish granitic material. It depicts the head of an individual (sex unknown) with a rattlesnake coiled atop it. The large triangular head of the snake rests on the coils while the tail and rattles wrap down along the neck of the individual.

The serpent/serpent-monster motif is widespread throughout the south-

Figure 10.6. Schild Figurine (after Perino 1971)

eastern United States. A composite overview of the mythological and symbolic aspects of this motif is available in Hudson (1976), Swanton (1946), and a number of other ethnohistorical works. The serpent motif among the Indians of the Eastern Woodlands is presumably of great antiquity and continued down to historic times, when ethnohistorical documents demonstrate that the peoples of the Southeast were concerned with both natural and supernatural serpents. As a motif, the serpent appears throughout the Southeast in temples, public structures, geometric decorations, tattoos, body painting, dance forms, and so forth.

The serpent as an Under World creature is associated with the attributes of lightning, thunder, rain, and water and with power over plants and other animals. In southeastern symbolism, the characteristics of the serpent are transferred to the serpent monster. This serpent monster is usually a composite beast with attributes of several animals. Regardless of form, these monsters are all associated with the Under World. This Under World has two aspects: It is the dwelling place of monsters, danger, and evil, but conversely it is also

Figure 10.7. Svehla Figurine (after Emerson 1995, figure 42)

the source of water, fertility, and power against evil. Symbolic and icono-graphic representations of underworld creatures are widespread in prehis-toric Mississippian and Caddoan art (Hamilton 1952; Howard 1968; Phillips and Brown 1978). There seems little doubt that the serpent creature por-trayed in the Birger sculpture, with its feline head and snake body, is related to the water monsters of the historic Southeast. As a class of creatures, un-derwater monsters can be said to be closely related to water, rain, lightning, and apparently fertility. These associations seem to be shared by all these monsters and are also commonly attributed to serpents. The serpent motif is dominant in the Birger, West, Schild, and Svehla effigies.

The relation of the figurines' motifs is to the concept of agricultural pur-suits. The hoe, in combination with the vines and gourds emerging from the Birger serpent monster's body, is a rendering of the natural process of regen-cration using agricultural motifs. Although more schematic, this same "ag-ricultural" motif is postulated for the Schild, Willoughby, and Sponemann figurines. The agricultural motif is the primary one in the Keller figurine.

The Keller, McGehee, Willoughby, and Sponemann effigies are concerned with the procreation of corn and sunflower (?) plants. The plant and agricultural motifs are significant because of their rarity in non-Cahokian Mississippian iconography.

The dominance of the female figure in these carvings recalls the important historic Corn Mother myths (Witthoft 1949). Prentice (1986), in a thorough compilation of relevant Native American symbolism from ethnohistoric, ethnographic, and archaeological sources, supports the Birger figurine identification as a Mississippian Earth Mother figure. Such Earth Mother concepts "include the wearing of a short skirt, association with the great monster serpent, the giving of plants to humankind (most notably corn, pumpkins, and tobacco), use of the tumpline, the giving of the sacred bundles to humankind (sacred bundles were normally carried on the back with a tumpline), and association with death concepts" (Prentice 1986, 254).

Perhaps Prentice's (1986, 254) most important point is the overlapping and polysemous nature of the symbolic world and "how notably the death goddess, the lunar goddess, the 'Old Woman,' and the 'Grandmother' deities of the Eastern Woodlands share each other's traits and merge in their identifying characteristics." This leads him to follow Hultkrantz (1957) in arguing that these "deities" are but facets of the "Earth Mother"—a concept that I too can accept. In fact, it becomes clear that many of the same sets of traits are also repeated in the other figurines recovered from the BBB Motor and Sponemann sites, and that these represent other facets of the Earth-Mother myth. The Keller figurine contains a female in a short skirt holding a plant stalk, with corn cobs and basket; the Sponemann figurine depicts a female wearing a turban (tumpline?) and backpack (?) with plants emerging from her palms; the Willoughby figurine female is in a short skirt kneeling in front of a basket and holding "plates" with plant vines around her head; the West female figurine is wrapped with serpents and wears a backpack; and the miscellaneous Sponemann site fragments include segments of baskets, snakes, vines, backpacks, and a hoe that are all associated with the figurines recovered from the site.

The similarity of these figurines' traits with those referenced by Prentice in correlating the Birger figurine with the Earth Mother are obvious. To reinforce the correlation, one might note that the basket and backpack motifs are interchangeable as "containers" used in the transport of "souls," seeds, bones, and so forth, and the baskets' vertical-rods motif can be easily related to the backpack "rods"—again with similar interpretations as lightning, rain, bones, and arrows. In these later figurines the emergence of the "corn" plants from the female's hands and body represent variations on the Corn Mother myth. (The detailed verification for these associations and others can be found in Prentice 1986, Witthoft 1949, and references included therein.) In fact, I would argue that, given the variation in motif representation between the figurines, the Birger, Schild, and West figurines represent the Earth Mother in all of its facets, while the Keller, Sponemann, and Willoughby figurines emphasize specifically the Corn Maiden aspect.

Cosmic Containers

Ramey-Incised ceramics were first designated a type by Griffin in 1949. These vessels are sharp-shouldered jars, usually with highly polished smudged or black-slipped surfaces and standardized trailed designs on their upfacing shoulders. Except for the often superior craftsmanship and the presence of decorations, they do not differ significantly from contemporary utilitarian ceramic forms. Such vessels have long been recognized as being distinct in a Cahokian ceramic assemblage that is primarily undecorated. They have been interpreted as simply a decorated utilitarian pottery form, as a horizon marker, or, conversely, a type with a long developmental history, a high-status ware, a ceremonial ware, and a signifier of a merchant class. Although suggestions are rampant concerning the significance of Ramey-Incised pottery, few studies have aimed at investigating these ceramics.

I have employed both connotative and formalistic approaches to Ramey design analysis to interpret their significance (Emerson 1989, 1995; cf. Shepard 1968, 259–60). The formalistic study was based on the principle of symmetry (discussed in detail by Birkoff [1933], simplified for archaeological use by Shepard [1948], and first applied to Ramey ceramics by Griffith [1962, 1981]). In this analysis nine categories of Ramey basic elements were recognized: the chevron, arc, trapezoid, scroll 1, scroll 2, wing, spiral, forked eye, and circle (figure 10.8). The frequency of the various basic elements shows that about one-third (33.5 percent) of the elements are in Category II (arc group), 18.9 percent are in Category I (chevrons), 11.9 percent are in Category VI (wing), while Category III (trapezoids) and Category IV (scroll 1) each comprise 10.6 percent of the collection. Although most recovered ceramic vessels are fragmentary, forty-eight examples of element asso-

ELABORATIONS WITHIN BASIC ELEMENT CATEGORIES		BBB MOTOR 11-Ms-595	JULIEN 11-S-63 11-S-660	CAHOKIA*	MITCHELL	RANGE 11-S-47	LABRAS LAKE 11-S-299	HORSESHOE LAKE 11-Ms-37	McCAIN	LILY LAKE 11-S-341
Category I	a 			5	1					2
	b 			6						
	c 				2					
	d 			4						1
	e 	3								
	f 		1							
	g 	2								
	h				1					
	i 	1			6			1		
Category II	a			11						
	b 		4	20	7	1				
	c 			2	2					
	d 			3						
	e 				1					
	f 		2	13	4	1				2
	g 			2						
	h 				1					

(continued on next page)

*Includes materials from various UIUC excavations in the Cahokia area
(see Griffith 1981, note 1; and O'Brien 1972a).

Figure 10.8. Categories of Ramey-Incised Design Elements
(after Emerson 1989, chart 1)

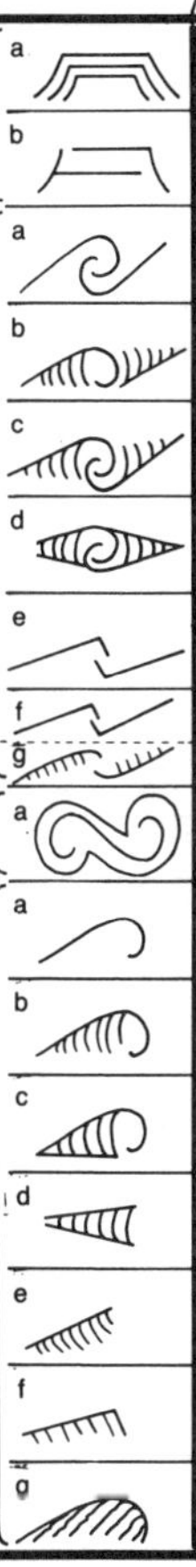

ELABORATIONS WITHIN BASIC ELEMENT CATEGORIES			BBB MOTOR 11-Ms-595	JULIEN 11-S-63 11-S-660	CAHOKIA*	MITCHELL	RANGE 11-S-47	LABRAS LAKE 11-S-299	HORSESHOE LAKE 11-Ms-37	McCAIN	LILY LAKE 11-S-341
Category III	a			1	1						2
	b				2						
Category IV	a		2		1						
	b				1			2			
	c				8	1					
	d				2						
	e				1						
	f g				6						
Category V	a				1						
Category VI	a			1							1
	b			2					1		
	c				1						
	d				2						
	e			1	10						
	f			1	1						
	g		1								

(continued on next page)

*Includes materials from various UIUC excavations in the Cahokia area
(see Griffith 1981, note 1; and O'Brien 1972a).

Figure 10.8. Categories of Ramey-Incised Design Elements
(after Emerson 1989, chart 1)

211

ELABORATIONS WITHIN BASIC ELEMENT CATEGORIES	BBB MOTOR 11-Ms-595	JULIEN 11-S-63 / 11-S-660	CAHOKIA*	MITCHELL	RANGE 11-S-47	LABRAS LAKE 11-S-299	HORSESHOE LAKE 11-Ms-37	McCAIN	LILY LAKE 11-S-341
Category VII — a (design element)									
Category VIII — a (design element)			1						
Category VIII — b (design element)		1	1						
Category VIII — c (design element)	1	2	2						
Category IX — a (design element)			3						
Combination Category X — a (design element)	2 1	3 2	5 4						
Combination Category X — a (design element)	2	3	5						
Combination Category X — b (design element)		2 1	2 2						
Combination Category X — b (design element)		2	2						
Combination Category X — (design element)			1 1						
Combination Category X — c (design element)			1						
Combination Category X — (design element)				3 3					
Combination Category X — d (design element)				3					
Combination Category XI — a (design element)				5 2					
Combination Category XI — (design element)				4					
Combination Category XII — a (design element)	1 1	1	1	1 2	1	2		2 3	
Combination Category XII — a (design element)	1		1	1					2
Combination Category XII — b (design element)					3 3				
Combination Category XII — (design element)					3				

*Includes materials from various UIUC excavations in the Cahokia area (see Griffith 1981, note 1; and O'Brien 1972a).

Figure 10.8. Categories of Ramey-Incised Design Elements (after Emerson 1989, chart 1)

212

ciations are recorded. These associations take two forms; 48 percent involve the association of identical basic elements, while 52 percent involve the association of different elements (see Pauketat and Emerson 1991). If one considers the element associations as a whole, there are two major pairings observable: one pairing is Category xia-type combinations, comprised of Categories iv and vi (22.9 percent); and 20.8 percent of the pairings involve Categories iiia and vii elements. There were minor groupings consisting of Category ii elements (14.6 percent) and pairs of Category i (10.4 percent).

This initial attempt (i.e., Emerson 1989, 1994) to quantify Ramey symbols is essential to demonstrate that the symbolism is homogeneous, tightly focused, and interpretable with respect to symbolic meanings. Some symbolic connotations, based on symbolic patterning, can be observed here (see fuller discussions in Emerson 1989, 1995). For example, within Categories i and ix of basic elements, a full 63.7 percent of the sample motifs relate to the chevron arc (Categories i and ii). Such motifs are likely related to the sky arch, bird, and Upper World continuum but also with an Under World and fertility association. One aspect of this study has been to show that the Upper World and Under World are not mutually exclusive but may be linked through a specific set of symbols. The other dominant symbolic motifs revolve about the scroll, spiral, and circle, and represent 27.8 percent of those recorded here. Again, symbolically, I argue that these are primary Under World, serpent, and water motifs (Emerson 1995). Two minor symbol motifs are the forked eye (4.5 percent, Category viii) and the trapezoid (3.4 percent, Category iii). In the first instance the forked eye is assumed to have a "Thunderer" association (water, rain, etc.), while the trapezoid is an earth and mound symbol (the greatest fertility icon of all, Knight 1986).

It is the extreme homogeneity of Ramey iconography, with more than 90 percent of the symbols falling into two closely related groups, that is so remarkable. As Pauketat and I argued (1991), the Ramey symbols represent a visual portrayal of a tightly integrated Cahokian cosmos. This "oneness" is reinforced by an examination of the combination categories (x and xii) that document the close association of what might be seen as unrelated symbols. Based on formal analysis alone, there is no reason to argue for the association of the chevron, scroll, and trapezoidal forms. Each, stylistically, could be seen as a separate and distinct symbolic form. Yet, it is exactly the linkage of these disparate symbols that is illustrated in the combination categories, that is, trapezoid with scroll (Category x) and scroll with chevron (Category

XII). These linkages are also visible in the co-occurrence of design elements documented in figure 10.9.

In 1989, I suggested that such vessels were, in fact, important ceremonial containers that may have been centrally produced and distributed as part of Cahokian fertility ritualism. Historically, such concepts were expressed in agricultural and socially integrating ceremonies such as the Busk and Green Corn ceremonies. Such ritualism was pervasive in the Eastern Woodlands (Witthoft 1949). Based on a number of scattered lines of evidence (see Emerson 1989), Ramey ceramics may have functioned as specialized ritual vessels. The integrating mechanism of Mississippian society may have included a number of centralized religious ceremonies that occurred at various times throughout the year. Dispersed rural communities were associated with rituals at secondary mound centers, which, in turn, were tied ritually to Cahokia. An important aspect of the ritual paraphernalia of such ceremonies may have been the manufacture and distribution of the semisacred Ramey ceramics. The manufacture of such vessels may have been limited to specific times of the year and manufactured in limited quantities, probably by potters who were associated with each specific lineage and community ritual group. At the end of such ceremonies, these vessels may have been dispersed throughout the scattered communities as the participants returned to their homes.

More recently, Pauketat and I (1991) have elaborated on our understanding of the "use" of Ramey-Incised ceramics as a mediator in Cahokian elite-commoner interactions. Succinctly, we argued for the use of Ramey symbolism within the context of "rites of intensification" that are "calendrically based, community-focused rites that play a critical role in the resolution of cosmological discontinuities in the annual ritual sequence . . . (that) are based on community-wide participation, which requires a symbolic text both highly visible and understandable to the masses. This text, we contend(ed), is Ramey iconography" (Pauketat and Emerson 1991, 919–20). These rites of intensification are assumed to be those associated with the pan-Eastern Woodlands Green Corn or Busk ceremonialism—evidence for whose existence is plentiful in Cahokia-Mississippian culture (Emerson 1989; Fortier 1992). During such festivals, elite distribution would result in the widespread distribution of both these vessels and their message—a message that we argued, reinforced and naturalized political centralization and elite supremacy.

214

	#	%
	4	8.3
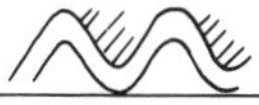	1	2.1
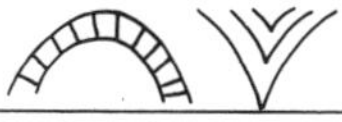	1	2.1
	1	2.1
	2	4.2
	4	8.3
	1	2.1
	1	2.1
	3	6.3
	3	6.3
	2	4.2
	11	22.9
	3	6.2
	1	2.1
	10	20.8

Figure 10.9. Co-occurrence of Ramey Design Elements (after Emerson 1995, figure 45)

Cosmic Messengers

Ramey-Incised ceramics and red goddesses served to convey the Cahokian cosmos to the populace. As manifest in these objects, a Cahokian cosmos involved a dualistic, quadripartitioned world that revolved around the procreation of agricultural crops, fertility, life forces, and purity. Furthermore, the distribution of such ritual items suggests that such beliefs played a dominant role in the ritual continuance and lifeways of the rural populace.

Both Brown (1985, 103–4) and Knight (1986, 675–76) have sought to facilitate our comprehension of Mississippian religion and ritualism by introducing the concept of the "cult" (in the sense of Turner 1964, 1969, 1974). "Cult institutions . . . [are defined as] a set of rituals all having the same general goal, all explicitly rationalized by a set of similar or related beliefs, and all supported by the same social group" (Wallace 1966, 75, cited in Knight 1986). Each cult would have associated symbols or *sacra*, including "representational art, artifacts, and icons that by inference appear to have been charged with conventional supernatural meanings, in the context of ritual activity or display" (Knight 1986, 675; Turner 1964).

Knight (1986), in an elaboration of Mississippian religious institutional organization, suggests "the formal articulation of two powerful and complementary cult organizations into a structure of dyadic type." He saw the pairing of a cult of nobility and one of fertility in Mississippian religion as reflecting a worldwide duality of such cult linkages (cf. Turner 1969). In addition, he argued for the recognition of an "organized priesthood." While extensively documented in the ethnohistoric literature, few researchers have dealt with the role or the importance of such priests, shamans, or "jugglers." However Knight (1986, 681), using documented accounts, notes that such priests were responsible for "the maintenance of temples and ossuaries, administration of mortuary ritual, the maintenance of sacred fires and responsibilities connected with their supernatural aspects, and the preparation of ritual medicines. The roles of priests intermeshed with both chiefly practice (especially mortuary) and with community rites of intensification. [They] . . . were occupationally specialized ritual groups . . . restricted in membership to certain age graded and normally sex bound initiates."

The relationship between these Mississippian cults is proposed to resemble a "dyadic structural type" with the chiefly warrior cult being opposed by the communally based fertility cult with the ancestor and mortuary priesthood playing a pivotal role as mediators. Such a scenario is similar to that outlined by Brown (1985), in which he saw the dialectic opposition of the nobility to the fertility cult mediated by a warrior cult. Both researchers stress the intrinsic conflict within a system of Mississippian cults due to the social connotations of each cult. The cult of the nobility carries with it restricted membership, most likely based on kin ties and manifestations of *power over* the actions of others. Such a cult focuses on creating spiritual, social, and spatial *distance* between social groups. The fertility cult, on the other hand, is conceived to be communal by its very nature. The iconography of such cults delves into the very symbolic core and deeply held values of the social group to promote unity often, as Pauketat and I have argued, through rites of intensification (Emerson 1989, 1994; Pauketat 1994a; Pauketat and Emerson 1991).

Cahokian Cults

The recognition of cults is essential to our study of Cahokian religion and ideology. Religions are best conceived of as comprised of multiple cults— they are pluralistic (Knight 1986). This is critical to understanding and identifying the appropriate "sacra," and it also establishes the critical nature of ensuring a commonalty of archaeological context. Each cult has its own developmental history, and cults may or may not co-vary as they wax and wane. Conversely, cults may be in accord or in opposition to one another. The motives, symbolism, and ritual of the Cahokian elite have different aspirations than the leadership at the small rural ceremonial centers of dispersed villages. Cults should not be automatically conceived of as integrative mechanisms; they may just as easily serve as divisive mechanisms (cf. Eister 1974).

There exists a dialectical relationship between these two cult forms that is universal in its appearance, that is, the poised conflict between an elite cult of the nobility and a cult of the earth, of fertility, of the masses (cf. Turner 1969, 99; 1974, 185). This dichotomy might be seen in Mississippian life as Brown's (1985) distinction between chiefly iconography and the serpent and fertility cults or Knight's (1986) iconic warfare and cosmogony, and platform mound complexes. The identification of these distinct cults is primary to establishing and understanding their relationship. One of the difficult tasks facing us is deriving some measure of the power relationships between the hierarchical levels in Mississippian society. Here I will argue that the relative strength of these cults as illustrated in the rural areas is one such subjective measure. Specifically, the ability of the elite to control the fertility symbolism and rituals at rural centers is a direct measure of their control over the rural population, and that the expropriation of the fertility cult by the elite was most marked in Stirling times.

It is useful, then, to examine the developmental history of this fertility cult within the context of small rural centers around Cahokia (cf. Emerson 1995). Fertility symbolism by no means originates with the onset of the Mississippi Period in the American Bottom. Kelly (1990a, 129–30) has documented the presence of the cross-in-circle motif in the courtyard, central post and four pits, and four quarters of Emergent Mississippian villages after A.D. 800. Such an association is strengthened by connections to ceremonial structures with multiple hearths facing the square. He suggests a "fire-sun-fertility" symbolic content for these complexes. This association is continued and expanded during the late Emergent Mississippi Period (cf. Kelly 1990a, 1990b) with the identification of circle and cross motifs, busk related renewal ceremonies, and the appearance of the large plazas bordered by elite structures in large villages.

The onset of the Lohmann-phase consolidation sees the first clear demonstration of elite controlled ceremonial construction in the rural countryside (Emerson 1995, chapter 9). This is most apparent at the Range site where the civic and ceremonial node (figure 10.10) includes a large (ca. 58 square meters) multi-walled, single-post, communal gathering structure with interior benches and cooking areas, four rectangular wall-trench structures that appear to be both residential and storage facilities. Across a courtyard (figure 10.11) lie two large rectangular wall-trench structures, one containing many ceremonially killed vessels, and a large rectangular pit with more than thirty ceramic vessels, some ceremonially killed, and items such as a discoidal, shell hoes, beads, a hematite abrader, multiple grinding and abrading tools, bifacial tools, and so forth. Hannenberger, in noting that this was the only Lohmann pit to contain such a mixture of red cedar, tobacco, effigy bowls, ceremonially killed vessels, shell objects, and engraved sherds, suggests an association with fertility and world renewal ceremonies (Hannenberger and Mehrer n.d.).

The correlation of this component with Busk fertility ceremonialism is apparent and demonstrated in the presence of a large ceremonial "world renewal pit" containing ritual artifacts and plants. This Lohmann civic and ceremonial node appears to have served as a special facility where commu-

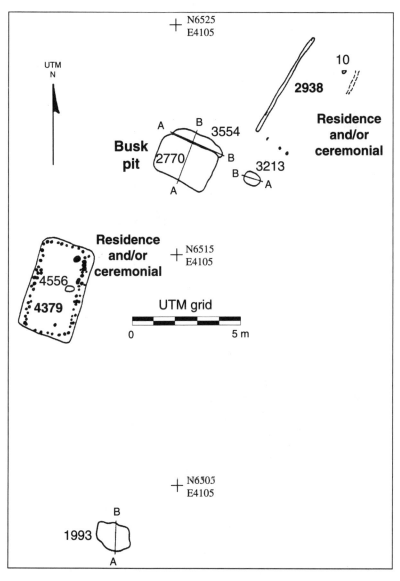

Figure 10.10. Lohmann-Phase Ceremonial Node at the Range Site (after Emerson 1995, figure 6)

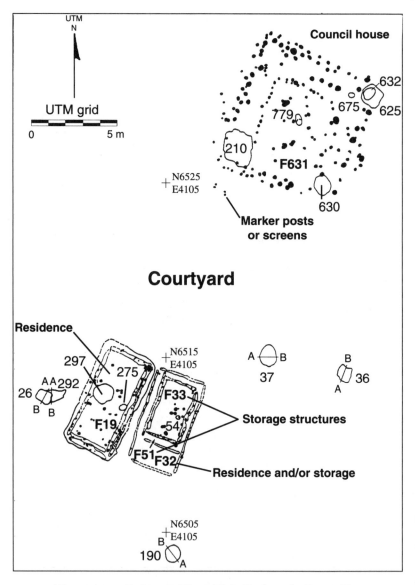

Figure 10.11. Lohmann-Phase Civic Node at the Range Site
(after Emerson 1995, figure 5)

nal activities were carried out, perhaps the residence of individuals trained to conduct such rituals. The community nature of the ceremony is reinforced by the presence of the large communal structure and suggests the participation of many individuals in such rituals. The community nature of the activities may also be adduced from the presence of possible food (?) storage facilities. If the evidence from the ethnographic record is appropriate here, the individuals associated with performing these rituals should be drawn from the local, dispersed-village civic leadership and, consequently, should not be considered religious or political specialists per se. It would indicate that the location served both civic and ritual functions, and was not restricted to cult activities alone. Such an explanation may explain the presence of the massive communal structure, which may have functioned as a council house for the local leaders.

A similar community atmosphere is present in the late Lohmann priest and mortuary ceremonial node at the BBB Motor site (figure 10.12; Emerson 1995, chapter 9). The structures indicate that, while one may possibly have served as a residence for a local priest or shaman, the other, with its internal benches, appears to have had a storage or ceremonial use. While this may mark the appearance of Lohmann-phase mortuary specialists—perhaps an actual priesthood as Knight's model would suggest—mortuary ritual appears still to have had community aspects involving a number of other individuals. The BBB Motor Lohmann mortuary complex indicates the clear presence of low-level elite in the countryside with an ascribed membership. Whether these individuals are a lineage segment of the ruling elite at Cahokia or a "superior" lineage segment of the rural population is not clear. Interestingly, there are few blatant symbolic referents in the mortuary setting, and no connection to the fertility cult per se is demonstrable.

The Lohmann phase is a dramatic break with the previous Emergent Mississippian rural pattern of farmsteads, hamlets, and villages. In such a countryside, power resided in the hands of the kin-based, corporate group. The Lohmann countryside, however, is comprised only of farmsteads and nodal centers that may have been directly organized and created by the Cahokian elite. There is evidence that an elite rural hierarchy tied to the civic and ceremonial centers, and very likely the creation of mortuary ritual specialists housed in small elite mortuary sites like BBB Motor, are the holders of rural power. With the appearance of elite individuals fulfilling specific political, religious, and mortuary ritual roles, and the disappearance of rural kin

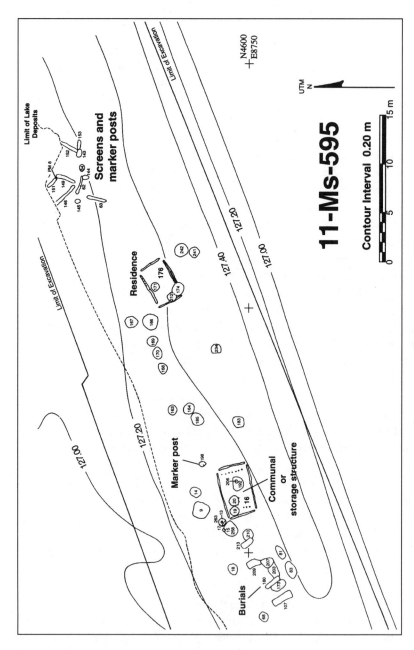

Figure 10.12. Lohmann-Phase Priest/Mortuary Ceremonial Node at the BBB Motor Site (after Emerson 1995, figure 9)

groups, a process begins that will result in the even further migration of power from kin-based groups toward elite patron-client relationships during the Stirling phase (cf. Pauketat 1991, 1994a, chapter 2).

As in most discussions of cultural change in the American Bottom, a dramatic shift can be seen in rural ceremonial complexes with the beginning of the Stirling phase. At least three specialized nodal complexes can be distinguished during this period—a temple and mortuary ceremonial node, civic nodes, and Busk ceremonial node (Emerson 1995, chapter 9). At least some evidence suggests that there may have been a chronological shift in the use and emphasis of these rural centers.

The most common and best known Stirling-phase rural centers are the classic civic nodes. These centers typically include residential, storage, and other specialized buildings in association with purification sweat houses. I believe that these Stirling-phase sites represent local civic nodes from which political control was exerted over the surrounding households. Typically, such nodes are centrally and accessibly located within a dispersed village and contain both residences and specialized storage or cooking facilities. While the presence of such facilities bespeaks either the existence of storage or "feasting," activities that exceed that of the local inhabitants, they are not on the community scale such as recognized at the Range Lohmann–phase complex. In fact, no community-scale "architecture" exists at these sites. There is little evidence of cult activity such as noted at either the earlier Range Lohmann civic-ceremonial node or the later BBB Motor or Sponemann ceremonial nodes. While it is clear that their inhabitants had access to the standard magicoritual materials and vessels, missing is any evidence of Busk ceremonialism such as "renewal dumps" or the critical red cedar wood.

I find a similar situation existing regarding the isolated temple and mortuary ceremonial node at the BBB Motor site (figure 10.13), that is, a specialized rather than communally oriented function. The two structures are specialized rather than generalized, with one serving as a facility for the sacred fire and the other as a temple. While I suggested it was possible that mortuary specialists were developing during the Lohmann phase, I believe that the Stirling component at BBB Motor indicates the existence of a full-time, organized mortuary priesthood, probably in residence at the temple. The developing complexity of the ritual paraphernalia, hallucinogenic medicines, mortuary ceremonialism (as evidenced by the grave house and corpse ma-

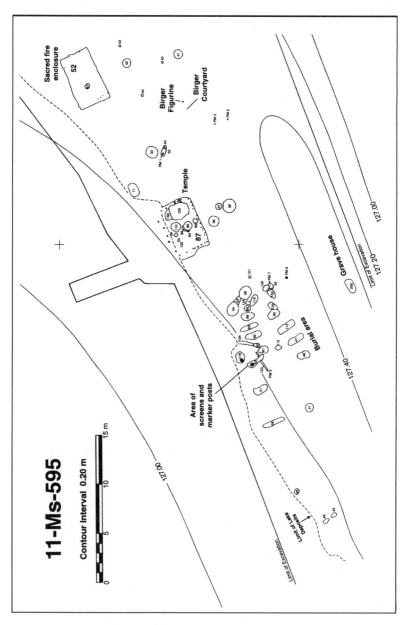

Figure 10.13. Stirling-Phase Temple/Mortuary Ceremonial Node at the BBB Motor Site (after Emerson 1995, figure 14)

224

nipulations), and the elaborate organizational pattern of the site indicate such activities were in the hands of trained specialists. The isolated site location, size, and layout also indicates that these ceremonies were not communally oriented, or at least not for public participation. An additional argument for the presence of a specialized priesthood at this time is the recovery of shaman figurines and depictions from the graves of individuals who may have been priests (Emerson n.d.b.).

The site evidence indicates that there has been a fusion of fertility and mortuary cult symbolism from the previous Lohmann phase. Religious fertility paraphernalia was totally absent from the earlier adjacent "ancestral" Lohmann mortuary complex, yet now it is an integral part of the Stirling-phase temple and mortuary complex. The mortuary complex also suggests the presence of rural elite with an ascribed membership. Whether these individuals are a lineage segment of the ruling elite at Cahokia or a "superior" lineage segment of the rural population is not clear.

The development of fertility cult ritual and symbolism reached its climax in the rural areas with the late–Stirling Sponemann ceremonial node (figure 10.14).In this case we have a large fertility cult complex complete with multiple specialized buildings, including a temple structure, storage buildings, ritual activity buildings, sacred fire enclosure, "world renewal dumps," benches, isolated wall trenches, and, perhaps, a large accompanying set of high-status residences. Here we find a rich accompanying assemblage of ritual plants, vessels, cult figurines, exotic artifacts, and so forth. It is similar to the BBB Motor site temple area but with a complete absence of mortuary facilities. I think there can be little doubt that Sponemann was staffed by religious specialists who were part of a permanent priesthood. However, similar to BBB Motor's ritual zone, I do not see any evidence for the encouragement of large-scale public participation. The organization, location, and layout suggest attempts to limit access rather than facilitate group access.

What does this imply for rural Mississippian political and cult organization during the Stirling phase? It strongly argues for a breakup of the Lohmann pattern that was marked by a division between a civic or cult leader operating from a communal or cult base and an emerging mortuary priesthood. The Stirling civic nodal sites, with a virtual absence of cult paraphernalia or symbolism, indicate the emergence of local political leadership with a political rather than cult basis. On the other hand, at this time a highly organized and specialized mortuary and cult priesthood appeared at sites such as BBB

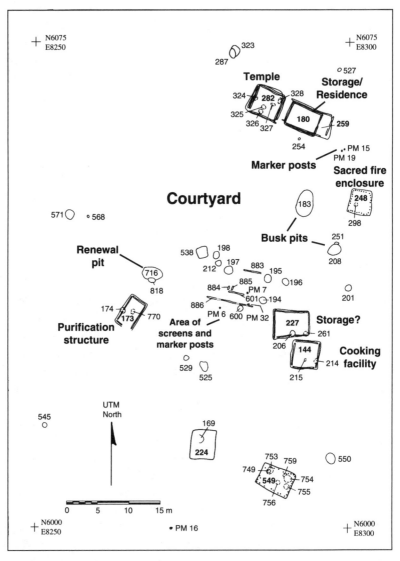

Figure 10.14. Stirling-Phase "Busk" Ceremonial Node at the Sponemann Site (after Emerson 1995, figure 19)

Motor and Sponemann. Moreover, such sites do not seem to have been communally oriented as one might predict in the case of fertility cults but instead were restricted in accessibility. This suggests that ritual access may have been limited to the rural elite—certainly a seemingly inappropriate role for cults that characteristically act to integrate a dispersed community. However, it is in keeping with the suggestion that many of the Stirling-phase symbols (e.g., Ramey-Incised) served as much to naturalize the dominance of the elite as to integrate the social classes (see Emerson 1989; Pauketat and Emerson 1991). I suggest that this phenomenon is the result of the elite expropriation of the fertility cult as part of their centralization of power and their increased consolidation of the rural population (Emerson 1995).

Initiation of the Moorehead and Sand Prairie phases resulted in significant changes in ritual and religious activity in the countryside. No demonstrable organized cult activities are recognizable in the excavated Moorehead rural sites. The only communal structure is the "men's house" from Julien, and, while it contained magicoritual materials and artifacts, there is no indication it served as a cult facility. Kelly (1984) has suggested that Wells Incised plates now played an important role in American Bottom ritual. If they did, their use represents a shift in Cahokian symbolic referents since these plates carry unambiguous sun symbols. While such sun symbolism is not new at Cahokia, its dominance would certainly indicate a reemphasis in ritual direction.

By early Sand Prairie times, the total emphasis of cult activity is focused on mortuary practices as demonstrated in the dispersed villages' communal, bounded cemeteries such as at Florence Street (Emerson, Milner, and Jackson 1983) or East St. Louis Stone Quarry (Milner 1983a). Nonmortuary organized cult symbolism was absent at this time. The disappearance of cults may simply reflect the total breakdown of all large-scale organized social and political functions, which appears to represent the end of hierarchical Mississippian society within the area.

Conclusions

In this chapter I have recognized a structured Cahokian cosmos as a four-sided place of oppositions depicted in this world in the material images they created. This quadripartite world is reflected in their greatest icon, the platform mound; in the great mound and plaza designs; in organization of their smallest ritual centers; in the central post and pits complex; in the cosmic wood circles; and even in the ceramic designs of their ritual pottery. It was a cosmology that also revolved about a set of dualisms—of oppositions. Their world revolved about the Upper and Lower Worlds as reflected, for example, in their stone fertility figurines and the elaborate cosmological iconography of their art.

This research has also amply demonstrated the presence of a recognizable Middle Mississippian agricultural fertility cult by as early as A.D. 900 and its emergence as a significant force in Cahokia during the eleventh and twelfth centuries. Initial analysis of the BBB Motor stone figurines provided extensive iconographic evidence for the presence of a Cahokian "Earth Mother" cult (Emerson 1982, 1984, 1989; Prentice 1986). This has been supported by the additional evidence supplied by the Sponemann-site figurines. I have demonstrated that a number of these figurines, such as the Keller, Sponemann, and Willoughby depictions, are symbolic of a specific Earth Mother variant, the Corn Maiden. The symbolism of these figurines is supported by the interpretation of the extensive Ramey iconography that also speaks of Under World and Upper World symbolism. These lines of evidence are also encouraged by the broader cultural symbolism of earthen mounds, the quadripartite world, and plaza organization.

Furthermore, this fertility symbolism complex was most assuredly part of the cultural milieu of the commoners, that is, a society-wide, shared cult, but with the onset of the Stirling phase this cult was appropriated by the elite as a tool for the domination of the commoners. That expropriation of the fertility cult as part of the dominant ideology by the Cahokian elite during the Lohmann-Stirling transition was a major ideological tool in creating and sanctifying elite sacredness and consolidating elite *power over*. The manipulation of fertility cosmology through a system of "rites of intensification" and associated symbols of authority served to naturalize the inherent social inequality that was a major hallmark of Stirling life.

Vernon James Knight Jr.

11

Some Developmental Parallels between Cahokia and Moundville

The Cahokia phenomenon has attracted the interest of several generations of scholars interested in explaining its complexity. Common to much of this intellectual activity is the notion of Cahokia's uniqueness on the continent of North America. This conception is without doubt justifiable. The Cahokia center was built on a uniquely grand scale, and the timing of its rise as a unified polity also appears to be singularly precocious in relation to counterparts such as Lake George, Etowah, or Moundville. There is a sense, though, in which Cahokia is an awkward beast. Although it is evident to most people that Cahokia is one of several large Mississippian ceremonial centers and belongs in that category, its untidy bulk tugs forcefully at the seams of textbook-variety generalizations by which its lesser counterparts might be accommodated. Add to this the perverse fact that Cahokia is not even geographically in the Southeast, and we have the unsettling result that the story of southeastern prehistory might be more comfortably told if Cahokia did not exist.

Nevertheless, Cahokia does exist, and it would be frivolous to ignore the fact that its appearance was part of a more general southeastern cultural and historical phenomenon. Despite local differences in many particulars, the rise and fall of native southeastern polities over the period of A.D. 1000 to 1500 constitutes a series of linked events. Something may be gained in this essay, therefore, from viewing Cahokia as a southeastern paramount chiefdom, if not a particularly normal one, that is likely to have developed with internal dynamics duplicated elsewhere in the Mississippian world.[1] My counterpoint will be the Moundville chiefdom in Alabama. Moundville is another Mississippian center that has attracted ample scholarly attention, much of it by a reasonably focused group of archaeologists.

Moundville also has been a centerpiece in theoretical discussions on the development of chiefdom-type societies. Moundville is an enlightening comparison with Cahokia, not merely as a chiefdom society, but also because the modern research emphases on the two chiefdoms have differed in ways that are sometimes complementary. On the one hand, we know far more about rural settlement in the American Bottom than we do in the Black Warrior valley. On the other hand, secondary mound centers are more systematically studied in the Black Warrior valley. At the moment, more is known about tribute mobilization of plant and animal foods in the Moundville case, and probably more is known about the contents of the mounds at the main center as well, in comparison to Cahokia; but at Cahokia, with its large blocks of space excavated by a stripping technique, we have comparatively better data on domestic and nonmounded public architecture than at Moundville.

To begin, I will briefly explore the question of what explanatory value might or might not lie in calling Cahokia "southeastern" and "Mississippian." Then, I will proffer what I perceive to be some meaningful parallels in our current understandings of the developmental trajectories of Cahokia and Moundville. Finally, a short space will be reserved for thinking about the significance of the parallels I have drawn. For a general outline of what happened in the Cahokia sequence I mostly depended upon the recent syntheses by Timothy Pauketat (1991, 1992). For the timing of that sequence, I used the calibrated chronology published by Robert Hall (1991, 10).

Is Cahokia Southeastern?

Cahokia is a "southeastern" polity, not because it embraced maize agriculture, nor because it developed a certain level of complexity, but rather because at the moment at which it passed the threshold to embrace a chiefly hierarchy, Cahokia also remodeled itself *culturally* with its eyes fixed firmly to the south.[2] The ingredients were spooned from the same cultural porridge-pot that contributed to the makeup of Moundville and numerous other Mississippian polities, a mix stirred and simmered for more than two millennia in the gulf region. If it were merely a case of the shoplifting of Varney tradition shell-tempered pottery from northeast Arkansas, along with its forms and modes of decoration, that would be easy to dismiss as an unimportant bit of diffusion. Likewise, were it simply a matter of the adoption of wall-trench architecture at Cahokia, or of Coles Creek–style fineware, that too could be regarded as merely a veneer. But the makeover ran deeper than this.

The new elements reached all the way from exclusive features of elite culture to common, domestic forms. The best single illustration of the profundity of this change is the adoption of platform-mound ceremonialism, a southeastern ritual practice raised up on the Gulf Coastal Plain in the first millennium B.C. and nurtured on the Chattahoochee River and in many other places over the centuries that followed. I have contended that the renewal of such mounds was a ritual act whose meanings survived into the historic era (Knight 1989a). On the part of the commoners who contributed their labor to build them, this was, arguably, a religious rite, expressive of cycles of purification. On the part of the nobility, this was also an expression of fealty to the divine wellsprings of hereditary office, dedicated in monumental architecture.

Thus platform mound building, if we understand it correctly, is not just a borrowed trait but the expression of an entire cult complex. It is not just the elite appropriation of an old symbol but the adoption of a full-blown ceremonial complex having specific behavioral associations both for leaders and for followers. The proximate source was, without much doubt, Coles Creek culture in the lower Mississippi valley. The appearance of mound and plaza complexes in the American Bottom is an homage to the power of southern ideas in Cahokia's transformation.[3]

What this adoption *really* means is still anybody's guess, but the pattern was repeated many times, resulting in very similar looking polities across the Southeast. In seeking to account for this phenomenon, we must be careful to avoid even the faintest coloration of our thinking by an acculturation model. Such a model has, in the past, cast the adoption of Mississippian culture at Cahokia in terms that imply that something identifiable as Mississippian culture was already somewhere out there, presumably thriving in an embryonic southeastern heartland and available for mimicry by the locals, should they have the good fortune of not being displaced by the "Mississippian" people themselves. This heartland plus acculturation and radiation formula has been invoked to explain the appearance of Mississippian culture virtually everywhere (B. Smith 1984), but it was a chimera.

At the time Cahokia first adopted these southeastern characteristics, there was no Mississippian culture to emulate, no cultural configuration anywhere on the landscape having that particular conjunction of characteristics. Certainly Coles Creek culture had no such configuration, despite the vitality of its mound ceremonialism, because such things as maize agriculture, an elite prestige-goods economy, and shell-tempered pottery were just as foreign to Coles Creek at that time as to Cahokia. Robert Hall's comments, written-writing in the 1960s, have a prescient ring.

> I will suggest that in the Cahokia area [the local Late Woodland tradition] probably served as a host for culturing certain ideas and practices in circulation after A.D. 800 which came to have an identity as Mississippian. . . . Our image of what Mississippi meant then was determined in part by the inventory of traits that certain cultures happened to have at a point in time when they lifted themselves by their own bootstraps, or were assisted in lifting themselves, to a new level of socio-economic organization. Interaction among these peoples served to erase some of the differences that existed, and migrations extended the area of interaction even further. (1967, 180–81)

Thus Cahokia became a "southeastern" polity more by synergism and convergence than by mimicry.[4] That it did so is all the more intriguing because the people responsible for it were much more likely to have been central Siouan linguistically, and therefore more closely related historically to the Osage or Omaha of the Plains, than some group with better southeastern credentials. Moreover, most of Cahokia's apparent extraregional influence was directed northward, not southward (Emerson and Lewis, eds., 1991; Pauketat and Emerson, chapter 1; Stoltman, ed., 1991).

Moundville and Cahokia: Preliminary Observations

Moundville's developmental sequence overlaps Cahokia's in time (figure 11.1). In fact, recognizably Mississippian cultural configurations appeared in both places at about the same time, estimated at A.D. 1050, following in both places upon a certain gestation during which maize agriculture was intensified and shell-tempered pottery adopted in small amounts. But there is an important difference in the timing of the expansion of regional political control in the two areas. In the American Bottom, according to Pauketat's scenario, expansion occurred at the beginning of the Lohmann phase, ca. A.D.

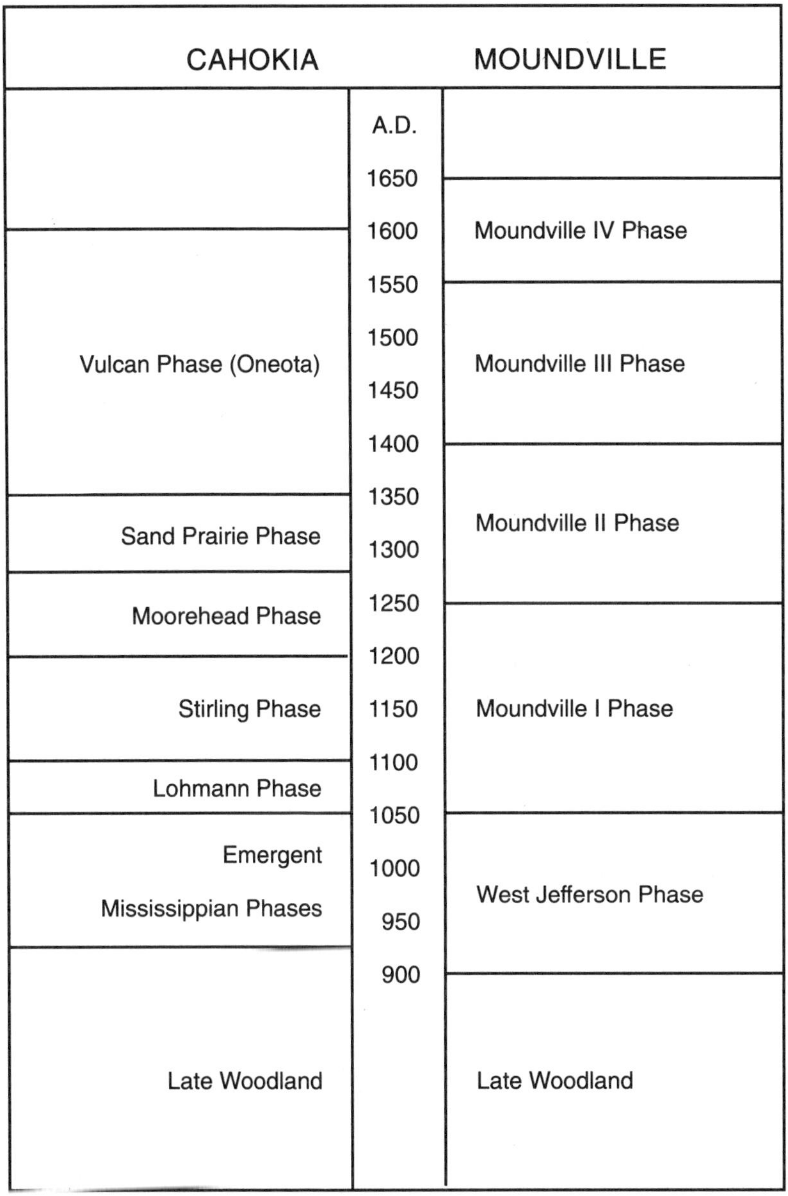

CAHOKIA		MOUNDVILLE
	A.D.	
	1650	
	1600	Moundville IV Phase
	1550	
Vulcan Phase (Oneota)	1500	Moundville III Phase
	1450	
	1400	
	1350	Moundville II Phase
Sand Prairie Phase	1300	
Moorehead Phase	1250	
	1200	
Stirling Phase	1150	Moundville I Phase
	1100	
Lohmann Phase	1050	
Emergent	1000	
Mississippian Phases	950	West Jefferson Phase
	900	
Late Woodland		Late Woodland

Figure II.1. Sequences for Cahokia and Moundville Compared in Calendar Years. Sources: Hall (1991) for Cahokia; Steponaitis (1983) and Peebles (1987a, b) for Moundville.

1050. At Moundville, the same event took place in the middle of the Moundville I phase, no earlier than about A.D. 1150. As Moundville's career as a paramountcy was just beginning, Cahokia was already at its Stirling phase (A.D. 1100–1200) apogee.[5] This forces the question: Was Cahokia's early prominence in any manner a stimulus for events far to the south of it?

Moundville's political trajectory is an independent case, an assertion that naturally affects any comparison with Cahokia. I have already remarked that the rise of all Mississippian polities represents a chain of historically linked events; some clarification, nevertheless, is in order on this point. We must first distinguish between two kinds of historical linkages. We may have societies that are linked merely by their mutual adoption of the conceptual core of Mississippian "superculture," a spread of ideas about hierarchy, ritual, and so forth, by low-level communication networks operating nonsystematically across a broad area. Undoubtedly we also have cases where a more direct interaction is responsible, that is, where the idea of parity with one's neighbors was a strong motivating factor in the adoption of Mississippian forms. A tendency toward a parity of scale in adjacent late Mississippian societies is very evident in the chronicles of sixteenth-century Spaniards who explored the Southeast, and there is reason to suspect that such pressures were commonplace at an earlier time. Thus secondary chiefdom formation and competitive expansion using the idiom of Mississippian culture is a distinct possibility (Anderson 1990a, 195–96).

The historical linkage between Cahokia and Moundville is plainly of the first kind. At Moundville there is scant evidence for any contact at all, much less competitive pressure, from its precocious cousin 680 kilometers to the north. From among Moundville's artifact collections, which number in seven figures, not so much as a single potsherd of Ramey-Incised, nor a single notched triangular point of Burlington chert has so far been identified.[6] A very small number of Mill Creek hoe chips and biface fragments from southern Illinois sources have been noted, but such items are considered "exotic" even at Cahokia, and there is no convincing evidence that Cahokia directly controlled the exchange of Mill Creek chert (Cobb 1989; Pauketat 1992, 41). Conversely, I am not aware of anything found at Cahokia to which a Moundville source is attributed.[7] Moundville and Cahokia probably did participate at times in the same or related networks of generalized exchange involving widely traded exotic commodities, but I am not convinced of any causal evolutionary role in this mutual participation (cf. Peebles 1986, 30; Brown et al. 1990, 256–57; Kelly 1991a).

So, for all practical purposes, the developmental history of Cahokia may be treated as independent from that of Moundville. We may be justified in treating any developmental similarities as the consequence of parallel stimulations to generally similar cultural and natural systems, without the complication of factoring out mutual interactions.

The Sequences Compared

In order to visualize better the congruence of the two sequences, I have prepared an illustration (figure 11.2) in which both sequences have been lifted from their actual calendar positions and artificially aligned, so that the match point is the time at which each region became politically consolidated. By "zeroing" the sequences to this reference point, the comparative tempo of events can be highlighted. The calendrical time scale is replaced by a scale in years, in which positive numbers are shown for years after consolidation, and negative numbers for years predating consolidation. In the margins of this drawing is an outline of the main features and events in each chronology by which they can be compared. I will discuss them briefly in turn.

Intensification of Maize Agriculture

In the Cahokia sequence, evidence of the intensification of maize agriculture comes at the beginning of the Emergent Mississippian stage. It is viewed by John Kelly (1987, 217) as the most significant element marking the onset of that stage. In the Moundville sequence, maize intensification is seen by the late West Jefferson phase, the terminal Woodland phase in the Black Warrior valley (M. Scarry 1986, 409). The time lag between maize intensification and broad-scale political consolidation in the two cases is about the same: about 125 years for Cahokia and 150 years for Moundville.

Emergence of Small, Independent Chiefdoms

In both sequences, the achievement of regional political consolidation appears to be preceded by a brief interval during which the local populace coalesced into some number of independent, small-scale polities. The evidence is clearest in the Moundville region, where rural house clusters at the beginning of the Moundville I phase are probably allied to small single-mound centers such as Site 1Tu50 and Mound X at Moundville (Steponaitis 1992,

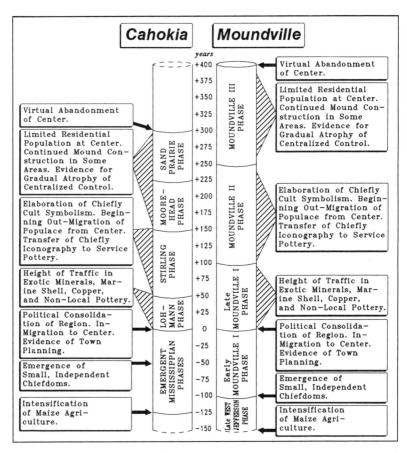

Figure II.2. Comparative Developmental Sequences for Cahokia and Moundville. Aligned on a time scale "zeroed" to the initial political centralization of each region.

10–11). Both the house clusters and the centers are culturally Mississippian by this date in nearly every respect. For the American Bottom region, Pauketat (1991, 63–77) has assembled evidence for a similar coalescence of "ranked" political formations by the late Emergent Mississippian Edelhardt phase, focused on early centers such as the Lunsford-Pulcher site and Cahokia itself. Emerson (1991a, 234) has suggested that by this time there may have been as many as "a half-dozen civic-ceremonial centers supporting simple chiefdoms" in the American Bottom. Unfortunately, the existence of platform mound and plaza construction at this date is not fully verified, though researchers strongly suspect it (cf. Kelly 1990a, 135). In fact, Dalan (1993a, 177–79), Holley (Holley, Dalan, and Smith 1993, 313–16), and their colleagues interpret their data as showing that portions of Cahokia's Monks Mound and adjacent Grand Plaza were already under construction at this time.

In both cases this initial appearance of simple chiefly centers follows close upon the heels of the first evidence for maize intensification by a span of mere decades, about seventy-five years in the Cahokia area and only fifty years in the Moundville area. Perhaps even more striking is the apparent brevity of this period of small-scale polities. No more than a century elapsed in the Black Warrior valley before these small polities were engulfed by the expanding paramountcy centered at Moundville. The corresponding interval in the Cahokia sequence is half that.

Political Consolidation of the Region

According to our current reconstructions, a sweeping political expansion incorporating the region into a single tributary system occurred at Cahokia at the beginning of the Lohmann phase (Pauketat 1993a), and at Moundville by the late Moundville I phase (Scarry and Steponaitis 1992, 2).[8] There is no evidence in either case that the ascendancy was gradual or piecemeal, and there is no better symbol of the power of the newborn paramountcies than the incredibly opulent burial of a Lohmann-phase noble found by Fowler in Cahokia's Mound 72 (Fowler 1991).

Similarities in the two cases are evident in the transformation of the Cahokia and Moundville sites into regional capitals. In both instances, political consolidation was accompanied by large-scale in-migration, resulting in an expanded residential population at the primary center (Lopinot 1993; Pauketat 1991, 224–27; Steponaitis 1993). Centralized "town planning" is clearly in evidence in both cases, and mound and plaza construction at the primary centers was expanded dramatically over the previous period (Collins and Chalfant 1993; Knight 1989c, 1993; Pauketat 1991, 307–9).

Importation of Nonlocal Goods in the Early Paramountcies

In both the Lohmann phase at Cahokia and the late Moundville I phase at Moundville, there is as yet a curious scarcity of evidence of chiefly cult paraphernalia and iconography. There is instead a noticeably similar pattern of the importation of nonlocal wealth of a different sort. The materials in question are not associated with mound architecture but rather most prominently with certain residential areas at the centers, where they signal craft production (Welch 1991a, 134–71).

In both cases such traffic is presaged by low-level exchange of various nonlocal commodities in preceding years, but the volume is now significantly expanded (Pauketat 1991, 309–10, 1992, 39; Steponaitis 1991, 205–6; Welch 1991b). Imported minerals such as exotic chert, mica, galena, copper, pigments, and fine-grained rocks suitable for axe making are conspicuous components of the trade. Marine shell is also important. Imported pottery vessels appear with regularity. In fact, it is one of the more intriguing parallels between our two cases that grog-tempered fineware vessels bearing Caddoan and lower Mississippi valley engraved motifs were especially prized at both Cahokia and Moundville, to the point that local potters in both places seem to have been moved to produce some rather good forgeries (Pauketat 1991, 121, 285–86; Welch 1989, 10–11).[9]

This parallel expansion of nonlocal imports associated with craft production—particularly minerals—in the early history of the two paramountcies seems especially significant since the two instances are emphatically not synchronous. It would be difficult, in light of this fact, to attribute the commonality to any mutual historical stimulus, such as the emergence and proliferation of new broad-scale exchange networks.

Divine Chiefships and Associated Events

Pauketat characterizes Stirling-phase Cahokia as a period that saw the maturation of a "sacral chiefship," marked by a distancing of the hereditary nobility from the affairs of commoners (1991, 323). Despite a paucity of modern excavations of elite Stirling-phase mortuary contexts (Pauketat 1991, 91), it seems clear that the view from Monks Mound at this time was indeed a majestic one. This is the phase to which the Post-Circle Monuments or woodhenges at Cahokia may be assigned. To this phase also belong the iconographically splendid stone figurines from ceremonial contexts at the BBB Motor site (Emerson and Jackson 1984, 254–61) and the Sponemann site (Fortier 1992).

The corresponding interval in Moundville's development was the

Moundville II phase. Various elite mortuaries dating to this phase, on mound summits arranged around the plaza, have yielded the bulk of the paraphernalia associated with what I have characterized as the warfare-cosmogony cult (Knight 1986, 680) at Moundville, a cult probably extolling supernatural powers claimed by the paramount and his kin. In particular, the mortuaries found by Clarence Moore in the final stages of Mounds C and D, with their tombs containing the burials assigned by Peebles to the highest-ranking segment of his "superordinate dimension" (i.e., nobility) at the site, belong to the Moundville II phase (Steponaitis 1983, 157). Here, probably, are the semidivine paramounts themselves, like the personage in Mound C that H. Newell Wardle colorfully described in the following passage.

> Of his costume, not a trace is left, yet there is enough of green and fragile ornament to give some idea of the splendor of his appearance when all this copperwork flashed red-gold in the southern sun. At the back of his head he wore a long and slender strip of copper, thrust in the hair like the honors-feather of a modern chief. At the left a curious hook-shaped hair-ornament of copper was secured by a pin of bison-horn. Around his neck hung a double string of pierced pearls from which depended three gorgets of sheet copper. The uppermost, circular in form, seems to have framed, so to speak, an exquisite pendant of carved amethyst. This unique gem of aboriginal art is a human head. . . . Below the annular gorget lay a second disk, the centre of which was occupied by an eight-pointed star. Lower on his chest had hung a pendant of peculiar form, rounded above, pointed below, showing, by excisions in the sheet copper, the swastika and the triangle. Wrists and ankles had been encircled by strings of round wooden beads, each covered with the precious copper. Across the knees lay the long and slender [copper] head of the ceremonial battle-axe once borne by the great chief of Mound C. Near by was found a lump of mineral pitch, most probably paint for some great ceremony of the land of shades. (Wardle 1906, 203)[10]

At both Cahokia and Moundville, mound building continued at a brisk pace, undoubtedly drawing in the tributary labor available from the entire chiefdom. But with a seeming irony, these corresponding phases, just as they show the maturation of the paramountcy, also bear clear evidence for a *decentralization* in one important regard. There now began an out-migration of people formerly living at the main centers. At Moundville, this is shown by a fourfold decrease in the overall amount of domestic refuse present. Former residential districts were converted into cemeteries, presumably used by nonresidents (Scarry 1993a, 240; Steponaitis 1993). At Cahokia, large tracts of former residential use in the central site area were converted into public plazas with special-purpose architecture. The few domiciles that remain are large in size and tend to be arranged with reference to nearby mounds (J. Collins 1990, 1993, 4; O'Brien 1993, 16–18; Pauketat 1991, 248, 1992, 36–37). These structures, which presumably housed various functionaries associated with the nobility, show a notable *decline* in the occurrence of exotic goods relative to the preceding phases.

Accompanying this centrifugal tendency in both the Cahokia and Moundville cases is the advent of a fascinating phenomenon. For the first time, elite iconography was transferred to the ordinary medium of service pottery and diffused outward, in what I have called, for Moundville, a "communalization" of the cult symbolism (Knight 1986, 682–83). At Cahokia this representational art occurs on the pottery type Ramey Incised, which appears in the Stirling phase. The corresponding item at Moundville is the type Moundville Engraved, *variety Hemphill*, which is first commonly produced late in the Moundville II phase. In both cases the pottery is probably made only at the regional center as a highly standardized product, but it ends up in patently non-elite contexts extending to the most remote farmsteads of the chiefdom (and beyond) (Mistovich 1986, 75–77; Pauketat and Emerson 1991; Welch 1991a, 138–49). Pauketat and Emerson (1991) think that the production and distribution of Ramey-Incised pottery in the American Bottom is a strategy for elite-commoner communication, perhaps a counter to the increasing practical alienation of the commoners from their leaders. A similar argument could be made for the production and distribution of engraved representational art on service pottery at Moundville. At any rate the abstruse symbolism of the elite now became, to some degree, the abstruse symbolism of everybody, in a move plainly orchestrated from the centers.

Decline

Both chiefdoms now entered into a protracted era of decline. While still retaining certain administrative and ceremonial functions at the main centers, there is increasing evidence of local autonomy at satellite communities. Although the process began somewhat earlier in the developmental trajectory of Cahokia than at Moundville, the duration of this "postclassic" era is essentially the same: 150 years. At Cahokia it is seen in the Moorehead and Sand Prairie phases, at Moundville in the Moundville III phase.

The residential population of both centers remained at a low level, probably consisting mostly of nobles and their retainers (Pauketat 1991, 325; Steponaitis 1993, 8). In the American Bottom, the rural population also was dispersed and reduced overall, perhaps accompanied by out-migration to the adjacent uplands in the Sand Prairie phase (Emerson 1991a, 230; Milner 1986, 232–34). At the primary centers mound building continued erratically at various locations, while other mounds were abandoned (Dalan 1993a, 193; Hall 1991, 14; Knight 1992), probably reflecting the variable fortunes of the kin groups associated with them. The elite mortuaries on mounds at Moundville were virtually, if not entirely, abandoned. However, at least for the Moundville chiefdom, there is evidence that provisioning of the local nobility continued without abatement (Welch 1991a, 132–33), while the primary center itself assumed the character of a necropolis. For both chiefdoms, traffic in nonlocal goods continued at a level much lower than previously (Pauketat 1992, 39; Peebles 1987a, 32–33; Steponaitis 1991, 209–12). The production of service pottery bearing chiefly iconography carried over into the Moorehead phase at Cahokia and into the Moundville III phase at Moundville, dropping out somewhat later. The overall picture is one of the slow atrophy of centralized authority, while, in the face of that, maintaining a status quo in the ceremonial importance of the primary centers that was remarkably long-lived.

Virtual Abandonment of the Primary Center

The evidence for centralized authority seems to vanish rather abruptly in each of the two cases with the virtual abandonment of both primary centers. However, in both cases this apparent collapse may be less an event than the culmination of a long process, where chiefly authority finally erodes below the point of archaeological visibility. No evidence at present points to anything catastrophic, such as conquests, conflagrations, or disease epidemics. Looking at the time elapsed from initial political consolidation to abandonment, Moundville lasted about a century longer than Cahokia. Cahokia itself endured as a polity for about three hundred years.

Developmental Differences between the Two Systems

I do not wish to close this discussion by leaving the impression that Moundville's and Cahokia's developments were parallel in *every* important respect. Some differences need to be stressed as in any meaningful comparative discussion. I will make brief mention of two such dissimilarities.

Perhaps the most important difference is the issue of scale. By all available measures, the Cahokia system was much larger than Moundville's. Lacking any concrete measures, we can say that the background demography of the two systems contrast: While the American Bottom was densely populated during the Emergent Mississippian stage, the corresponding terminal Woodland population of the Black Warrior valley was quite modest, even relative to neighboring river valleys. The scale of both Mississippian systems at their height has been debated and downsized in recent years (Milner 1990, 1993; Steponaitis 1993). But even a "lesser Cahokia," to use George Milner's term, remains on a scale that dwarfs Moundville.[11] The demographic difference quite possibly lies behind the somewhat speedier tempo of development for Cahokia, seen graphically in figure 11.2.

Second, the role of warfare in the history of the two systems may have been quite different. Moundville's palisade, built to defend the entire occupied area of the site, was first erected at a time corresponding to the initial political consolidation of the region, that is, during the late Moundville I phase (Scarry 1993, 264–65). It was rebuilt several times but was abandoned during the Moundville II phase when the paramountcy was at its height. In contrast, the inner palisade at Cahokia was built and maintained during the twelfth century A.D. to defend only the site's inner precinct, and at a time when the site's residential population was already in decline (Iseminger et al. 1990).[12]

Conclusion

Having compared the pattern of development in two large, native, pre-state polities in eastern North America, Cahokia and Moundville, I have demonstrated that the two sequences bear an overall resemblance to each other and that there are many specific correspondences at similar points within both sequences. Some of these resemblances are comparatively unremarkable, whereas others are relatively unanticipated and therefore pose intriguing questions to be answered in our ongoing attempts to build satisfying theoretical accounts.

Of general comparative interest is the brevity of the "warm-up time" between initial intensification of maize agriculture and the relatively sudden political consolidation of the region under a hereditary regime. Only 125 to 150 years separates egalitarian, village-level societies from their maize-growing offspring who lived as tributaries to quite large regionally centralized polities. This accelerated timing will fly against any gradualist model of the development of complexity.

A related curiosity is the extraordinarily short time during which these regions experienced organization under simple or petty chiefdoms. While in many other areas of the Mississippian world this emergent mode of hierarchical organization—several local communities bound under the chiefly rule of a small center—was the stable pattern, here it is a phase reduced to near archaeological invisibility, an eye-blink of no more than a few generations. It is as if the *initial* submission to hereditary leadership, plus the adoption of Mississippian cultural forms, was all that was needed in these regions to set the table for the first convenient opening to expand into a paramountcy. One may wonder if there is not a demographic threshold at work here, below which a paramountcy is impossible to maintain, and above which it is inevitable.

The respective roles of nonlocal craft goods on the one hand, and iconography on the other, have remarkably parallel histories in the two chiefdoms. Both pass through a stage, just after regional political consolidation, during which the acquisition of exotic materials and craft manufactures was important at a broad scale, not just among the nobility. Although the paramountcies were fully functional at this stage, there is as yet very little evidence for the display of an exclusive iconography touting the supernatural abilities of the leadership. A second stage is then apparent during which we see the proliferation of chiefly symbolism, but during which the traffic in exotic goods not directly related to this symbolism is curtailed. From here on we see a communalization of elite symbols. The iconography of chiefly supernatural power is conspicuously transferred to more ordinary media, such as service pottery manufactured at the primary centers and delivered outward to common households. The integrative functions of the latter seem, in fact, to replace the role played at the beginning by a prestige-goods economy.

Both primary centers lived a double life. They began their careers as full-blown towns, packed with residents orchestrated spatially to an overall plan.

These centers were demographic magnets, attracting people from a broad area. Then, at the apparent height of centralized authority, the residential functions of these centers were abruptly subordinated to their public and ceremonial functions. As the public architecture reached its most grandiose dimensions, people moved away. Thereafter, each center probably had a residential component limited to the nobility and their retainers. Central planning broke down, and the architectural emphasis became oriented to specific mounds.

These polities lasted three hundred to four hundred years, nearly half of which time, in each case, was in an apparently devolved and decentralized condition following an earlier spurt of aristocratic exorbitance and focus on the paramountcy. The later stage is characterized by erratic new construction of public architecture, generally low levels of traffic in foreign luxuries, and, perhaps surprisingly, the total absence of military defense. Of special interest is the length of time each polity was able to survive in this manner before finally withering away. This merely raises unanswerable questions, pointing to the need for more data on how the aristocracy was functioning during this interval.

The fact of several centuries of survival brings up a final observation, which may help to contextualize this comparison. Among Mississippian systems, longevity is apparently proportional to size on the one hand, and to the degree of sustained contact with a higher-order system on the other. David Hally's data from the Georgia area, dealing mainly with simple Mississippian chiefdoms rather than regional paramountcies, show that they seldom lasted for more than a century. These small chiefdoms rose and fell with steady regularity for several hundred years across a volatile political landscape (Hally 1992; cf. Anderson 1990b). But there are other small Mississippian systems with well-documented histories (not treated by Hally) that seem to defy this pattern and to last much longer. Good examples are found at the Lubbub Creek mound center on the Tombigbee River (Blitz 1993) and the Cemochechobee center on the Chattahoochee River (F. T. Schnell, Knight, and G. S. Schnell 1981). The only thing that appears to set these systems apart is their proximity to Moundville and Roods Landing respectively, both large and long-lived paramount chiefdoms.[13]

An adequate account of the development of paramountcies in this part of the world must also reconcile itself to another independent source of data. These are the chronicles of the Spanish interior expeditions of the sixteenth century. They describe a number of regional-scale tributary chiefdoms from present-day Georgia to Arkansas, with names such as Ichisi, Cofitachequi, Coosa, and Pacaha. And despite the many shortcomings of these accounts, they leave no doubt that these systems were true paramountcies, politically manipulating areas as large, or even larger, than the areas believed to have been dominated by Cahokia and Moundville. Moreover, the archaeological units corresponding to these political systems are known with a fair amount of certainty, and therefore would seem to be a good basis for model building.[14]

The problem is this: These systems show few or no *archaeological* traces of having been paramountcies at all. No really large civic-ceremonial centers, no obvious class distinctions among burials, and no evidence of regional economic integration are apparent. The best-documented case is that of the paramount chiefdom of Coosa, which presents itself to us archaeologically as a *series of simple chiefdoms* arranged like a string of beads down the ridge and valley province of the southern Appalachians (Hally, Smith, and Langford 1990). The individual village clusters making up the paramount chiefdom maintained their own pottery traditions and showed few signs of any contribution to or connection with the three-mound center at Carters Quarters, Georgia. In sum, these late Mississippian paramount chiefdoms of the sixteenth-century Southeast are archaeologically invisible (cf. Hally, Smith, and Langford 1990, 132–34).

In view of our notions about Cahokia and Moundville and their development, this is a very important discrepancy, one which we cannot hope to resolve fully in this chapter. Two suggestions, however, do seem worth making. The first is, that it is without doubt critical to our understanding of the situation to bear in mind that the sixteenth-century paramountcies were all somewhere in their first century of development. Some were rather clearly on the rise. In time, without European interference, it is entirely conceivable that the paramount chiefdom of Pacaha in the Mississippi valley, given its rich and populous environment, could have achieved the scale and stability of a Moundville or even a Cahokia. Others, for any number of potential reasons, may have collapsed prematurely, in which case we would scarcely know of their existence from the archaeological evidence alone (see Anderson 1990a, 26–83).

The lesson to be learned from this may be as follows. In a political landscape of simple chiefdoms, opportunities for the consolidation of paramountcies under the influence of a charismatic chief must have arisen repeatedly throughout the Mississippian Southeast. The pushes and pulls would have been several: preadaptation of local systems through development of rank hierarchies, the fortunes of warfare, peer-polity competition, the desire to participate in the magnificence of a local god-chief, and the opening up of new channels for traffic in culturally perceived valuables. Perhaps the few prehistoric paramountcies we know about are the ones that survived long enough to develop stable archaeological signatures of the kind we have been discussing. They were not, or at least were no longer, *opportunistic* paramountcies, like those sixteenth-century forms that seem to have been held together largely by political strategems and intimidation. Our prehistoric exemplars had become, by contrast, *structural* paramountcies, with culturally encoded hierarchical properties whose inertia alone could carry them forward.[15]

There is a second point to be made in light of the sixteenth-century historical record. The cultural baggage carried by these late Mississippian societies, diffused over several centuries, was different from the milieu out of which Cahokia and Moundville arose. And in the urge to ferret out developmental regularities that might have broader evolutionary significance, it cannot be forgotten that specific preexisting cultural configurations always have determinative roles in how the game is played out. Here is a possible case in point. I have said that Cahokia and Moundville independently reached a point at which a chiefly iconographic system became communalized and transferred to media suitable for consumption as common wealth items. Now, by the fifteenth-century A.D., for reasons probably having to do with interregional exchange, this phenomenon became general across the Southeast, in simple and complex polities alike. In some instances, particularly in the central Mississippi valley and northern Gulf Coast, engraved iconography on pottery comparable to Moundville's became common. In most other areas, however, the iconographic message was carried by engraved marine-shell gorgets, once an exclusive medium but now very frequently found in the graves of ordinary people. I suggest that this is a case of iconographic communalization parallel to that seen on pottery.

Would-be paramounts in the sixteenth century could no longer claim *that* iconography, with its references to the supernatural power of snake monsters, thunder spirits, cosmic centers, and so forth, as an instrument of exclusion. Presumably these images were still perceived as sources of great power, but common ones, not very suitable for gods-on-earth. Earlier generations of Mississippian paramounts would take folkloric references and make them their own. They would mold and transform them by the power of the imagery of exclusion: mystical, shamanic, and above all, owned (Knight 1989b). New generations of paramounts, if they insisted on their divinity and the divine right of their heirs to govern forever, would have to achieve the same symbolic exclusion. There is no evidence that they ever did achieve it.

David G. Anderson

12

The Role of Cahokia in the Evolution of Southeastern Mississippian Society

During the half millennium or so before European contact, agricultural chiefdoms of varying levels of complexity were present across much of the southeastern United States, an area that has been variously defined but in most accounts is taken to mean the states south of the Ohio River and from just west of the Mississippi valley eastward to the Atlantic Ocean (B. Smith 1986, 1–2).[1] By almost any definition, the American Bottom lies at or just beyond the margins of the Southeast. In spite of this, the events that transpired in this area during the interval from roughly A.D. 900 to 1300 influenced developments in societies across the Southeast at this time and afterward by playing a major role in the emergence, character, spread, and evolution of Mississippian culture.[2] Such a view, while appreciably at odds with prevailing interpretations about the development of Mississippian culture, provides a better fit with available evidence than do positions that minimize the role of the American Bottom area.

During its heyday from about A.D. 1050 to 1200, during the Lohmann and Stirling phases, Cahokia appears to have been the center of a paramount chiefdom dominating the American Bottom, with other simple and complex chiefdoms under its direct or indirect control. In this regard it is like many other such societies that were present in the Southeast during the Mississippian era (Milner 1990). Most of the Mississippian towns and centers that have been found elsewhere in the Southeast could fit comfortably in the area circumscribed by Monk's Mound, just one of more than one hundred mounds making up the core of Cahokia; however, some investigators have found it difficult to accept that Monk's Mound and Cahokia were organizationally similar societies (e.g., compare the views of Milner 1990, 1991, and Pauketat 1994a, and the various authors in this volume, who hold that Cahokia was a paramount chiefdom, with those of Fowler 1974 or O'Brien 1989, who see it as a proto-state or state). Analyses of mortuary, settlement, and artifactual data (e.g., as summarized in Milner 1990 and Pauketat 1994a), however, clearly indicate that it is the scale of Cahokia that is different, not the basic political structure, which conforms to that of chiefdom society, in which leadership positions were kin-based and hereditary, with ruling elites drawn from ranked clans and lineages (Knight 1990). Just as chiefdoms in other parts of the world, such as in Polynesia and Africa, ranged markedly in size and organizational complexity, so, too, did they within the Mississippian world, which had its own equivalents of the simple and complex chiefdoms represented ethnographically by societies like Tikopia and Hawaii, or the Plateau Tonga and the Swazi (e.g., Colson and Gluckman 1951; Goldman 1970; Sahlins 1958). The Lohmann-phase population estimates for Cahokia provided by Pauketat and Lopinot in this volume, at ten thousand to fifteen thousand, fall within the range expected of chiefdoms, albeit toward the upper end of the scale (Feinman and Neitzel 1984).

The Nature and Evolution of the Cahokia Chiefdom

The emergence and evolution of chiefdom political organization in the American Bottom followed a course similar to that of many other Mississippian societies, as Knight has persuasively argued in chapter 11 (see also Holley n.d.; Milner 1990); that is, the chiefdom centered at Cahokia went through a process of emergence, expansion, and then collapse such as that observed in chiefdoms across the Southeast and indeed worldwide, a process that at the regional scale can be described as cycling (Anderson 1990a, 1994a, 1–11; Earle 1991a, 13–14). It is at a regional scale of analysis, in fact, that we can best appreciate the size, complexity, and impact of Cahokia. At the same time, as Stoltman (1991, 352) has rightly cautioned, we must be careful to avoid adopting a strict minimalist stance, downplaying Cahokia and equating it to merely one Mississippian chiefdom among many, since its large size, early emergence, and obvious impact on surrounding societies, particularly those to the north and northwest, clearly set it apart.

Although the amount of construction undertaken in the immediate Cahokia area is unprecedented in the Mississippian world, the actual scale or geographic extent of the polity, or at least its central core, does not appear very atypical. The spatial extent and duration of Mississippian polities have been the subject of appreciable work in recent years, and it appears that few centers were occupied continuously for more than a century or so, or exercised direct control over areas much more than 40 kilometers in extent (Hally 1992, 1993). Mississippian chiefdoms, in fact, appear to have been organizationally incapable of exerting direct control over societies much more than 20 or 30 kilometers away, although this certainly did not preclude the emergence of patterns of less direct control—the acknowledgment of power relationships characteristic of complex or paramount chiefdoms—encompassing much larger areas. The existence of a critical distance or zone of direct control equivalent to one or, at the most, two days round-trip travel time has been widely observed in early complex societies (Johnson 1982; Renfrew 1975). Interestingly, such an area around Cahokia closely corresponds to the northern part of the American Bottom, encompassing centers from Lunsford-Pulcher in the south to Grassy Lake in the north, and including the Mitchell, East St. Louis, and St. Louis centers. This was likely the core area of the Cahokia polity, something that is, in fact, widely accepted in the literature (e.g., Milner 1990; R. Hall 1991; Pauketat 1994a).

The number of large centers occurring in close proximity to one another in the northern American Bottom—of which the Cahokia, East St. Louis, and St. Louis mound groups are merely the largest, however—immediately raises questions about their relationship to one another. Although the occupational histories of these sites are not fully worked out (and for some of them this may no longer be possible), it is likely that many were contemporaneous. If so, the question is whether each distinctive center or group of mounds was a subsidiary chiefdom in a complex or paramount chiefdom organizational structure. Such an arrangement does not seem at all probable, since the northern American Bottom appears to be much too small and circumscribed an area to support several independent or distinct political entities. Mounds occur almost continuously from St. Louis to Cahokia with few breaks, suggesting instead the presence of a number of wealthy, outlying communities or neighborhoods whose elites, while overseeing events in their immediate areas, were closely related and played primary roles in Cahokian society and ceremony. Although the Mississippi itself would have been an appreciable barrier to east-west interaction, the presence of the St. Louis and East St. Louis centers, instead of indicating the existence of separate or even rival polities, may instead have been part of a greater Cahokia, what Pauketat has called the "Central Political-Administrative Complex" (1994a, 5, 81). I suggest that a greater Cahokia is literally what is represented by these sites or groupings of mounds.

That is, I assume that the Cahokia, East St. Louis, and St. Louis mound complexes, which are all within 8 kilometers of one another, were linked together. The reason for this, quite simply, would be to demarcate and control access to the sacred landscape that was the core of Cahokia proper with its numerous mounds, woodhenges, and plazas, as well as to serve the more secular role of controlling traffic along the Mississippi waterway. While the mound groups along the river would have been points of entry for religious travelers, having population centers with canoes on opposing banks would also have made it all but impossible for anyone to pass through the area without coming under challenge.[3] That Mississippian populations could have effectively controlled movement along the river can be seen from the accounts of the de Soto expedition, which was harassed and nearly overwhelmed by fleets of war canoes in their final retreat down the Mississippi River in 1543. The Spanish, in fact, lost more men in this battle than in any other they fought on land, including at Mauvila (Vega in Shelby 1993, 504–18; Lafferty 1994, 201). Of course, the positioning of settlements and centers in the Central Political-Administrative Complex, while having the potential to control trade through the use of force, may have achieved the same effect more benignly, by dramatically highlighting the location and prominence of Cahokia (see also R. Hall 1991, 21). There is some suggestion, in fact, that direct exchange during the early years of Cahokia's ascendancy may have been largely one way, toward the center, which may have proven an irresistible attraction for peoples over large areas (Fowler 1991, 25; J. Kelly 1991a, 72). Whatever the organization of the central core, the outlying centers in the northern American Bottom, like Mitchell and Lunsford-Pulcher, were likely more typical subsidiary chiefly centers, whose elites, while subordinate to those in the central precincts, still controlled activities in their individual areas.

The duration of Cahokia as a political center also does not appear atypical in the Mississippian world or among chiefdom societies in general. The heyday of the site, at least as the apex of a complex and powerful chiefdom, was during the Lohmann and Stirling phases, a span of approximately 150 years. Although the site continued to be occupied for more than another century during the subsequent Moorehead and Sand Prairie phases, monumental construction soon ceased and population gradually but steadily declined, as did evidence for long-distance exchange and interaction. The complex or paramount chiefdom present earlier appears to have collapsed during the Moorehead phase and, by the end of this interval during the late Sand Prairie phase, it is debatable whether even a simple chiefdom was present in the area. Hally (1992), in an examination of the occupational histories of several dozen Mississippian centers in the South Appalachian area, has shown that continuous occupation at chiefly centers—interpreted by the presence of a series of successive, uninterrupted stage construction episodes in the center's platform mounds, or by only minor changes in its ceramic assemblages—rarely exceeded 100 to 150 years, or more than four to six mound stages, and many were occupied for much shorter intervals (see also D. Anderson 1994a, 127–28). Assuming each stage represented the death or replacement of one elite by another, and that this occurred about once a generation, or every 20 to 30 years or so, this evidence (which has been duplicated in many other parts of the region) suggests Mississippian chiefdoms rarely lasted more than a few generations at any given center.

Cahokia thus provides particularly dramatic testimony of the organizational instability of chiefdoms. Of course, as power rotated over the regional landscape, some centers were reoccupied after lying abandoned for varying lengths of time or else continued to be occupied while no longer serving as chiefly centers. The latter fate appears to have befallen Cahokia. That the central area continued to be inhabited well past the period of dynamic political leadership was likely, as Pauketat has eloquently put it, due to the "inertia of Cahokia as a sacred location." As we have seen from the preceding chapter by Knight, this was not atypical in the Mississippian world. Moundville resembles Cahokia in that it was a dynamic polity early on (i.e., in the decades around A.D. 1200), characterized by extensive growth, a large population, and evidence for widespread interaction, yet one that soon thereafter went into a long period of apparent decline. Like Cahokia, the occupation and use of the Moundville area may have continued much longer than otherwise because the ceremonial center had taken on a sacred aspect. Parenthetically, if Cahokia was the center of a vibrant chiefly polity for 150 years, it probably witnessed the succession of a half a dozen to a dozen or more paramount elites. If Mound 72 truly contains the remains of two such rulers, many more remain to be found around Cahokia, assuming their burial mounds have not been destroyed. That the Mound 72 burials date to the Loh-mann phase further suggests that later Stirling-phase burials, interred when elite legitimization strategies may have been at their height, may be even more elaborate than those found in Mound 72.[4]

The Cahokia and Moundville cases also suggest that chiefly polity dura-tion was apparently not scale dependent, that is, tied to the size of the support population, or the degree to which labor was mobilized for monumental con-struction or crop production. In other words, larger chiefdoms did not neces-sarily last longer than smaller ones. That chiefly centers persisted in some areas longer than others, as at Cahokia and Moundville, appears to have been due to their individual historical trajectories and position in the regional political and ceremonial landscape, as moderated by factors such as climate, resource structure, and physiography. Why do chiefdoms have such a short life span? As I and a number of other authors have argued, there are a great many social and environmental factors promoting organizational instability in chiefdoms, of which the fact that succession to power was based on kin-ship—and any number of a chief's close kin were thus qualified to take his or her place—was perhaps the single most important factor, all but ensuring incessant factional competition and warfare between rival elites in these societies (D. Anderson 1990b, 1994a; Pauketat, chapter 2). Understanding the factors behind the growth and collapse of individual Mississippian soci-eties, however, requires the consideration of a wide range of possible causal mechanisms, as well as historical circumstances. Essentially, such an ex-amination requires the use of a diachronic, multiscalar, analytical perspec-tive that examines conditions shaping each society over time and at a number of scales of analysis, including the site, locality, and region (Anderson 1994a, n.d.).[5]

Cahokia's External Connections

Cahokia's relationship with societies outside the American Bottom, partic-ularly in areas to the south, is not well understood at the present. I do not mean by this that artifactual evidence for contact with other societies is lack-ing. Far from it (e.g., recent summaries of primary data include those by Griffin 1993; J. Kelly 1991a; Lafferty 1994; Milner 1990, 1991; and Pauketat 1994a). Just what this evidence means, however, is still unclear and has prompted appreciable debate (cf. Milner 1990, 1991 and Griffin 1993, with Dincauze and Hasenstab 1989 or P. O'Brien 1989). If Cahokia was the center of a complex or paramount chiefdom during the period of its ascendancy (i.e., a chiefdom that exerted control over other simple chiefdoms or, in the case of a paramount chiefdom, over both simple and complex chiefdoms), then questions that immediately arise are where these subsidiary polities were located, and what the nature was of their interaction with societies in the American Bottom. A fairly appreciable literature documents Cahokian contacts in the Eastern Woodlands (e.g., see references in Emerson and Lewis, eds., 1991, Griffin 1993, and Stoltman, ed., 1991). While its relations with societies to the north have received appreciable attention, particularly in the shaping of the Oneota culture (Emerson 1991a; Goldstein 1991; Griffin 1960; Stoltman 1986), there has been little discussion of potential subsidiary polities of impacts outside the American Bottom in areas to the south (see discussions in Brain 1989; R. Lewis 1991; Morse and Morse 1990; S. Williams and Brain 1983). Large quantities of raw materials like Mill Creek chert from southern Illinois and igneous rock from the St. Francois Mountains of northern Arkansas and southern Missouri are present at Cahokia, however, which may derive from exchange or direct procurement or, alternatively, tribute (Pauketat 1994a, 145–59, chapter 2).

Other raw materials like shell, mica, and copper are present at Cahokia in appreciable quantity and come from much greater distances, probably from the Great Lakes, the South Appalachians, and the Gulf or south Atlantic coast. Cahokia clearly participated in a regional exchange network, of a kind that has existed in one form or another in the Eastern Woodlands since the Archaic Period, albeit with varying levels of intensity (Anderson 1994c; Brown et al. 1990; Lafferty 1994; Peregrine 1992). Long-distance interaction was fairly quiescent in the Eastern Woodlands following the demise of Middle Woodland Hopewellian culture, but reemerged dramatically during the early Mississippian era after A.D. 900 or so, ultimately peaking in intensity over the region around A.D. 1200, at the height of the Southeastern Ceremonial Complex (Muller 1989). The rise of simple chiefdoms in several parts of the region during the latter part of the Emergent Mississippi Period from ca. A.D. 800 to 1000 has been closely tied to long-distance exchange, by fostering a process of competitive emulation among the region's elites, who made use of extralocal prestige goods to demonstrate their power and control over distant forces (Brown et al. 1990; J. Clark and Blake 1994; Helms 1979; Pauketat 1994a, 20–21).

This renewal in long-distance exchange may be linked, in part, to the rise of Cahokia, whose own newly emergent elites may have helped create a demand for extralocal materials, and who were certainly strategically situated to direct their flow in the midcontinent (see J. Kelly 1980, 1991a, 1991b). Controlling a major waterway, and maintaining a massive civic-ceremonial center, parenthetically, may have reduced or obviated the need for Cahokia to control lesser chiefdoms at appreciable distances. Rather than enforcing tributary relations over large areas, people and goods may well have gravitated to Cahokia, in part because of the impressiveness and sacredness of the center, and in part because it was astride the continent's principal transportation corridor, a location all but impossible to avoid or miss. Cahokia clearly emerged where it did, at least in part, because its location offered tremendous potential for interaction with societies over large areas (Clark and Blake 1994, 19–20; Peregrine 1991).

Given its massive size and complex organizational structure, however, it is quite likely that Cahokia physically dominated surrounding societies over appreciable distances by force or arms if and when its ideas or ceremony were insufficient, or when its inferred control over trade and transportation came under challenge. Views that the complex political entity present in the American Bottom between ca. A.D. 1050 and 1200 cast a long shadow of threat, demanding and receiving massive quantities of tribute from across much of the midcontinent, however, have been justifiably discredited in recent years (cf. Dincauze and Hasenstab 1989; Griffin 1993; Milner 1990, 1991). In part, the reason for this is that only minimal evidence for Cahokian presence, much less overt control, has been found at sites outside of the American Bottom area, and also because the American Bottom appears to have been largely self-sufficient, at least in terms of agricultural food production (Milner 1990). The elite burials in Mound 72, with their numerous sacrificed retainers, do suggest, however, that secular power was not at all unknown to the rulers of Cahokia and could have been resorted to as needed to advance their agendas.

Some evidence suggests that deer and wood found at societies in the American Bottom were obtained from over an appreciable area, for example, suggesting Cahokia may have maintained extensive hunting and resource procurement territories, areas likely formed and maintained through the subordination of neighboring societies (L. Kelly, chapter 4; Lopinot and Woods 1993). Given the large numbers of people inferred to have been present in the American Bottom, appreciable hunting territories would likely have to have been maintained to harvest enough deer hides and meat for use in clothing as well as a source of animal protein (Gramly 1977; Turner and Santley 1979). By maintaining sufficient hunting territories to meet their needs, the societies in the American Bottom would not have had to receive tribute in the form of foodstuffs from across large areas to survive or even live in relative plenty. Given interannual variation in rainfall and hence crop production in the Southeast, being dependent on other societies could have been quite destabilizing. It is evident from regional rainfall patterns that when crops failed they usually did so over fairly appreciable areas, rendering tribute flow an unlikely means of supporting large populations or accommodating food shortages, at least in agricultural chiefdoms. Maintaining appreciable stored food reserves would have been a more viable strategy (D. Anderson et al. 1995).

Griffin (1993) has summarized the limited direct evidence for Cahokian contacts in the Southeast (see also summaries in Brain 1991; J. Kelly 1991a, 1991b; Milner 1990, 1991), data that have been used to advance the argument that Cahokian control over these societies was minimal. Southeastern Mississippian centers with evidence for interaction with Cahokia, typically the presence of a few sherds of Cahokia or Cahokia-like pottery, include Obion and Shiloh on the Tennessee River of southwestern Tennessee, the Banks site in northeast Arkansas, the Winterville site in northeast Mississippi, and the Shell Bluff site in west-central Mississippi (Griffin 1993; Phillips 1970, 258–60). In the Ohio River valley, similar materials have been found at the Kincaid and Angel centers in southern Illinois and Indiana, at the Turpin site in southern Ohio, and at the Annis mound-and-village site on the Green River in Kentucky (Griffin 1993, 6–8). Large numbers of ceramics from the general vicinity of the Ohio-Mississippi confluence have, in turn, been found in the American Bottom, particularly during the end of the Emergent Mississippi Period, indicating that extensive interaction with this area likely took place at this time (J. Kelly 1991a, 86; Milner 1991, 37).

The lack of a common Cahokian material culture and ceramic technology over a large area, and particularly in the central and lower Mississippi valley to the south of the American Bottom, however, cannot be used to disprove the existence of subsidiary polities, or Cahokian impacts on or outright suppression of outlying polities. The various chiefdoms making up the sixteenth-century province of Coosa located in northern Georgia and eastern

Tennessee, for example, had distinctive ceramic assemblages, and the paramountcy cross-cut two major ceramic traditions, Dallas and Lamar (Hally, Smith, and Langford 1990). All but invisible archaeologically, the recognition of Coosa relies as much on ethnohistorical analysis as on archaeology, a form of data that is not available unfortunately from the eleventh- through thirteenth-century Southeast. It is still possible to delimit the extent of prehistoric complex chiefdoms, as archaeological work with the Coosa province has indicated (Hally et al. 1990). Through the examination of settlement data, in fact, it is possible to recognize potential constituent polities (inferred by the presence of clusters and size hierarchies of sites) and then, by examining population levels or the number and size of mounds in use, estimate their relative power and importance.

Whether or not subsidiary polities at appreciable distances were subordinate to Cahokia is unknown at the present. As I have suggested above, by controlling the waterways, Cahokia may not have needed to dominate physically or directly control societies at great distances, employing an organizational structure like that assumed for sixteenth-century paramount chiefdoms such as Coosa or Cofitachequi (Hudson et al. 1985, 1987). This is not to say that Cahokian elites could not have cast their weight around as needed to maintain their position; chiefly altruism is not a characteristic of complex chiefdoms. The emergence of the complex chiefdom at Moundville, for example, is thought to have been tied to the abandonment of a series of Mississippian societies in northern Alabama, the suppression of elite ambitions, and the elimination of fortification sites to the west along the Tombigbee (Blitz 1993). Comparable events may have occurred with the emergence of Cahokia as a dominant power during the Lohmann phase or shortly afterward. In particular, a major power struggle for control of the Mississippi River may have occurred between the societies of the American Bottom and the Cairo Lowlands early in the Mississippian era, with the latter area clearly losing out.

The Cairo Lowlands of southeast Missouri, like Cahokia, includes a major expanse of bottomland near a major confluence, in this case with the Ohio instead of the Illinois and Missouri Rivers as at Cahokia. During the Emergent Mississippi Period from ca. A.D. 800 to 1050, both areas were characterized by large population concentrations and major centers, and witnessed appreciable organizational change. Some evidence suggests that the societies in the Cairo Lowlands were actually more organizationally complex and technologically advanced earlier; the Hoecake site, in fact, may have been the center of the most complex polity in the entire Mississippi valley in the ninth century (Morse and Morse 1983, 215, 1990, 162, 165). There is evidence for appreciable interaction between the two areas, however, and much of what is thought of as classic Middle Mississippian technology as exemplified at Cahokia (i.e., shell-tempered pottery, red-filming of pottery, microliths, wall-trench houses, the bow and arrow, a town/dispersed hamlet settlement pattern) appears to have first appeared in the Cairo Lowlands (Morse and Morse 1983, 216–17, 230, 1990, 162–66; J. Kelly et al. 1984, 157). Much of what we think of as Mississippian material culture and technology, in fact, likely arose from the highly fertile interaction that occurred between these two areas during the Emergent Mississippi Period.

That a paramount chiefdom comparable to Cahokia in size and power did not develop in the Cairo Lowlands during the Early Mississippi Period, I suggest, is because such an entity arose first in the American Bottom, probably during the Lohmann phase. This society had a vested interest in controlling—or at least assuring that no one else restricted access to—the great navigable waterways of the midcontinent that funneled travelers, pilgrims, and traders to Cahokia. Just as Moundville suppressed societies around it (Steponaitis 1991), I suspect we shall eventually recognize evidence for similar behavior on the part of Cahokia. The most likely area of such impact, if control of major waterways was deemed important, would have probably been in the Cairo Lowlands and Ohio confluence area (Lafferty 1994, 199; Lewis 1991, 290). Our understanding of Mississippian developments in the Cairo Lowlands, unfortunately, is imperfect due to the minimal fieldwork and reporting that has occurred in this area, at least when compared with the American Bottom. During the tenth and eleventh centuries when Cahokia was at its height, its elites may have stifled the ambitions of their neighbors to the south, much as the Moundville chiefdom a century or so later apparently suppressed and left defenseless societies along the Tombigbee (Blitz 1993). Major fortifications do appear at centers in the Cairo Lowland in the twelfth century, however, and it is after this time that these centers reach their greatest extent (Lewis 1991, 281–92; Morse and Morse 1990, 169). The appearance of fortifications in the Cairo Lowlands later in the Mississippi Period may reflect the emergence of societies capable of challenging Cahokia, which by this time was itself in decline.

Cahokia and the Shaping of the Mississippian World

Cahokia's impact on contemporaneous societies in the Southeast is usually assumed to have been fairly minimal, with little direct evidence for interaction noted (e.g., Emerson and Lewis, eds., 1991; Griffin 1993; but see Williams and Brain 1983). This "minimalist" stance (after Stoltman 1991, 351) is best represented by the following quotes:

> In terms of the broad sweep of eastern North American cultural evolution, Cahokia's impact was a pulse that once felt was soon gone. Moreover, its influence would have become rapidly attenuated with distance from the American Bottom. (Milner 1991, 4)

> During the subsequent Stirling phase, Cahokia rose to dominance as the largest Mississippian site in Eastern North America. Prior to this, evidence for Cahokia's influence outside the American Bottom was minimal, especially in the lower Mississippi valley. (J. Kelly 1991a, 84)

Griffin (1993, 12), not surprisingly, given his life's work with materials from across eastern North America—making him more aware than anyone of the limited artifactual evidence for Cahokian domination—has perhaps summarized this traditional or standard position best of all:

> Most of the modern myths about Cahokia have resulted from a gross overestimate of its population at 30,000 or more, which has been used to bolster the concept that Cahokia was a "state." To some archaeologists, this, in turn, made Cahokia the primary and most prominent society in Mississippian times, a Rome of the eastern United States, establishing trade controlling centers and dominating much of the east from A.D. 1000–1200, with a ripple effect lasting to the seventeenth century. It has been suggested that the central Illinois Valley Mississippian populations were busy providing crop plants to feed the overpopulated American Bottom, while Mill Creek societies of northwest Iowa were sending dried buffalo meat to Cahokia in exchange for Cahokia products. This interpretation explains why there are so few buffalo bones at Cahokia. The myths can be said to result from two views. The first is that Cahokia had little effect in those areas to the north and northwest, areas where there is the most evidence for contact. *The second myth comes in overemphasizing Cahokia's role in producing cul-*

tural change in those areas where very little or no evidence of Cahokia materials are found. (Griffin 1993, 11–12; emphasis added)

Current archaeological theory and evidence forces me to take a diametrically different position (outlined below), although I fully agree with the scholars quoted above that if ceramic artifacts are the criteria by which Cahokian influence is to be assessed, its role in the evolution of Eastern Woodland culture does indeed appear to have been fairly minimal. I also agree that little new ceramic data are likely to appear in the years ahead that will change this picture appreciably (although, as I shall argue, there are other kinds of artifactual evidence that may shed more light on this matter). As already noted, if anything, more artifacts and raw materials (ceramics and otherwise) apparently gravitated *to* early Cahokia than went out *from* it, or at least went out from it much beyond the reaches of the American Bottom, particularly to areas to the south. While the ceramic evidence clearly appears to be telling us one thing, I suggest we need to look beyond isolated categories of artifacts to the kinds of cultural systems that were present. Viewed this way, it seems extremely implausible that so complex and primary a political formation as Cahokia could have had as minimal effect as that implied by the comments above.

The importance of the ideas offered by Pauketat and Emerson in their various chapters in this volume, ideas encompassing the formation and spread of ideologies, and how a dominant ideology can create a cultural hegemony, *is that they provide a theoretical framework by which one can understand how a society like Cahokia could have profoundly influenced developments at great distances.* They supply the framework without resorting to admittedly fallacious arguments requiring the control by American Bottom elites of societies over vast areas, the need for a state-level organizational hierarchy, or the existence of tributary networks extending from Iroquoia to the Gulf of Mexico. While Cahokia certainly could have dominated societies at appreciable distances, if nothing else by threat of conquest, it apparently did not. Neither did it need to, except perhaps when its interests were directly threatened. The acknowledgment of Cahokia's special place in the order of things and in ceremony and religion—that is, the acceptance and appropriation of its dominant ideology by outlying societies—however, was more important and had a far greater impact than anything Cahokia's elites could have achieved through conquest. While the scale of Cahokian political economy may have been largely restricted to the American Bottom, its ideological domination extended over a much greater area.[6]

Quite simply, I believe the Mississippian ideology that emerged at Cahokia in the Lohmann phase acted as a trigger, sparking evolutionary change in the societies around it, which in turn had a ripple effect over a much larger area.[7] I thus believe that it is no coincidence that complex chiefdoms appeared in several parts of the Southeast between A.D. 1100 and 1250, and that a panregional exchange network peaked at about this same time. I believe that these events were a direct reaction and response by societies across the region to events and processes originating in the American Bottom, albeit adopted or modified as circumstances warranted. Likewise, when Cahokia gradually collapsed after A.D. 1200, nothing, and certainly no one society, stepped in to fill the void. Instead a series of complex or paramount chiefdoms with spheres of influence that were, at best, subregional in scale emerged in a number of areas (Payne 1994; Scarry n.d.). Long-distance exchange and monumental construction appear to have declined significantly across the region, while warfare appears to have increased. The character of the later Mississippi Period, with its isolated warring chiefdoms and colorless ceremony, at least when compared with what came before, was likely shaped, at least in part, by the decline of Cahokia. The heart of the Mississippian world, the ideas of power, complexity, and ceremony that bound the region together, were gone. The idea of Cahokia lived on but imperfectly in its successor societies.

Cahokia was extremely complex, had established far-reaching exchange contacts, and had an elaborate religious and ceremonial infrastructure in place at a very early time level when compared with developments in other parts of the Mississippian world. The Cahokia paramount chiefdom, which had emerged by A.D. 1050–1100 in the American Bottom, vastly exceeded anything seen before or since elsewhere in the region. This society was an order of magnitude larger in scale than the incipient hierarchies seen to the south in the Coles Creek area during the earlier Late Woodland era and was far beyond the simple chiefdoms reported from elsewhere in the Southeast at this time. A marked increase in the occurrence of extralocal raw materials characterizes the Lohmann phase (A.D. 1050–1100), indicating Cahokian contacts were far-reaching at an early time level (Pauketat 1994a, 141–67). The elaborate religious complex centered on Cahokia during the Stirling phase (A.D. 1100–1200), finally, emphasized truly epic-scale monumental construction and, no doubt, public ceremony.

These ingredients led to the formation of dominant ideology that set in play a process of competitive emulation and reaction across the region. That such may have been the case can be seen from an inspection of the dates offered for the Mississippian emergence and for complex chiefdom formation in various parts of the Southeast. Outside of the Mississippi valley the Mississippian emergence is usually placed between roughly A.D. 900 and 1000 (uncalibrated) at the earliest (D. Anderson n.d.). Complex chiefdom formation, the emergence of subregional-scale polities like those represented by Wilbanks-phase Etowah, Moundville II, or Lake Jackson, furthermore, did not occur in most parts of the region until A.D. 1100 or later (uncalibrated radiocarbon years), well after the Lohmann phase. In the eastern part of the region in the Carolinas, in fact, complex chiefdoms did not emerge until well after the Stirling phase.

While specific artifacts are admittedly few and far between, I believe, nevertheless, that events in the American Bottom between ca. A.D. 900 and 1250 profoundly shaped the character and evolution of Mississippian societies throughout the Southeast, even in areas where people never saw a Ramey-Incised pot or met anyone who had visited Monks Mound. At least some of the complex chiefdoms the Spanish encountered in the sixteenth century, such as Coosa and Cofitachequi, were known (and either feared or respected!) by societies hundreds of kilometers away. It seems eminently reasonable to assume that eleventh- and twelfth-century Cahokia, sitting astride the continent's major waterway, would have had a similar, if not vastly greater, reputation and impact on its surroundings.

Thus, while what we commonly think of as major facets of Mississippian technology and social organization (i.e., intensive maize agriculture and simple chiefdoms) may have indeed arisen or were rapidly adopted in a number of areas during the Emergent Mississippi Period (Phillips, Ford, and Griffin 1951, 451; B. Smith 1990), where Mississippian ideology arose (in the sense of Knight 1986; Pauketat 1994a; Pauketat and Emerson, chapter 1) and how it spread appears to be another matter entirely. The emergence and subsequent spread of Mississippian ideology, I believe, owes a great deal to events that took place at Cahokia, and even more specifically to the actions of Lohmann- and subsequent Stirling-phase elites during the period from roughly A.D. 1050 to 1100. Specific aspects of this Mississippian ideology that appear to have formed in the American Bottom included an agricultural fertility cult, views of the world order and cosmos that were reflected in iconography and mound-plaza layouts, and the sacred status of the chiefly elite (see, in particular, Emerson, chapter 10, for a more detailed discussion of Cahokian elite ideology).[8] It is possible, in fact, that what we think of as classic southeastern Mississippian culture did not even exist until the constellation of technological, organizational, and ideological attributes crystallized in the American Bottom around A.D. 1050, during the Lohmann phase "Big Bang." While Cahokia thus admittedly exerted little direct control over southeastern societies, its presence had a profound impact throughout the region. In a very real sense, much of what we think of as Mississippian across the region appears to be the idea of Cahokia writ large.[9]

Cahokia played a major role in the establishment of the Mississippian ideology and hence world view and in this regard can be said to have fostered or led an interregional hegemony of sorts. Pauketat describes the impact that Cahokia had on other societies in the Eastern Woodlands, simply by virtue of its existence, most eloquently in chapter 1, while simultaneously noting that such an idea has received little systematic examination. Many of the solutions to the problem of complex political formation, that is, the emergence of complex chiefdoms ruled by hereditary elites with appreciable secular as well as sacred power and authority, were first worked out successfully in early Cahokia. These ideological solutions were likely widely copied, not necessarily in a calculated fashion, but rather as the inevitable result of groups buying into the ideology of power that emanated from Lohmann- and Stirling-phase Cahokia. This is not to say that all of the pieces to this organizational and ideological puzzle were developed at Cahokia—much of what happened was undoubtedly based on ideas and processes under way in other contemporaneous and previous middle and lower Mississippi valley (and even Gulf Coastal) societies—but merely that the package first came together in a coherent and wildly successful manner at Cahokia.[10]

All of this, of course, requires some revision to our thinking about the so-called "analogy or process" model of Mississippian emergence that has become widely adopted in recent years, which holds that "the widespread cultural-developmental similarities of Mississippian societies are perceived and explained in terms of independent and isolated cultural responses to similar challenges." That is, there may be more truth to what Bruce Smith (1990, 2) has described as the "homology or historical relatedness position" than we have assumed in recent years, that is, that the emergence of Mississippian culture across the Eastern Woodlands was, at least in part, due to the spread of ideas, if not people. Viewing the emergence and spread of Mississippian culture as being, in part, the spread of a dominant ideology in the face of competing and subsidiary ideologies, I believe, is more satisfying theoretically than resorting to descriptively sound but otherwise nonexplanatory arguments describing the Mississippian emergence as "a large interconnected set of nested developmental black boxes resting in the interpretive shadow of the homology-analogy dilemma" (B. Smith 1990, 2–3). Ideological domination, whether imposed or adopted willingly, furthermore, subsumes prestige goods exchange which, as Smith (1990, 7–8, summarizing arguments by Brown, Kerber, and Winters 1990) correctly noted, "fueled the parallel interactive transformational processes within different regions."

Avenues for Future Research

One way to better understand Cahokia is through the explicit comparison of its organization and operation with that of other southeastern Mississippian societies, drawing insight from other areas wherever possible. Regarding the correlates of organizational change, the dramatic restructuring of the social and physical landscape that characterizes Lohmann-phase Cahokia is paralleled in other Mississippian societies, albeit at a much smaller scale. The emergence of the Moundville paramount chiefdom, for example, witnessed changes in the location, size, and fortification of outlying centers, and in some nearby areas whole populations were removed or relocated (Blitz 1993; Knight, chapter 11; Peebles 1987a, 1987b; Steponaitis 1978, 1991). The provisioning of elites with choice meaty elements, something noted at Cahokia by Lucretia Kelly in chapter 4, has also been observed in other southeastern Mississippian societies, and the diversity of subsistence remains at both centers and outlying sites has likewise been used to assess the impact of such provisioning on commoner populations (Jackson and Scott 1995; Scott 1983, 1985).

How did Cahokian elites dominate other societies? Did they insist upon tribute and, if so, of what kind? If they required formal acknowledgment of their power and abilities, was this sealed through marriage alliances and gifts of wealth items, as was characteristic between contact period elites (e.g., Smith and Hally 1992)? Given that there is little evidence for massive trade, perhaps our attention should focus on possible contexts in which exchanges of preciosities and raw materials, and perhaps women, could have occurred.

264

DNA analyses of human skeletal remains, particularly the Mound 72 males and females, might reveal the extent of Cahokia's regional sphere of influence by determining whether they came from local or outside groups.

How did the Lohmann-phase "Big Bang" occur, if Pauketat's scenario stands the test of time and further research? Could it have been the result of the actions of one or a few people and, if so, how do individuals come up with and then implement ideas about transforming social landscapes? Outside sources of innovation are clearly not very plausible; there are no local Quetzalcoatl myths or Mesoamerican artifacts to offer the facile, but undoubtedly to some the very comforting, solution of an external origin, although all this would really do is move the question one step back in time, to why such things happened at Tula or some other such Mesoamerican center. From my limited reading of history, it appears that innovations are usually adopted if they confer advantages that are widely perceived and at the same time do not threaten the established order of things, or at least the order of the powerful. They can also, of course, be imposed by the powerful upon the powerless, who have no choice in their acceptance. Given the dramatic nature of the settlement changes that occurred during the Lohmann phase in the American Bottom, I strongly suspect that at least part of the process entailed a major centralization of coercive power, the nature and extent of which are, again, well documented in early historic accounts of southeastern chiefdom societies (e.g., Anderson 1994a 68–93, 1994b; DePratter 1983; Smith and Hally 1992).

The relationship or interplay between dominant and subordinate or alternative ideologies is also a potentially fruitful area of study, both at Cahokia and elsewhere in the Mississippian world (e.g., Saitta 1994; see also Emerson, chapter 10; Pauketat, chapter 2). Resistance to domination may help to explain why "traditional" or "Woodland-like" adaptations (or at least ceramic technologies) occur in some parts of the Southeast away from ceremonial centers; these cases suggest that the local Mississippian elites were not very successful in transforming the social landscape. The failure of Mississippian culture to take root along the middle and northern Atlantic seaboard also may reflect a resistance to ideology by local populations who did not feel compelled to buy into it. Part of this regional patterning may, of course, be due to regional physiographic structure. The Atlantic coast is isolated from the interior Southeast by the Appalachian Mountains, and the regular exchange of preciosities and prestige goods, something that was likely integral to spreading Mississippian ideology, may have been difficult in this area; that the area was largely outside of an earlier Hopewellian world was likely for similar reasons.

The probable movement of people out of Cahokia, albeit primarily to the north, provides evidence that migration occurred in at least this part of the Mississippian world (just as population movement is commonly observed in ethnographic chiefdoms), and that it is a process that should not be ignored elsewhere in the Southeast. Population changes in the central and northern Mississippi valley, accordingly, may give us clues to the origin or disappearance of Mississippian societies elsewhere. In spite of forceful arguments to the contrary (e.g., B. Smith 1984), for example, current evidence indicates that "the only reasonable conclusion for the present is that the Macon Plateau site was settled by people who were not natives of central Georgia" (M. Williams 1994, 137). Other striking examples of population movement or relocation include the wholesale abandonment of major portions of the Savannah, Tennessee, and (possibly) the central Mississippi valleys (Anderson 1994a; S. Williams 1990). How much was population movement and relocation caused by political factors, and how much by biological necessity? Is it possible, for example, that the size and the success of the Cahokian system may have led to an overabundance of elites in the American Bottom, who then had to be relocated through marriage alliances or military force?

Finally, the potential of dendrochronology for both improving American Bottom chronology as well as delimiting the effects of climatic variability on the political history of central Mississippi valley societies should be explored anew, given the vast improvements in this form of analysis that have occurred in the Southeast in recent years (Stahle, Cleaveland, and Hehr 1985; D. Anderson, Stahle, and Cleaveland 1995). In particular, it is possible to obtain very precise dates through the wiggle matching of a series of radiocarbon dates obtained at set-year intervals on log or wood post segments from preserved architectural features, by examining the secular radiocarbon curve against a series of temporally precisely separated samples for a best fit (Clark and Renfrew 1972; Pearson 1986). It is also possible to explore year-to-year climatic variability during the Emergent Mississippi Period, particularly spring (growing season) rainfall, using bald cypress dendrochronological reconstructions. Did the Lohmann-phase transformation occur during a period conducive to the generation of major agricultural surpluses, and did the Moorehead-phase decline occur during conditions of greater uncertainty? Answers to these kinds of questions are within our grasp and should be the subject of research in the near future.

Conclusions

Like Pauketat and Emerson, I agree that ideology is at the very foundation of complex cultural systems and that it is reflected in and can be explored through the examination of material remains such as artifacts, architecture, and the use of space (see also Kus 1983). I particularly like Emerson's ideas (chapter 10) that much of what we think of as Mississippian iconography and world view originated during the Lohmann and subsequent Stirling phases and was incorporated into material culture, and specifically prestige-goods that had widespread circulation. In this regard, I concur with Emerson's statement (chaper 10) that Cahokia "disproportionately contributed to Mississippiandom." Cahokia can thus be seen as occupying the apex of a regional hegemony, fostering a dominant ideology that came to be copied, emulated, or coopted by societies around it. While the spread of Cahokian ideology was unquestionably fostered by prestige-goods exchange, we must take care to avoid assuming that the exchange itself, or the baubles being passed along, were what was important (Saitta 1994). Instead, the circulation of these prestige goods marked the spread of a dominant ideology that became, and reinforced, the idea of "Mississippian."

It is time to accept that Cahokia likely had a major impact on the Mississippian world. As we have seen, we can accept this view without assuming that the classic Southeastern Ceremonial Complex (scc) was a manifestation of Cahokian-elite legitimization strategies, or that waves of migrating elites poured out from an American Bottom heartland, or that war parties from Cahokia exacted tribute from and ruled societies across the Eastern Woodlands. Mississippian ideology and culture, the idea that was Cahokia, spread very rapidly over the Southeast in the years just after A.D. 1050. That Mississippian culture spread widely across the Southeast rather than in areas to the north suggests that its accompanying ideology was closely tied to the elite mobilization of agricultural surpluses, specifically those generated by the intensive cultivation of maize, and that it was ideally suited to societies that were already fairly complex, at the level of simple chiefdoms. Cahokia expansion to the north, as a consequence, may have been following a path of least resistance; that is, if societies to the south quickly adopted the organizational and ideological system originating in the American Bottom, they may have soon been in a good position to challenge intruders. Thus, because the *idea* of Cahokia spread quickly to the south, where maize agriculture was feasible and complex societies were already in place, the *people* of Cahokia could not. That sites with appreciable evidence for Cahokian contact, like Aztalan, are in Wisconsin instead of Arkansas or Louisiana is thus not altogether surprising.

Timothy R. Pauketat and Thomas E. Emerson

13
Conclusion:
Cahokia and the Four Winds

By the fifteenth century A.D., Cahokia had been scattered to the four winds, leaving behind only archaeological traces of the central capital and its surrounding domain, bereft of the human ideas, actions, and interactions that had defined its history. The preceding chapters offer a new synthesis of Cahokia's place in the Mississippian world. Cahokia, to the authors of these chapters, was about agriculture and appropriation, production and power, ideology and authority, and monuments and mobilization. The Cahokian polity has been called a native southeastern chiefdom, with all that this classification implies, but it was also unique in its scale, developmental trajectory, and panregional effect.

More than anything else, the chapters in this volume bespeak a nonstate-level political, economic, and social behemoth. The great scale of the Cahokian polity, relative to other southeastern chiefdoms, most assuredly was due in part to its location in an expanse of Mississippi River floodplain and to local demographic preconditions (Fowler 1974, 1975; Milner 1990). For Cahokia to have become Cahokia, the resource-mobilization potential of the region must have far exceeded the sum total necessary to provision individual Emergent Mississippian communities. This simple conclusion leads us to a more important insight into Cahokia and the rest of Mississippiandom. Cahokia was more than the remains of the machinations of a few powerful elite rulers who imposed their individual wills upon a preexisting community. Cahokia *was* community, writ large.

The abrupt, political ascent of Cahokia, as evidenced in Lohmann-phase monument building, craft manufacturing, stylistic homogenization, demographic centralization, and the central and rural community and household reorganization, is revealing of a social and ideological "coalition" or movement in the American Bottom in which more than the elite held a stake (see Emerson 1991a; Pauketat 1994a). Whatever was happening at the level of the political ruler (and ignoring ideology for the moment), it seems likely that the web of communities of the bottom were linked or, better, usurped by a coalition of high- and low-ranked people for whom community-writ-large (i.e., Cahokia) was a shared interest. Limited, if not strategic, violence might have been the stick behind the carrot-of-reward given the loyal follower of the early Cahokian order. Estimating the size of the Cahokian stick, so to speak, is difficult at best. It may be that violence was a minor component of the Big Bang in the Bottom, affirming an if-you-build-it-they-will-come theory of civilization.

Violence and coercion, of course, are difficult to see archaeologically, especially if not endemic to an entire population. Warfare or feuds among high-ranking Emergent Mississippian families may have been central to the events of ca. A.D. 1050. To be sure, people did come to Cahokia after A.D. 1050, and it seems unlikely that coercion could have been largely responsible for this boom phase (Pauketat and Lopinot, chapter 6). The actual means by which people came to Cahokia over the span of a few decades, and by which Cahokia's population increased some five to ten times what it had been, may have included whole corporate-kin groups native to the region (and perhaps some from beyond), who resettled in the vicinity of the mounds and plazas of the new or revamped capital. The demographic circumstances of these various groups would then correlate with the labor investments and the political fortunes of each mound-and-plaza segment or subcommunity (if not subchief) of Cahokia.

That the rural settlements and fields in the vicinity of Cahokia were a Mississippian phenomenon that appeared with the Lohmann phase suggests a relationship between the centralized changes of A.D. 1050 and those of the entire northern American Bottom proper at A.D. 1050 (Emerson 1995, chapter 9). Unlike the manner in which rural, dispersed Mississippian farmsteads have been depicted by others, it is likely that the Lohmann-phase homesteads, farmsteads, nodal settlements, and field houses were as much caught up in the web of early Cahokian change as central Cahokia was itself.[1] These were neither isolated farmers nor autonomous households, although they undoubtedly were able to feed themselves and then some. Rather, the rural folk of the northern American Bottom, if we can indeed call them rural, probably relied upon centers for their very social existence, not to mention for periodic religious and economic services. Many of the relatives and affines of rural folk undoubtedly resided at Cahokia or at smaller local centers. Important community events would have taken place in centers. Even relatively small kin-group functions might have been feasible only at Cahokia and the secondary centers.

To note the functional relationships between the rural folk and Cahokia, however, is not to deemphasize the serious impact and potential breakdown of the traditional kin order that accompanied the events of A.D. 1050. If our inferences withstand future scrutiny, then the Emergent Mississippian–Mississippian transition was a brief episode during which a few (high-ranking) overlords of Cahokia extended control over the social lives of all individuals within the northern American Bottom (Emerson 1995, chapter 9; Pauketat 1994a, chapter 2). This control meant that some ruler or rulers were capable of regularly extracting labor and produce from the farming communities of the floodplain and, perhaps, the surrounding upland hills. Owing some portion of their labor and produce—both crops and craft goods—to high-ranking Cahokian patrons initially may have been rationalized as obligations to kin (in the sense of Sahlins 1972). But as time wore on, an "elite ideology" diffused across the landscape, and a cultural hegemony usurped the values, beliefs, and meanings of Emergent Mississippian tradition (Pauketat 1994a).

The result was a Stirling-phase "divine chiefship" and an elite Cahokian ideology that emanated out from Cahokia (Emerson 1995; Pauketat 1994a). A local vehicle for the dispersion of the goods and ideas of twelfth-century Cahokia was the Ramey-Incised pot, distinctly shaped and decorated at Cahokia or other centers with the iconography of a Cahokian cosmos (Emerson 1989, chapter 10; Pauketat and Emerson 1991). The simple design fields of these pots contained motifs suggestive of order, symbolizing the four directions, four cosmological partitions, or the four winds (figure 13.1). These pots, distributed out from Cahokia, were material symbols of the relationship between the Cahokian elite and the American Bottom commoner (Pauketat and Emerson 1991).

Ramey-Incised pots are signatures of domination. They attest to the limited redistribution of medicines, comestibles, and ideology from centers out to rural folk, but it is unlikely that redistributions came close to matching the

0 ——————— 5
centimeters

Figure 13.1. A Quadripartite Ramey-Incised Design Field (vessel Cb-14, adapted from Pauketat 1996)

provisions previously appropriated by centers (see L. Kelly, chapter 4; Lopinot, chapter 3). Cahokia could not have been built merely on communal sharing. It did not gradually evolve as a self-sufficient community or mercantile center. In its radically and abruptly transformed landscape and in its distinctive craft products, Cahokia was constructed through the appropriated resources from the entire region, returning or redistributing itself and its ideology to those who would be dominated. In fact, at upward of ten thousand people, Lohmann-phase Cahokia may have depended on rural produce. Otherwise, seasonal shortfalls in production might have spelled doom for a Cahokian political economy (see Anderson 1994a). Surplus production by rural residents, encouraged if not controlled by chiefs, would have ensured the stability of the Cahokian web of communities and kin groups (see H. Wright 1984).[2] By the Stirling and Moorehead phases, tributary relations may have been a component of elite and non-elite ideologies, although the demographic and political demise of Cahokia is revealing of the solution for those resisting such relations—simply leaving (cf. Pauketat 1992; Pauketat and Lopinot, chapter 6).

If accurate, our view of a regionally integrated, early-Cahokian political economy sets the American Bottom apart from other, purportedly less-integrated, southeastern chiefdoms (e.g., Muller 1987; Muller and Stephens 1991). The Moundville polity, like its earlier Cahokian counterpart, exceeded the resource and labor constraints of its immediate environs to loom over potential rival chiefdoms in contiguous regions (Steponaitis 1991). Like Cahokia, Moundville's early development may be described as meteoric (Knight, chapter 11). The reason for both Moundville's and Cahokia's meteoric rise to regional prominence perhaps resides in their sociohistorical antecedents; that is, small-scale, ranked organizations or incipient chiefdoms defined the preconsolidation political landscapes of their respective regions.[3]

While Dean Saitta's (1994) characterization of early Cahokia as a communal formation (with communally subsumed classes) ignores the political dynamics attested in Cahokian data (Pauketat 1994a), he and others (Brown and Kelly 1995; Knight 1986, 1989a; Muller 1986a) have identified the importance of communal relations within Mississippiandom.[4] The senior author has elsewhere argued that where ideologies or world views incorporated such a communal ethic, the regional dynamics or the historical trajectory of the polity may have included punctuated leaps in the scale of regional integration (Pauketat 1994a, 37). This may be explained as symptomatic of the means by which the communal ethic was breached by an emerging tributary political economy. Where social stratification and tributary economics were already entrenched, as in the late Mississippian world, the communal ethic would not have required large-scale political consolidation to overcome the local resistance to political development (Pauketat 1994a, 27; see Knight, chapter 11).

Cahokia, therefore, was in part so large and its beginning so abrupt precisely because it was, for all practical purposes, the first of the large Mississippian domains (cf. Fowler 1974, 33; Griffin 1952, 362). And because it was so large and its political economy so expansive, Cahokia was able to exert an unmistakable influence on its neighbors along the Mississippi River and beyond. Cahokian influences probably would not have been a function of direct economic control. A Cahokian political ideology emanated out from this preeminent center, emulated to greater or lesser degree by neighbors and would-be tribute takers elsewhere in the Southeast and midcontinent.

Direct controls over the labor and goods of distant neighbors could have been effected by Cahokian war parties, occasionally extracting the cooperation of foreign political leaders. But direct control was limited by the logistical realities of canoe transport and the political realities of chiefdoms. Not only were canoes limited in terms of the quantity of goods or people that could have been carried, but even a Mississippian behemoth like Cahokia would have had difficulty maintaining or resupplying a sizeable long-distance task force or war party. Not only did the technology not exist for regular tribute mobilizations from afar, but the political administration that would have been capable of managing the details of such regular tributary relations—a state bureaucracy—was not to be found along the Mississippi River. Simply put, there might have been little reason, beyond the periodic offensive, for the people of distant domains (more than 100 kilometers from Cahokia) to cooperate with or submit to Cahokia.

Some sense of the boundaries of a Cahokian political economy are evidenced in a quantitative analysis of the archaeological record of the American Bottom. Of the "exotic" artifact types at Cahokia but derived from outside the American Bottom proper, about half originate from sources located no more than 150 kilometers from the northern American Bottom (table 13.1). In terms of artifact quantities in one large sample of Cahokia's domestic refuse, less than 1 percent of lithic artifact weight or count (excluding hearth rocks, limestone, and sandstone) consists of exotic artifacts from sources beyond a 150-kilometer radius of Cahokia (Pauketat 1996). On the other hand, more than 66 percent of this same sample is made up of Burlington-chert, Mill Creek–chert and St. Francois Mountain–diabase debitage derived from sources 30 to 100 kilometers south of the northern American Bottom. Cahokia was not at the center of a vast panregional trade network (*contra* Dincauze and Hasenstab 1989; Lafferty 1994; Peregrine 1991), if by that is meant a regular if not regulated exchange of "commodities." It was at the center of an intensive local exchange network typified by

274

Table 13.1. Exotic Artifacts at Cahokia

Artifact	Common Refuse	Uncommon Deposits	Finished Objects
Available within 150 Kilometers of Northern American Bottom			
Barite crystals	x		crystals
Burlington chert	x	x	bifacial tools, expedient tools
Cobden chert	x		arrowheads (debitage)
Flintclay (a.k.a. "fireclay")		x	figurines, pipes
Galena	x		pigment stones, paraphernalia
Hematite	x		pigment stones
Hixton-like orthoquartzites	x	?	bifacial tools, expedient tools
Kaolin chert	x	x	bifacial tools, expedient tools
Mill Creek chert tools	x	x	large bifacial tools
Plagioclase crystals	x		small crystals
Pottery	x	x	southern Illinois and Missouri wares
Quartz crystals	x		small crystals
Quartzite	x	x	discoidals
St. Francois Mt. diabase	x	x	axeheads
Available at Distances beyond 150 Kilometers from Northern American Bottom			
Alligator and shark teeth		x	ornament, club spurs
Anculosa gastropod shells		x	beads
Catlinite		x	pipe
Fluorite	x		crystals, beads
Fort Payne chert	x	x	arrowheads (see Mound 72 cache)
Hixton silicified sediment	x	x	bifacial tools, expedient tools
Great Lakes copper	x	x	ornaments
Long-Stemmed spatulate axeheads		x	Appalachian metamorphic rock
Marine shell	x	x	beads, pendants, dippers
Mica (muscovite)	x	x	ornaments, glitter
Pitken-like chert	x	x	arrowheads (see Mound 72 cache)
Pottery	x	x	Coles Creek, etc., wares
Quartz crystals	x	x	large crystals, arrowheads

the acquisition of raw materials and the centralized transformation of these materials into Cahokian symbols (Pauketat, chapter 2). Exotic goods originating more than 150 kilometers from Cahokia, not being abundant in Cahokia's domestic refuse, were likely acquired intermittently by Cahokians themselves or carried to the region by visiting pilgrims and dignitaries (Pauketat and Emerson, chapter 1).

Such long-distance communications and interactions, though not causing the rise of Cahokia, were at the heart of the Mississippianization of the Southeast. Cahokian influences, or a Cahokian strain of "political culture,"

275

altered in some ways the long-term development of significant portions of the Eastern Woodlands (Pauketat 1994a, 183–84). If we consider the early dates of the Cahokian experiment, then recognizing that the rest of the Mississippian world owes some debt to the Cahokians and their counterparts up and down the Mississippi River is plausible (Anderson, chapter 12; Knight, chapter 11). The extent of this debt and a precise understanding of the processes of Mississippianization remain to be fully delineated.

If Cahokia was unique in the terms laid out in this volume, then archaeologists are forced to consider other polities and other phases of Mississippian development as equally unique. In other words, political, cultural, social, and economic variation existed across the Southeast contingent upon local historical factors, landscape constraints, and supralocal interactions. What tied these variant populations together was not a uniform "adaptation" that predetermined history, but the formation of a panregional Mississippian milieu, including an emanating Cahokian political culture (*contra* Muller and Stephens 1991; B. Smith 1978). Each regional population to greater or lesser extent would have been affected by (i.e., emulated) and would have contributed to (i.e., emanated) this supralocal Mississippian culture depending on the local ideological negotiations of community and authority (cf. Renfrew 1987). Mississippianism would have been a culture of political organization, agricultural production, craft manufacturing, social relations, and other "elite" knowledge negotiated and transformed locally and transmitted via long-distance lines of communication (see J. Brown, Kerber, and Winters 1990; Drechsel 1994; Helms 1992b; Knight 1986; Pauketat 1994a). Mississippianism itself, then, is to be understood vis-à-vis a long-term developmental trajectory, made up of shorter-term political booms and busts.

While regional Mississippian developments varied, the archaeology of all of these groups has much to reveal about how people, at various phases of political and cultural development, conceded to or resisted the desires of authority. Southeastern people figure prominently in an understanding of the transformation from communalism to hierarchy (e.g., Nassaney 1992). Yes, the present volume's theoretical emphasis on the historical processes of domination and ideology is at odds with earlier adaptationist or eco-functionalist paradigms in archaeology. But our new synthesis of Cahokia cannot easily nor profitably be pigeonholed as either "processual" or "postprocessual" (see Barker and Pauketat 1992, 3; McGuire 1992; Preucel 1991). Our new synthesis does not assume an established position in the debate over

Cahokian sociopolitical complexity. Nor does it straddle the middle of the debate.

An older synthesis told of a highly integrated and functionally diverse four-tiered settlement system orchestrated by the urban center of Cahokia that controlled "various resources, transportation, and communication" locally and with "outside areas" (Fowler 1974, 27). This synthesis was tied to the (cultural-materialist) proposition that Cahokian urbanization was caused by improved agricultural technology, trade, and concomitant population growth (Fowler 1974, 1975). A later synthesis challenged this four-tiered integrated model owing to burgeoning evidence of intersettlement functional redundancy and settlement size–occupation span correlations (Emerson 1991a; Emerson and Milner 1981, 1982; Milner 1990, 20–21; Milner et al. 1984). The "Cahokia cultural system," according to Milner (1990), was not unlike other "complex chiefdoms" of the Southeast. It was most certainly not a mercantile center with an economic network spanning the eastern United States. And it was not an overpopulated urban development (Milner 1991).[5] Yet, like the older statement, the later synthesis followed a familiar cultural-materialist path. Cahokia's rise and its demise were still seen as direct results of environment and population growth (J. Kelly 1990a; Lopinot and Woods 1993; Milner 1990, 1991). These older and later researchers argued over little more than size, semantics, and social-evolutionary taxonomy, expressed as state (Fowler 1975; O'Brien 1989, 1991, 1992) versus chiefdom (Milner 1990), high population density (Gregg 1975a) versus low population density (Milner 1991), and full-time craft specialization (Yerkes 1983, 1991) versus no specialization (Muller 1984, 1986b, 1987).

Cahokia was not an urban center with an internally differentiated state government, but it was also not simply another Mississippian center like any other Mississippian center. Moreover, the processes of change were not restricted to the simple causal effects of environment, population growth, or agricultural production. Cahokian development was contingent upon such things, but it was also underlaid by a much more complex set of processes involving political ideologies, disparate interests and identities, actions, and interactions. These complex processes involved subsets of the regional population dominating, resisting, or collaborating with others such that regional development followed a course that was generated from within (see Steponaitis 1983, 173).

Cahokia's dissolution and the scattering of its residents to the four winds likewise may have been a process generated from within (Emerson 1991a; Pauketat 1992). Given the well-known instability of chiefdoms, Cahokia stood little chance of lasting beyond a couple of centuries. The significance of its drawn-out ending, however, lies in the transformation of central Cahokia from a political capital to a sacred center and cemetery (see Knight, chapter 11; Pauketat, chapter 2). Its demise might have witnessed short-lived political resurgences, if the East Plaza (J. Kelly, chapter 8) and the regional Moorehead-phase demographic pattern (Pauketat and Lopinot, chapter 6) have been properly characterized. In fact, ongoing research by Emerson may point toward a more abrupt ending to the Moorehead-phase Cahokia-Mississippian world. A number of small rural cemeteries, formerly thought to have spanned the Sand Prairie phase (A.D. 1275–1350), now appear to date to a narrow window of time at the end of the Moorehead phase or beginning of the Sand Prairie phase (Emerson, Hedman, and Williams 1996). This would be entirely consistent with residential-site data that bear out the larger Moorehead-phase population in the American Bottom compared to the meager Sand Prairie–phase occupation (e.g., Emerson, Milner, and Jackson 1983; Melbye 1963; Milner 1983b, 1984a). And it may mean that the winds of change were a little stiffer at A.D. 1300 than previously had been realized.

With these winds at their backs, the Cahokians left the American Bottom and scattered across the midcontinent and Southeast. Neither Cahokia's beginning nor its end can be reduced to simple eco-functionalist or adaptationist equations. Such causal factors or prime movers, though easy to grasp, are insufficient to explain Cahokia and the rest of Mississippiandom. The Cahokian world was never static. It was never unidimensional or internally homogeneous. And it was not merely a large duplicate of every other Mississippian polity. To explain Cahokian development, we must explain its history of domination, as interest groups vied with one another, promulgating their ideologies and accommodating those of others, in the process exerting a cultural force beyond the American Bottom. The Mississippian world was, at least in part, "Cahokia writ large" (Anderson, chapter 12). Historical understanding of this world will come only by recognizing the dynamic Cahokian past, a past that gave shape and meaning to the Mississippian world. Such recognition will finally place Cahokia and the four winds of Mississippiandom on our charts of American history.

Notes

I. INTRODUCTION

1. Mississippian is a broad cultural category applied by archaeologists to certain precontact peoples in southeastern North America, the Mississippi River drainage, and the eastern margins of the Great Plains. It is best described as consisting of a set of social and religious elements, or social and cultural traditions, closely related to agricultural production and falling between the years A.D 1000 to 1600 (Griffin 1985; Knight 1986; B. Smith 1986; Steponaitis 1986).

2. Griffin's chronology was based on the collections of A. R. Kelly (1933), Titterington (1938), and Griffin and Spaulding (1951), among others.

3. The regional chronology, tied to an absolute radiocarbon scale, is usually presented without being calibrated relative to past fluctuations in atmospheric radiocarbon (Bareis and Porter 1984; J. Kelly 1990a). For present purposes, however, Robert Hall's (1991, figure 1.3) calibrated revision is adopted. This calibrated chronology, adjusting for prehistoric episodes of greater or lesser radioactive carbon in the atmosphere, better serves the current examination of Cahokian development. It has been adopted elsewhere with the provision that future recalibrations are anticipated (Pauketat 1994a, 47).

4. Examples are Porter's ([1969] 1977) market-economy scenario or Gibbon's (1974) Cahokian-state perspective.

5. They also impart a Western-European economic logic to a Native American phenomenon and deny active roles for non-Cahokian native groups.

6. Panregional communication systems, like Mobilean trade jargon (Drechsel 1994) or Plains sign language (Hollow and Parks 1980, 83), may have facilitated long-distance interaction between diverse linguistic groups.

7. Documentation includes Anderson 1991, 1994a; Barth 1991; Blitz 1993; Brain 1988; Chapman 1980; Conrad 1991; Early 1988; Emerson and Lewis, eds., 1991; Garland 1992; Hoffman 1990; Jenkins and Krause 1986; Jeter and Williams 1989; Kidder 1992; Knight, chapter 11; Lewis 1991; Moffat 1991; Morse and Morse 1983; Muller 1986a; M. O'Brien, Warren, and Lewarch 1982; Perttula 1992; Rodell 1991; Sabo and Early 1990; Schnell et al. 1981; Steponaitis 1991; Stoltman, ed., 1991; Tiffany 1991a, 1991b; Webb 1987; Wesler 1991a, 1991b, 1991c; S. Williams 1990; Williams and Brain 1983.

8. Various southeastern and eastern Plains peoples played "chunky," a game with two opposing sides that took place in a yard or plaza. Swanton (1979, 682) states

that there "were evidently several different varieties, but all made use of a smooth stone roller and two long slender poles, often supplied with short cross-pieces midway of their length. While there were usually only two active participants, numbers of onlookers wagered quantities of property on the outcome. The essence of the game was to start the roller along a smooth piece of ground with which every town was supplied, after which the two players threw their poles after it with the idea of hitting the stone, coming as near it as possible when the stone came to rest, or preventing the opponent's stick from accomplishing either of these results."

9. Documentation includes Anderson 1990a, 1994a; Barker and Pauketat 1922; Pauketat 1991, 1994a; J. Scarry 1990, 1992; Steponaitis 1983, 169–74; Welch 1991a.

10. Causal factors, including population growth and climate change, cannot lie outside the gestalt. The inception of the Neo-Atlantic and Pacific climatic episodes at about A.D. 900 and 1200, respectively, have been used to explain both the rise and fall of particular Mississippian "adaptations," including Cahokia (Baerris and Bryson 1965; Griffin 1961; R. Hall 1991, 23; Rindos and Johannessen 1991, 44). They explain little, in fact, about the reasons why political centralization or decentralization occurred or why it took a different shape at Cahokia versus other Mississippian complexes.

2. POLITICAL ECONOMY

1. Social theorists agree that subordinate ideologies persist even under conditions of domination. Ethnic identities and ideologies are not pure, unchanging, or internally consistent. Entire groups never share an ideology en masse, as ideologies constantly change by incorporating elements of others in the context of dominant-subordinate relations (see Comaroff and Comaroff 1991; McGuire 1992, 141–42; Pauketat 1994a, 14–16).

2. At Tract 15A, Cahokia, 15 percent of late Lohmann-phase features contained 800 grams of the axehead-making waste per cubic meter of feature fill. This figure far exceeds the density of any other kind of igneous rock at any site or portion of Cahokia (Pauketat 1994a, 158–59, 177–78). There is little evidence of shell-bead manufacturing at Tract 15A which contrasts greatly with Kunnemann Tract evidence. Likewise, unlike Tract 15A, there are no indications of axehead-making activities in excavated ICT-II (Gums 1993) or Kunnemann-Tract samples (Pauketat 1993c), except for a cache of hypertrophic celts reported from Mound 12.

3. A household cluster or domestic zone consists of the building or buildings and all facilities (pits, hearths, racks, etc.) and activity areas associated with a single household (Pauketat 1989, 295; cf. Winter 1976).

4. The fourteen massive "stages" of Reed et al. (1968) and Skele (1988) are probably not construction stages, per se, but possible periods of inactivity leading to mineraloid precipitation and soil development. All evidence from the four terraces points toward a gradual building up of Monks Mound with *many* stage enlargements and blanket mantles (see Benchley 1974, 1975; Collins and Chalfant 1993; Emerson and Woods 1993; Reed et al. 1968). Doubtless, each mound had a unique construction history. This is especially true of Monks Mound.

5. Production of these mobilized materials is poorly served by the notion of "task specialization," as this has been portrayed in Mississippian literature (Milner 1990, 13; Muller 1984, 1986b, 1987; Yerkes 1991).

4. PATTERNS OF FAUNAL EXPLOITATION

1. A large Lohmann faunal assemblage was identified by Chmurny (1973) from fills of the sub-Mound 51 borrow pit at Cahokia. However, the deer element data were not presented in NISP and therefore cannot be used here. Also, since it is not certain from where the faunal debris in this borrow pit originated and because the association to other artifactual debris (domestic vs. elite garbage) is unknown, it has not been included in this paper.

6. POPULATION DYNAMICS

1. The former include those who have worked at Cahokia proper, some of whom may have been influenced by a Mexican-state model, and others who have worked with Cahokia-influenced groups to the north (see papers in Stoltman, ed., 1991). The latter include certain southeastern archaeologists who appear predisposed to extrapolate from other southeastern complexes to the American Bottom.

2. The first of these walls was built during the late Stirling phase, and the last was constructed during the Moorehead phase (J. Anderson 1977; Pauketat 1987a, 1990).

3. Not only did buildings not last one hundred years, but Gregg's (1975b) Stirling-phase assignations were not based on an analysis of archaeological context and, subsequent to such an analysis, his assignations are known to be erroneous (Pauketat 1994a, 1996).

4. Stirling-phase Cahokians might have been living in higher densities than earlier ones around the margins of the site. Sites like Olszewski (Hanenberger 1990b; Pauketat and Koldehoff 1988) or Sponemann (Jackson et al. 1992) may be the remains of these marginal Cahokians (Pauketat 1994a, 186).

5. Many of the 1:1.5 ratio appear to be late Emergent Mississippian, probably Edelhardt phase, sites. Moreover, the Mississippi Period is, of course, allotted three centuries while the Emergent Mississippi Period is allowed about two centuries, making the rural-site ratio even more weighted in favor of Emergent Mississippian sites.

6. Within a circular catchment 5 kilometers in diameter centered on Monks Mound, about 40 percent of the 78.5 square kilometers (or about 30 square kilometers) would have been cultivable (ignoring all other residential occupations and constraints on land access). Given an average of about one hectare of land per household (three to five individuals), in accordance with the agricultural requirements in underdeveloped countries (Revelle 1966, table 3), this ideal catchment could have supported between nine thousand and fifteen thousand people.

7. The entire region could have supported the speculated numbers of people under a Cahokian umbrella with few subsistence or dietary problems. It would certainly seem, given limited bioanthropological data, that the American Bottom residents were as healthy as the healthiest of Mississippians in the Southeast (Milner 1992, 67).

7. SETTLEMENT AND SOCIAL STRUCTURES

1. This paper reports work sponsored by the Illinois Historic Preservation Agency and performed by the Southern Illinois University at Edwardsville, Contract Archaeology Program. The Iowa Office of the State Archaeologist and the Office of the Vice President for Research, The University of Iowa, provided assistance and support for this paper. Thanks are extended to Lucy Hansen for drafting figures 7.1–7.10. Discussions with Fred Finney, Bill Green, and Tim Pauketat were fruitful in bringing this paper to its final form.

8. SOCIOPOLITICAL ACTIVITY AT EAST ST. LOUIS AND CAHOKIA

1. I would like to recognize the following institutions and persons who were instrumental in the research and preparation of this paper. First and foremost, the excavations at East St. Louis were conducted by the Office of Contract Archaeology at Southern Illinois University at Edwardsville under the auspices of the Illinois Department of Transportation (IDOT) and the Federal Highway Administration. John Walthall of IDOT was instrumental in providing the necessary support throughout this project. Although I cannot name all the people who participated in the excavations, those who were there from beginning to end were Charles O. Witty, Mike Morelock, and Roger Williamson. I am especially indebted to Bonnie Gums who filled in when needed and who endured belligerent backhoe oper-

ators. For the comparative architectural material from Cahokia, funding for a study of Public Architecture at Cahokia was provided by a Funded University Research grant (F-ss328) from Southern Illinois University at Edwardsville. Mera Hertel prepared the various maps used throughout this article. As usual her talents are greatly appreciated. The support of Sam Pearson, dean of Social Science, and William I. Woods, coordinator for the Office of Contract Archaeology, also is gratefully acknowledged. Helpful comments on early drafts of the manuscript were provided by Tim Pauketat, Brad Koldehoff, and Charles O. Witty. Finally, I would like to thank Tim Pauketat and Tom Emerson, editors of this volume, for including this paper and for exercising tolerance and patience throughout the process of writing it.

2. The mounds were probably the symbolic substructures for the abodes of high-ranking individuals, sacred temples housing the dead, or the ritual edifices in which ceremonies of the living were conducted. The symbolic themes that dominated Mississippian ceremonies probably incorporated the ideas of renewal or rebirth, fertility, and purification. Rituals that portrayed these themes would have been conducted within the plazas and sacred temples of the Cahokia core and the other centers. These concepts, which are expressed in a number of ways and through a number of media, were further extended to incorporate the various monuments both mound and nonmound alike (e.g., Pauketat and Emerson 1991). Even simple shapes such as the circle and the square were pivotal building blocks of Mississippian symbolism.

3. It is important to emphasize that what we perceive in this plan is the final product of three hundred years of construction. What is readily visible (the earthen platforms) often served as the foundations for larger buildings. Not readily visible (except through excavation) were the remains of other large architectural edifices that for various reasons were not erected on such platforms, yet served also to demarcate a plaza precinct. For example, the early architectural history of the Murdock mound is replete with such evidence (H. Smith 1969; figure 8.3). Thus, as in the case of each mound center, the history of each Cahokian mound is unique. Each mound's use, however, may not have been continuous nor was its initial erection necessarily synchronous with the construction of other mounds. It was in essence an orchestrated crescendo of construction and reconstruction over two centuries. An excellent example of the discontinuities is apparent in the relocation of the East Plaza after the Stirling phase to the area outside and east of the palisade.

4. The social organization of such groups as the Osage, Omaha, Ioway, and Winnebago has a bearing on understanding some of the principles of social organization at Cahokia. For example, most of these groups, as with many of the southeastern groups, exhibit two major divisions or moieties (e.g., Bailey 1995). These clans had specific social obligations and ritual roles, generally the respon-

sibility of a clan religious specialist. Most positions of leadership were hereditary (see Fletcher and LaFlesche 1972, 202).

9. REFLECTIONS ON CAHOKIAN HEGEMONY

1. In this paper, I shall use the term "elite" to refer to that segment of the Cahokian population that exercises hegemonic control over some portion of the general population. Thus, in this context, I consider "eliteness" as being related to political and religious *power over* rather than solely as a function of restricted membership in a kin group.
2. The early Spoon River Eveland site provides an excellent example of the wholesale emplacement of a settlement form associated with a much higher level of political and social organization into a frontier area. The presence of this site type provides additional strength to Conrad's hypothesis (1991) that the Spoon River Middle Mississippian cultures originated from a movement of Cahokian elite and their attendant sociopolitical systems into the area.
3. The small sites documented by Blitz are extremely unusual and do not conform to the American Bottom definition of a rural "farmstead."
4. Circular structures make their first appearance at Cahokia during the Lohmann phase (cf. Mehrer 1988; Pauketat 1994a).

10. ELITE IDEOLOGY AND THE MISSISSIPPIAN COSMOS

1. Notes on file at the Missouri Historical Society made by Gerald Fowke at the accessioning of the B&O figurine in the late nineteenth century.

11. DEVELOPMENTAL PARALLELS BETWEEN CAHOKIA AND MOUNDVILLE

1. In this paper I will use the term "paramountcy" as a synonym for a complex or multitiered chiefdom (Wright 1984, 42–43), thus sidestepping Anderson's (1990b, 21) distinction between paramount and complex chiefdoms, which, although perhaps ethnographically sound, is not yet fully developed in its archaeological application.
2. In the early 1960s Joseph Vogel wrote, "That there was a steady rain of influence onto the American Bottoms out of the south is evident. That these new traits are absorbed into the existent pattern is also evident" (1964, 26). It has been noted with irony that this "steady rain" produced a Cahokia that "looks *stylistically* very much like its southern Mississippian neighbors," only late in the game, during the Sand Prairie phase, when Cahokia was already in decline (Hall 1991, 15, emphasis added).

3. That the southern contacts remained important through time is attested to by the predominance of southern source areas among the nonlocal commodities found at American Bottom sites (Kelly 1991a, 64).

4. This suggestion is, of course, hardly novel. It conforms to the general model of Mississippian development articulated four decades ago by Phillips, Ford, and Griffin in their classic Mississippi valley study (1951, 451; see also B. Smith 1984, 19–20).

5. I am, of course, assuming that both chronologies are right, an admittedly precarious position. Despite the possibility of future adjustments, I believe it is well enough established that Cahokia's political expansion predated Moundville's, and that is enough for the present argument.

6. A disclaimer is in order to the effect that only a small faction of these collections has been analyzed in any detail, but even if such items are present, they are extraordinarily rare.

7. Cahokia did manage to acquire fairly large quantities of marine shell from the Gulf Coast, a trade that might be expected to have involved Moundville, but there is no evidence of this. The social landscape of the Southeast during Cahokia's Lohmann and Stirling phases (ca. A.D. 1050–1200) was largely a patchwork of rather diminutive simple chiefdoms, any number of which may have been involved. The precise sources of this shell and the mechanisms for its exchange are at this writing unknown. I am aware, in addition, that much of Moundville's iconography is in a style or styles believed to be derivative from the Braden style group of Phillips and Brown, which James Brown (1989, 193–98) is increasingly convinced originated in the American Bottom area. How this style transmission occurred is an intriguing problem in which the traffic in embossed copper prestige goods is almost certainly implicated.

8. The incorporation is cleverly expressed by Pauketat (1993a) as the "Big Bang in the Bottom."

9. Alternatively, perhaps, we have actual Caddoan-bred potters at both sites adapting to the local materials. Neutron-activation analysis of Moundville sherds lends preliminary support to such an idea (Welch 1991b, 15).

10. Wardle neglects to mention additional pearl beads found at the ankles of this individual.

11. By one generous estimate, the primary center at Cahokia covers some 1,340 hectares, an area about half of which was too low for habitation. Moundville covers only about 100 hectares; its entire mound group would fit quite neatly within the inner palisade surrounding the central precinct at Cahokia. Cahokia has more than one hundred mounds; Moundville has twenty-six. Monks Mound at Cahokia has a volume estimated at 615,144 cubic meters; Moundville's Mound B has a volume of about 112,000 cubic meters (Morgan 1980, xxxi). Taking these

disparate measures into account, we can say that Cahokia at its height was very roughly five times larger than Moundville.

12. An alert reader will notice that Cahokia's and Moundville's efforts at defense are actually completely synchronous. The point here, though, is that they come at *different* times in the developmental trajectory of the two systems.

13. Lubbub Creek is 53 kilometers from Moundville. Cemochechobee is 47 kilometers from Roods Landing.

14. There will be some who will surely debate this, but even if it was not so, my point would still be valid. There are no other archaeological cultures on the landscape at this time level that are more complexly organized than the ones identified.

15. I am grateful to Richard Krause for suggesting this distinction.

12. EVOLUTION OF SOUTHEASTERN MISSISSIPPIAN SOCIETY

1. I would like to thank Tim Pauketat and Tom Emerson for encouraging me to write this paper and for detailed technical comments and assistance in tracking down references. The comments of Jim Brown, John Kelly, Jim Knight, George Milner, Dan F. Morse, Dean Saitta, and Vin Steponaitis were also most helpful. Of course, the ideas presented here, while an amalgam of many sources, remain the responsibility of the author.

2. All dates used here are calibrated and follow Robert Hall's 1991 Cahokia chronology; uncorrected radiocarbon dates, which are used over much of the Southeast to date Mississippian events, fall somewhat earlier.

3. A similar perspective is advanced by John Kelly (1991a), in his discussion of Cahokia as a "gateway" community, and also by Peregrine (1991, 1992), in his discussion of the strategic location of Cahokia within the waterways of the East.

4. Evidence for elaborate burials and mortuary facilities has been observed at a number of major centers in the northern American Bottom, and not just at Cahokia, including from the Big Mound in St. Louis, the "Cemetery Mound" at the East St. Louis site, and the large mound at Mitchell, as well as from the Harding and Powell Mounds at Cahokia itself. John Kelly (1994a, 30, 50), in a discussion of this evidence, has suggested that the elite burials in Mound 72 "may represent an earlier, Lohmann-phase precursor to these massive mortuary monuments," most of which he (tentatively) attributes to the Stirling and Moorehead phases. He further suggests that the Harding (or Rattlesnake) Mound at Cahokia may well contain similar, spectacular mortuary assemblages.

The nature of later paramount elite mortuary treatment is not well known, although the limited evidence from the above sites (many of which were destroyed in the last century, and our records are sparse about their contents) suggests there may have been a change from spectacular individual burials (albeit with numerous sacrificial retainers) in the Lohmann phase to collective interments in elaborate, submound charnel facilities later. Dean Saitta, in commenting on an earlier version of this manuscript, has suggested that later, Stirling-phase elite legitimization strategies may have taken different directions than those evidenced by the Mound 72 burials, which come from an early period in the site's history. That is, once political control was achieved, elaborate burial ceremony may have been less necessary as a means of legitimizing the position of the elite (see Pauketat 1992, 42). The extensive monumental construction attributed to Stirlingphase Cahokia, in this view, may indicate more energy was directed to legitimizing and maintaining the idea of a sacred landscape, rather than the position of individual elites.

Finally, Kelly (1994a, 50) has suggested that the capping observed at some mortuary mounds in the northern American Bottom may represent the "symbolic retirement of these lineages," something that was likely tied to the actual retirement (i.e., death) of the individuals comprising them. Whether such retirements were the result of factional competition or more innocuous demographic processes is unknown. The elaborate burials at all of these centers clearly indicate, however, that political power, while perhaps ultimately residing at Cahokia, was nonetheless spread over the landscape. Some of Cahokia's elites quite likely came from these "outlying" centers and returned to them in death (Milner 1984c).

5. Jill Neitzel has done an excellent job of stimulating multiscalar analyses in the Southeast and Southwest alike, first through the symposium "Great Towns and Regional Polities: Cultural Evolution in the U.S. Southwest and Southeast" held at the 57th Annual Meeting of the Society for American Archaeology in Pittsburgh in 1992. Later she was responsible for a week-long seminar at the Amerind Foundation in Dragoon, Arizona, in 1994. The edited papers are currently undergoing review for publication in book form and should be available in 1997.

6. Ideological "domination" need not imply universal or unequivocal acceptance of all parts of the dominant ideology by affected populations. Indeed, people invariably appropriate some aspects of the ideologies they are exposed to (often transforming them to suit their own needs in the process), while simultaneously resisting other parts.

7. Mississippian societies and "influence" clearly varied across the Southeast, and although I believe the spread and emulation of a Cahokian-based ideology were critically important to shaping what came to be known as Mississippian culture over the larger region, obviously the role played by physiography and resource structure, historical conditions, and interaction potential in such a spread must be acknowledged. This is what is meant by a "ripple effect," that societies influenced by Cahokia in turn influenced societies at a greater remove, and so on,

bearing in mind that local conditions could and did prevent the ideology from spreading or being accepted everywhere in the region.

8. The idea that Cahokia played a major role in the origins of what has come to be called the Southeastern Ceremonial Complex (SECC), that is, in the shaping Mississippian religion and iconography (the latter being a material expression of the former, although the "classic" SECC is still taken to refer to a time period as well, from ca. A.D. 1250 to 1350), is increasingly viewed as plausible. Brown and Kelly (1995), for example, in a major treatment of the evolution of the SECC, have argued that the origin for the Braden iconographic style, as well as an early appearance for many classic SECC motifs, appears to be at Cahokia. These same authors infer an evolution from Late Woodland and Emergent Mississippian "birdman" motifs found at sites in the Midwest to the falcon warrior motifs of the classic SECC, as exemplified on the Rogan plates and Spiro shell engravings.

The late and post-Cahokian flourishing of the SECC from ca. A.D. 1250 to 1350, like the widespread emergence of paramount chiefdoms about this time or slightly earlier, may have actually been stimulated by the decline of Cahokia. Instead of one preeminent center that was the source of all sacredness and ceremony, there were now many centers of varying size and influence, each with its own ceremonies and rituals (the individual expressions of a shared Mississippian religion, after Knight 1986) and each participating in a regional interaction and exchange network. The idea of Mississippian that first crystallized in the northern American Bottom was powerfully augmented and transformed during its spread across the region, and as the political landscape changed.

9. Conditions were ripe for the emergence and spread of an ideology like that which we now call Mississippian around A.D. 900 to 1100. Societies over the region were adopting intensive agriculture, populations were growing, and warfare appears to have been increasing. Experiments in the formation of complex organization and ceremony are evident not only in the Central Mississippi valley (i.e., in the American Bottom and the Cairo Lowlands), but across the region, from the Coles Creek societies of the lower Mississippi valley to a range of so-called "Emergent Mississippian" societies as far east as the South Appalachian area and the Florida Gulf Coast (B. Smith 1990). Political and ideological systems that enabled people to better adapt to these changing conditions would have probably quickly spread.

Cahokian ideology, in the form of Mississippian religion, exchange, and elite political behavior, also may have been able to fill the apparent ideological void that characterizes parts of the Late Woodland Southeast, following the collapse of the earlier Middle Woodland period, Hopewellian ritual and interaction. That Mississippian culture failed to spread everywhere across the East appears to be, in part, because it was an ideology tied to an organizational form—the chiefdom—and an economic foundation—intensive maize agriculture. Only when these conditions were present did the ideology have a chance of being accepted or differentially appropriated.

10. This point must be stressed. The ideology that crystallized at Cahokia certainly did not spring full-blown from nothing but had to have been based, at least in part, on myths, motifs, and ceremonies from antecedent and contemporaneous societies over the surrounding region. It would be foolish to deny the existence and history of the regional cultural landscape within which Cahokia arose. This is not to deny that much of what later came to known as Mississippian religion and ceremony could not have crystallized at Cahokia. What appears to have spread widely, however, was ceremony, iconography, and political structure, rather than the more obvious or mundane accoutrements of the Cahokian lifestyle, such as Ramey-Incised pots or wall-trench architecture.

13. CONCLUSION

1. Reference is to the American Bottom as seen by Mehrer (1995), and by others in the guise of eco-functionalism and adaptationism (Emerson and Milner 1981, 1982; Milner 1990; Milner et al. 1984, 186; Muller 1978, 1986a).

2. Alternative "bottom-up" explanations that fail to consider political-administrative centers as part and parcel of rural Mississippian communities beg the question of why rural-settlement changes occurred in the first place. The best-fit explanation at present is that rural life within at least a 10-kilometer radius of Cahokia was simply an extension of the centralized Mississippian phenomenon. It is perhaps noteworthy that most of the residents within such a radius would have been able to see Monks Mound in its final form (elevated 30 meters above the floodplain).

3. A cursory comparison, however, of the rural organization of the Black Warrior and Tombigbee valleys reveals that the American Bottom farmstead-homestead-nodal settlement pattern is different from the Moundville and Summerville "farmstead" pattern (see Blitz 1993; Knight, chapter 11). Moundville and Summerville include large and multiple-household settlements that have yet to be seen in the northern American Bottom proper. Besides the fact that a Cahokian polity might have been five to ten times the size of a Moundville polity, Cahokia's reshaping of the rural landscape may have been unparalleled by other southeastern developments. Again, the Cahokian polity, in its scale and organization, was historically unique.

4. The pre-Mississippian ethic itself may be seen as the means whereby regional control was arrested by Cahokians. Cahokian patrons or overlords (once in control) would have redefined the meanings of community, appropriating them for the sake of perpetuating political control (Pauketat and Emerson 1996). To see only Mississippian communalism at Cahokia, as does Saitta (1994), is to fall

289

prey to the same usurpation of community that resulted in the Lohmann phase. Cahokian political ideology, it seems, continues to sway contemporary thought.

5. At the fringe of various syntheses have been adaptationists and neo-Darwinists who emphasize Cahokia as a minimal chiefdom or redistributional adaptation (e.g., Mehrer 1995; Muller 1986a, 1987; O'Brien, Warren, and Lewarch 1982, 81) and "world-systems" advocates who prefer to see Cahokia as an economic core exploiting its far-flung periphery (Dincauze and Hasenstab 1989; O'Brien 1991, 1992; Peregrine 1991, 1992). Neither position is theoretically current or an entirely appropriate fit to the archaeological data.

References Cited

Abercrombie, Nicholas, Stephen Hill, and Bryan S. Turner

1980   *The Dominant Ideology Thesis.* London: George Allen and Unwin.

Ahler, Steven R., and Peter J. DePuydt

1987   *A Report on the 1931 Powell Mound Excavations, Madison County, Illinois.* Illinois State Museum Reports of Investigations 43. Springfield.

Ambrose, Stanley H.

1987   Chemical and isotopic techniques of diet reconstruction in eastern North America. In *Emergent Horticultural Economies of the Eastern Woodlands*, edited by W. F. Keegan, pp.87–107. Center for Archaeological Investigations Occasional Paper 7. Carbondale IL.

Anderson, David G.

1990a   Political change in chiefdom societies: Cycling changes in the late prehistoric southeastern United States. Ph.D. diss., University of Michigan, Ann Arbor. Ann Arbor: University Microfilms.

1990b   Stability and change in chiefdom-level societies: An examination of Mississippian political evolution on the South Atlantic slope. In *Lamar Archaeology: Mississippian Chiefdoms in the Deep South*, edited by M. Williams and G. Shapiro, pp.187–213. Tuscaloosa: University of Alabama Press.

1991   Examining prehistoric settlement distribution in eastern North America. *Archaeology of Eastern North America* 19:1–22.

1994a   *The Savannah River Chiefdoms: Political Change in the Late Prehistoric Southeast.* Tuscaloosa: University of Alabama Press.

1994b   Factional competition and the political evolution of Mississippian chiefdoms in the southeastern United States. In *Factional Competition in the New World*, edited by Elizabeth M. Brumfiel and John W. Fox, pp.61–76. Cambridge: Cambridge University Press.

1994c   Exploring the antiquity of interaction networks in the east. Paper presented at the annual meeting of the Southeastern Archaeological Conference, 9–12 November 1994, Lexington KY.

n.d.   Examining chiefdoms in the Southeast: An application of multiscalar analysis. Manuscript prepared for the seminar "Great Towns and Regional Polities: Cultural Evolution in the U.S. Southwest and Southeast," organized by Jill Neitzel, 5–12 March 1994, Amerind Foundation, Dragoon AZ.

Anderson, David G., David W. Stahle, and Malcolm R. Cleaveland
1995   Paleoclimate and the potential food reserves of Mississippian societies: A case study from the Savannah River valley. *American Antiquity* 60:258–86.

Anderson, James
1973   A Cahokia palisade sequence. In *Explorations into Cahokia Archaeology*, edited by M. Fowler, pp.89–99. Illinois Archaeological Survey Bulletin 7. Urbana.

1977   A Cahokia palisade sequence. In *Explorations into Cahokia Archaeology* (2d revised edition), edited by M. Fowler, pp.89–99. Illinois Archaeological Survey Bulletin 7. Urbana.

Asch, David L., and Nancy B. Asch
1978   The economic potential of *Iva annua* and its prehistoric importance in the lower Illinois valley. In *The Nature and Status of Ethnobotany*, edited by R. I. Ford, pp.300–341. University of Michigan, Museum of Anthropology, Anthropological Papers 67. Ann Arbor: Museum of Anthropology.

1985   Archeobotany. In *Smiling Dan: Structure and Function at a Middle Woodland Settlement in the Illinois Valley*, edited by B. D. Stafford and M. B. Sant, pp.327–401. Kampsville Archeological Center Research Series 2. Kampsville IL: Center for American Archeology.

Asch, Nancy B., and David L. Asch
1975   Plant remains from the Zimmerman site—grid A: A quantitative perspective. In *The Zimmerman Site: Further Excavations at the Grand Village of Kaskaskia*, by M. K. Brown, pp.116–20. Illinois State Museum Reports of Investigations 32. Springfield.

1981   Archeobotany of Newbridge, Carlin, and Weitzer sites—the White Hall components. In *Faunal Exploitation and Resource Selection: Early Late Woodland Subsistence in the Lower Illinois Valley*, by B. Styles, pp.275–91. Evanston IL: Northwestern University Archeology Program.

Baerreis, David A., and Reid A. Bryson
1965   Climatic episodes and the dating of the Mississippian cultures. *Wisconsin Archeologist* 46 (4): 203–20.

Bailey, Garrick A., editor
1995   *The Osage and the Invisible World: From the Works of Francis La Flesche*. Norman: University of Oklahoma Press.

Banerjee, S. K.
1981   Experimental methods of rock magnetism and paleomagnetism. In *Advances in Geophysics*, vol.23, edited by B. Saltzman, pp.25–99. New York: Academic Press.

Banerjee, S. K., J. W. King, and J. A. Marvin
1981   A rapid method for magnetic granulometry with application to environmental studies. *Geophysical Research Letters* 8:333–36.

Bareis, Charles J.

1963   University of Illinois projects. In *Second Annual Report: American Bottoms Archaeology, 1 July 1962–30 June 1963*, edited by M. L. Fowler, pp.3–8. Urbana: Illinois Archaeological Survey.

1967   Interim report on preliminary site examination undertaken in Archaeological Section A of FAI 255 south of business 40 in the interstate portion of Area s-34-4 of the Cahokia site, St. Clair County, Illinois. Department of Anthropology Research Reports 1, Urbana.

1975a   Report of 1971 University of Illinois–Urbana excavations at the Cahokia site. In *Cahokia Archaeology: Field Reports*, edited by M. L. Fowler, pp.9–11. Illinois State Museum Research Series, Papers in Anthropology 3. Springfield.

1975b   Report of 1972 University of Illinois–Urbana excavations at the Cahokia site. In *Cahokia Archaeology: Field Reports*, edited by M. L. Fowler, pp.12–15. Illinois State Museum Research Series, Papers in Anthropology 3. Springfield.

Bareis, Charles J., and Donald Lathrap

1962   University of Illinois projects. In *First Annual Report: American Bottoms Archaeology, 1 July 1961–30 June 1962*, edited by M. L. Fowler, pp.3–9. Urbana: Illinois Archaeological Survey.

Bareis, Charles J., and James W. Porter, editors

1984   *American Bottom Archaeology*. Urbana: University of Illinois Press.

Barker, Alex W., and Timothy R. Pauketat

1992   Introduction: Social inequality and the native elites of southeastern North America. In *Lords of the Southeast: Social Inequality and the Native Elites of Southeastern North America*, edited by A. W. Barker and T. R. Pauketat, pp.1–10. Archeological Papers of the American Anthropological Association, No.3. Washington DC: American Anthropological Association.

Barth, Robert J.

1991   The emergence of the Vincennes culture in the lower Wabash drainage. In *Cahokia and the Hinterlands: Middle Mississippian Cultures of the Midwest*, edited by T. E. Emerson and R. B. Lewis, pp.257–63. Urbana: University of Illinois Press.

Benchley, Elizabeth D.

1974   Mississippian secondary mound loci: A comparative functional analysis in a time-space perspective. Ph.D. diss., Department of Anthropology, University of Wisconsin, Milwaukee.

1975   Summary field report of excavations on the southwest corner of the first terrace of Monks Mound: 1968, 1969, 1971. In *Cahokia Archaeology: Field Reports*, edited by M. L. Fowler, pp.16–24. Illinois State Museum Research Series, Papers in Anthropology 3. Springfield.

1977   Preliminary report of an archaeological site feasibility study for the proposed interpretive center at the Cahokia mounds historic site, East St. Louis, Illinois. Manuscript on file, Illinois Historic Preservation Agency, Springfield.

Benchley, Elizabeth D., and P. DePuydt

1982   Final report of the 1980 test excavations at the interpretive center tract, Cahokia mounds historic site. Report of Investigations No.61. Archaeological Research Laboratory, University of Wisconsin, Milwaukee.

Bender, Margaret M., David A. Baerreis, and R. L. Stevenson

1981   Further light on carbon isotopes and Hopewell agriculture. *American Antiquity* 46:346–53.

Binford, Lewis R.

1978   *Nunamuit Ethnoarchaeology*. New York: Academic Press.

1984   *Faunal Remains from Klasies River Mouth*. New York: Academic Press.

Birkoff, G. D.

1933   *Aesthetic Measure*. Cambridge: Harvard University Press.

Blitz, John H.

1993   *Ancient Chiefdoms of the Tombigbee*. Tuscaloosa: University of Alabama Press.

Bloch, Maurice

1989   From cognition to ideology. In *Ritual, History and Power: Selected Papers in Anthropology*, by M. Bloch, pp.106–36. London School of Economics, Monographs on Social Anthropology 58. London: Athlone Press.

Bogan, A. F.

1980   A comparison of late prehistoric Dallas and Overhill Cherokee subsistence strategies in the Little Tennessee River valley. Ph.D. diss., University of Tennessee, Knoxville.

Boserup, Ester

1965   *The Conditions of Agricultural Growth: The Economics of Agrarian Change Under Population Pressure*. Chicago: Aldine.

Bozell, John R.

1993   Vertebrate fauna. In *Temples for Cahokia Lords: Preston Holder's 1955–1956 Excavations of Kunnemann Mound*, by Timothy R. Pauketat, pp.107–23. University of Michigan Museum of Anthropology Memoir 26. Ann Arbor.

Brackenridge, Henry M.

1962   *Views of Louisiana Together with a Journal of a Voyage Up the Missouri River*. 1811. Reprint, Chicago: Quadrangle Books.

Bradley, Richard

1984   Studying monuments. In *Neolithic Studies: A Review of Some Current Research*, edited by R. Bradley and J. Gardiner, pp.61–66. BAR British Series 133. Oxford: BAR.

Brain, Jeffrey P.
1978   Late prehistoric settlement patterning in the Yazoo Basin and Natchez Bluffs regions of the Lower Mississippi valley. In *Mississippian Settlement Patterns*, edited by B. D. Smith, pp.331–68. New York: Academic Press.
1988   *Tunica Archaeology*. Peabody Museum of Archaeology and Ethnology. Cambridge: Harvard University.
1989   Winterville: Late prehistoric culture contact in the Lower Mississippi valley. Mississippi Department of Archives and History Archaeological Report 23. Jackson MS.
1991   Cahokia from the southern periphery. In *New Perspectives on Cahokia: Views from the Periphery*, edited by J. B. Stoltman, pp.93–100. Monographs in World Archaeology 2. Madison WI: Prehistory Press.

Bronson, Bennet
1972   Farm labor and the evolution of food production. In *Population Growth: Anthropological Implications*, edited by B. Spooner, pp.190–218. Cambridge: MIT Press.

Brouk, Michael
1978   A Middle Mississippian crematory burial. *Central States Archaeological Journal* 25:122–28.

Brown, James A.
1976a   The Southern cult reconsidered. *Midcontinental Journal of Archaeology* 1:115–35.
1976b   Spiro studies, volume 4, The artifacts. Third Annual Report of Caddoan Archaeology-Spiro Focus Research, Part 2. Norman: University of Oklahoma Research Institute.
1985   The Mississippian Period. In *Ancient Art of the American Woodland Indians*, pp.93–145. New York: Harry N. Abrams.
1989   On style divisions of the Southeastern Ceremonial Complex: A Revisionist perspective. In *The Southeastern Ceremonial Complex: Artifacts and Analysis*, edited by P. Galloway, pp.183–204. Lincoln: University of Nebraska Press.

Brown, James A., and John E. Kelly
1995   Cahokia and the beginnings of the Southeastern Ceremonial Complex. Manuscript in preparation, dated 25 June 1995.

Brown, James A., Richard A. Kerber, and Howard D. Winters
1990   Trade and the evolution of exchange relations at the beginning of the Mississippian Period. In *The Mississippian Emergence*, edited by B. D. Smith, pp.251–80. Washington DC: Smithsonian Institution Press.

Brumfiel, Elizabeth M., and Timothy K. Earle
1987   Specialization, exchange, and complex societies: An introduction. In *Spe-*

cialization, Exchange, and Complex Societies, edited by E. M. Brumfiel and T. K. Earle, pp. 1–9. Cambridge: Cambridge University Press.

Bushnell, David I., Jr.

1904   The Cahokia and surrounding mound groups. Papers of the Peabody Museum of American Archaeology and Ethnology, vol. 3, no. 1. Cambridge: Harvard University.

1922   Archaeological reconnaissance of the Cahokia and related mound groups. Explorations and field work of the Smithsonian Institution in 1921. *Smithsonian Miscellaneous Collections* 72 (15): 92–105. Washington DC.

Butler, Brian

1977   Mississippian settlement in the Black Bottom, Pope and Massac Counties, Illinois. Ph.D. diss., Department of Anthropology, Southern Illinois University, Carbondale. Ann Arbor: University Microfilms.

Carneiro, Robert L.

1981   The chiefdom: Precursor of the state. In *Transitions to Statehood in the New World*, edited by G. Jones and R. Kantz, pp. 37–79. Cambridge: Cambridge University Press.

Casselberry, Samuel E.

1974   Further refinement of formulae for determining population from floor area. *World Archaeology* 6:117–22.

Champion, Timothy C.

1989   Introduction. In *Centre and Periphery: Comparative Studies in Archaeology*, edited by T. C. Champion, pp. 1–21. London: Unwin Hyman.

Chapman, Carl H.

1980   *The Archaeology of Missouri, II*. Columbia: University of Missouri Press.

Chmurny, William W.

1973   The ecology of the Middle Mississippian occupation of the American Bottom. Ph.D. diss., Department of Anthropology, University of Illinois at Urbana.

Clark, A.

1990   *Seeing Beneath the Soil: Prospecting Methods in Archaeology*. London: B.T. Batsford Ltd.

Clark, John E., and Michael Blake

1994   The power of prestige: Competitive generosity and the emergence of rank societies in lowland Mesoamerica. In *Factional Competition in the New World*, edited by Elizabeth M. Brumfiel and John W. Fox, pp. 17–30. Cambridge: Cambridge University Press.

Clark, R. M., and Colin Renfrew

1972   A statistical approach to the calibration of floating tree-ring chronologies using radiocarbon dates. *Archaeometry* 14:5–19.

Clayton, Lawrence A., Vernon James Knight Jr., and Edward C. Moore, editors
1993   *The De Soto Chronicles: The Expedition of Hernando de Soto to North America in 1539–1543*. Tuscaloosa: University of Alabama Press.

Cobb, Charles R.
1989   An appraisal of the role of Mill Creek chert hoes in Mississippian exchange systems. *Southeastern Archaeology* 8:79–92.

Cohen, Mark N.
1977   *The Food Crisis in Prehistory: Overpopulation and the Origins of Agriculture*. New Haven: Yale University Press.

Cole, F-C., R. Bell, J. Bennett, J. Caldwell, N. Emerson, R. MacNeish, K. Orr, and R. Willis
1951   *Kincaid: A Prehistoric Illinois Metropolis*. Chicago: University of Chicago Press.

Collins, James M.
1990   *The Archaeology of the Cahokia Mounds ICT-II: Site Structure*. Illinois Cultural Resources Study 10. Illinois Historic Preservation Agency, Springfield.
1993   Cahokia settlement and social structures as viewed from the ICT-II. Paper presented at the 58th annual meeting of the Society for American Archaeology, St. Louis.

Collins, James M., and Dale R. Henning
1996   The Big River phase: Emergent Mississippian cultural expression on Cahokia's near frontier, the northeast Ozark rim, Missouri. Manuscript in the possession of the author.

Collins, James M., and Michael L. Chalfant
1993   A second-terrace perspective on Monks Mound. *American Antiquity* 58:319–32.

Colson, Elizabeth, and Max Gluckman
1951   *Seven Tribes of Central Africa*. Manchester: Manchester University Press.

Comaroff, Jean, and John Comaroff
1991   *Of Revelation and Revolution: Christianity, Colonialism, and Consciousness in South Africa*. Chicago: University of Chicago Press.

Conant, A. J.
1877   The mounds and their builders or traces of prehistoric man in Missouri. In *The Commonwealth of Missouri*, edited by C. R. Barns, pp. 1–122. St. Louis: Bryan, Brand and Co.

Conrad, Lawrence
1991   The Middle Mississippian cultures of the central Illinois valley. In *Cahokia and the Hinterlands: Middle Mississippian Cultures of the Midwest*, edited by T. E. Emerson and R. B. Lewis, pp. 119–63. Urbana: University of Illinois Press.

Cook, Della C.
1984   Subsistence and health in the lower Illinois valley: Osteological evidence. In *Paleopathology at the Origins of Agriculture*, edited by M. N. Cohen and G. J. Armelagos, pp.235–69. Orlando: Academic Press.

Cook, Sherburne F.
1972   Prehistoric demography. *Addison-Wesley Modular Publications* 16:1–42.

Cowan, C. Wesley
1985   Understanding the evolution of plant husbandry in eastern North America: Lessons from botany, ethnography and archaeology. In *Prehistoric Food Production in North America*, edited by R. I. Ford, pp.205–43. University of Michigan, Museum of Anthropology, Anthropological Papers 75. Ann Arbor.

Crabtree, J. P.
1990   Zooarchaeology and complex societies: Some uses of faunal analysis for the study of trade, social status and ethnicity. In *Archaeological Method and Theory*, vol.2, edited by Michael B. Schiffer, pp.155–206. Tucson: University of Arizona Press.

Crites, Gary D., and R. Dale Terry
1984   Nutritive value of maygrass, *Phalaris caroliniana. Economic Botany* 38:114–20.

Culin, Stewart
1907   Games of the North American Indians. Twenty-fourth Annual Report of the Bureau of American Ethnology. Washington DC: Smithsonian Instititution.

Dalan, Rinita A.
1993a   Landscape modification at the Cahokia mounds site: Geophysical evidence of culture change. Ph.D. diss., Department of Anthropology, University of Minnesota.

1993b   Issues of scale in archaeogeophysical research. In *Effects of Scale on Archaeological and Geoscientific Perspectives*, edited by J. K. Stein and A. R. Linse, pp.67–78. Boulder CO: Geological Society of America Special Paper 283.

Dalan, Rinita A., and Subir K. Banerjee
1996   Soil magnetism, an approach for examining archaeological landscapes. *Geophysical Research Letters* (23:185–88).

Dalan, Rinita A., George R. Holley, and Harold W. Watters Jr.
1993   An assessment of Moorehead's investigations at Mound 56, Cahokia Mounds State Historic Site. Unpublished report submitted to the Illinois Historic Preservation Agency, Springfield. Southern Illinois University at Edwardsville.

Dalan, Rinita A., George R. Holley, Melvin L. Fowler, and William R. Iseminger
1989   A reconsideration of the Central Palisade at the Cahokia site. Paper presented at the 54th annual meeting of the Society for American Archaeology, Atlanta.

DeBoer, Warren R.
1988   Subterranean storage and the organization of surplus: The view from eastern North America. *Southeastern Archaeology* 7:1–20.
1993   Like a rolling stone: The chunkey game and political organization in eastern North America. *Southeastern Archaeology* 12:83–92.

Deetz, James
1990   Prologue: Landscapes as cultural statements. In *Earth Patterns: Essays in Landscape Archaeology*, edited by W. M. Kelso and R. Most, pp. 1–4. Charlottesville: University Press of Virginia.

Demarest, Arthur A., and Geoffrey W. Conrad, editors
1992   *Ideology and Pre-Columbian Civilizations*. Sante Fe: School of American Research Press.

De Montmollin, Olivier
1989   *The Archaeology of Political Structure: Settlement Analysis in a Classic Maya Polity*. Cambridge: Cambridge University Press.

Denny, Sidney G., William I. Woods, and Brad Koldehoff
1983   Upland Mississippian settlement/subsistence systems of the Cahokia region. Paper presented at the 48th annual meeting of the Society for American Archaeology, Pittsburgh.

DePratter, Chester B.
1983   Late prehistoric and early historic chiefdoms in the southeastern United States. Ph.D. diss., University of Georgia. Ann Arbor: University Microfilms.

Dincauze, Dena F., and Robert J. Hasenstab
1989   Explaining the Iroquois: Tribalization on a prehistoric periphery. In *Centre und Periphery: Comparative Studies in Archaeology*, edited by T. C. Champion, pp.67–87. London: Unwin Hyman.

Divale, William T.
1977   Living floor area and marital residence: A replication. *Behavior Science Research* 12 (2): 109–15.

Dorothy, Lawrence G.
1980   The ceramics of the Sand Point site (20BG14), Baraga County, Michigan: A preliminary description. *Michigan Archaeologist* 26 (3–4): 39–90.

Douglas, John
1976   Collins: A late Woodland Ceremonial Complex in the Woodfordian. Ph.D. diss., University of Illinois. Ann Arbor: University Microfilms.

Douglas, Mary, and Baron Isherwood
1979   *The World of Goods: Towards a Theory of Consumption*. New York: Allen Lane.

Drechsel, Emanuel J.
1994   Mobilean jargon in the "prehistory" of southeastern North America. In *Perspectives on the Southeast: Linguistics, Archaeology, and Ethnohistory*, edited by P. B. Kwachka, pp.25–43. Athens: University of Georgia Press.

Drennan, Robert D.
1987   Regional demography in chiefdoms. *In Chiefdoms in the Americas*, edited by R. Drennan and C. A. Uribe, pp.307–23. Lanham MD: University Press of America.

1991   Pre-Hispanic chiefdom trajectories in Mesoamerica, Central America, and northern South America. In *Chiefdoms: Power, Economy, and Ideology*, edited by T. Earle, pp.263–87. Cambridge: Cambridge University Press.

Drennan, Robert D., and C. A. Uribe
1987   Introduction. In *Chiefdoms in the Americas*, edited by R. Drennan and C. A. Uribe, pp. vii–xix. Lanham MD: University Press of America.

Drennan, Robert D., and C. A. Uribe, editors
1987   *Chiefdoms in the Americas*. Lanham MD: University Press of America.

Dunavan, Sandra L.
1993   Reanalysis of seed crops from Emge: New implications for Late Woodland subsistence-settlement systems. In *Foraging and Farming in the Eastern Woodlands*, edited by C. M. Scarry, pp.98–114. Gainesville: University of Florida Press.

Duncan, Carol Diaz-Granados
1993   Prehistoric petroglyphs and pictographs of Missouri: Reflections of power, wealth, and sex—nothing's changed. Paper presented at the 1993 Midwest Archaeological Conference, Milwaukee.

Dye, David H.
1994   The art of war in the sixteenth-century central Mississippi valley. In *Perspectives on the Southeast: Linguistics, Archaeology, and Ethnohistory*, edited by P. B. Kwachka, pp.44–60. Athens: University of Georgia Press.

Earle, Timothy K.
1987   Chiefdoms in archaeological and ethnohistorical perspective. *Annual Review of Anthropology* 16:279–308.

1989   The evolution of chiefdoms. *Current Anthropology* 30:84–88.

1991a   The evolution of chiefdoms. In *Chiefdoms: Power, Economy, and Ideology*, edited by T. Earle, pp.1–15. Cambridge: Cambridge University Press.

1991b   Property rights and the evolution of chiefdoms. In *Chiefdoms: Power, Economy, and Ideology*, edited by T. Earle, pp.71–99. Cambridge: Cambridge University Press.

Early, Ann M.

1988 Standridge: Caddoan settlement in a mountain environment. Arkansas Archeological Survey Research Series No.29. Fayetteville.

Easton, David

1959 Political anthropology. In *Biennial Review of Anthropology 1959*, edited by Bernard Siegal, pp.210–62. Stanford: Stanford University Press.

Eberhart, S. A., L. H. Penny, and G. F. Sprague

1964 Intra-plot competition among maize single-crosses. *Crop Science* 4:467–71.

Ehrenberg, M.

1989 *Women in Prehistory*. London: British Museum Publications.

Eister, Allan W.

1974 Religious institutions in complex societies: Difficulties in the theoretic specification of functions. In *The Social Meanings of Religions*, edited by W. Newman, pp.71–79. Chicago: Rand McNally.

Ember, Melvin

1973 An archaeological indicator of matrilocal versus patrilocal residence. *American Antiquity* 38:177–82.

Emerson, Thomas E.

1982 Mississippian stone images in Illinois. Illinois Archaeological Survey Circular 6. Urbana.

1983 The Bostrom figure pipe and the Cahokia effigy style in the American Bottom. *Midcontinental Journal of Archaeology* 8:257–67.

1984 The Stirling phase occupation. In *The BBB Motor Site*, by T. Emerson and D. Jackson, pp.197–321. American Bottom Archaeology, FAI-270 Reports 6. Urbana: University of Illinois Press.

1989 Water, serpents, and the underworld: An exploration into Cahokia symbolism. In *The Southeastern Ceremonial Complex: Artifacts and Analysis*, edited by P. Galloway, pp.45–92. Lincoln: University of Nebraska Press.

1991a Some perspectives on Cahokia and the northern Mississippian expansion. In *Cahokia and the Hinterlands: Middle Mississippian Cultures of the Midwest*, edited by T. E. Emerson and R. B. Lewis, pp.221–36. Urbana: University of Illinois Press.

1991b The Apple River Mississippian culture of northwestern Illinois. In *Cahokia and the Hinterlands: Middle Mississippian Cultures of the Midwest*, edited by T. E. Emerson and R. B. Lewis, pp.164–82. Urbana: University of Illinois Press.

1992 The Mississippian dispersed village as a social and environmental strategy. In *Late Prehistoric Agriculture: Observations from the Midwest*, edited by W. I. Woods, pp.198–216. Studies in Illinois Archaeology, 8. Springfield: Illinois Historic Preservation Agency.

1995 Settlement, symbolism, and hegemony in the Cahokian countryside. Ph.D. diss., Department of Anthropology, University of Wisconsin, Madison.

n.d. a The Svehla effigy elbow pipe and spud: Mississippian elite sacra from the Sutter collection. Manuscript in preparation.

n.d. b Mississippian stone shamans. Manuscript in preparation.

Emerson, Thomas E., and Douglas K. Jackson

1984 *The BBB Motor Site (11-Ms-595)*. American Bottom Archaeology, FAI-270 Site Reports 6. Urbana: University of Illinois Press.

1987 *The Marcus Site*. American Bottom Archaeology, FAI-270 Site Reports 17, part 2. Urbana: University of Illinois Press.

Emerson, Thomas E., and George R. Milner

1981 The Mississippian occupation of the American Bottom: The communities. Paper presented at the 26th annual Midwest Archaeological Conference, Madison WI.

1982 Community organization and settlement patterns of peripheral Mississippian sites in the American Bottom. Paper presented at the 47th annual meeting of the Society for American Archaeology, Minneapolis.

1988 Internal structure, distribution, and relationships among low-level Mississippian communities in Illinois. Paper presented at the 53d annual meeting of the Society for American Archaeology, Phoenix.

Emerson, Thomas E., and James A. Brown

1992 The late prehistory and protohistory of Illinois. In *Calumet and Fleur-de-Lys: Archaeology of Indian and French Contact in the Midcontinent*, edited by J. A. Walthall and T. E. Emerson, pp.77–128. Washington DC: Smithsonian Institution Press.

Emerson, Thomas E., and W. I. Woods

1990 The slumping of the Great Knob: An archaeological and geotechnic case study of the stability of a great earthen mound. In *Sixth International Conference on the Conservation of Earthen Architecture*, Adobe 90 Preprints, pp.219–24. Los Angeles: The Getty Conservation Institute.

1993 Saving the Great Nobb: A case study in the preservation of Cahokia's Monks Mound through passive management. *Illinois Archaeology* 5 (1–2): 100–107.

Emerson, Thomas E., George R. Milner, and Douglas Jackson

1983 The Florence Street site. American Bottom Archaeology, FAI-270 Site Reports 2. Urbana: University of Illinois Press.

Emerson, Thomas E., Kristin Hedman, Mary Simon, and Valerie Williams

1996 New data and preliminary insights into the Cahokian collapse. Paper presented at the 61st annual meeting of the Society for American Archaeology, New Orleans.

Emerson, Thomas E., and R. Barry Lewis, editors

1991 *Cahokia and the Hinterlands: Middle Mississippian Cultures of the Midwest.* Urbana: University of Illinois Press.

Esarey, Duane, and Timothy R. Pauketat

1992 *The Lohmann Site: An Early Mississippian Center in the American Bottom.* American Bottom Archaeology, FAI-270 Site Reports 25. Urbana: University of Illinois Press.

Farnsworth, Kenneth B., and Thomas E. Emerson

1989 The Macoupin Creek figure pipe and its archaeological context: Evidence for Late Woodland–Mississippian interaction beyond the northern border of Cahokia settlement. *Midcontinental Journal of Archaeology* 14:18–37.

Feinman, Gary, and Jill Neitzel

1984 Too many types: An overview of sedentary prestate societies in the Americas. *Advances in Archaeological Method and Theory*, vol.7, pp.39–102. New York: Academic Press.

Finney, Fred A.

1985 *The Carbon Dioxide Site.* American Bottom Archaeology, FAI-270 Site Reports 11, part 1. Urbana: University of Illinois Press.

1993 Spatially isolated structures in the Cahokia locality: Short-term residences or special-purpose shelters? *Illinois Archaeology* 5 (1–2): 381–392.

Finney, Fred A., and James B. Stoltman

1991 The Fred Edwards site: A case of Stirling phase culture contact in southwestern Wisconsin. In *New Perspectives on Cahokia: Views from the Periphery*, edited by J.. Stoltman, pp.229–52. Madison WI: Prehistory Press.

Fletcher, Alice C., and Francis La Flesche

1972 The Omaha Tribe, vols.1–2. Lincoln: University of Nebraska Press.

Ford, Richard I.

1974a Appendix 2: Floral identifications. In *Late Woodland Settlement and Subsistence in the Lower Kaskaskia River Valley*, by L. Carl Kuttruff, pp.225–31. Ph.D. diss., Department of Anthropology, Southern Illinois University, Carbondale.

1974b Northeastern archaeology: Past and future directions. *Annual Review of Anthropology* 3:385–413.

Fortier, Andrew C.

1985 *The Robert Schneider Site.* American Bottom Archaeology, FAI-270 Site Reports 11, part 2. Urbana: University of Illinois Press.

1991a Features. In The Sponemann Site 2, by D. K. Jackson, A. C. Fortier, and J. A. Williams, pp.49–124. Department of Anthropology, University of Illinois at Urbana-Champaign, FAI-270 Archaeological Mitigation Project 83.

1991b Stone figurines. In The Sponemann Site 2, by D. K. Jackson, A. C. Fortier, and J. A. Williams, pp.277–303. Department of Anthropology, University of Illinois at Urbana-Champaign, FAI-270 Archaeological Mitigation Project Report 83.

1991c Interpretation. In The Sponemann Site 2, by D. K. Jackson, A. C. Fortier, and J. A. Williams, pp.339–48. Department of Anthropology, University of Illinois at Urbana-Champaign, FAI-270 Archaeological Mitigation Project Report 83.

1992 Stone figurines. In *The Sponemann Site 2: The Mississippian and Oneota Occupations*, by D. K. Jackson, A. C. Fortier, and J. A. Williams, pp.277–303. American Bottom Archaeology, FAI-270 Site Reports 24. Urbana: University of Illinois Press.

Fortier, Andrew C., Fred A. Finney, and Richard B. Lacampagne
1983 *The Mund Site* (11-S-435). American Bottom Archaeology, FAI-270 Site Reports 5. Urbana: University of Illinois Press.

Fortier, Andrew C., Thomas O. Maher, and Joyce A. Williams
1991 *The Sponemann Site: The Formative Emergent Mississippian Sponemann Phase Occupations*. American Bottom Archaeology, FAI-270 Site Reports 23. Urbana: University of Illinois Press.

Fowler, Melvin L.
1969a Middle Mississippian agricultural fields. *American Antiquity* 34:365–75.

1969b The Cahokia site. In *Explorations into Cahokia Archaeology*, edited by Melvin L. Fowler, pp.1–30. Illinois Archaeological Survey, Bulletin 7. Urbana.

1974 Cahokia: Ancient capital of the Midwest. *Addison-Wesley Module in Anthropology* 48:3–38.

1975 A Pre-Columbian urban center on the Mississippi. *Scientific American* 233 (2): 92–101.

1977 The Cahokia site. In *Explorations into Cahokia Archaeology*, 2d edition, edited by M. L. Fowler, pp.1–42. Illinois Archaeological Survey, Bulletin 7. Urbana.

1978 Cahokia and the American Bottom: Settlement archaeology. In *Mississippian Settlement Patterns*, edited by B. D. Smith, pp.455–78. New York: Academic Press.

1989 The Cahokia atlas: A historical atlas of Cahokia archaeology. Studies in Illinois Archaeology, 6. Springfield: Illinois Historic Preservation Agency.

1991 Mound 72 and early Mississippian at Cahokia. In *New Perspectives on Cahokia: Views from the Periphery*, edited by J. B. Stoltman, pp.1–28. Madison WI: Prehistory Press.

Fowler, Melvin L., and James Anderson
1975 Report of 1971 excavations at Mound 72, Cahokia Mounds State Park. In

Cahokia Archaeology: Field Reports, edited by M. L. Fowler, pp.25–27. Illinois State Museum Papers in Anthropology 3. Springfield.

Fowler, Melvin L., and Robert L. Hall

1972   Archaeological phases at Cahokia. Research Series, Illinois State Museum papers in Anthropology 1. Springfield.

1975   Archaeological phases at Cahokia. In Perspectives in Cahokia Archaeology, pp.1–14. Illinois Archaeological Survey, Bulletin 10. Urbana.

1978   Late prehistory of the Illinois area. In *Handbook of North American Indians* 15:560–68. Washington DC: Smithsonian Institution.

Fried, Morton H.

1975   *The Notion of Tribe*. Menlo Park CA: Cumings.

Friedman, Jonathan A.

1992   The past in the future: History and the politics of identity. *American Anthropologist* 94:837–59.

Friedman, Jonathan A., and Michael Rowlands

1978   Notes towards an epigenetic model of the evolution of "civilization." In *The Evolution of Social Systems*, edited by J. Friedman and M. Rowlands, pp.201–76. Pittsburgh: University of Pittsburgh Press.

Fritz, Gayle J.

1990   Multiple pathways to farming in precontact eastern North America. *Journal of World Prehistory* 4 (4): 387–476.

1992   "Newer," "better" maize and the Mississippian emergence: A critique of prime mover explanations. In *Late Prehistoric Agriculture: Observations from the Midwest*, edited by W. I. Woods, pp.19–43. Studies in Illinois Archaeology, 8. Springfield: Illinois Historic Preservation Agency.

1993   Early and Middle Woodland period paleoethnobotany. In *Foraging and Farming in the Eastern Woodlands*, edited by C. M. Scarry, pp.39–56. Gainesville: University Press of Florida.

Fritz, Gayle J., and Tristram R. Kidder

1993   Recent investigations into prehistoric agriculture in the lower Mississippi valley. *Southeastern Archaeology* 12:1–14.

Gallagher, James P.

1989   Processes of agricultural intensification in the temperate upper Midwest of North America. In *Foraging and Farming: The Evolution of Plant Exploitation*, edited by D. R. Harris and G. C. Hillman, pp.572–84. London: Unwin Hyman.

1992   Prehistoric field systems in the upper Midwest. In *Late Prehistoric Agriculture: Observations from the Midwest*, edited by W. I. Woods, pp.95–135. Studies in Illinois Archaeology, 8. Springfield: Illinois Historic Preservation Agency.

Gallagher, James P., and Robert F. Sasso

1987   Investigations into Oneota ridged field agriculture on the northern margin of the Prairie Peninsula. *Plains Anthropologist* 32:141–51.

Gallagher, James P., Robert F. Boszhardt, Robert F. Sasso, and Katherine Stevenson

1985   Oneota ridged field agriculture in southwestern Wisconsin. *American Antiquity* 50:605–12.

Garland, Elizabeth Baldwin

1992   The Obion site: An early Mississippian center in Western Tennessee. Mississippi State University, Cobb Institute of Archaeology, Report of Investigations, 7.

Geertz, Clifford

1973   *Interpretation of Cultures*. New York: Basic Books.

Gergen, R. D., and W. R. Iseminger

1987   1987 testing of Mound 50 at Cahokia Mounds State Historic Site 11-S-34. Unpublished report submitted to the Cahokia Mounds Museum Society, Collinsville IL.

Gibbon, Guy E.

1974   A model of Mississippian development and its implications for the Red Wing area. In *Aspects of Upper Great Lakes Anthropology*, edited by E. Johnson, pp.129–37. Minnesota Prehistoric Archaeology Series 11.

Gibbon, Guy E., and Clark A. Dobbs

1991   The Mississippian presence in the Red Wing area, Minnesota. In *New Perspectives on Cahokia: Views from the Periphery*, edited by J. B. Stoltman, pp.281–305. Madison WI: Prehistory Press.

Giddens, Anthony

1979   *Central Problems in Social Theory*. London: Macmillan Press.

Gladfelter, Bruce

1981   Developments and direction in geoarchaeology. In *Advances in Archaeological Method and Theory*, vol.4, edited by Michael B. Schiffer, pp.343–64. New York: Academic Press.

Gladfelter, Bruce G., Barney W. Nashold, and Robert L. Hall

1979   A geomorphic, magnetic, and archaeological investigation of the Dunham Tract, Cahokia Mounds site, July–August 1976. Unpublished report submitted to the Illinois Department of Conservation. Department of Anthropology, University of Illinois at Chicago Circle.

Goldman, Irving

1970   *Ancient Polynesian Society*. Chicago: University of Chicago Press.

Goldstein, Lynne

1991   The implications of Aztalan's location. In *New Perspectives on Cahokia: Views from the Periphery*, edited by J. B. Stoltman, pp.209–27. Madison WI: Prehistory Press.

Goodman, Alan H., John Lallo, George J. Armelagos, and Jerome C. Rose

1984 Health changes at Dickson Mounds, Illinois (A.D. 950–1000). In *Paleo-pathology at the Origins of Agriculture*, edited by M. N. Cohen and G. J. Armelagos, pp.271–305. Orlando: Academic Press.

Goodman, Claire G.

1984 *Copper Artifacts in Late Eastern Woodlands Prehistory*, edited by Anne-Marie Cantwell. Kampsville IL: Center for American Archaeology.

Gramly, Richard Michael

1977 Deerskins and hunting territories: Competition for a scarce resource of the northeastern woodlands. *American Antiquity* 42:601–5.

Grayson, D. K.

1984 *Quantitative Zooarchaeology: Topics in the Analysis of Archaeological Faunas*. New York: Academic Press.

Green, William, and Roland L. Rodell

1994 The Mississippian presence and Cahokia interaction at Trempealeau, Wisconsin. *American Antiquity* 59:334–59.

Gregg, Michael L.

1975a A population estimate for Cahokia. In *Perspectives in Cahokia Archaeology*, pp.126–36. Illinois Archaeological Survey, Bulletin 10. Urbana.

1975b Settlement morphology and production specialization: The Horseshoe Lake site, a case study. Ph.D. diss., Department of Anthropology, University of Wisconsin, Milwaukee.

Griffin, James B.

1941 Report on pottery from the St. Louis area. *The Missouri Archaeologist* 7 (2): 1–17.

1949 The Cahokia ceramic complexes. In *Proceedings of the Fifth Plains Conference for Archaeology*, edited by J. L. Champe, pp.44–58. Lincoln: University of Nebraska.

1952 Culture periods in eastern United States archeology. In *Archeology of Eastern United States*, edited by J. B. Griffin, pp.352–64. Chicago: University of Chicago Press.

1960 A hypothesis for the prehistory of the Winnebago. In *Culture in History*, edited by S. Diamond, pp.809–65. New York: Columbia University Press.

1961 Some correlations of climatic and cultural change in eastern North America prehistory. *Annals of the New York Academy of Science* 95 (1): 710–17.

1967 Eastern North American archaeology: A summary. *Science* 156 (3772): 175–91.

1977 The University of Michigan excavations at the Pulcher site in 1950. *American Antiquity* 42:462–90.

1983 The midlands. In *Ancient North Americans*, edited by J. D. Jennings, pp.243–301. New York: W. H. Freeman and Company.

307

1984   A historical perspective. In *American Bottom Archaeology*, edited by C. J. Bareis and J. W. Porter, pp. xv–xvii. Urbana: University of Illinois Press.

1985   Changing concepts of the prehistoric Mississippian cultures of the eastern United States. In *Alabama and the Borderlands: From Prehistory to Statehood*, edited by R. Reid Badger and L. A. Clayton, pp.40–63. Tuscaloosa: University of Alabama Press.

1992   Fort Ancient has no class: The absence of an elite group in Mississippian societies in the central Ohio valley. In *Lords of the Southeast: Social Inequality and the Native Elites of Southeastern North America*, edited by A. W. Barker and T. R. Pauketat, pp.53–59. Archeological Papers of the American Anthropological Association, 3. Washington DC: American Anthropological Association.

1993   Cahokia interaction with contemporary southeastern and eastern societies. *Midcontinental Journal of Archaeology* 18:3–17.

Griffin, James B., and Albert C. Spaulding

1951   The central Mississippi valley archaeological survey, season 1950—a preliminary report. *Journal of the Illinois State Archaeological Society* 1 (3): 74–81, 84.

Griffith, Roberta Jean

1962   Ramey Incised pottery. Master's thesis, Department of Art, Southern Illinois University, Carbondale.

1981   Ramey Incised pottery. Illinois Archaeological Survey, Circular 5. Urbana.

Gums, Bonnie L.

1993   Groundstone tools, modified rock, and exotic materials. In *The Archaeology of the Cahokia Mounds ICT-II: Testing and Lithics*, pt.3. Illinois Cultural Resources Study 9. Springfield: Illinois Historic Preservation Agency.

Gums, Bonnie L., and George R. Holley

1991   Archaeology at the Cahokia Mounds State Historic Site: Limited excavations at the Falcon Drive-In, St. Clair County, Illinois. Archaeology Program Research Report No.8, Southern Illinois University at Edwardsville.

Gums, Bonnie L., Rodney C. De Mott, Neal H. Lopinot,

George R. Holley, and Lucretia S. Kelly

1989   Archaeological investigations for the Mississippi River Transmission Corporation Alton Line in Madison and St. Clair Counties, Illinois. Unpublished report submitted to the Illinois Historic Preservation Agency, Springfield. Southern Illinois University at Edwardsville.

Haas, Mary R.

1979   Southeastern languages. In *The Languages of Native America: Historical and Comparative Assessment*, edited by L. Campbell and M. Mithun, pp.299–326. Austin: University of Texas Press.

Hall, Abigail F., John E. Kelly, and Brad Koldehoff

1995   The nature and context of the Mississippian occupation on the southern pe-
        riphery of the Powell Tract. Paper presented at the 40th Midwest Archae-
        ological Conference, South Beloit IL.

Hall, Robert L.

1966   Cahokia chronology. Paper presented at the annual meeting of the Central
        States Anthropological Society, St. Louis.

1967   The Mississippian heartland and its Plains relationship. *Plains Anthropolo-
        gist* 12:175–83.

1975   Chronology and phases at Cahokia. In *Perspectives in Cahokia Archaeol-
        ogy*, pp.15–31. Illinois Archaeological Survey, Bulletin 10. Urbana.

1976   Ghosts, water barriers, corn, and sacred enclosures in the Eastern Wood-
        lands. *American Antiquity* 41 (3): 360–64.

1977   An anthropocentric perspective for eastern United States prehistory. *Ameri-
        can Antiquity* 42:499–518.

1979   In search of an ideology of the Adena-Hopewell climax. In *Hopewell Ar-
        chaeology: The Chillicothe Conference*, edited by D. Brose and N. Greber,
        pp.259–78. Kent OH: Kent State University Press.

1980   An interpretation of the two-climax model of Illinois prehistory. In *Early
        Native America: Prehistoric Demography, Economy, and Technology*,
        edited by D. L. Browman, pp.401–62. The Hague: Mouton.

1985   Medicine wheels, sun circles, and the magic of world center shrines. *Plains
        Anthropologist* 30:181–93.

1989   The cultural background of Mississippian symbolism. In *The Southeastern
        Ceremonial Complex*, edited by P. Galloway, pp.239–78. Lincoln: Univer-
        sity of Nebraska Press.

1991   Cahokia identity and interaction models of Cahokia Mississippian. In *Ca-
        hokia and the Hinterlands: Middle Mississippian Cultures of the Midwest*,
        edited by T. E. Emerson and R. B. Lewis, pp.3–34. Urbana: University of
        Illinois Press.

Hally, David J.

1988   The archaeology and settlement plan of the King site. In *The King Site: Con-
        tinuity and Contact in Sixteenth-Century Georgia*, edited by R. L. Blakely,
        pp.3–16. Athens: University of Georgia Press.

1992   Platform mound construction and the instability of Mississippian chief-
        doms. Paper presented at the 49th annual meeting of the Southeastern Ar-
        chaeological Conference, Little Rock AR.

1993   The territorial size of Mississippian chiefdoms. In *Archaeology of Eastern
        North America: Papers in Honor of Stephen Williams*, edited by James B.
        Stoltman, pp.143–68. Archaeological Report No. 25. Jackson: Mississippi
        Department of Archives and History.

Hally, David J., Marvin T. Smith, and James B. Langford Jr.

1990   The archaeological reality of De Soto's Coosa. In *Columbian Consequences*, vol. 2, Archaeological and Historical Perspectives on the Spanish Borderlands East, edited by D. H. Thomas, pp.121–38. Washington DC: Smithsonian Institution Press.

Halstead, Paul, and John O'Shea, editors

1989   *Bad Year Economics: Cultural Responses to Risk and Uncertainty.* Cambridge: Cambridge University Press.

Hamilton, Henry W.

1952   The Spiro Mound. *Missouri Archaeologist* 14:1–276.

Hanenberger, Ned H.

1990a   The Karol Rekas site (11-Ms-1255). In *Selected Early Mississippian Household Sites in the American Bottom*, by D. K. Jackson and N. H. Hanenberger, pp.425–509. American Bottom Archaeology, FAI-270 Site Reports 22. Urbana: University of Illinois Press.

1990b   The Olszewski site (11-S-465). In *Selected Early Mississippian Household Sites in the American Bottom*, by D. K. Jackson and N. H. Hanenberger, pp.253–423. American Bottom Archaeology, FAI-270 Site Reports 22. Urbana: University of Illinois Press.

Hanenberger, Ned H., and Mark W. Mehrer

n.d.   The Range site 3 (11-S-47): Mississippian and Oneota occupations. Draft manuscript submitted to the Illinois Department of Transportation by the FAI-270 Archaeological Mitigation Project.

Hargrave, Michael L., Gerald A. Oetelaar, Neal H. Lopinot,

Brian M. Butler, and Deborah Billings

1983   The Bridges site (11-Mr-11): A Late Prehistoric settlement in the Central Kaskaskia valley. Center for Archaeological Investigations, Research Paper 38. Carbondale: Southern Illinois University.

Harl, Joseph L.

1991   An alternative explanation for the shift from a Late Woodland to a Mississippian lifestyle based on evidence from the Bridgeton site (23SL442) and other sites along the Lower Missouri River valley. Master's thesis, Department of Anthropology, Washington University, St. Louis.

Harlan, H. V., and M. L. Martini

1938   The effects of natural selection in a mixture of barley varieties. *Journal of Agricultural Research* 57:189–99.

Harn, Alan D.

1971   An archaeological survey of the American Bottom in Madison and St. Clair Counties, Illinois. Illinois State Museum, Reports of Investigations 21 (pt.2). Springfield.

1978   Mississippian settlement patterns in the central Illinois River valley. In *Mississippian Settlement Patterns*, edited by Bruce D. Smith, pp.233–68. New York: Academic Press.

1980   Comments on the spatial distribution of Late Woodland and Mississippian ceramics in the general Cahokia sphere. *Rediscovery* (Journal of the Illinois Association for the Advancement of Archaeology) 1:17–26.

1991   The Eveland site: Inroad to Spoon River Mississippian society. In *New Perspectives on Cahokia: Views from the Periphery*, edited by J. B. Stoltman, pp.129–53. Madison WI: Prehistory Press.

Helms, Mary W.

1979   *Ancient Panama: Chiefs in Search of Power*. Austin: University of Texas Press.

1988   *Ulysses' Sail: An Ethnographic Odyssey of Power, Knowledge, and Geographical Distance*. Princeton NJ: Princeton University Press.

1992a   Long-distance contacts, elite aspirations, and the age of discovery in cosmological context. In *Resources, Power, and Interregional Interaction*, edited by E. M. Schortman and P. A. Urban, pp.157–74. New York: Plenum Press.

1992b   Political lords and political ideology in southeastern chiefdoms: Comments and observations. In *Lords of the Southeast: Social Inequality and the Native Elites of Southeastern North America*, edited by A. W. Barker and T. R. Pauketat, pp.185–94. Archeological Papers of the American Anthropological Association, 3. Washington DC: American Anthropological Association.

1993   *Craft and the Kingly Ideal: Art, Trade, and Power*. Austin: University of Texas Press.

Henning, Dale R.

1967   Mississippian influences on the eastern Plains border: An evaluation. *Plains Anthropologist* 12:184–94.

Hines, P.

1977   On social organization in the Middle Mississippian: States or chiefdoms? *Current Anthropology* 18:337–38.

Hodder, Ian

1990   *The Domestication of Europe*. Oxford: Basil Blackwell.

1991   *Reading the Past*. 2d edition. Cambridge: Cambridge University Press.

1992   *Theory and Practice in Archaeology*. London: Routledge.

Hoehr, Peter

1980   Utilitarian artifacts from the Cahokia site. In *Cahokia Brought to Life*. 2d printing, edited by R. E. Grimm, pp.41–45. St. Louis: Greater St. Louis Archaeological Society.

Hoffman, Michael P.

1990   The terminal Mississippian Period in the Arkansas River valley and Quapaw ethnogenesis. In *Towns and Temples Along the Mississippi*, edited by D. H. Dye, pp.208–26. Tuscaloosa: University of Alabama Press.

1994   Ethnic identities and cultural change in the protohistoric period of eastern Arkansas. In *Perspectives on the Southeast: Linguistics, Archaeology, and Ethnohistory*, edited by P. B. Kwachka, pp.61–70. Athens: University of Georgia Press.

Holley, George R.

1989   The archaeology of the Cahokia Mounds ICT-II: Ceramics. Illinois Cultural Resources Study 11. Springfield: Illinois Historic Preservation Agency.

1990   Investigations at the Kunnemann Tract, Cahokia Mounds Historic Site, Madison County, Illinois. Unpublished report submitted to the Illinois Historic Preservation Agency, Springfield. Southern Illinois University at Edwardsville.

1992   Late prehistoric towns in the Southeast. Paper presented at the 57th annual meeting of the Society for American Archaeology, Pittsburgh.

1995   Microliths and the Kunnemann Tract: An assessment of craft production at the Cahokia site. *Illinois Archaeology* 7:1–68.

n.d.   Late prehistoric towns in the Southeast. Manuscript prepared for the seminar "Great Towns and Regional Polities: Cultural Evolution in the U.S. Southwest and Southeast," organized by Jill Neitzel, 5–12 March 1994, Amerind Foundation, Dragoon AZ.

Holley, George R., Rinita A. Dalan, and Harold W. Watters Jr.

1992   Archaeological investigations at the Rouch Mound Group, Cahokia Mounds State Historic site. Unpublished report submitted to the Illinois Historic Preservation Agency, Springfield. Southern Illinois University at Edwardsville.

Holley, George R., Rinita A. Dalan, and Philip A. Smith

1993   Investigations in the Cahokia site Grand Plaza. *American Antiquity* 58:306–19.

Holley, George R., Neal H. Lopinot, Rinita A. Dalan, and William I. Woods

1990   South Palisade investigations. In *The Archaeology of the Cahokia Palisade*. Illinois Cultural Resources Study No. 14. Springfield: Illinois Historic Preservation Agency.

Holley, George R., Neal H. Lopinot, William I. Woods, and John E. Kelly

1989   Dynamics of community organization at prehistoric Cahokia. In *Households and Communities*. Proceedings of the 21st annual Chacmool Conference, edited by S. MacEachern, D. J. W. Archer, and R. D. Garvin, pp.339–49. Calgary: University of Calgary.

Holley, George R., Rinita A. Dalan, Neal H. Lopinot, and Philip A. Smith

1990   Investigations in the Grand Plaza, Cahokia Mounds Historic site, St. Clair County, Illinois. Unpublished report submitted to the Illinois Historic Preservation Agency, Springfield. Southern Illinois University at Edwardsville.

Hollinger, R. Eric

1993   Investigating Oneota residence through domestic architecture. Master's thesis, Department of Anthropology, University of Missouri–Columbia.

Hollow, Robert C., and Douglas R. Parks

1980   Studies in Plains linguistics: A review. In *Anthropology on the Great Plains*, edited by W. R. Wood and M. Liberty, pp.68–97. Lincoln: University of Nebraska Press.

Holt, Julie Zimmerman

1993   Subsistence at the Assembly of God Church site: A Late Woodland–Emergent Mississippian community in the Uplands of St. Clair County, Illinois. Master's thesis, Department of Anthropology, New York University.

Howard, James H.

1968   The Southern Ceremonial Complex and its interpretations. Missouri Archaeological Society Memoir 6. Columbia.

Howland, Henry R.

1877   Recent archaeological discoveries in the American Bottom. *Bulletin* (Buffalo Society of Natural Sciences) 3 (5): 204–11.

Hudson, Charles

1976   The *Southeastern Indians*. Knoxville: University of Tennessee Press.

Hudson, Charles M., Marvin T. Smith, David J. Hally, Richard Polhemus, and Chester B. DePratter

1985   Coosa: A chiefdom in the sixteenth-century United States. *American Antiquity* 50:723–37.

1987   In search of Coosa: Reply to Schroedl and Boyd. *American Antiquity* 52:840–57.

Hughes, Randall, and Thomas E. Emerson

1995   Preliminary sourcing of Cahokia Middle Mississippian flint clay figurines. Paper presented at the annual Southeastern Archaeological Conference, Knoxville TN.

Hultkrantz, Ake

1957   The North American Indian Orpheus Tradition. The Ethnological Museum of Sweden, Monograph Series, Publication 2. Stockholm

Iseminger, William R.

1990   Features. In *The Archaeology of the Cahokia Palisade: The East Palisade Investigations*, edited by W. R. Iseminger et al., pp.18–38. Illinois Cultural Resources Study 14. Springfield: Illinois Historic Preservation Agency.

Iseminger, William R., and John E. Kelly
1995   Partitioning the sacred precinct. *Cahokian* (summer): 3–5.
Iseminger, William R., Timothy R. Pauketat, Brad Koldehoff,
Lucretia S. Kelly, and Leonard Blake
1990   East Palisade excavations. In *The Archaeology of the Cahokia Palisade, Part 1*. Illinois Cultural Resource Study 14. Springfield: Illinois Historic Preservation Agency.

Jackson, Douglas K.
1990a   The Esterlein site (11-Ms-598). In *Selected Early Mississippian Household Sites in the American Bottom*. American Bottom Archaeology, FAI-270 Site Reports 22. Urbana: University of Illinois Press.
1990b   The Willoughby site (11-Ms-610). In *Selected Early Mississippian Household Sites in the American Bottom*. American Bottom Archaeology, FAI-270 Site Reports 22. Urbana: University of Illinois Press.
1990c   The Sandy Ridge farm site (11-S-660). In *Selected Early Mississippian Household Sites in the American Bottom*. American Bottom Archaeology, FAI-270 Site Reports 22. Urbana: University of Illinois Press.

Jackson, Douglas K., and Lawson M. Smith
1979   Report of archaeological testing for the Chalfin Bridge project undertaken at the Johanings site (11-Ms-242) on FAS-1857, Monroe County, Illinois. Manuscript on file at the Department of Anthropology, University of Illinois, Urbana.

Jackson, Douglas K., and Ned H. Hannenberger
1990   *Selected Early Mississippian Household Sites in the American Bottom*. American Bottom Archaeology, FAI-270 Site Reports 22. Urbana: University of Illinois Press.

Jackson, Douglas K., Andrew C. Fortier, and Joyce A. Williams
1992   *The Sponemann Site 2 (11-Ms-517): The Mississippian and Oneota occupations*. American Bottom Archaeology, FAI-270 Site Reports 24. Urbana: University of Illinois Press.

Jackson, H. Edwin, and Susan L. Scott
1995   The faunal record of the southeastern elite: The implications of economy, social relations, and ideology. *Southeastern Archaeology* 14:103–19.

Jenkins, Ned J., and Richard A. Krause
1986   *The Tombigbee Watershed in Southeastern Prehistory*. University: University of Alabama Press.

Jeter, Marvin D., and G. Ishmael Williams Jr.
1989   Late prehistoric cultures, A.D. 1000–1500. Archaeology and bioarchaeology of the lower Mississippi valley and trans-Mississippi South in Arkansas and Louisiana. Arkansas Archeological Survey Research Series 37. Fayetteville.

References

Johannessen, Sissel

1984   Paleoethnobotany. In *American Bottom Archaeology*, edited by C. J. Bareis and J. W. Porter, pp.197–214. Urbana: University of Illinois Press.

1985   Plant remains. In *The Dohack Site*, by A. B. Stahl, pp.249–69. American Bottom Archaeology, FAI-270 Site Reports 12. Urbana: University of Illinois Press.

1988   Plant remains and culture change: Are paleoethnobotanical data better than we think? In *Current Paleoethnobotany*, edited by C. A. Hastorf and V. S. Popper, pp.145–66. Chicago: University of Chicago Press.

1993   Farmers of the Late Woodland. In *Foraging and Farming in the Eastern Woodlands*, edited by C. M. Scarry, pp.57–77. Gainesville: University Press of Florida.

Johannessen, Sissel, and Paula G. Cross

1993   The social context of food at Cahokia. Paper presented at the 58th annual meeting of the Society for American Archaeology, St. Louis.

Johnson, Gregory A.

1973   Local exchange and early state development in southwestern Iran. University of Michigan, Museum of Anthropology, Anthropological Paper No. 37. Ann Arbor.

1978   Information sources and the development of decision-making organizations. In *Social Archaeology Beyond Subsistence and Dating*, edited by C. L. Redman, M. Berman, E. Curtin, T. Langhorne, N. Versaggi, and J. Wanser, pp.87–112. New York: Academic Press.

1982   Organizational structure and scalar stress. In *Theory and Explanation in Archaeology: The Southampton Conference*, edited by Colin Renfrew, M. J. Rowlands, and Barbara A. Segraves, pp.389–421. New York: Academic Press.

Johnson, Jay K.

1987   Cahokia core technology in Mississippi: The view from the south. In *The Organization of Core Technology*, edited by J. K. Johnson and C. A. Morrow, pp.187–205. Boulder CO: Westview Press.

Keller, Kenneth J., John E. Kelly, and Charles O. Witty

1994   Cahokia's western periphery: Recent investigations on the Fingerhut Tract. Paper presented at the joint Southeastern Archaeological and Midwest Archaeological Conference, Lexington KY.

Kelly, Arthur R.

1933   Some problems of recent Cahokia archaeology. *Transactions of the Illinois State Academy of Science* 25 (4): 101–3.

1938   A Preliminary Report on Archaeological Explorations at Macon, Georgia. Smithsonian Institution, Bureau of American Ethnology, Bulletin 119. Washington DC: GPO.

315

1964   Notes on a prehistoric cultivated field in Macon, Georgia. *Southeast Archaeological Conference Bulletin* 3, pp.49–51.

Kelly, John E.

1980   Formative developments at Cahokia and the adjacent American Bottom: A Merrell Tract perspective. Ph.D. diss., Department of Anthropology, University of Wisconsin at Madison.

1984   Wells Incised plates: Their context and affinities with O'Byam Incised. Paper presented at the Paducah Ceramics Conference, Paducah KY.

1987   Emergent Mississippian and the transition from Late Woodland to Mississippian: The American Bottom case for a new concept. In *The Emergent Mississippian: Proceedings of the Sixth Mid-South Archaeological Conference, June 6–9, 1985*, edited by R. A. Marshall, pp.212–26. Occasional Papers 87-01. Mississippi State: Cobb Institute of Archaeology, Mississippi State University.

1990a   The emergence of Mississippian culture in the American Bottom region. In *The Mississippian Emergence*, edited by B. Smith, pp.113–52. Washington DC: Smithsonian Institution Press.

1990b   Range site community patterns and the Mississippian emergence. In *The Mississippian Emergence*, edited by B. Smith, pp.67–112. Washington DC: Smithsonian Institution Press.

1990c   The realm of public architecture at Cahokia. Paper presented at the 52d annual meeting of the Southeastern Archaeological Conference, Mobile AL.

1991a   Cahokia and its role as a gateway center in interregional exchange. In *Cahokia and the Hinterlands: Middle Mississippian Cultures of the Midwest*, edited by T. E. Emerson and R. B. Lewis, pp.61–80. Urbana: University of Illinois Press.

1991b   The evidence for prehistoric exchange and its implications for the development of Cahokia. In *New Perspectives on Cahokia: Views from the Periphery*, edited by J. B. Stoltman, pp.65–92. Madison WI: Prehistory Press.

1991c   The Pulcher tradition and its role in the development of Mississippian in the American Bottom. Paper presented at the 48th annual meeting of the Southeastern Archaeological Conference, Jackson MS.

1991d   Myth-conceptions about Cahokia's urbane character. Paper presented in the symposium "Exploring and Exploding Myths About Cahokia," organized by J. E. Kelly, 56th annual meeting of the Society for American Archaeology, New Orleans.

1992a   Moorehead's investigations in the American Bottom. Paper presented at the 37th annual meeting of the Midwest Archaeological Conference, Grand Rapids MI.

1992b   The impact of maize on the development of nucleated settlements: An American Bottom example. In *Late Prehistoric Agriculture: Observations from the Midwest*, edited by William I. Woods, pp.167–97. Studies in Illinois Archaeology No. 8. Springfield: Illinois Historic Preservation Agency.

1993a   The discovery, debate, and destruction of American Bottom mounds: A prelude to the preservation of Cahokia Mounds. Paper presented at the 38th annual meeting of the Midwest Archaeological Conference, October, Milwaukee WI.

1993b   The Pulcher site: An archaeological and historical overview. *Illinois Archaeology* 5:434–51.

1993c   Redefining Cahokia: Prince(ples) and elements of community organization. Paper presented at the 50th annual meeting of the Southeastern Archaeological Conference, 3–6 November, Raleigh NC.

1994a   The archaeology of the East St. Louis mound center: Past and present. *Illinois Archaeology* 6:1–57.

1994b   The Curtis Steinberg and Finger sites. Manuscript on file, Illinois Transportation Archaeological Research Program, Department of Anthropology, University of Illinois, Urbana.

1994c   Redefining Cahokia: Principles and elements of community organization. Paper presented at conference on "The Ancient Skies and Sky Watchers of Cahokia: Woodhenges, Eclipses, and Cahokia Cosmology," organized by M. Fowler, Cahokia Mounds State Historic Site.

1995   *The Fingers and Curtiss Steinberg Road Sites: Two Stirling Phase Mississippian Farmsteads in the Goose Lake Locality*. Transportation Archaeological Research Reports Number 1. Urbana: Illinois Transportation Archaeological Research Program.

Kelly, John E., Steven J. Ozuk, and Joyce Williams

1990   *The Range Site 2: The Emergent Mississippian Dohack and Range Phase Occupations*. American Bottom Archaeology, FAI-270 Site Reports 20. Urbana: University of Illinois Press.

Kelly, John E., Andrew C. Fortier, Steven J. Ozuk, and Joyce A. Williams

1987   *The Range Site: Archaic through Late Woodland Occupations*. American Bottom Archaeology, FAI-270 Site Reports 16. Urbana: University of Illinois Press.

Kelly, John E., Steven J. Ozuk, Douglas K. Jackson, Dale L. McElrath, Fred A. Finney, and Duane Esarey

1984   Emergent Mississippian period. In *American Bottom Archaeology*, edited by C. J. Bareis and J. W. Porter, pp.128–57. Urbana: University of Illinois Press.

Kelly, Lucretia S.

1979   Animal resource exploitation by early Cahokia populations on the Merrell Tract. Illinois Archaeological Survey Circular 4. Urbana.

1987   Patrick phase faunal remains. In *The Range Site: Archaic Through Late Woodland Occupations*, edited by J. E. Kelly, A. C. Fortier, S. J. Ozuk, and J. A. Williams, pp.350–400. American Bottom Archaeology, FAI-270 Site Reports 16. Urbana: University of Illinois Press.

1990a   Dohack phase faunal analysis. In *The Range Site 2: The Emergent Mississippian Dohack and Range Phase Occupations*, edited by J. E. Kelly, S. J. Ozuk, and J. A. Williams, pp.237–65. American Bottom Archaeology, FAI-270 Site Reports 20. Urbana: University of Illinois Press.

1990b   Faunal remains. In *The Archaeology of the Cahokia Palisade, East Palisade Investigations*, by W. R. Iseminger, T. R. Pauketat, B. Koldehoff, L. S. Kelly, and L. Blake, pp.109–34. Illinois Cultural Resources Study 14. Springfield: Illinois Historic Preservation Agency.

1990c   Range phase faunal analysis. In *The Range Site 2: The Emergent Mississippian Dohack and Range Phase Occupations*, by J. E. Kelly, S. J. Ozuk, and J. A. Williams, pp.487–511. American Bottom Archaeology, FAI-270 Site Reports 20. Urbana: University of Illinois Press.

1991   Zooarchaeological remains. In *The Archaeology of the Cahokia Mounds ICT-II: Biological Remains*, by N. H. Lopinot, L. S. Kelly, G. R. Milner, and R. Paine, pp.1–78. Illinois Cultural Resources Study 13. Springfield: Illinois Historic Preservation Agency.

1993   Faunal remains. In An assessment of Moorehead's investigations at Mound 56, Cahokia Mounds State Historic Site, by R. A. Dalan, G. R. Holley, and W. Watters Jr. Unpublished report submitted to the Illinois Historic Preservation Agency. Southern Illinois University at Edwardsville.

1994   Assessing the role of faunal remains at the Cahokia site. Paper presented at the 51st annual meeting of the Southeastern Archaeological Conference, Lexington KY.

Kent, Susan

1990   A cross-cultural study in segmentation, architecture, and the use of space. In *Domestic Architecture and the Use of Space*, edited by Susan Kent, pp.127–52. Cambridge: Cambridge University Press.

Kidder, Tristram R.

1990   The timing and consequences of the introduction of maize agriculture in the lower Mississippi valley. Paper presented at the 55th annual meeting of the Society for American Archaeology, Las Vegas.

1992   Coles Creek period social organization and evolution in northeast Louisiana. In *Lords of the Southeast: Social Inequality and the Native Elites of Southeastern North America*, edited by A. W. Barker and T. R. Pauketat, pp.145–

318

62. Archeological Papers of the American Anthropological Association Number 3. Washington DC: American Anthropological Association.

King, J. W., S. K. Banerjee, J. Marvin, and O. Ozdemir

1982   A comparison of different magnetic methods for determining the relative grain size of magnetite in natural materials: Some results in lake sediments. *Earth and Planetary Science Letters* 59:404–19.

Kirchoff, Paul

1955   The principles of clanship in human society. *Davidson Journal of Anthropology* I:I–IO.

Klein, Richard G.

1989   Why does skeletal part representation differ between smaller and larger bovids at Klasies River Mouth and other archaeological sites? *Journal of Archaeological Science* 6:363–81.

Knight, Vernon James, Jr.

1981   Mississippian Ritual. Ph.D. diss., Department of Anthropology, University of Florida. Ann Arbor: University Microfilms.

1986   The institutional organization of Mississippian religion. *American Antiquity* 51:675–87.

1989a   Symbolism of Mississippian mounds. In *Powhatan's Mantle: Indians in the Colonial Southeast*, edited by P. H. Wood, G. A. Waselkov, and M. T. Hatley, pp.279–91. Lincoln: University of Nebraska Press.

1989b   Some speculations on Mississippian monsters. In *The Southeastern Ceremonial Complex: Artifacts and Analysis*, edited by P. Galloway, pp.205–10. Lincoln: University of Nebraska Press.

1989c   Certain aboriginal mounds at Moundville: 1937 excavations in Mounds H, I, J, K, and L. Paper presented at the 46th annual Southeastern Archaeological Conference, Tampa FL.

1990   Social organization and the evolution of hierarchy in southeastern chiefdoms. *Journal of Anthropological Research* 46:1–23

1992   Preliminary report on excavations at Mound Q, Moundville. Paper presented at the 49th annual meeting of the Southeastern Archaeological Conference, Little Rock AR.

1993   Moundville as a diagrammatic ceremonial center. Paper presented at the 58th annual meeting of the Society for American Archaeology, St. Louis.

Kohl, Phil

1987   The use and abuse of world systems theory: The case of the pristine west Asian state. *Advances in Archaeological Method and Theory*, vol.11, pp.1–35. New York: Academic Press.

Koldehoff, Brad

1987   The Cahokia flake tool industry: Socioeconomic implications for late prehistory in the central Mississippi valley. In *The Organization of Core Technology*, edited by J. Johnson and C. Morrow, pp.151–86. Boulder CO: Westview Press.

1989   Cahokia's immediate hinterland: The Mississippian occupation of Douglas Creek. *Illinois Archaeology* 1:39–68.

1990   Household specialization: The organization of Mississippian chipped-stone-tool production. Master's thesis, Department of Anthropology, Southern Illinois University, Carbondale.

Koldehoff, Brad, Timothy R. Pauketat, and John E. Kelly

1993   The Emerald site and the Mississippian occupation of the central Silver Creek valley. *Illinois Archaeology* 5 (1–2): 331–43.

Kramer, Carol

1982   Ethnographic households and archaeological interpretation. *American Behavioral Scientist* 25 (6): 663–75.

Kristiansen, Kristian

1991   Chiefdoms, states, and systems of social evolution. In *Chiefdoms: Power, Economy, and Ideology*, edited by Timothy K. Earle, pp.16–43. Cambridge: Cambridge University Press.

Krupp, E. C.

1977   Cahokia, corn, commerce, and the cosmos. *Griffith Observer* 4:10–20.

Kus, Susan M.

1983   The social representation of space: Dimensioning the cosmological and the quotidian. In *Archaeological Hammers and Theories*, edited by J. A. Moore and A. S. Keene, pp.277–98. New York: Academic Press.

Kuttruff, L. Carl

1974   Late Woodland settlement and subsistence in the Lower Kaskaskia River valley. Ph.D. diss., Department of Anthropology, Southern Illinois University, Carbondale.

Lafferty, Robert H., III

1994   Prehistoric exchange systems in the lower Mississippi valley. In *Prehistoric Exchange Systems in North America*, edited by Timothy G. Baugh and Jonathon E. Ericson, pp.177–213. New York: Plenum Press.

Larrain, Jorge

1979   *The Concept of Ideology*. Athens: University of Georgia Press.

Larson, L. H., Jr.

1989   The Etowah site. In *The Southeastern Ceremonial Complex: Artifacts and Analysis*, edited by P. Galloway, pp.133–41. Lincoln: University of Nebraska Press.

Lekson, Stephen H.

1994   Chaco, Cahokia, and complexity. Paper presented in the symposium "Prehistoric Cultures as Complex Adaptive Systems," at the annual meeting of the Society for American Archaeology, Anaheim CA.

Lewis, R. Barry

1991   The early Mississipppi Period in the confluence region and its northern relationships. In *Cahokia and the Hinterlands: Middle Mississippian Cultures of the Midwest*, edited by T. E. Emerson and R. B. Lewis, pp.274–94. Urbana: University of Illinois Press.

Lewis, T. M. N., and M. Kneberg

1946   *Hiwassee Island: An Archaeological Account of Four Tennessee Indian Peoples*. Knoxville: University of Tennessee Press.

Lightfoot, Kent G.

1984   *Prehistoric Political Dynamics: A Case Study from the American Southwest*. De Kalb: Northern Illinois University Press.

Lightfoot, Kent, and Steadman Upham

1989   Complex societies in the prehistoric American Southwest: A consideration of the controversy. In *The Sociopolitical Structure of Prehistoric Southwestern Societies*, edited by S. Upham , K. C. Lightfoot, and R. A. Jewett, pp.3–30. Boulder CO: Westview Press.

Little, Elizabeth A.

1987   Inland waterways in the Northeast. *Midcontinental Journal of Archaeology* 12:55–76.

Lopinot, Neal H.

1991   Archaeobotanical remains. In *The Archaeology of the Cahokia Mounds ICT-II: Biological Remains*, part 1. Illinois Cultural Resources Study 13. Springfield: Illinois Historic Preservation Agency.

1992a   Spatial and temporal variability in Mississippian subsistence: The archaeobotanical record. In *Late Prehistoric Agriculture*, edited by W. I. Woods, pp.44–94. Studies in Illinois Archaeology, 8. Springfield: Illinois Historic Preservation Agency.

1992b   Archaeobotany. In *The Pettit Site (11-Ax-253), Alexander County, Illinois*, edited by P. A. Webb, pp.261–93. Center for Archaeological Investigations Research Paper 58. Carbondale: Southern Illinois University.

1993   Demographic restructuring and political unification in the northern American Bottom. Paper presented at the 58th annual meeting of the Society for American Archaeology, St. Louis.

1994   A new crop of data on the Cahokian polity. In *Agricultural Origins and Development in the Midcontinent*, edited by W. Green, pp.127–53. Office of the State Archaeologist, Report 19. Iowa City.

1995   Archaeobotanical remains. In *Woodland and Mississippian Occupations at the Hayti Bypass Site, Pemiscot County, Missouri*, edited by M. D. Conner,

321

pp.221–62. Center for Archaeological Research, Special Publication 1. Southwest Missouri State University, Springfield.

Lopinot, Neal H., and William I. Woods

1993　Wood overexploitation and the collapse of Cahokia. In *Foraging and Farming in the Eastern Woodlands*, edited by C. M. Scarry, pp.206–31. Gainesville: University Press of Florida.

Lopinot, Neal H., Alan J. Brown, and George R. Holley

1989　Archaeological investigations on the western periphery of the Cahokia site, St. Clair and Madison Counties, Illinois. Archaeology Program Research Report No. 4. Southern Illinois University at Edwardsville.

1993　Archaeological investigations on the western periphery of the Cahokia site. *Illinois Archaeology* 5:407–20.

Lopinot, Neal H., Gayle J. Fritz, and John E. Kelly

1991　The archaeological context and significance of *Polygonum erectum* achene masses from the American Bottom region. Paper presented at the 14th Annual Ethnobiology Conference, St. Louis.

Lopinot, Neal H., M. Denise Hutto, and David P. Braun

1982　Archaeological investigations at the Kingfish site, St. Clair County, Illinois. Center for Archaeological Investigations Research Paper 25. Carbondale: Southern Illinois University.

Lyman, R. L.

1984　Bone density and differential survivorship of fossil classes. *Journal of Anthropological Archaeology* 3:259–99.

1991　Taphonomic problems with archaeological analyses of animal carcass utilization and transport. In *Beamers, Bobwhite, and Blue-points: Tributes to the Career of Paul W. Parmalee*, edited by J. R. Purdue, W. E. Klippel, and B. W. Styles, pp.125–38. Illinois State Museum Scientific Papers, vol.23, and the University of Tennessee, Department of Anthropology Report of Investigations No. 52.

Lyman, R. L., L. E. Houghton, and A. L. Chambers

1992　The effect of structural density on marmot skeletal part representation in archaeological sites. *Journal of Archaeological Science* 19:557–73.

McAdams, William H.

1882　Antiquities. In *History of Madison County, Illinois*, pp.58–64. Edwardsville IL: W. R. Brink.

McElrath, Dale L.

1983　Mississippian chert exploitation: A case study from the American Bottom. Paper presented at the 48th annual meeting of the Society for American Archaeology, Pittsburgh.

322

McElrath, Dale L., and Fred A. Finney

1987   *The George Reeves Site.* American Bottom Archaeology, FAI-270 Site Reports 15. Urbana: University of Illinois Press.

McElrath, Dale L., Joyce A. Wiliams, Thomas O. Maher, and Michael C. Meinkoth

1987   *The Radic Site.* American Bottom Archaeology, FAI-270 Site Reports 17, part 1. Urbana: University of Illinois Press.

McGimsey, C. R., and M. D. Wiant

1984   Limited archaeological investigations of Monks Mound (11-Ms-38): Some perspectives on its stability, structure, and age. Studies in Illinois Archaeology No. 1. Springfield: Illinois Historic Preservation Agency.

McGuire, Randall H.

1992   *A Marxist Archaeology.* San Diego: Academic Press.

McNeill, J. D.

1980   *Electromagnetic Terrain Conductivity Measurement at Low Induction Numbers.* Technical Note TN-5. Mississauga, Ontario, Canada: Geonics Limited.

Marshall, F., and T. Pilgram

1991   Meat versus within-bone nutrients: Another look at the meaning of body part representation in archaeological sites. *Journal of Archaeological Science* 18:149–63.

1993   NISP vs. MNI in quantification of body part representation. *American Antiquity* 58 (2): 261–69.

Marx, Karl, and Frederick Engels

1989   *The German Ideology*, edited by C. J. Arthur. New York: International Publishers.

Mason, Ronald J., and Gregory Perino

1961   Microblades at Cahokia, Illinois. *American Antiquity* 26:553–57.

Mathews, John J.

1961   *The Osages.* Norman: University of Oklahoma Press.

Mehrer, Mark W.

1988   The settlement patterns and social power of Cahokia's hinterland households. Unpublished Ph.D. diss., Department of Anthropology, University of Illinois, Urbana.

1995   *Cahokia's Countryside: Household Archaeology, Settlement Patterns, and Social Power.* DeKalb: Northern Illinois University Press.

Mehrer, Mark W., and James M. Collins

1989   Household archaeology at Cahokia and its hinterlands. Paper presented in the symposium "Households and Settlements in the Mississippian Period" at the 54th annual meeting of the Society for American Archaeology, Atlanta.

1995   Household archaeology at Cahokia and its hinterlands. In *Mississippian*

Communities and Households, edited by J. D. Rogers and B. D. Smith, pp.32–57. Tuscaloosa: University of Alabama Press.

Meillassoux, Claude

1973   On the mode of production of a hunting band. In *French Perspectives in African Studies*, edited by P. Alexandre, pp.187–203. Oxford: Oxford University Press.

Melbye, F. Jerome

1963   The Kane burial mounds. Archaeological Salvage Report Number 15. Carbondale: Southern Illinois University Museum.

Metcalfe, D., and K. T. Jones

1988   A reconsideration of animal body part indices. *American Antiquity* 53 (3): 486–504.

Michals, L. M.

1990   Faunal exploitation and chiefdom organization at Moundville, Alabama. Paper presented at the 55th annual meeting of the Society for American Archaeology, Las Vegas.

1992   The nature of faunal exploitation in Mississippian societies. Paper presented at the 57th annual meeting of the Society for American Archaeology, Pittsburgh.

Milner, George R.

1983a   *The Turner and DeMange Sites*. American Bottom Archaeology, FAI-270 Site Reports 4. Urbana: University of Illinois Press.

1983b   *The East St. Louis Stone Quarry Site Cemetery*. American Bottom Archaeology, FAI-270 Site Reports 1. Urbana: University of Illinois Press.

1984a   The Julien site (11-S-63). American Bottom Archaeology, FAI-270 Site Reports 7. Urbana: University of Illinois Press.

1984b   *The Robinsons Lake Site*. American Bottom Archaeology, FAI-270 Site Reports 10. Urbana: University of Illinois Press.

1984c   Social and temporal implications of variation among American Bottom Mississippian cemeteries. *American Antiquity* 49:468–88.

1986   Mississippian period population density in a segment of the central Mississippi valley. *American Antiquity* 51:227–38.

1987   Range phase human remains. In *The Range Site 2: The Emergent Mississippian Dohack and Range Phase Occupations*, by J. E. Kelly, S. J. Ozuk, and J. A. Williams, p.513. American Bottom Archaeology, FAI-270 Site Reports 20. Urbana: University of Illinois Press.

1990   The late prehistoric Cahokia cultural system of the Mississippi River valley: Foundations, florescence, and fragmentation. *Journal of World Prehistory* 4 (1): 1–43.

1991   American Bottom Mississippian culture: Internal developments and external relations. In *New Perspectives on Cahokia: Views from the Periphery*, edited by J. B. Stoltman, pp.29–47. Madison WI: Prehistory Press.

1992a Health and cultural change in the late prehistoric American Bottom, Illinois. In *What Mean These Bones? Studies in Southeastern Bioarchaeology*, edited by M. L. Powell, pp.52–69. Tuscaloosa: University of Alabama Press.

1992b Human skeletal remains. In *The Lohmann Site: An Early Mississippian Center in the American Bottom*, by D. Esarey and T. R. Pauketat. American Bottom Archaeology, FAI-270 Reports 25. Urbana: University of Illinois Press.

1993 Cahokia in a regional context. Paper presented at the 58th annual meeting of the Society for American Archaeology, St. Louis.

Milner, George R., and Richard Paine

1991 Human skeletal remains. In *The Archaeology of the Cahokia Mounds ICT-II: Biological Remains*, part 3. Illinois Cultural Resources Study 13. Springfield: Illinois Historic Preservation Agency.

Milner, George R., and Thomas E. Emerson

1981 The Mississippian occupation of the American Bottom: The farmsteads. Paper presented at the Midwestern Archaeological Conference, Madison WI.

Milner, George R., Thomas E. Emerson, Mark W. Mehrer,
Joyce A. Williams, and Duane Esarey

1984 Mississippian and Oneota Period. In *American Bottom Archaeology*, edited by C. J. Bareis and J. W. Porter, pp.158–86. Urbana: University of Illinois Press.

Miracle, Preston

1996a Faunal remains. In *The Archaeology of Downtown Cahokia: The Tract 15A and Dunham Tract Excavations*, by Timothy R. Pauketat. Urbana: Illinois Archaeological Survey (in press).

1996b Human remains. In *The Archaeology of Downtown Cahokia: The Tract 15A and Dunham Tract Excavations*, by Timothy R. Pauketat. Urbana: Illinois Archaeological Survey (in press).

Mistovich, Tim S.

1986 Excavations at Sites 1Tu265 and 1Tu423, Oliver Lock and Dam, Tuscaloosa, Alabama. Report of Investigations 51. Office of Archaeological Research, University of Alabama, Tuscaloosa.

Mochon, Marion J.

1972 Language, history, and prehistory: Mississippian lexico-reconstruction. *American Antiquity* 37:478–503.

Moffat, Charles R.

1991 Mississippian in the upper Kaskaskia valley: New data from Lake Shelbyville and new interpretations. In *Cahokia and the Hinterlands: Middle Mississippian Cultures of the Midwest*, edited by T. E. Emerson and R. B. Lewis, pp.239–56. Urbana: University of Illinois Press.

325

Moorehead, Warren K.
1922   *The Cahokia Mounds: A Preliminary Paper*. Urbana: University of Illinois.
1923   *The Cahokia Mounds: A Report of Progress on the Exploration of the Cahokia Group*. Urbana: University of Illinois Press.
1929   *The Cahokia Mounds*. Bulletin 26 (4). Urbana: University of Illinois.
Morgan, William N.
1980   *Prehistoric Architecture of the Eastern United States*. Cambridge. MIT Press.
Morse, Dan F.
1990   The Nodena phase. In *Temples and Towns Along the Mississippi*, edited by D. H. Dye, pp.69–97. Tuscaloosa: University of Alabama Press.
Morse, Dan F., and Phyllis A. Morse
1983   *Archaeology of the Central Mississippi Valley*. New York: Academic Press.
1990   Emergent Mississippian in the central Mississippi valley. In *The Mississippian Emergence*, edited by B. D. Smith, pp.153–73. Washington DC: Smithsonian Institution Press.
Muller, Jon
1978   The Kincaid system: Mississippian settlement in the environs of a large site. In *Mississippian Settlement Patterns*, edited by B. D. Smith, pp.269–92. New York: Academic Press.
1984   Mississippian specialization and salt. *American Antiquity* 49:489–507.
1986a   *Archaeology of the Lower Ohio River Valley*. Orlando: Academic Press.
1986b   Pans and a grain of salt: Mississippian specialization revisited. *American Antiquity* 51:405–9.
1987   Salt, chert, and shell: Mississippian exchange and economy. In *Specialization, Exchange, and Complex Societies*, edited by E. Brumfiel and T. Earle, pp.10–21. Cambridge: Cambridge University Press.
1989   The Southern cult. In *The Southeastern Ceremonial Complex: Artifacts and Analysis*, edited by Patricia Galloway, pp.11–26. Lincoln: University of Nebraska Press.
Muller, Jon, and Jeanette E. Stephens
1991   Mississippian sociocultural adaptation. In *Cahokia and the Hinterlands: Middle Mississippian Cultures of the Midwest*, edited by T. E. Emerson and R. B. Lewis, pp.297–310. Urbana: University of Illinois Press.
Munson, Patrick J.
1971   An archaeological survey of the Wood River Terrace and adjacent bottoms and bluffs in Madison County, Illinois. Illinois State Museum Reports of Investigations 21, part 1. Springfield.
Narroll, Raoul
1962   Floor area and settlement pattern. *American Antiquity* 27: 587–89.

Nash, C. H.
1972   Chucalissa: Excavations and burial through 1963. Occasional Papers No. 6, Anthropological Research Center, Memphis State University, Memphis TN.

Nassaney, Michael S.
1992   Communal societies and the emergence of elites in the prehistoric American Southeast. In *Lords of the Southeast: Social Inequality and the Native Elites of Southeastern North America*, edited by A. W. Barker and T. R. Pauketat, pp.111–43. Archeological Papers of the American Anthropological Association 3. Washington DC: American Anthropological Association.

Netting, Robert McC.
1982   Some truths about household size and wealth. *American Behavioral Scientist* 25 (6): 641–62.

Nicklas, T. Dale
1994   Linguistic provinces of the Southeast at the time of Columbus. In *Perspectives on the Southeast: Linguistics, Archaeology, and Ethnohistory*, pp.1–13. Athens: University of Georgia Press.

Norris, F. Terry
1975   Horseshoe Lake State Park Archaeological Survey. Manuscript on file at Cahokia Mound State Park, Illinois State Museum.

Oberg, Kalervo
1955   Types of social structure among the lowland tribes of South and Central America. *American Anthropologist* 57:472–87.

O'Brien, Michael J., Robert E. Warren, and Dennis E. Lewarch
1982   *The Cannon Reservoir Human Ecology Project: An Archaeological Study of Cultural Adaptations in the Southern Prairie Peninsula*. New York: Academic Press.

O'Brien, Patricia J.
1972a   A formal analysis of Cahokia ceramic from the Powell Tract. Illinois Archaeological Survey Monograph 3. Urbana.
1972b   Urbanism, Cahokia, and Middle Mississippian. *Archaeology* 25 (3): 88–197.
1989   Cahokia: The political capital of the "Ramey" state? *North American Archaeologist* 10:275–92.
1991   Early state economics: Cahokia, capital of the Ramey state. In *Early State Economics*, edited by Henri J. M. Claessen and Pieter van de Velde, pp.143–75. London: Transaction Publishers.
1992   The "world-system" of Cahokia within the Middle Mississippi tradition. *Review* 15 (3): 389–417.
1993   The social dynamics of Cahokia's Tract 15B. Paper presented at the 58th annual meeting of the Society for American Archaeology, St. Louis.

1994   Prehistoric politics: Petroglyphs and the political boundaries of Cahokia. *Gateway Heritage* (summer): 30–47. Quarterly magazine of the Missouri Historical Society.

O'Shea, John M., and John Ludwickson

1992   Omaha chieftainship in the nineteenth century. *Ethnohistory* 39:316–52.

Parker, Kathryn E.

1989a   Archaeobotanical assemblage. In *The Holding Site: A Hopewell Community in the American Bottom*, by A. C. Fortier, T. O. Maher, J. A. Williams, M. C. Meinkoth, K. E. Parker, and L. S. Kelly, pp.429–64. American Bottom Archaeology, FAI-270 Site Reports 19. Urbana: University of Illinois Press.

1989b   Botanical remains from the Samson Bluff site. Manuscript on file at the Department of Anthropology, University of Illinois, Urbana.

1991   Sponemann phase archaeobotany. In *The Sponemann Site: The Formative Emergent Mississippian Sponemann Phase Occupations*, by A. C. Fortier, T. O. Maher, and J. A. Williams, pp.377–419. American Bottom Archaeology, FAI-270 Site Reports 23. Urbana: University of Illinois Press.

1992a   Plant remains from archaeological excavations at the Walmart site (11-Ms-1369). Manuscript on file at Archaeological Consultants, Normal IL.

1992b   Archaeobotany. In *The Sponemann Site 2: The Mississippian and Oneota Occupations* (11-Ms-517), by D. K. Jackson, A. C. Fortier, and J. A. Williams, pp.305–24. American Bottom Archaeology, FAI-270 Site Reports 22. Urbana: University of Illinois Press.

1993   Plant remains from archaeological testing at the Fingerhut site (11-S-34/7). Manuscript on file at Great Lakes Ecosystems, Indian River, Michigan.

1994   Plant remains from archaeological investigations at the GSC#1 site, Madison County, Illinois. Manuscript on file at Hanson Engineers, Inc., Springfield, Illinois.

Pauketat, Timothy R.

1987a   A burned domestic dwelling at Cahokia. *Wisconsin Archeologist* 68 (3): 212–37.

1987b   A functional consideration of a Mississippian domestic vessel assemblage. *Southeastern Archaeology* 6:1–15.

1987c   Mississippian domestic economy and formation processes: A response to Prentice. *Midcontinental Journal of Archaeology* 12 (1): 77–88.

1989   Monitoring Mississippian homestead occupation span and economy using ceramic refuse. *American Antiquity* 54:288–310.

1990   Ceramics. In *The Archaeology of the Cahokia Palisade: The East Palisade Investigations*, by W. R. Iseminger, T. R. Pauketat, B. Koldehoff, L. S. Kelly, and L. Blake, pp.39–76. Illinois Cultural Resources Study 14. Springfield: Illinois Historic Preservation Agency.

1991 The dynamics of pre-state political centralization in the North American midcontinent. Ph.D. diss., Department of Anthropology, University of Michigan, Ann Arbor.

1992 The reign and ruin of the lords of Cahokia: A dialectic of dominance. In *Lords of the Southeast: Social Inequality and the Native Elites of Southeastern North America*, edited by A. W. Barker and T. R. Pauketat, pp. 31–52. American Anthropological Association, Archeological Papers 3. Washington DC: American Anthropological Association.

1993a Big bang in the bottom: Political consolidation and Mississippianism at Cahokia. Paper presented at the 58th annual meeting of the Society for American Archaeology, St. Louis.

1993b Preliminary observations of building density at Cahokia's Tract 15A and Dunham Tract. *Illinois Archaeology* 5 (1–2): 402–6.

1993c Temples for Cahokia lords: Preston Holder's 1955–1956 excavation of Kunnemann Mound. University of Michigan, Museum of Anthropology, Memoir 26. Ann Arbor.

1994a *The Ascent of Chiefs: Cahokia and Mississippian Politics in Native North America.* Tuscaloosa: University of Alabama Press.

1994b The place of post-circle monuments in Cahokian political history. Paper presented at conference on "The Ancient Skies and Sky Watchers of Cahokia: Woodhenges, Eclipses, and Cahokian Cosmology," organized by M. Fowler, Cahokia Mounds State Historic Site.

1994c Molding pots and traditions at early Cahokia. Paper presented at the Southeastern Archaeological Conference, Lexington KY.

1995 The Halliday site and the limits of Cahokian dominance. Paper presented at the Southeastern Archaeological Conference, Knoxville TN.

1996 The archaeology of downtown Cahokia: The Tract 15A and Dunham Tract excavations. Illinois Archaeological Survey Monograph. Urbana. In press.

1997 Specialization, political symbols, and the crafty elite of Cahokia. *Southeastern Archaeology* 16 (in press).

Pauketat, Timothy R., and Alex W. Barker

n.d. Mounds 65 and 66 at Cahokia: Additional details of the 1927 excavations. Manuscript in the possession of the authors.

Pauketat, Timothy R., and Brad Koldehoff

1988 Salvage data recovery at the Olszewski Site: A small Mississippian community in the American Bottom. *Rediscovery* (Journal of the Illinois Association for Advancement of Archaeology) 3:31–50.

Pauketat, Timothy R., and Mark A. Rees

1996 Early Cahokia project 1994 excavations at Mound 49, Cahokia (11-S-34-2).

Unpublished report submitted to the Illinois Historic Preservation Agency, Springfield. Early Cahokia Project Papers 2, University of Oklahoma, Norman.

Pauketat, Timothy R., and Thomas E. Emerson

1991   The ideology of authority and the power of the pot. *American Anthropologist* 93:919–41.

1996   The production of hegemony and Mississippianism. Paper presented at the 13th annual Visiting Scholar Conference "Material Symbols: Culture and Economy in Prehistory," Southern Illinois University at Carbondale.

Pauketat, Timothy R., Mark A. Rees, and Stephanie L. Pauketat

1996   An archaeological survey of the Horseshoe Lake State Recreation Area, Madison County, Illinois. Unpublished report submitted to the Illinois Department of Conservation. Illinois State Museum, Quaternary Studies Program, Technical Report Number 95-899-34. Springfield.

Payne, Claudine

1994   Mississippian capitals: An archaeological investigation of Precolumbian political structure. Ph.D. diss., University of Florida, Gainesville.

Paynter, Robert, and Randall H. McGuire

1991   The archaeology of inequality: An introduction. In *The Archaeology of Inequality*, edited by R. H. McGuire and R. Paynter, pp. 1–11. Oxford: Basil Blackwell.

Peale, T. R.

1862   Ancient mounds at St. Louis Missouri, in 1819. In *Annual Report of the Smithsonian Institution for the Year 1861*, pp. 386–91. Washington DC.

Pearson, G. W.

1986   Precise calendrical dating of known growth-period samples using a "curve fitting" technique. *Radiocarbon* 28:292–99.

Peebles, Christopher S.

1978   Moundville phase. In *Mississippian Settlement Patterns*, edited by Bruce D. Smith, pp. 369–416. New York: Academic Press.

1986   Paradise lost, strayed, and stolen: Prehistoric social devolution in the Southeast. In *The Burden of Being Civilized: An Anthropological Perspective on the Discontents of Civilization*, edited by M. Richardson and M. C. Webb, pp. 24–40. Southern Anthropological Society Proceedings 18. Athens: University of Georgia Press.

1987a Moundville from 1000 to 1500 A.D. as seen from 1840 to 1985 A.D. In *Chiefdoms in the Americas*, edited by Robert D. Drennen and Carlos A. Uribe, pp. 21–41. Lanham MD: University Press of America.

1987b The rise and fall of the Mississippian in western Alabama: The Moundville and Summerville phases, A.D. 1000 to 1600. *Mississippi Archaeology* 22:1–31.

Peebles, Christopher S., editor
1983   Excavations in the Lubbub Creek archaeological locality: Prehistoric agricultural communities in west-central Alabama. Unpublished report submitted to the United States Army Corps of Engineers, Mobile AL.

Peebles, Christopher S., and Susan M. Kus
1977   Some archaeological correlates of ranked societies. *American Antiquity* 42:421–48.

Peet, Stephen D.
1903   The Mound Builders. 2d edition. Chicago: Office of the American Antiquarian.

Peregrine, Peter
1991   A graph-theoretic approach to the evolution of Cahokia. *American Antiquity* 56:66–75.
1992   *Mississippian Evolution: A World-System Perspective.* Madison WI: Prehistory Press.

Perino, Gregory
1957   Cahokia. *Central States Archaeological Journal* 3:84–88.
1971   The Mississippian component at the Schild site (No.4), Greene County, Illinois. In *Mississippian Site Archaeology in Illinois: I.* Illinois Archaeological Survey, Bulletin 8. Urbana.
1980   Cahokia notes. In *Cahokia Brought to Life*, edited by R. E. Grimm, pp.61–67. St. Louis: Greater St. Louis Archaeological Society.
n.d.   Untitled manuscript on Mound 34 on file at the University of Michigan, Museum of Anthropology, Ann Arbor.

Perttula, Timothy K.
1992   *The Caddo Nation: Archaeological and Ethnohistorical Perspectives.* Austin: University of Texas Press.

Phillips, Philip
1970   *Archaeological Survey in the Lower Yazoo Basin, Mississippi, 1947–1955.* 2 vols. Papers of the Peabody Museum of Archaeology and Ethnology 60. Cambridge: Harvard University.

Phillips, Philip, and James A. Brown
1978   *Pre-Columbian Shell Engravings from the Craig Mound at Spiro, Oklahoma*, part 1. Cambridge MA: Peabody Museum Press.
1984   *Pre-Columbian Shell Engravings from the Craig Mound at Spiro, Oklahoma*, part 2. Cambridge MA: Peabody Museum Press.

Phillips, Philip, James A. Ford, and James B. Griffin
1951   *Archaeological Survey in the Lower Mississippi Alluvial Valley, 1940–1947.* Papers of the Peabody Museum of American Archaeology and Ethnology 25. Cambridge: Harvard University.

Porter, James W.

1974   Cahokia archaeology as viewed from the Mitchell site: A satellite community at A.D. 1150–1200. Ph.D. diss., Department of Anthropology, University of Wisconsin at Milwaukee. Ann Arbor: University Microfilms.

1977   The Mitchell site and prehistoric exchange systems at Cahokia: A.D. 1000
± 300. In *Explorations into Cahokia Archaeology*, edited by M. Fowler,
pp.137–64. 1969. Reprinted, Illinois Archaeological Survey Bulletin 7. Urbana.

Prentice, Guy

1986   An analysis of the symbolism expressed by the Birger Figurine. *American
Antiquity* 51:239–66.

Prentice, Guy, and Mark Mehrer

1981   The Lab Woofie site (11-S-346): An unplowed Mississippian site in the
American Bottom region of Illinois. *Midcontinental Journal of Archaeology*
6:33–53.

Preucel, Robert W., editor

1991   Processual and postprocessual archaeologies: Multiple ways of knowing the
past. Center for Archaeological Investigations, Occasional Paper 10. Carbondale IL.

Price, James E.

1978   The settlement pattern of the Powers phase. In *Mississippian Settlement Patterns*, edited by Bruce D. Smith, pp.201–32. New York: Academic Press.

Price, James E., and James B. Griffin

1979   *The Snodgrass Site of the Powers Phase of Southeast Missouri*. Museum of
Anthropology, University of Michigan, Anthropological Papers No. 66.
Ann Arbor.

Pulcher, Ronald E.

1985   St. Louis harbor project pedestrian survey, Madison County, Illinois. St.
Louis District Cultural Resource Management Reports 24. St. Louis: U.S.
Army Corps of Engineers.

Purdue, J. R., B. W. Styles, and M. C. Masulis

1989   Faunal remains and white-tail deer exploitation from a Late Woodland upland encampment: The Boschert site (23SC609), St. Charles County, Missouri. *Midcontinental Journal of Archaeology* 14 (2): 146–63.

Reed, Nelson A.

1977   Monks and other Mississippian mounds. In *Explorations in Cahokia Archaeology*, edited by M. L. Fowler, pp.31–42. Illinois Archaeological Survey, Bulletin 7. Urbana.

Reed, Nelson A., James W. Bennett, and James W. Porter

1968   Solid core drilling of Monks Mound: Technique and findings. *American Antiquity* 33:137–48.

References

Renfrew, Colin

1975   Trade as action at a distance: Questions of integration and communication. In *Ancient Civilization and Trade*, edited by J. A. Sabloff and C. C. Lamborg-Karlovsky, pp. 1–60. Albuquerque: University of New Mexico Press.

1987   Introduction: Peer polity interaction and socio-political change. In *Peer Polity Interaction and Socio-Political Change*, edited by C. Renfrew and J. F. Cherry, pp. 1–18. Cambridge: Cambridge University Press.

Revelle, Roger

1966   Population and food supplies: The edge of the knife. In *Prospects of the World Food Supply*, compiled by J. George Harrar, pp. 24–47. Washington DC: National Academy of Sciences.

Riley, Thomas J.

1987   Ridged-field agriculture and the Mississippian economic pattern. In *Emergent Horticultural Economies of the Eastern Woodlands*, edited by W. F. Keegan, pp. 295–304. Center for Archaeological Investigations Occasional Paper 7. Carbondale: Southern Illinois University.

Riley, Thomas J., and Glen Freimuth

1979   Field systems and frost drainage in the prehistoric agriculture of the upper Great Lakes. *American Antiquity* 44:271–85.

Riley, Thomas J., and Gregory Walz

1992   AMS dating of maize from the Middle Woodland Holding site (11-Ms-118) in the American Bottom of Illinois. Paper presented at the 49th annual meeting of the Southeastern Archaeological Conference, Little Rock AR.

Riley, Thomas J., Charles R. Moffat, and Glen Freimuth

1981   Prehistoric raised fields in the upper Midwestern United States: An innovation in response to marginal growing conditions. *North American Archaeologist* 2:103–13.

Riley, Thomas J., Gregory R. Walz, Charles J. Bareis,
Andrew C. Fortier, and Kathryn E. Parker

1994   Accelerator mass spectrometry (AMS) dates confirm early Zea mays in the Mississippi River valley. *American Antiquity* 59 (3): 490–98.

Rindos, David, and Sissel Johannessen

1991   Human-plant interactions and cultural change in the American Bottom. In *Cahokia and the Hinterlands: Middle Mississippian Cultures of the Midwest*, edited by T. E. Emerson and R. B. Lewis, pp. 35–45. Urbana: University of Illinois Press.

Riordan, Robert

1975   Ceramics and chronology: Mississippian settlement in the Black Bottom, southern Illinois. Ph.D. diss., Department of Anthropology, Southern Illinois University at Carbondale. Ann Arbor: University Microfilms.

333

Rodell, Roland L.

1991   The Diamond Bluff site complex and Cahokia influence in the Red Wing locality. In *New Perspectives on Cahokia: Views from the Periphery*, edited by J. B. Stoltman, pp. 253–80. Madison WI: Prehistory Press.

Rogers, J. Daniel, and Bruce D. Smith, editors

1995   *Mississippian Communities and Households*. Tuscaloosa: University of Alabama Press.

Rollings, Willard H.

1992   *The Osage: An Ethnohistorical Study of Hegemony on the Prairie-Plains*. Columbia: University of Missouri Press.

Rose, Jerome, and Janice Cohen

1974   Skeletal biology, Mound 72. Paper presented at the 39th annual meeting of the Society for American Archaeology, Washington DC.

Rowlands, Michael

1987   Centre and periphery: A review of a concept. In *Centre and Periphery in the Ancient World*, edited by M. Rowlands, M. Larsen, and K. Kristiansen, pp. 1–11. Cambridge: Cambridge University Press.

Sabo, George, III, and Ann M. Early

1990   Prehistoric culture history. In *Human Adaptation in the Ozark and Ouachita Mountains*, by G. Sabo III, A. M. Early, J. C. Rose, B. A. Burnett, L. Vogele Jr., and J. P. Harcourt, pp. 34–120. Arkansas Archeological Survey Research Series 31, Fayetteville.

Sahlins, Marshall D.

1958   *Social Stratification in Polynesia*. Seattle: University of Washington Press.

1972   *Stone Age Economics*. Chicago: Aldine.

Saitta, Dean J.

1994   Agency, class, and archaeological interpretation. *Journal of Anthropological Archaeology* 13:201–27.

Salisbury, E. J.

1974   Seed size and mass in relation to environment. *Proceedings of the Royal Botanical Society* 186:83–88.

Salzer, Robert J.

1975   Excavations at the Merrell Tract of the Cahokia site: Summary field report, 1973. In *Cahokia Archaeology: Field Reports*, edited by M. L. Fowler. Illinois State Museum Research Series, Papers in Anthropology 3:1–8. Springfield.

Sasso, Robert F., R. Boszhardt, J. Knox, J. Theler, K. Stevenson, J. Gallagher, and C. Stiles-Hanson

1985   Prehistoric ridge field agriculture in the Upper Mississippi valley. Mississippi Valley Archaeology Center Reports of Investigations 38. La Crosse: University of Wisconsin.

Scarry, John

1990   Mississippian emergence in the Fort Walton area: The evolution of the Cayson and Lake Jackson phases. In *The Mississippian Emergence*, edited by B. Smith, pp.227–50. Washington DC: Smithsonian Institution Press.

1992   Political offices and political structure: Ethnohistoric and archaeological perspectiveson the native lords of Apalachee. In *Lords of the Southeast: Social Inequality and the Native Elites of Southeastern North America*, edited by A. W. Barker and T. R. Pauketat, pp.163–83. Archaeological Papers of the American Anthropological Association No.3. Washington DC: American Anthropological Association.

n.d.   How great were the southeastern polities? Variation in scale, productivity, and complexity among the Mississippian Societies. Manuscript prepared for the seminar "Great Towns and Regional Polities: Cultural Evolution in the U.S. Southwest and Southeast," organized by Jill Neitzel, 5–12 March 1994, Amerind Foundation, Dragoon AZ.

Scarry, C. Margaret

1986   Change in plant procurement and production during the emergence of the Moundville chiefdom. Ph.D. diss., Department of Anthropology, University of Michigan. Ann Arbor: University Microfilms.

1993a   Archaeological investigations of the Riverbank stabilization project at Moundville. Draft report of investigations submitted to Mobile District Corps of Engineers, Mobile AL.

1993b   Introduction. In *Foraging and Farming in the Eastern Woodlands*, edited by C. M. Scarry, pp.3–11. Gainesville: University Press of Florida.

1993c   Variability in Mississippian crop production strategies. In *Foraging and Farming in the Eastern Woodlands*, edited by C. M. Scarry, pp.78–90. Gainesville: University Press of Florida.

Scarry, C. Margaret, editor

1993   *Foraging and Farming in the Eastern Woodlands*. Gainesville: University Press of Florida.

Scarry, C. Margaret, and Vincas P. Steponaitis

1992   Between farmstead and center: The natural and social landscape of Moundville. Paper presented in the Fryxell Symposium at the 57th annual meeting of the Society for American Archaeology, Pittsburgh.

Schamback, Frank F., and Frank Rackerby, editors

1982   Contributions to the archeology of the Great Bend region. Arkansas Archeological Survey Research Series 22. Fayetteville.

Schnell, Frank T., Vernon J. Knight Jr., and Gail S. Schnell

1981   *Cemochechobee: Archaeology of a Mississippian Ceremonial Center on the Chattahoochee River*. Gainesville: University Press of Florida.

Scollar, I., A. Tabbagh, A. Hesse, and I. Herzog
1990   *Archaeological Prospecting and Remote Sensing*. Cambridge: Cambridge University Press.

Scott, Susan L.
1983   Analysis, synthesis, and interpretations of faunal remains from the Lubbub Creek Archaeological Locality. In *Studies of the Material Remains from the Lubbub Creek Archaeological Locality*, edited by C. Peebles, pp.274–381. Prehistoric Agricultural Communities in West Central Alabama, vol.2. Report submitted to the U.S. Army Corps of Engineers, Mobile District, by the University of Michigan, Museum of Anthropology, Ann Arbor.

1985   Analysis of faunal remains recovered at the Rucker's Bottom site (9EB91), Elbert County, Georgia. In *Prehistoric Human Ecology along the Upper Savannah River: Excavations at the Rucker's Bottom, Abbeville, and Bullard Site Groups*, assembled by David G. Anderson and Joseph Schuldenrein, pp.639–64. Atlanta Interagency Archeological Services Division, National Park Service, Russell Papers, Atlanta.

Service, Elman R.
1962   *Primitive Social Organization*. New York: Random House.

1975   *Origins of the State and Civilization*. New York: Norton.

Shanks, Michael, and Christopher Tilley
1982   Ideology, symbolic power, and ritual communication: Reinterpretation of Neolithic mortuary practices. In *Symbolic and Structural Archaeology*, edited by I. Hodder, pp.129–54. Cambridge: Cambridge University Press.

Sharer, Robert J., and Wendy Ashmore
1987   *Archaeology: Discovering Our Past*. Palo Alto CA: Mayfield.

1987   *Social Theory and Archaeology*. Albuquerque: University of New Mexico Press.

Shelby, Charmion, translator
1993   La Florida, by the Inca. In *The De Soto Chronicles: Expedition of Hernando De Soto to North America in 1539–43*, edited by L. A. Clayton, V. J. Knight Jr., and E. C. Moore, pp.25–559. Tuscaloosa: University of Alabama Press.

Shennan, Stephen J.
1982   Exchange and ranking: The role of amber in the earlier Bronze Age of Europe. In *Ranking, Resource and Exchange*, edited by C. Renfrew, pp.33–45. Cambridge: Cambridge University Press.

1987   Trends in the study of later European prehistory. *Annual Review of Anthropology* 16:365–82.

Shepard, Anna O.
1948   A symmetry of abstract design with special reference to ceramic description. Carnegie Institute of Washington Publication 574, Contribution 47:211–92. Washington DC: Carnegie Institute.

1968   *Ceramics for the Archaeologist.* Washington DC: Carnegie Institution of Washington.

Sherratt, Andrew

1990   The genesis of megaliths: Monumentality, ethnicity, and social complexity in Neolithic north-west Europe. *World Archaeology* 22:147–67.

Skele, Mikels

1988   The great knob: Interpretations of Monks Mound. Studies in Illinois Archaeology No.4. Springfield: Illinois Historic Preservation Agency.

Smith, Bruce D.

1978   Variation in Mississippian settlement patterns. In *Mississippian Settlement Patterns*, edited by B. D. Smith, pp.479–503. New York: Academic Press.

1984   Mississippian expansion: Tracing the historical development of an explanatory model. *Southeastern Archaeology* 3 (1): 13–32.

1986   The archaeology of the southeastern United States: From Dalton to DeSoto, 10,500–500 B.P. In *Advances in World Archaeology*, edited by F. Wendorf and A. E. Close, pp.1–92. New York: Academic Press.

1987   The independent domestication of indigenous seed-bearing plants in eastern North America. In *Emergent Horticultural Economies of the Eastern Woodlands*, edited by W. F. Keegan, pp.3–47. Center for Archaeological Investigations, Occasional Paper 7. Carbondale: Southern Illinois University Press.

1990   Introduction: Research on the origins of Mississippian chiefdoms in eastern North America. In *The Mississippian Emergence*, edited by B. D. Smith, pp.1–8. Washington DC: Smithsonian Institution Press.

1992a   Hopewellian farmers of eastern North America. In *Rivers of Change: Essays on Early Agriculture in Eastern North America*, by Bruce D. Smith, pp.201–48. Washington DC: Smithsonian Institution Press.

1992b   Mississippian elites and solar alignments: A reflection of managerial necessity, or levers of social inequality? In *Lords of the Southeast: Social Inequality and the Native Elites of Southeastern North America*, edited by A. W. Barker and T. R. Pauketat, pp.11–30. Archeological Papers of the American Anthropological Association 3. Washington DC: American Anthropological Association.

Smith, Harriet M.

1969   The Murdock Mound: Cahokia site. In *Explorations into Cahokia Archaeology*, edited by M. L. Fowler, pp.49–88. Illinois Archaeological Survey Bulletin 7. Urbana.

1973   The Murdock Mound: Cahokia site. In *Explorations into Cahokia Archaeology*, 1st revised edition. Edited by M. L. Fowler, pp.49–88. Illinois Archaeological Survey Bulletin 7. Urbana.

1977   The Murdock Mound: Cahokia site. In *Explorations into Cahokia Archaeol-*

ogy, 2d revised edition. Edited by M. L. Fowler, pp.49–88. Illinois Archaeological Survey Bulletin 7. Urbana.

Smith, Marvin T., and David J. Hally

1992   Chiefly behavior: Evidence from sixteenth-century Spanish accounts. In *Lords of the Southeast: Social Inequality and the Native Elites of Southeastern North America*, edited by A. W. Barker and T. R. Pauketat, pp.99–109. Archeological Papers of the American Anthropological Association 3. Washington DC: American Anthropological Association.

Smith, Marvin T., and Mark Williams

1994   Mississippian mound refuse disposal patterns and implications for archaeological research. *Southeastern Archaeology* 13 (1): 27–35.

Smith, Michael E.

1993   New World complex societies: recent economic, social, and political studies. *Journal of Archaeological Research* 1:5–41.

Snaydon, R. W.

1980   Plant demography in agricultural systems. In *Demography and Evolution in Plant Populations*, edited by O. T. Solbrig, pp.131–60. Berkeley: University of California Press.

Spencer, Charles

1982   *The Cuicatlán Cañada and Monte Albán*. New York: Academic Press.

1987   Rethinking the chiefdom. In *Chiefdoms of the Americas*, edited by R. Drennan and C. A. Uribe, pp.369–89. Lanham MD: University Press of America.

Speth, John D., and Susan L. Scott

1989   Horticulture and large-mammal hunting: The role of resource depletion and the constraints of time and labor. In *Farmers as Hunters: The Implications of Sedentism*, edited by S. Kent, pp.71–79. Cambridge: Cambridge University Press.

Stahl, Ann B.

1985   *The Dohack Site*. American Bottom Archaeology, FAI Site Reports 12. Urbana: University of Illinois Press.

Stahle, David W., Malcolm K. Cleaveland, and John G. Hehr

1985   Tree-ring dating of baldcypress and the potential for millennia-long chronologies in the Southeast. *American Antiquity* 50:796–802.

Steponaitis, Vincas P.

1978   Location theory and complex chiefdoms: A Mississippian example. In *Mississippian Settlement Patterns*, edited by Bruce D. Smith, pp.417–53. New York: Academic Press.

1981   Settlement hierarchies and political complexity in nonmarket societies: The formative period of the valley of Mexico. *American Anthropologist* 83:320–63.

1983   *Ceramics, Chronology, and Community Patterns: An Archaeological Study at Moundville*. New York: Academic Press.

1986   Prehistoric archaeology in the southeastern United States, 1970–1985. *Annual Review of Anthropology* 15:363–404.

1991   Contrasting Patterns of Mississippian Development. In *Chiefdoms: Power, Economy, and Ideology*, edited by T. Earle, pp.193–228. Cambridge: Cambridge University Press.

1992   Excavations at 1Tu50, an early Mississippian center near Moundville. *Southeastern Archaeology* 11:1–13.

1993   Population trends at Moundville. Paper presented at the 58th annual meeting of the Society for American Archaeology, St. Louis.

Steward, Julian H., editor

1948   *Handbook of South American Indians*, vol.4, *The Circum-Caribbean Tribes*. Smithsonian Institution, Bureau of American Ethnology, Bulletin 143.

Stoltman, James B.

1986   The appearance of the Mississippian cultural tradition in the Mississippi valley. In *Prehistoric Mound Builders of the Mississippi Valley*, edited by J. B. Stoltman, pp.26–34. Davenport IA: Putnam Museum.

1991   Cahokia as seen from the peripheries. In *New Perspectives on Cahokia: Views from the Periphery*, edited by J. B. Stoltman, pp.349–54. Madison, WI: Prehistory Press.

Stoltman, James B., editor

1991   *New Perspectives on Cahokia: Views from the Periphery*. Madison WI: Prehistory Press.

Story, Dee Ann

1988   Cultural history of the Native Americans. In *The Archaeology and Bioarchaeology of the Gulf Coast Plain: Volume 1*, by D. A. Story, J. A. Guy, B. A. Burnett, M. D. Freeman, J. C. Rose, D. G. Steele, B. W. Olive, and K. J. Reinhard, pp.163–366. Arkansas Archeological Survey Research Series 38. Fayetteville.

Styles, Bonnie W., and J. R. Purdue

1996   Animal exploitation. In *Middle-Late Woodland Subsistence and Ceramic Technology in the Central Mississippi Valley: Selected Studies from the Burkemper Site, Lincoln County, Missouri*, edited by M. J. O'Brien. Illinois State Museum, Reports of Investigations 52. Springfield.

Sumner, C.

1979   *Reading Ideologies: An Investigation into the Marxist Theory of Ideology and Law*. London: Academic Press.

Sunesan, C. A.

1949   Survival of four barley varieties in mixture. *Journal of Agronomy* 41:459–61.

Swanton, John R.

1931   *Source Material for the Social and Ceremonial Life of the Choctaw Indians.* Bureau of American Ethnology, Bulletin 103. Washington DC.

1946   *The Indians of the Southeastern United States.* Bureau of American Ethnology, Bulletin 137. Washington DC.

1979   *The Indians of the Southeastern United States.* Washington DC: Smithsonian Institution Press.

Thomas, Cyrus

1907   Cahokia or Monk's Mound. *American Anthropologist* 9:362–65.

Thompson, R., and F. Oldfield

1986   *Environmental Magnetism.* London: Allen and Unwin.

Tiffany, Joseph A.

1991a   Modeling Mill Creek-Mississippian interaction. In *New Perspectives on Cahokia: Views from the Periphery,* edited by J. B. Stoltman, pp.319–47. Madison WI: Prehistory Press.

1991b   Models of Mississippian culture history in the western Prairie Peninsula: A perspective from Iowa. In *Cahokia and the Hinterlands: Middle Mississippian Cultures of the Midwest,* edited by T. E. Emerson and R. B. Lewis, pp.183–92. Urbana: University of Illinois Press.

Titterington, Paul F.

1938   *The Cahokia Mound Group and Its Village Site Materials.* St. Louis: Privately published.

Trenbath, B. R.

1974   Biomass productivity of mixtures. *Advances in Agronomy* 26:177–210.

1976   Plant interaction in mixed crop communities. In *Multiple Cropping,* edited by R. I. Papendick, P. A. Sanchez, and G. B. Triplet, pp.129–69. Madison WI: American Society of Agronomy.

Trigger, Bruce G.

1968   The determinants of settlement patterns. In *Settlement Archaeology,* edited by K. C. Chang, pp.53–78. Palo Alto CA: National Press Books.

1990   Monumental architecture: A thermodynamic explanation of symbolic behaviour. *World Archaeology* 22 (2): 119–32.

Turner, E. Randolph, and Robert S. Santley

1979   Deer skins and hunting territories reconsidered. *American Antiquity* 44:810–16.

Turner, Victor

1964   Betwixt and between: The liminal period in rites de passage. In *Symposium on New Approaches to the Study of Religion,* edited by J. Helm, pp.4–20.

Proceedings of the American Ethnological Society. Seattle: University of Washington Press.

1969   *The Ritual Process: Structure and Anti-Structure*. Chicago: Aldine.

1974   *Dramas, Fields, and Metaphors: Symbolic Action in Human Society*. Ithaca: Cornell University Press.

Upham, Steadman

1987   A theoretical consideration of middle range societies. In *Chiefdoms in the Americas*, edited by R. Drennan and C. A. Uribe, pp.345–68. Lanham MD: University Press of America.

Upham, Steadman, Kent G. Lightfoot, and Roberta A. Jewett, editors

1989   *The Sociopolitical Structure of Prehistoric Southwestern Societies*. Boulder CO: Westview Press.

Vehik, Susan C.

1993   Dhegiha origins and Plains archaeology. *Plains Anthropologist* 38:231–52.

Vogel, Joseph O.

1964   *A Preliminary Report on the Analysis of Ceramics from the Cahokia Area at the Illinois State Museum*. Springfield: Illinois State Museum.

1975   Trends in Cahokia ceramics: preliminary study of the collections from Tracts 15A and 15B. In *Perspectives in Cahokia Archaeology*, pp.32–125. Illinois Archaeological Survey Bulletin 10. Urbana.

Wagner, Gail E.

1987   Uses of plants by the Fort Ancient Indians. Ph.D. diss., Department of Anthropology, Washington University, St. Louis.

Wagner, Robert W.

1959   An analysis of the material culture of the James Ramey Mound. Master's thesis, Department of Anthropology, University of Illinois, Urbana.

Walthall, John A.

1981   Galena and aboriginal trade in eastern North America. Illinois State Museum, Scientific Papers 27. Springfield.

Wardle, H. Newell

1906   The treasures of prehistoric Moundville. *Harpers Monthly Magazine* 112:200–210.

Waring, Antonio J.

1968   The Southern Cult and Muskogean ceremonial. In *The Waring Papers*, edited by S. Williams, pp.30–69. Papers of the Peabody Museum of Archaeology and Ethnology 58. Cambridge: Harvard University.

Waring, Antonio J., Jr., and Preston Holder

1945   A prehistoric ceremonial complex in the southeastern United States. *American Anthropologist* 47:1–34.

Webb, Paul A.

1987   Excavations at the New Massilon site (11-Wy-44), Wayne County, Illinois. Center for Archaeological Investigations, Research Paper 54. Carbondale: Southern Illinois University.

Webster, Gary S.

1990   Labor control and emergent stratification in prehistoric Europe. *Current Anthropology* 31:337–66.

Welch, Paul D.

1989   Chronological markers and imported items from the roadway excavations at Moundville. Paper presented at the 46th annual meeting of the Southeastern Archaeological Conference, Tampa FL.

1990   Mississippian emergence in west-central Alabama. In *The Mississippian Emergence*, edited by B. D. Smith, pp.197–225. Washington DC: Smithsonian Institution Press.

1991a   *Moundville's Economy*. Tuscaloosa: University of Alabama Press.

1991b   Control over goods and the political stability of the Moundville chiefdom. Paper presented at the 56th annual meeting of the Society for American Archaeology, New Orleans.

Wesler, Kit W.

1989   Archaeological excavations at Wickliffe Mounds, 15BA4: Mound D, 1987. Wickliffe Mounds Research Center Report No.3. Wickliffe KY.

1991a   Archaeological excavations at Wickliffe Mounds, 15BA4: North village and cemetery, 1988–1989. Wickliffe Mounds Research Center Report No.4. Wickliffe KY

1991b   Aspects of settlement patterning at Wickliffe (15BA4). In *The Human Landscape in Kentucky's Past: Site Structure and Settlement Patterns*, edited by C. Stout and C. K. Hensley, pp.106–27. Kentucky Heritage Council, Frankfort.

1991c   Ceramics, chronology, and horizon markers at Wickliffe Mounds. *American Antiquity* 56:278–90.

Wesler, Kit W., and Sarah W. Neusius

1987   Archaeological excavations at Wickliffe Mounds, 15BA4: Mound F, Mound A addendum, and mitigation for the Great River road project, 1985 and 1986. Wickliffe Mounds Research Center Report No.2. Wickliffe KY.

Wetterstrom, Wilma

1978   Plant foods from the Gypsy Joint site. In *Prehistoric Patterns of Human Behavior: A Case Study in the Mississippi Valley*, by B. D. Smith, pp.101–15. New York: Academic Press.

Weymouth, John W.

1986   Geophysical methods of archaeological site surveying. In *Advances in Ar-*

chaeological Method and Theory, vol.9, edited by M. B. Schiffer, pp.311–95. New York: Academic Press.

Whalley, Lucy A.

1983   Plant remains from the Turner site. In *The Turner and DeMange Sites*, by G. R. Milner, pp.213–33. American Bottom Archaeology, FAI-270 Site Reports 4. Urbana: University of Illinois Press.

1984   Plant remains from the Stirling phase. In *The BBB Motor Site*, by T. E. Emerson and D. K. Jackson, pp.321–35. American Bottom Archaeology, FAI-270 Site Reports 6. Urbana: University of Illinois Press.

Whiting, John W. M., and Barbara Ayres

1968   Inferences from the shape of dwellings. In Settlement Archaeology, edited by K. C. Chang. Palo Alto CA: National Press Books.

Willey, Gordon R.

1966   *An Introduction to American Archaeology*, vol.1. Englewood Cliffs NJ: Prentice-Hall.

Williams, Kenneth

1975   Preliminary summation of excavations at the east lobes of Monks Mound. In *Cahokia Archaeology: Field Reports*, edited by M. L. Fowler, pp.21–24. Illinois State Museum, Papers in Anthropology 3. Springfield.

Williams, J. Mark

1994   The origins of the Macon Plateau site. In *Ocmulgee Archaeology 1936–1986*, edited by David J. Hally, pp.130–37. Athens: University of Georgia Press.

Williams, Mark, and Gary Shapiro

1990   Paired towns. In *Lamar Archaeology: Mississippian Chiefdoms in the Deep South*, edited by M. Williams and G. Shapiro, pp.163–74. Tuscaloosa: University of Alabama Press.

Williams, Samuel C.

1930   *Adair's History of the American Indians*. Johnson City TN: Watauga Press.

Williams, Stephen

1990   The vacant quarter and other late events in the lower valley. In *Towns and Temples along the Mississippi*, edited by D. H. Dye, pp.170–80. Tuscaloosa: University of Alabama Press.

Williams, Stephen, and Jeffrey P. Brain

1983   *Excavations at the Lake George Site, Yazoo County, Mississippi, 1958–1960*. Papers of the Peabody Museum of Archaeology and Ethnology, vol.74. Cambridge: Harvard University.

Williams, Stephen, and John M. Goggin

1956   The long-nosed god mask in eastern United States. *The Missouri Archaeologist* 18 (3): 1–72.

Winter, Marcus C.

1976   The archaeological household cluster in the Valley of Oaxaca. In *The Early Mesoamerican Village*, edited by K. V. Flannery, pp.25–31. Academic Press: New York.

Witthoft, John

1949   Green Corn ceremonialism in the Eastern Woodlands. University of Michigan, Museum of Anthropology, Occasional Contributions 13. Ann Arbor.

Wittry, Warren L.

1960   Report of Phase 3 Archaeological Salvage Project: FAI. Route 70. Illinois State Museum, Preliminary Reports Series 1. Springfield.

1961   Report of Phase 3 Archaeological Salvage Project, FAI 255, Section 60-6-1, Tract 15A, Project 1-70-1. Unpublished report, Illinois State Museum, Springfield.

1969   The American woodhenge. In *Explorations into Cahokia Archaeology*, edited by M. Fowler, pp.43–48. Illinois Archaeological Survey Bulletin 7. Urbana.

1977   The American woodhenge. *In Explorations into Cahokia Archaeology*, 2d revised edition, edited by M. Fowler, pp.43–48. Illinois Archaeological Survey Bulletin 7. Urbana.

1980   Cahokia woodhenge update. *Archaeoastronomy* 3:12–14.

Wittry, Warren L., and Joseph O. Vogel

1962   Illinois State Museum projects. In *First Annual Report: American Bottoms Archaeology, July 1, 1961–June 30, 1962*, edited by M. Fowler, pp.14–30. Urbana: Illinois Archaeological Survey.

Wittry, Warren L., John C. Arnold, Charles O. Witty, and Timothy R. Pauketat

1994   *The Holdener Site: Late Woodland, Emergent Mississippian, and Mississippian Occupations in the American Bottom Uplands*. American Bottom Archaeology, FAI-270 Reports 26. Urbana: University of Illinois Press.

Wolf, Eric

1966   Kinship, friendship, and patron-client relations in complex societies. In *The Social Anthropology of Complex Societies*, edited by Michael Banton, pp.1–22. London: Tavistock Publications.

1982   *Europe and the People without History*. Berkeley: University of California Press.

Woodburn, J.

1980   Hunters and gatherers today and reconstruction of the past. In *Soviet and Western Anthropology*, edited by E. Gellner, pp.95–117. London: Duckworth.

Woods, William I.

1985   Archaeological testing at the Cahokia Mounds Interpretive Center Tract—

Location II, St. Clair County, Illinois. Unpublished report submitted to the Illinois Historic Preservation Agency, Springfield.

Woods, William I., and George R. Holley

1989   Current research at the Cahokia site (1984–1989). In *A Cahokia Atlas: A Historical Atlas of Cahokia Archaeology*, by M. L. Fowler, Appendix 5. Studies in Illinois Archaeology 6. Springfield: Illinois Historic Preservation Agency.

1991   Upland Mississippian settlement in the American Bottom region. In *Cahokia and the Hinterlands: Middle Mississippian Cultures of the Midwest*, edited by Thomas E. Emerson and R. Barry Lewis, pp.46–60. Urbana: University of Illinois Press.

Wright, Henry T.

1977   Recent research on the origin of the state. *Annual Review of Anthropology* 6:379–97.

1984   Prestate political formations. In *On the Evolution of Complex Societies: Essays in Honor of Harry Hoijer 1982*, edited by T. K. Earle, pp.41–77. Malibu CA: Undena Publications.

Wright, Henry T., and Gregory Johnson

1975   Population, exchange, and early state formation in southwestern Iran. *American Anthropologist* 77:267–89.

Wright, Patti J.

1986   Analysis of plant remains from the Bridgeton Archaeological site (23SL442): Late Woodland and Emergent Mississippian assemblages. Master's thesis, Liberal Arts Program, Washington University, St. Louis.

Yerkes, Richard W.

1980   The Mississippian component. In *Investigations at the Labras Lake Site*, pp.143–264. Department of Anthropology, University of Illinois at Chicago Circle.

1983   Microwear, microdrills, and Mississippian craft specialization. *American Antiquity* 48:499–518.

1987   *Prehistoric Life on the Mississippian Floodplain: Stone Tool Use, Settlement Organization, and Subsistence Practices at the Labras Lake Site, Illinois*. Chicago: University of Chicago Press.

1991   Specialization in shell artifact production at Cahokia. In *New Perspectives on Cahokia: Views from the Periphery*, edited by J. B. Stoltman, pp.49–64. Madison WI: Prehistory Press.

Yoffee, Norman

1993   Too many chiefs? (or, Safe texts for the '90s). In *Archaeological Theory: Who Sets the Agenda?* edited by N. Yoffee and A. Sherratt, pp.60–78. Cambridge: Cambridge University Press.

345

The Contributors

DAVID G. ANDERSON is an archaeologist at the Southeast Archeological Center of the National Park Service in Tallahassee, Florida, working in the Technical Assistance and Partnerships Division. His technical interests include cultural resource management, modeling prehistoric population distributions, synthesizing extant archaeological research on locality to regional scales, and exploring the evolution of cultural complexity in eastern North America. The author of numerous papers and monographs on prehistoric archaeology in various parts of North America and the Caribbean, he received in 1990 the Lower Mississippi Survey's C. B. Moore award for excellence by a young scholar and in 1991 the Society for American Archaeology's dissertation prize. His most recent book, based on his doctoral research, is *The Savannah River Chiefdoms: Political Change in the Late Prehistoric Southeast* (University of Alabama Press, 1994).

JAMES M. COLLINS is an archaeologist on the staff of the Iowa Office of the State Archaeologist, The University of Iowa. He has been engaged in Midwestern and Plains archaeology since graduating from Middlebury College in 1976. Recent publications include articles in *American Antiquity* (1993), *Illinois Archaeology* (1993, 1994), *Plains Anthropologist* (1995), *Midcontinental Journal of Archaeology* (1996), and the *Journal of the Iowa Archeological Society* (1990, 1995); a chapter in *Mississippian Communities and Households* (University of Alabama Press, 1995); and two monographs: *The Archaeology of the Cahokia ICT-II: Site Structure* (Illinois Historic Preservation Agency, 1990) and *The Iowa River Greenbelt: An Archaeological Landscape (Iowa Office of the State Archaeologist,* 1991). Most recently, his attention has focused on the Woodland Tradition of the upper Mississippi River valley.

RINITA A. DALAN is a grant-supported researcher in the Office of Contract Archaeology, Southern Illinois University at Edwardsville. She has published a number of articles in both archaeological and geophysical journals on the application of exploration geophysical and soil magnetic methods to archaeological problems. Supported by a grant from the National Endow-

347

ment for the Humanities, she is currently working on a volume dealing with the use of the landscape concept within archaeological research.

THOMAS E. EMERSON received his undergraduate training in sociology and political science at the University of Wisconsin at Eau Claire and his M.A. and Ph.D. from the University of Wisconsin at Madison. He has been Director of the Illinois Transporation Archaeological Research Program, University of Illinois, since 1994. For the previous decade he served as Chief Archaeologist, Illinois Historic Preservation Agency, where he managed statewide archaeological review and compliance, shipwreck, archaeological research, burial, education, and publication programs. He has been involved in Eastern Woodlands archaeology for twenty-five years and has published widely on a number of topics, most recently on complex societies, ideology, and hegemony. He is coeditor of *Cahokia and the Hinterlands: Middle Mississippian Cultures of the Midwest* (University of Illinois Press, 1991).

JOHN E. KELLY serves as the Coordinator for the American Bottom Survey Division of the Illinois Transportation Archaeological Research Program at the University of Illinois at Urbana–Champaign. He received a B.A. in anthropology from Beloit College and an M.A. and Ph.D. from the University of Wisconsin at Madison. He has been involved in archaeological investigations in the American Bottom and Cahokia since 1969. He has published numerous articles and publications examining the late prehistory of the region, especially the Mississippian emergence. Of interest is a recent article in *Illinois Archaeology* entitled "The Archaeology of the East St. Louis Mound Center: Past and Present" (1994).

LUCRETIA S. KELLY is a doctoral candidate in the Department of Anthropology, Washington University–St. Louis. She received a B.A. in anthropology from Beloit College and an M.A. in anthropology from Washington University. She has been conducting zooarchaeological research in the American Bottom region and at the Cahokia site for the past twenty years. She has contributed fifteen chapters to published books or monographs, published one monograph, authored twenty-four chapters in technical reports, and presented nine professional papers. Of particular note is "Zooarchaeological Remains," in *The Archaeology of the Cahokia Mounds ICT-II: Biological Remains, Part II* (Illinois Historic Preservation Agency, Springfield, 1991).

348

VERNON JAMES KNIGHT JR. is an Associate Professor of Anthropology at the University of Alabama. His current research includes a long-term project of excavations, beginning in 1989, at the Moundville site. His recent publications include *The De Soto Chronicles*, coedited with Lawrence Clayton and Edward Moore.

NEAL H. LOPINOT is currently the Director of the Center for Archaeological Research, Southwest Missouri State University, Springfield. Having grown up along the American Bottom bluffs between Columbia and Dupo, he has M.A. (1977) and Ph.D. (1984) degrees from Southern Illinois University at Carbondale. His primary research interest is archaeobotany, although he maintains other interests that include field methods, lithic analysis, and ethnohistory. His regional focus has gradually shifted toward the Ozarks and the upper Lower Mississippi valley. He has authored over one hundred technical reports, book articles, and journal articles. Recent articles about the American Bottom have included "Wood Overexploitation and the Collapse of Cahokia" (1993) and "A New Crop of Data on the Cahokian Polity" (1994).

TIMOTHY R. PAUKETAT is an Associate Professor of Anthropology at the State University of New York Buffalo. He has an M.A. (1986) from Southern Illinois University at Carbondale and a Ph.D. (1991) from the University of Michigan. He has held positions at the University of Illinois and the University of Oklahoma and was the 1995 recipient of the Lower Mississippi Survey's C. B. Moore Award. His research interests lie in early civilizations, and he has been involved in archaeological research at and around Cahokia since 1980. The author of numerous articles and monographs, his most recent book is *The Ascent of Chiefs: Cahokia and Mississippian Politics in Native North America* (University of Alabama Press, 1994).

Index

abandonment, 120, 241
A.D. 1050, 5, 19, 69, 111, 121, 162, 178, 186, 189, 232, 234, 248, 255, 261, 262, 263, 267, 270, 271
AG Church, 75, 78
agency theory, 192
agricultural intensification, 59
agricultural surpluses, 267
agriculture, 269; defined, 53; role of, 53
Alabama, 28, 257
alienation, 240
amaranth, 61
American Bottom (region), 2, 5, 8, 18, 20, 27, 250, 271, 278; environment of, 64
Angel center, 256
Annis site, 256
Appalachians, 245, 252, 254, 265
archaeology of Cahokia (history), 2
Archaic period, 254
architecture, 171; circular and rectangular, 14; disappearance of, in Moorehead phase, 185; Interpretive Center Tract II, 113; monumental, 2, 14, 162, 165; of power, 171, 186, 188; public, 244; reconstruction of, 20; Tract 15A and Dunham Tract, 111; special purpose, 14, 174, 178, 240; used to estimate population, 104
Arkansas, 18, 230, 245, 254, 256, 268
Arkansas River, 199
artifacts: exotic, 172, 177–79, 181, 182, 238, 254, 274; of power, 171
Atlantic coast, 254, 265
authority, 169, 181, 269, 276; civic, 184
autonomy, rural, 176
axes of political system variation, 169
Ayres, B., 138
Aztalan, 18, 268

backswamp deposition, 93
Banks village, 256
Baytown, 63
BBB Motor site, 177, 178, 179, 184, 196, 198,
208, 221, 223, 225, 238; burial complex at, 177; exotica at, 198
Bennett, J., 104
Big Bang, 162, 263, 265
Binford, L., 72
Black Bottoms, 172
black drink, 177
Black Warrior Valley, 230, 235, 237, 242
Blitz, J., 173
borrow pits, 93, 96, 109
Boserup, E., 59
Brackenridge, H., 10–11, 103, 104, 147
Brown, J. A., 195, 216, 217
buildings: charnel, 185; circular, 150, 151, 155, 162, 179; density of, 113, 114; floor areas of, 113, 115; during Lohmann phase, 112, 113; longevity of, 106, 114, 115; L-shaped, 150, 162; at Monks Mound, 164; during Moorehead phase, 112, 114; single-post, 112, 114; size of, 114, 138; size modes of, 107; size of, relating to status, 106; specialized, 162; during Stirling phase, 114; storage shed, 159; wall-trench, 5, 114, 155, 159, 179, 181, 218; wall-trench and single-post, 153
bundled continua of variation, 169, 186
bureaucracy, 274
Burlington chert, 274
Busk ceremonial node, 223
Butler, B., 172

Cahokia: boundaries of, 107; cardinal axes of, 197; central precinct of, 90, 97, 98, 101, 242; climax of, 161; compared to Moundville, 235; compared to Philadelphia, 104; decline of, 120, 140, 188; Emergent Mississippian occupation of, 115; high-density residential area in, 107, 109; as an idea, 268; lesser, 242; at Lohmann-phase maximum, 121; as mercantile city, 3, 19, 27; scale of, 242, 274; sociopolitical structure of, 167; as southeastern polity, 229, 230, 232; temporal extent of, 252. See also community; population

351